International Organization

International Organization

Hylke Dijkstra, Andreas Kruck and Bernhard Zangl

BLOOMSBURY ACADEMIC
LONDON · NEW YORK · OXFORD · NEW DELHI · SYDNEY

BLOOMSBURY ACADEMIC
Bloomsbury Publishing Plc, 50 Bedford Square, London, WC1B 3DP, UK
Bloomsbury Publishing Inc, 1359 Broadway, New York, NY 10018, USA
Bloomsbury Publishing Ireland, 29 Earlsfort Terrace, Dublin 2, D02 AY28, Ireland

BLOOMSBURY, BLOOMSBURY ACADEMIC and the Diana logo are trademarks of
Bloomsbury Publishing Plc

First published in Great Britain 2006
Second edition published 2012
Third edition published 2019
This edition published 2025

Copyright © Hylke Dijkstra, Andreas Kruck and Bernhard Zangl 2006, 2012, 2019, 2025

Hylke Dijkstra, Andreas Kruck and Bernhard Zangl have asserted their right under the
Copyright, Designs and Patents Act, 1988, to be identified as Authors of this work.

Cover design: Darren Rumney / www.rumneydesign.co.uk
Cover image © David Fransolet / Getty Images

All rights reserved. No part of this publication may be: i) reproduced or transmitted in
any form, electronic or mechanical, including photocopying, recording or by means of
any information storage or retrieval system without prior permission in writing from the
publishers; or ii) used or reproduced in any way for the training, development or operation
of artificial intelligence (AI) technologies, including generative AI technologies. The rights
holders expressly reserve this publication from the text and data mining exception as per
Article 4(3) of the Digital Single Market Directive (EU) 2019/790.

Bloomsbury Publishing Plc does not have any control over, or responsibility for, any third-
party websites referred to or in this book. All internet addresses given in this book were
correct at the time of going to press. The author and publisher regret any inconvenience
caused if addresses have changed or sites have ceased to exist, but can accept no
responsibility for any such changes.

A catalogue record for this book is available from the British Library.

ISBN: HB: 978-1-3504-6133-8
PB: 978-1-3504-6134-5
ePDF: 978-1-3504-6131-4
eBook: 978-1-3504-6132-1

Typeset by Deanta Global Publishing Services, Chennai, India
Printed and bound in Great Britain

For product safety related questions contact productsafety@bloomsbury.com.

To find out more about our authors and books visit www.bloomsbury.com and
sign up for our newsletters.

CONTENTS

List of Boxes vii
List of Figures viii
List of Tables ix
List of Acronyms x
Preface xiv

1   Introduction 1

Part I Theory and history of international organizations

2   Theories of international organizations 15

3   History of international organizations 35

Part II Policymaking in international organizations

4   International organizations as political systems 65

5   Input: Actors' demands and support 83

6   Conversion: Decision-making in international organizations 101

7   Output: What international organizations produce 121

Part III Activities of international organizations

8   Peace, security and war 139

9   Trade, development and finance 167

10 Climate and the environment 195

11 Migration and human rights 213

12 Regional cooperation 236

Part IV Conclusion

13 The future of international organizations 263

References 279
Index 311

BOXES

1.1 International institutions, international regimes and international organizations 4

8.1 NATO and the war in Ukraine 159

9.1 The ten-point catalogue of the Washington Consensus 182

12.1 EU institutional structure 239

12.2 AU institutional structure 245

12.3 ASEAN institutional structure 250

12.4 MERCOSUR institutional structure 255

FIGURES

1.1 Total number of international organizations since 1800 2

4.1 The political system of international organizations 66

4.2 The institutional structure of international organizations 71

4.3 The institutional structure of the United Nations (UN) 72

5.1 The political system of international organizations (input) 84

6.1 The political system of international organizations (conversion) 102

7.1 The political system of international organizations (output) 122

8.1 Number of UN peacekeeping operations, 1948–2024 150

8.2 Number of global armed conflicts, 1946–2022 152

8.3 Burden sharing in NATO: Defence spending by selected allies (% of GDP) 164

9.1 Trade ratios of major economies and the world, 1970–2022 (ratio of imports + exports of goods and services to GDP, %) 175

9.2 Decrease of absolute poverty: population living on less than US$2.15 per day, 1981–2022 (%) 184

10.1 Total chlorofluorocarbon (CFC) production major states, 1986–2003 (ODP tons) 202

10.2 Global rise of temperature, 1880–present (yearly deviation from the average temperature in the period 1951–80, °C) 203

10.3 Annual CO_2 emissions (1946–date) of major economies (in billion tons) 210

11.1 Number of refugees and IDPs, 1951–2024 222

11.2 Proportion of 'free', 'partly free' and 'not free' countries, 1972–2024 (in % of overall number of states, based on Freedom House Country Ratings) 231

TABLES

1.1 Types of international organizations (scope) 6

1.2 Types of international organizations (function) 6

1.3 Types of international organizations (centralization) 7

2.1 The 'Prisoner's Dilemma' 20

2.2 Four contemporary theories of international organizations (IOs) 32

3.1 War and power politics as a stimulus for international organizations 38

3.2 International commerce as a stimulus for international organizations 43

3.3 Global economic crises as a stimulus for international organizations 47

3.4 Human rights violations as a stimulus for international organizations 54

3.5 Developmental disparities as a stimulus for international organizations 55

3.6 Environmental problems as a stimulus for international organizations 57

11.1 The main global Human Rights Conventions 226

11.2 Monitoring procedures of the Human Rights Council 228

12.1 Different forms of economic cooperation 241

ACRONYMS

AfCFTA	African Continental Free Trade Area
AFTA	ASEAN Free Trade Area
AMISOM	AU Mission in Somalia
AOSIS	Alliance of Small Island States
APEC	Asia-Pacific Economic Cooperation
ASEAN	Association of Southeast Asian Nations
ATMIS	AU Transition Mission in Somalia
ATTAC	Association for the Taxation of Financial Transactions and Aid to Citizens/Association pour la Taxation des Transactions Financières et l'Aide aux Citoyens
AU	African Union
BCBS	Basel Committee on Banking Supervision
BRICS	Brazil, Russia, India, China and South Africa
CAC	Codex Alimentarius Commission (FAO)
CCOL	Coordinating Committee on the Ozone Layer (UNEP)
CDF	Comprehensive Development Framework (World Bank)
CEPT	Common Effective Preferential Tariff (ASEAN)
CFCs	Chlorofluorocarbons
COP	Conference of the Parties
COREPER	Committee of Permanent Representatives (EU)
DSB	Dispute Settlement Body (WTO)
DSU	Dispute Settlement Understanding (WTO)
ECB	European Central Bank (EU)
ECF	Extended Credit Facility (IMF)
ECHR	European Convention for the Protection of Human Rights and Fundamental Freedoms (Convention on Human Rights)
ECJ	European Court of Justice (EU)
ECOSOC	Economic and Social Council (UN)
ECSC	European Coal and Steel Community (now EU)
EEAS	European External Action Service (EU)
EEC	European Economic Community (now EU)
EESC	European Economic and Social Committee (EU)
EFF	Extended Fund Facility (IMF)
EU	European Union
FAO	Food and Agriculture Organization (UN)

FCL	Flexible Credit Line (IMF)
G7/8	Group of Seven/Eight (leading industrial countries)
G20	Group of 20 (industrialized and emerging market countries)
G77	Group of 77 (developing countries)
GATS	General Agreement on Trade in Services (WTO)
GATT	General Agreement on Tariffs and Trade (WTO)
GDP	Gross domestic product
GEF	Global Environmental Facility (UN)
GMG	Global Migration Group (UN)
GOIC	Gulf Organization for Industrial Consulting
HCFCs	Hydrochlorofluorocarbons
HFCs	Hydrofluorocarbons
HIPC	Heavily Indebted Poor Countries (IMF)
HRC	Human Rights Council (UN)
IAEA	International Atomic Energy Agency
IBRD	International Bank for Reconstruction and Development (World Bank)
ICAO	International Civil Aviation Organization
ICC	International Criminal Court
ICJ	International Court of Justice (UN)
ICTR	International Criminal Tribunal for Rwanda
ICTY	International Criminal Tribunal for the Former Yugoslavia
IDA	International Development Association (World Bank)
IDP	Internally displaced people
IEO	Independent Evaluation Office (IMF)
IFC	International Finance Corporation (World Bank)
ILO	International Labour Organization
IMF	International Monetary Fund
IMO	International Maritime Organization
INC	Intergovernmental Negotiating Committee
IOM	International Organization for Migration
IPCC	Intergovernmental Panel on Climate Change
IRO	International Refugee Organization
ISAF	International Security Assistance Force (Afghanistan)
ITO	International Trade Organization
IWC	International Whaling Commission
KFOR	Kosovo Force (NATO)
MERCOSUR	Southern Common Market
MIGA	Multilateral Investment Guarantee Agency
NAB	New Arrangements to Borrow (IMF)
NAC	North Atlantic Council (NATO)
NAFTA	North American Free Trade Agreement
NAM	Non-Aligned Movement
NASA	National Aeronautics and Space Administration

NATO	North Atlantic Treaty Organization
NDPP	NATO Defence Planning Process
NGOs	Non-governmental organizations
NIEO	New international economic order
NPT	Nuclear Non-Proliferation Treaty (UN)
OAS	Organization of American States
OAU	Organization of African Unity (now AU)
ODP	Ozone Depletion Potential
OECD	Organisation for Economic Co-operation and Development
OHCHR	Office of the High Commissioner for Human Rights (UN)
OIC	Organization of Islamic Cooperation
OIHP	International Office for Public Hygiene
OPEC	Organization of the Petroleum Exporting Countries
OSCE	Organization for Security and Co-operation in Europe (see CSCE)
PfP	Partnership for Peace programme (NATO)
PSC	Peace and Security Council (AU)
R2P	Responsibility to protect
RCEP	Regional Comprehensive Economic Partnership (ASEAN)
RCF	Rapid Credit Facility (IMF)
RECs	Regional Economic Communities
SAP	Structural Adjustment Programme (IMF)
SBA	Stand-By Arrangement (IMF)
SCF	Standby Credit Facility (IMF)
SDRs	Special Drawing Rights (IMF)
SHAPE	Supreme Headquarters Allied Powers Europe (NATO)
TEU	Treaty on European Union
TFEU	Treaty on the Functioning of the European Union
TPRB	Trade Policy Review Body (WTO)
TRIPS	Agreement on Trade-Related Aspects of Intellectual Property Rights (WTO)
UN	United Nations
UNAMID	AU-UN mission in Darfur
UNCLOS	United Nations Convention on the Law of the Sea
UNCTAD	United Nations Conference on Trade and Development
UNDP	United Nations Development Programme
UNEP	United Nations Environment Programme
UNESCO	United Nations Educational, Scientific and Cultural Organization
UNFCCC	United Nations Framework Convention on Climate Change
UNFICYP	Peacekeeping Force in Cyprus (UN)
UNFPA	United Nations Population Fund
UNHCHR	United Nations High Commissioner for Human Rights

UNHCR	United Nations Refugee Agency
UNICEF	United Nations Children's Emergency Fund
UNIDO	United Nations Industrial Development Organization
UNIIMOG	United Nations Iran–Iraq Military Observer Group
UNMIK	United Nations Mission in Kosovo
UNMOVIC	UN Monitoring, Verification and Inspection Commission (Iraq)
UNRRA	UN Relief and Rehabilitation Agency
UNSCOM	United Nations Special Commission
UNRWA	Relief and Works Agency for Palestinian Refugees (UN)
UIC	International Union of Railways
UPR	Universal Periodic Review
UPU	Universal Postal Union
USA	United States of America
USMCA	United States, Mexico and Canada Agreement
VAT	Value-added tax
WFP	World Food Programme
WHO	World Health Organization
WMO	World Meteorological Organization
WTO	World Trade Organization
ZOPA	Zone of possible agreement

PREFACE

On the first day of his second term in office, Donald Trump signed executive orders to withdraw the United States from the Paris Agreement on Climate Change and the World Health Organization (WHO). He also renewed sanctions against officials of the International Criminal Court (ICC) in The Hague for investigating war crimes committed by US troops. This opening salvo of the second attempt at 'America First' indicates an ambition of President Trump to undo much of the world order established by his predecessors since 1945.

It is, however, not just Donald Trump and the United States challenging world order and its international organizations. The emerging powers, notably Brazil, China, Russia, India and South Africa (BRICS), have also long called for the reform of international organizations. They demand that their economic weight gets reflected in international economic organizations, such as the World Bank and the International Monetary Fund (IMF), while India wants a permanent seat on the United Nations (UN) Security Council. On behalf of the Global South, they demand climate justice and large financial support for energy transition. Brazil and South Africa have put global poverty and the future of Africa at the heart of their presidencies of the Group of 20 (G20). China along with other authoritarian regimes has taken on the UN Human Rights Council.

Serious challenges no doubt, these examples also show that international organizations are at the forefront of international politics at a time that the world order appears to be shifting away from the comforts of the post-Cold War era. That President Trump is withdrawing from the Paris Agreement and the WHO and is taking on the ICC tells us that these international organizations matter. Not just to international politics but also to domestic politics in the United States. Implementing the Paris Agreement implies energy transition across all layers of society, while the WHO provides countries with pandemic reporting requirements and prescribes public health advice. The ICC proceedings and arrest warrants severely restrict suspects of war crimes, which now include the Russian president and Israeli prime minister.

International organizations are similarly relevant for the emerging powers, which are vying for more equal representation with a symbolic seat at the diplomatic top table or are concerned about regime stability with respect to human rights condemnations. The BRICS as an institution has long prioritized, in its annual summit declarations, the reform of a variety of international organizations. Its reform proposals and demands may be at odds with the more liberal norms and policies that many of the established international organizations are pursuing, but the BRICS are taking a key interest in international organizations nonetheless.

It is against the background of this changing international environment that the fourth edition of this book, once again, seeks to open up the 'blackbox' of everyday politics inside international organizations. By considering international organizations as political systems that have to convert diverse inputs by a variety of actors into concrete policy output, this book takes the constitutional and institutional structure of international organizations seriously. As we argue, different types of international organizations will convert similar inputs into different outputs. This forces us to zoom in and take an interest in the nitty-gritty of how international organizations operate in practice. The fundamentals of this book therefore remain the same, even if we are aware of the limitations of international organizations and the challenges they face.

For the fourth edition the author constellation has changed. Originally published in German, the first English edition (2006) was written by Volker Rittberger and Bernhard Zangl. Andreas Kruck joined for the second edition (2012) and Hylke Dijkstra for the third (2019). Volker Rittberger passed away before the second edition became available. He remained the first author on the second and third editions highlighting the continuity of his intellectual approach to international organizations in this book. We continue to stand on the shoulders of Volker Rittberger, but we now take full responsibility for this new edition. We hope that he would have enjoyed reading the book. The new author order also reflects the work of Hylke Dijkstra on the third and fourth editions with Andreas Kruck and Bernhard Zangl gradually withdrawing as contributors.

We have tried to improve the book in several ways for this fourth edition. The chapters in Parts I and II of the book have been thoroughly updated to consider current events and the new findings in the rapidly expanding academic literature. The theory chapter, for instance, has been revised to highlight important advances in institutionalist, constructivist and critical theories. The chapters in Part III have also been revised and several new ones have been added. Chapter 8 includes a study of NATO and the importance of alliances. We have included migration and refugees as important topics in Chapter 11. There is a new Chapter 12 on regional cooperation with a discussion of the European Union (EU), African Union (AU), Association of Southeast Asian Nations (ASEAN) and Southern Common Market (MERCOSUR). The concluding Chapter 13 on the future of international organizations is also new and discusses a variety of challenges including legitimacy, gridlock, emerging powers and geopoliticization. We hope that readers find these revisions useful and that the book provides them with renewed stimulus to study the ins and outs of international organizations.

In these turbulent times, we dedicate this book to all the diplomats and officials working every single day within the political systems of the many international organizations trying to convert divergent inputs into coherent outputs.

Hylke Dijkstra, Andreas Kruck and Bernhard Zangl
Maastricht and Munich, February 2025

1

Introduction

International organizations are a relatively new phenomenon in international relations. They first emerged during the nineteenth century and became ever-more important over the course of the twentieth century. Today, international organizations are involved in nearly all issue areas – from A, as in Arms Control, to Z, as in Zones of Fishing. General purpose international organizations such as the United Nations (UN) or the European Union (EU) cover many different topics, while task-specific organizations such as the International Labour Organization (ILO) or the International Whaling Commission (IWC) specialize in specific issue areas. Some international organizations, like the UN, have a near-universal membership. Others restrict membership on the basis of criteria such as geography, economy, culture or religion; examples include the African Union (AU), the Organization of the Petroleum Exporting Countries (OPEC), the Organisation for Economic Co-operation and Development (OECD) and the Organization of Islamic Cooperation (OIC). All these international organizations contribute to establishing and implementing norms and rules which guide the management of transnational, cross-border problems, such as climate change, the proliferation of weapons of mass destruction or international terrorism. It is thus no exaggeration to say that it is difficult to understand contemporary world politics without referring to international organizations.

International organizations are, however, not only for diplomats, or for academics, to study. Ordinary citizens are also confronted by the work of international organizations, many of which have become familiar to even the most casual newspaper readers. The UN General Assembly has, for instance, repeatedly condemned Russia's aggression and its war against Ukraine. The work of some international organizations has also become fiercely contested. The World Health Organization (WHO) was criticized when it failed to bring the Covid-19 pandemic under control. Through a referendum, British voters decided to leave the EU, while Burundi and the Philippines have left the International Criminal Court (ICC). Emerging powers, such as Brazil, Russia, India, China and South Africa (BRICS), have challenged what they consider a Western bias across many international organizations. The fact that ordinary citizens pay attention is perhaps the best evidence of their significance: international organizations are no longer technical agencies; they are political bodies that have actual influence on people's lives.

The international organizations mentioned so far only represent a fraction of the approximately 350 international *governmental* organizations existing at present (Pevehouse et al. 2020), not to mention around 42,000 international *non-governmental* organizations (NGOs) (Union of International Associations n.d.). Figure 1.1 provides an overview of how the number of international organizations has developed since the beginning of the nineteenth century, showing a significant increase after the Second World War ended in 1945. Indeed, the post-war period can be characterized as an era of growing institutionalization of interstate relations. The number of international organizations has stabilized in more recent years. Yet the overall number of international organizations does not tell us everything. Since the Second World War, there have been increases in the political significance of, financial resources assigned to and number of civil servants working for international organizations. The growth in the number and significance of international organizations are discussed throughout this book.

This first chapter starts with a seemingly simple question: What are international organizations? The answer, however, is not straightforward. The chapter puts forward a definition, which requires international organizations to have three or more states as members, a plenary meeting at least every ten years and a permanent secretariat and correspondence

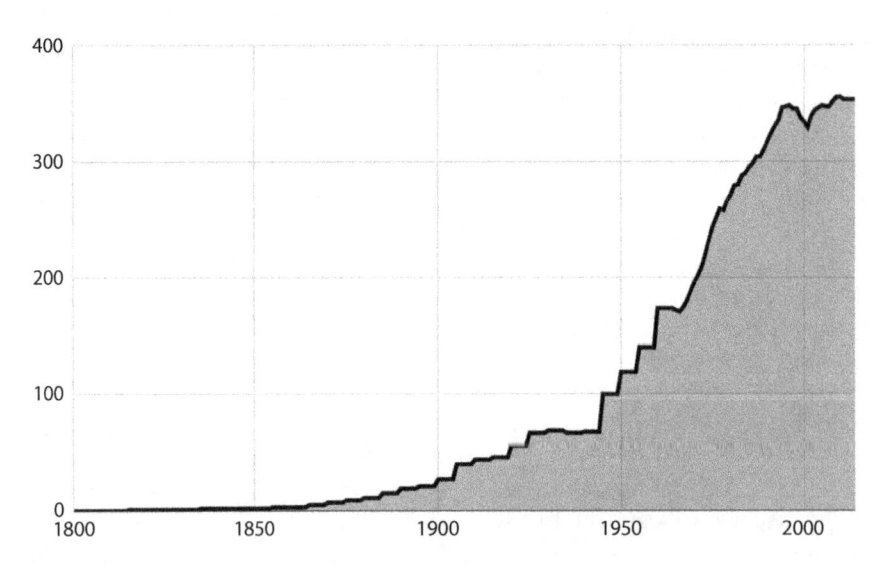

FIGURE 1.1 *Total number of international organizations since 1800. Source: Pevehouse et al. (2020).*

address (Pevehouse et al. 2020). As such, international organizations differ from other international institutions, such as international regimes (which do not have a secretariat) or NGOs (which do not have states as members). Yet even when we follow this restrictive definition, we are still left with approximately 350 international organizations of many shapes and sizes. The chapter therefore also introduces a typology that conceptualizes these international organizations along three different dimensions:

- *Task-specific* international organizations address a limited set of problems, while *general purpose* international organizations have a wide policy scope.
- *Programme* international organizations focus on setting norms and rules to address problems, while *operational* international organizations implement those norms and rules.
- *Centralized* international organizations have the authority to address problems themselves, while *decentralized* international organizations rely on the authority of their member states.

After discussing what international organizations are, this chapter asks how we can study them. It suggests three big questions:

- Why are international organizations created?
- How are decisions made and implemented within international organizations?
- How do the decisions and activities of international organizations affect international cooperation?

What are international organizations?

International organizations are obviously of practical importance. But how can they be conceptualized? Surprisingly, the term 'international organization' became part of scientific and everyday vocabulary only relatively recently. During the nineteenth century, expressions such as 'international public union', 'international office' or 'commission' were commonly used. A very early example is the Rhine River Commission, which was founded in the aftermath of the Congress of Vienna (1814–15). Its task was (and remains) to facilitate and coordinate the navigation of international traffic on the Rhine. Even today, we cannot simply determine an international organization by its name: the World Trade *Organization* (WTO) is clearly an international organization, yet the International Atomic Energy *Agency* (IAEA) is an international organization as well. A definition of international organizations is thus needed to distinguish them from other forms of governance, such as international regimes or NGOs.

As a starting point, it is important to point out that international organizations are a specific subcategory of international institutions. *International institutions* can be defined as 'persistent and connected sets of rules (formal and informal) that prescribe behavioral roles, constrain activity, and shape expectations' (Keohane 1989: 3). International institutions are a very broad category. For instance, the 'nuclear taboo' (Tannenwald 1999) – states refrain from using nuclear weapons even if they can – is also an international institution. After all, it is an example of a persistent informal rule (a norm), which constraints the use of the most powerful weapon and shapes expectations between states. Yet the nuclear taboo is clearly not an international organization: it does not have a building, it does not have member states, or a budget or staff. Instead it is part of the nuclear non-proliferation regime, which also includes the Treaty on the Non-Proliferation of Nuclear Weapons and the IAEA – all different sorts of international institutions aimed at reducing the threat and use of nuclear weapons.

BOX 1.1 INTERNATIONAL INSTITUTIONS, INTERNATIONAL REGIMES AND INTERNATIONAL ORGANIZATIONS

International institutions are 'persistent and connected sets of rules (formal and informal) that prescribe behavioral roles, constrain activity, and shape expectations' (Keohane 1989: 3). *International regimes* are 'implicit or explicit principles, norms, rules, and decision-making procedures around which actors' expectations converge in a given area of international relations' (Krasner 1983: 2). *International organizations* have three or more states as members, hold a plenary meeting at least every ten years and have a permanent secretariat and correspondence address (Pevehouse et al. 2020).

So what are international organizations? And how can we distinguish them from other international institutions? In this book, international organizations are defined as having (1) three or more states as members, (2) a plenary meeting at least every ten years (3) and a permanent secretariat and correspondence address (Pevehouse et al. 2020). It is important to discuss these three elements of the definition in greater detail:

- *Three or more states as members*: International organizations can be distinguished from, for instance, NGOs due to the fact that their membership predominantly consists of states. While the Universal Postal Union (UPU) is an international organization with 192 member states, the International Committee of the Red Cross

(ICRC) is not as it does not have states as its members. This part of the definition also makes international organizations *multilateral* (three or more states as members) rather than *bilateral* (two states as members).

- *A plenary meeting at least every ten years*: International organizations can be distinguished from ad hoc international conferences because they have a regular plenary meeting. When the international community organized, for instance, a donor conference for the people in Türkiye or Syria in 2023 following a devastating earthquake, this was a one-off event. Such conferences are therefore not international organizations. The ten years requirement is a minimum to be defined as an international organization. In many international organizations meetings are organized much more frequently, for example, in the EU where ministers meet almost every week. Some scholars therefore feel that a more restrictive definition, requiring more regular meetings, is appropriate. For instance, Volgy et al. (2008) have proposed a plenary meeting every four years, though most international organizations have a plenary meeting every year.

- *A permanent secretariat and correspondence address*: International organizations can be distinguished from regular international conferences or regimes because of a higher degree of institutionalization in the form of a permanent secretariat and correspondence address. Or, to put it differently, 'international organizations are palpable entities with headquarters and letterheads, voting procedures, and generous pension plans' (Ruggie 1992: 573). A secretariat can, however, be a modest affair. The Arctic Council, for instance, has a secretariat with only a dozen staff members. This is why several scholars suggest a stricter definition. Hooghe et al. (2017: 16), for instance, propose that the secretariat should consist of at least thirty permanent staff. As a result, they only identify seventy-six international organizations (compared to the 350 of Pevehouse et al. 2020). A permanent secretariat and correspondence address distinguish international organizations from informal international institutions, such as the Group of 20 (G20) which meets every year in a different host country (Vabulas and Snidal 2013).

While scholars debate the exact definition of international organizations, they largely agree that international organizations consist of states, are continuous and permanent. As its title suggests, international organizations are also the topic of this book. While we recognize their importance, we do not focus on NGOs, such as Amnesty International, Greenpeace or Transparency International, or multinational companies such as General Motors, Amazon or Citigroup. These actors may be involved in the work of international organizations, but they are not the topic of this book as such. Still, this leaves us with a wide variety of international organizations which are not necessarily always comparable. The UN, for example, may not have much in common with the Gulf Organization for Industrial Consulting (GOIC). And comparing them is a bit like comparing apples and oranges: both fruits are round and of similar size, but they have a different colour, taste and texture. The bigger challenge therefore is to create a typology *of* international organizations. We argue that international organizations can be classified according to their scope, function and centralization.

First of all, it is important to distinguish between *task-specific* international organizations and *general purpose* international organizations (Hooghe, Lenz and Marks 2019). They differ in terms of their scope (Koremenos, Lipson and Snidal 2001). Whereas task-specific international organizations focus on one or a limited number of issue areas, general purpose international organizations address a range of issue areas (see Table 1.1). The underlying rationale of both groups of international organizations is different (Hooghe, Lenz and Marks 2019). Task-specific international organizations are problem-driven – that is, a group of states want to address a problem in a specific issue area. For instance, the founding states of the Rhine River Commission wanted to solve navigation problems on the Rhine. General purpose international organizations, on the other hand, are community-driven: a group of member states, which share a purpose, set up an international organization to address a range of problems. For instance, the AU facilitates cooperation between states on the African continent. As such, general purpose international

TABLE 1.1 *Types of international organizations (scope)*

Type	Task-Specific	General Purpose
Scope	Few issue areas	Many issue areas
Examples	IAEA IMF World Bank WTO	AU EU UN

TABLE 1.2 *Types of international organizations (function)*

Type	Programme Organization	Operational Organization
Function	Setting norms and rules	Implementing norms and rules
Examples	ILO UN WTO	IAEA UNHCR World Food Programme (WFP)

organizations tend to have a smaller membership (Hooghe, Lenz and Marks 2019: Figure 4.2). Many of the international organizations with universal membership, on the other hand, are task-specific.

Secondly, international organizations can be distinguished with regard to their main function (see Table 1.2). *Programme* organizations deal primarily with programme formulation – that is, they determine the norms and rules to address international problems. The WTO, for example, sets the rules concerning global trade. The ILO sets international labour standards. The UN General Assembly adopts many resolutions concerning human rights. *Operational* organizations, on the other hand, concentrate on implementing those norms and rules. This includes both the monitoring of compliance by states with agreed norms and rules and actual implementation activities by the international organizations themselves. The IAEA is an example of the former. It 'verifies through its inspection system that States comply with their commitments ... to use nuclear material and facilities only for peaceful [i.e. non-military] purposes' (IAEA n.d.). The UN Refugee Agency (UNHCR) is another example of an operational organization. It implements the 1951 Refugee Convention and has a mandate to protect refugees and internally displaced people. This includes administering refugee camps around the world. Operational organizations often have large budgets to implement their mandates. While it is useful to distinguish international organizations on the basis of their functions, various international organizations not only develop norms and rules but also implement them. They thus combine programme and operational functions.

Finally, international organizations can also be distinguished according to the degree to which authority has been centralized within them (Table 1.3; Koremenos, Lipson and Snidal 2001). The centralization of authority is about its pooling in decision-making and the delegation of tasks to international organizations (Hooghe and Marks 2015). In *decentralized* international organizations, the member states make decisions by consensus and they are themselves in charge of implementation. An example is Asia-Pacific Economic

TABLE 1.3 *Types of international organizations (centralization)*

Type	Decentralized Organization	Centralized Organization
Authority	Consensus decision-making and implementation by states	Majority voting and implementation by international organizations
Examples	APEC North Atlantic Treaty Organization OPEC	EU IMF World Bank

Cooperation (APEC) consisting of twenty-one member states. While there is an APEC Secretariat (making it an international organization), the actual delegation of tasks is minimal and decision-making is by consensus. The same goes for OPEC. In *centralized* international organizations, on the other hand, states make decisions through majority voting and delegate the implementation of decisions to the secretariat, agencies and other organs of the international organizations. The International Monetary Fund (IMF) and World Bank as well as the EU are examples of international organizations with majority voting, where member states have also delegated considerable implementing authority.

How can we study international organizations?

It is important to define international organizations and classify them. Yet scholarship is not merely about systematic description. In this book, we raise three big (research) questions. The purpose is to make sense of the rapid increase in the number of international organizations since the nineteenth century. We also want to know how international organizations work – and, finally, how they affect international cooperation. These questions are introduced below and answered in the three sections of this book.

Why are international organizations created?

As mentioned earlier, international organizations first appeared in the nineteenth century and they have become particularly numerous since 1945. To put it differently, international organizations have not always been around. While evidence exists of diplomatic relations going as far back as 2550 BC (in Mesopotamia, modern-day Iraq) and, more recently, appearing in the modern state system which developed after the Treaties of Westphalia (1648), international organizations are very much a contemporary phenomenon. This raises the question of why states did not create international organizations earlier – or, in other words: What triggered the creation of all these international organizations over the past 200 years? It is fair to say that something must have changed in the international system. Was it the 'first wave' of globalization between 1870 and 1914, which required new forms of international governance to facilitate the rapidly increasing trade volumes? Was it about the prevention of future war following the millions of casualties from the two world wars of the twentieth century? Was it about the awareness of cross-border environmental problems which became a key issue on the international agenda in the 1970s? Or was it mainly about American hegemony in the post-war and particularly the post-Cold War period?

Understanding the changes that motivated the creation of international organizations is only the first step. We also need to know why states considered that international organizations could better address international problems than could other forms of governance. To go back to the definition, what is it precisely about multilateral cooperation (between three or more states), with regular meetings and permanence in the form of a secretariat, that makes international organizations better equipped for today's problems than other international institutions? Why not simply address cross-border problems on an ad hoc basis, as they come along, only with the involved states? Chapters 2 and 3 provide detailed answers to these questions. Chapter 2 focuses on the main international relations theories and how they regard international organizations. Chapter 3 provides a historical overview of the creation and development of international organizations.

How are decisions made and implemented within international organizations?

After we have studied why international organizations are created, the next logical question is: How do international organizations work? To answer this question, we can no longer treat international organizations as 'black boxes'. Rather than simply saying 'the WTO does this' or 'the UN did that', we need to look inside international organizations and study the actual 'machinery'. Which actors set the agenda and propose new norms and rules? Which actors call the shots and make the important decisions? Do all member states have an equal say, or are there more powerful member states, such as the five permanent members of the UN Security Council? Is implementation delegated to the secretariat or a specific agency? We argue in this book that international organizations are political systems. That means that all international organizations have their own constitutional and institutional structures as well as their procedures and practices. These structures, procedures and practices determine which actors within international organizations can make and implement decisions. As such, the political system of each international organization facilitates the process of policymaking. At the same time, it also constrains the different actors in that it tells them which procedures to follow.

While it is important to understand the constitutional and institutional structures of the individual international organizations and their procedures and practices, this is not the whole story. It is also important to know what the actors want to achieve in the context of an international organization. What are their interests and preferences? For instance, in the negotiations around the Paris Agreement on climate change, the Western countries wanted all states to submit ambitious proposals to reduce CO_2 emissions. The developing countries, on the other hand, wanted access to Western technology and financial compensation to pay for adaptation. Such preferences by the member states are *inputs* into the political system of an international organization. How such preferences are precisely channelled through international organizations and result in decisions is what we call the *conversion process*. The decisions, in turn, result in the *output* of international organizations, which includes policy programmes as well as operational activities. Chapter 4 discusses the constitutional and institutional structure of international organizations. Chapter 5 focuses on input, while Chapter 6 discusses conversion and Chapter 7 analyses output.

How do the decisions and activities of international organizations affect international cooperation?

After we know how decisions are made and implemented, we need to pay attention to the actual outputs of international organizations. What is the substance of the policy programmes by various international organizations, such as the UN, NATO or IMF? To what extent does the UN Charter limit aggressive behaviour by states? What type of rules govern the EU's internal market? Why can the United States not discriminate between French and Indian products under the WTO framework? What is the role of the IMF when countries have payment problems? What commitments have states made in terms of addressing climate change and global warming? And how important is the Universal Declaration of Human Rights? In addition to all these international rules and norms, we argue that we should pay particular attention to their actual implementation. International organizations have developed a whole range of operational activities that help states further specify rules and norms. In some cases, policy implementation is actually delegated to international organizations themselves. International organizations also have an important role to play in monitoring implementation as well as adjudicating in disputes among the member states and imposing sanctions on non-compliant member states. Indeed, we argue that operational activities have a significant impact on the effectiveness of international cooperation among states.

In Chapters 8–12, we address the outputs of international organizations and the effectiveness of this output across different policy areas. Chapter 8 focuses on questions of peace, security and war. It highlights the policy programme of the UN, which restricts the use of force, and the operational activities that the UN has developed: pacific settlement of disputes, peace enforcement and peacekeeping. We also address questions of collective defence in Europe provided by NATO. In Chapter 9, we focus on global trade, development and finance. We address how the output of the WTO has resulted in increased trade among the member states. We also focus on the World Bank and its role in providing development assistance and loans as well as the changing role of the IMF. The focus of Chapter 10 is on climate change and the environment. We contrast the climate change policies and the Paris Agreement with earlier international cooperation to protect the ozone layer. Chapter 11 is about migration and human rights. We zoom in on the UNHCR and the International Organization for Migration (IOM) while also discussing the negotiations of a human rights policy programme in the UN following the Second World War and the operational activities of the ICC. Finally, Chapter 12 is about regional cooperation in the context of international organizations in Europe, Africa, Asia and Latin America. The chapter clarifies the policy programmes and operational activities of the EU, AU, Association of Southeast Asian Nations (ASEAN) and Southern Common Market (MERCOSUR), four important regional organizations that address a variety of policy areas.

Discussion questions

1. How do international organizations differ from other international institutions?
2. Which types of international organizations can be distinguished? Please provide several examples.

Further reading

Abbott, Kenneth W. and Duncan Snidal (1998). 'Why States Act Through Formal International Organizations', *Journal of Conflict Resolution,* 42 (1): 3–32.

Pevehouse, Jon, Timothy Nordstrom, Roseanne McManus and Anne Spencer Jamison (2020). 'Tracking Organizations in the World: The Correlates of War IGO Version 3.0 Datasets', *Journal of Peace Research*, 57 (3): 492–503.

Ruggie, John Gerard (1992). 'Multilateralism: The Anatomy of an Institution', *International Organization,* 46 (3): 561–98.

PART I

Theory and history of international organizations

2

Theories of international organizations

In this chapter, we look at several theories of international organizations. International organizations are complex. They often have many different member states which all have specific preferences. They also have different constitutional and institutional structures. The day-to-day practice of an international organization can indeed be a mystery to anyone who has not been working on that specific international organization for a long time. The purpose of theory is to structure and simplify such complexity. This allows us to identify patterns, trends and causal relationships not only *within* an international organization but also *across* international organizations. For instance, by studying regional cooperation in Europe (the European Union (EU)), we may also be able to say something about the prospects of regional cooperation in Africa, Asia or Latin America (the African Union (AU), Association of Southeast Asian Nations (ASEAN) and Southern Common Market (MERCOSUR)) (see also Chapter 12). The aim of theory is therefore to generalize and to put the daily practices into a broader context. By developing and then applying theories, we can better explain and occasionally predict developments in international organizations.

In the area of international relations there are many different theories. In this book, we consider four of the most dominant theories. *Realist theory* stresses the importance of power: the power of states is largely based on their military capabilities, such as the number of soldiers and weapons. International organizations are, for realists, simply forums where states diplomatically fight out their conflicts. *Institutionalist theory*, on the other hand, is problem-driven. It argues that states – due to globalization – increasingly face cross-border and international problems, such as global warming. International organizations help states to address these problems collectively. They facilitate the process of cooperation between states. *Constructivist theory* argues that international problems are not simply 'out there', but that they are 'socially constructed'. The perception of problems matters. For instance, only relatively recently we started to pay attention to human rights in international relations; previously human rights were simply perceived as domestic matters. Finally, a diverse group of *critical theories*, including Marxist, feminist, postcolonial and green theories, stress the hierarchies in international relations. International organizations, according to these theories, reproduce inequalities to the benefit of powerful states and elites. These four theories not only suggest different reasons for why international organizations are created but also provide us with alternative explanations for how international organizations are designed and what the effects of international organizations are.

Realist theory

While realist theory is occasionally traced to the political philosophers Thucydides, Machiavelli and Hobbes, we consider *classical realism* as introduced by Carr (1939) and Morgenthau (1948) and *neo-realism*, which has become a central theory since the late 1970s (Waltz 1979; Gilpin 1981; Grieco 1988; Mearsheimer 2001). These theories claim that the state is the primary actor in international politics. In realist analyses, other actors such as non-governmental organizations (NGOs), multinational companies or international organizations are left out or are assigned a secondary role. Realists also do not distinguish between different types of states – for instance, democracies or autocracies. The only thing that matters are *the differences in the power of states* measured by material capabilities such as soldiers and weapons. Informed by history, philosophy and the experience of the two world wars, classical realists hold that it is an important part of human nature to strive for power. Neo-realism does not assume that all humans are 'power hungry'. Rather, it claims that the anarchical structure of the international system requires states to pursue a security-oriented policy of maximizing their capabilities in order to survive (Waltz 1990: 29–37).

Realists consider that power in international politics differs from political power in domestic politics (Morgenthau 1948). In domestic politics, the struggle for power between politicians and parties is constrained because the state has a monopoly on the use of force. In international politics, however, the struggle for power between states can escalate into violence, because there is no supranational authority capable of constraining states. In other words, 'wars occur because there is nothing to prevent them' (Waltz 1959: 232). This implies that there is no guarantee of survival for states. Therefore, all states are responsible for their own survival. Because states cannot trust other states to come to their rescue, they have to provide for their own security. They can do so through maximizing their military capabilities. This comes with a catch: the efforts of one state to enhance its security by enlarging its capabilities may be perceived by other states as threatening. This leads to a vicious circle of distrust, competition and strife for power. States are thus caught in a situation known as the 'security dilemma' (Herz 1950). If they do not orient their policy according to this 'self-help' imperative, they will inevitably perish (Waltz 1979: 79–101). Yet, if they do, they end up in competition for security which also entails the risk of escalation.

According to realist theory, international organizations are of little help in addressing this power struggle. International organizations cannot change human nature. They also cannot transform the anarchical structure of the international system, in which states constantly have to maximize their own capabilities in order to survive, into a hierarchical structure. Long-term international cooperation is also almost impossible to achieve: even if states can benefit from cooperation in the short term, there is always the risk that today's friend may become tomorrow's enemy (Mearsheimer 1995: 11). This makes international cooperation inherently instable, as states must ensure that other states do not benefit more from cooperation than they do themselves (Grieco 1988). Cooperation thereby takes place against the backdrop of mistrust, concerns about relative gains and cheating and is likely short-lived. Rather, for realists, international organizations are established as forums for powerful states to discuss their business. International organizations are also used by powerful states to implement their power politics more effectively and to pursue their self-interest. International organizations are only established when it is in the interest of powerful states. Similarly, international organizations can only succeed – and indeed survive – if they have the support of powerful states.

While realists make their argument with gusto and are capable of pointing out the shortcomings of international organizations in an anarchical world, realist theory has greater difficulty to explain the significant increase in the number and authority of international organizations in the post-Second World War and post-Cold War period (see Chapter 1). To explain why international organizations are created, realist theory offers two arguments. First, realists note that international organizations mostly govern in the area of trade and commerce and other domains of 'low politics', whereas realist theory is concerned with 'a small number of big and important things' in the field of security (Waltz 1986: 329). For realists, regulating internet standards is simply not as important as nuclear warfare. Second, realists argue that international organizations are created under a condition of hegemony. In other words, Western cooperation since the Second World War was only possible because the omni-powerful United States allowed its allies substantial gains of cooperation as well (Kindleberger 1974; Gilpin 1987). This is, however, the exception and not the rule. Without the United States, realists argue, we would not have had so many international organizations. Once the hegemon declines in strength or withdraws its support for international organizations, the relevant organizations falter accordingly. Realists also argue that even powerful states like the United States occasionally make 'foolish' decisions in international relations, such as believing in international organizations, which will then likely backfire (Carr 1939; Morgenthau 1948; Mearsheimer 1995, 2019).

When powerful states do decide to create international organizations, they design those international organizations to reflect their own interests (e.g. Krasner 1991; Gruber 2000; Drezner 2007). From a realist perspective, the decision-making procedures of international organizations will thus be set up in a way that privileges the most powerful member states, for instance, by giving them a disproportionate share of voting rights or special voting rights. Examples are the system of weighted voting in the International Monetary Fund's (IMF's) and the World Bank's Executive Boards, which favour Western industrialized states and in particular the United States. Or consider the United Nations (UN) Security Council: the five most powerful countries insisted that they would have a veto to stop the Security Council doing anything to hurt their interests. In many international organizations we therefore find skewed decision-making procedures that promote rather than mitigate imbalances in power.

While realists have traditionally not paid much attention to international organizations, more recent scholarship uses power-based explanations to uncover how international organizations favour strong states in everyday policymaking. Scholars have studied, for instance, the informal channels through which states can assert their power: when international organizations deal with crisis situations, strong states often take a lead role (Stone 2011). Powerful states are also good at lobbying the permanent secretariats of international organizations, because of their informal contacts, and placing their own nationals in senior positions (Urpelainen 2012; Kleine 2013; Dijkstra 2017; Parízek 2017). In other words, they often use international organizations and the permanent secretariats to exert power over weaker states (Manulak 2017). While such power-based explanations go beyond neo-realism in its purest form, they are relevant in understanding the design of international organizations.

Institutionalist theory

Institutionalism includes a wide variety of different theoretical approaches. The common theme in institutionalist theories is that states try to address *international and cross-border problems* through the creation of international organizations. Many institutionalists share the realists' view of an anarchic international system. In contrast to realists, however, institutionalists view cooperation through international organizations as a way of taming the struggle for power. In international politics, according to institutionalists, the interests of different states are usually neither mutually exclusive nor harmoniously in agreement. Instead, states have a common interest in reaping joint gains from cooperation while, at the same time, each individual state has some incentive to refrain from cooperation (Keohane 1984, 1989).

As a result of globalization, states have become ever-more interdependent and their relations ever-more complex. This often leads to problems that no state can master alone. Even powerful states now depend on other states' cooperation and, institutionalists argue, they often do so through international organizations (Keohane and Nye 1977). Institutionalist theory considers international organizations as central to international relations, and we therefore discuss this theory in greater length here.

There are various institutional theories that explain how states can address international and cross-border problems. Older theories, such as federalism and functionalism, for instance, suggest that different sort of problems can be most effectively dealt with by different levels of government (Friedrich 1968; Mitrany 1933, 1966; Haas 1964, 1968). Taking inspiration from the division of labour in federal states, for instance, in the United States, Germany or Brazil, they argue that international organizations can serve as a 'world government' for some of the largest international problems, such as climate change. We focus in this book, however, on *neo-institutionalism* – also known as neoliberal institutionalism – as it has become the most prominent institutionalist theory (Keohane 1984; Abbott and Snidal 1998; Koremenos, Lipson and Snidal 2001; Hooghe, Lenz and Marks 2019). It provides what is considered the 'standard explanation' of why states establish international organizations. It can also explain why international organizations are designed in different ways. Neo-institutionalism is furthermore increasingly used to examine the day-to-day operations of international organizations.

The starting point of neo-institutionalism is that international institutions can help states to cooperate successfully in the pursuit of common interests when these interests are neither totally aligned nor mutually exclusive. The so-called 'Prisoner's Dilemma' exemplifies such a constellation of interest. It models the situation of two suspects arrested by the police. As the police have insufficient evidence, they offer each of the (separated) suspects the same deal. If one testifies (*defects* from the other) for the prosecution against the other and the other remains silent (*cooperates* with the other), the betrayer goes free. The silent accomplice will receive a full ten-year sentence. If both remain silent (*cooperate*), both prisoners are sentenced to only one year in jail for a minor charge. If each betrays the other, each receives a five-year sentence. The dominant strategy of each prisoner will be to betray the other (*defect*) because, independently of what suspect B does, suspect A is better off when employing a defective strategy. Despite the joint interest in cooperation, both suspects have strong incentives to defect from cooperation. This typically results in an outcome where both will be worse off than if they had cooperated (see Table 2.1).

The Prisoner's Dilemma game can be applied to a wide range of situations in international politics, including arms races or trade wars between states (see Chapters 8–12). From a neo-institutionalist perspective, international organizations are created to help states address this dilemma (Abbott and Snidal 1998; Keohane 1989). They can provide reliable information

TABLE 2.1 *The 'Prisoner's Dilemma'*

		Player B	
		Cooperate	*Defect*
Player A	Cooperate	1/1	10/0
	Defect	0/10	5/5

10 = ten years in jail; 0 = prisoner goes free. Each player prefers defection, while the other cooperates, to mutual cooperation. However, both consider mutual cooperation more beneficial than mutual defection. The worst outcome for each player is to cooperate while the other defects.

about the other parties' cooperation, thereby reducing mutual uncertainty (Hasenclever, Mayer and Rittberger 1997: Chapter 3). They can also reduce the transaction costs of cooperation, such as the preparation and completion of contracts (e.g. treaties, laws and resolutions) and the monitoring and enforcement of those contract provisions (Coase 1960). International organizations thus remove various obstacles to cooperation. As they help states to realize joint gains of cooperation, states have an interest in establishing and maintaining them. In constellations such as the Prisoner's Dilemma, states create international organizations as instruments that help their cooperation (Keohane 1984: 80).

Neo-institutionalist theory provides an explanation for why states create international institutions including international organizations. It also pays considerable attention to the *institutional design* of international institutions (Koremenos, Lipson and Snidal 2001). The argument is that the design of international institutions differs depending on the problems states seek to address. Dealing with human rights violations may require a different set of institutions than tackling global warming. Some problems might require the establishment of formal international organizations whereas others can be tackled more effectively or efficiently in informal institutions (e.g. Abbott and Snidal 2021; Westerwinter, Abbott and Biersteker2021; Reykers et al. 2023). Institutionalists, however, not only consider how different problems require different sorts of institutions. They are also attentive to what is politically achievable. They highlight, for instance, that establishing international organizations through a formal treaty is typically much more difficult than setting up informal institutions or ad hoc coalitions.

In Chapter 1, we have introduced different typologies of international organizations and institutionalists make an important distinction between so-called task-specific and general purpose international organizations (Hooghe, Lenz and Marks 2019). In task-specific organizations, a group of member states tries to address a limited number of problems. Through the International Whaling Commission (IWC), for instance, member states try to regulate whaling and preserve whale stocks through catch limits in order to avoid extinction. This has several implications in terms of the *scope* and *membership* of international organizations. Task-specific international organizations tend to have a limited scope and a large membership (Koremenos, Lipson and Snidal 2001; Hooghe, Lenz and Marks 2019). The scope of the IWC, for instance, is limited to environmental and scientific cooperation. Yet to be effective, it is important for the IWC that as many states with fishing fleets become members. If only half of those states participate, it does not work. Several task-specific organizations, such as the Rhine River Commission, have a more limited memberships, but also in this case all the relevant states are included.

These task-specific organizations contrast with general purpose organizations, such as regional organizations (e.g. AU and MERCOSUR) and the United Nations (UN). The cooperation logic differs in that a community of similar states decides to address a whole range of problems collectively. General purpose organizations therefore have a large scope and a limited membership (Koremenos, Lipson and Snidal 2001; Hooghe, Lenz and Marks 2019). The EU is an example of an international organization that does almost everything. It has an internal market but also a security policy and a variety of programmes from social cohesion to public health. At the same time, the EU has a clearly restricted membership, as only European countries can join. General purpose organizations tend to be quite flexible in that they can increase their scope when new cooperation problems appear for their member states (Jupille, Mattli and Snidal 2013; Hooghe, Lenz and Marks 2019), while task-specific organizations tend to stick to their mandates. The UN is, of course, an interesting 'outlier' as it deals with a large scope and has a universal membership. At the same time, it also makes sense to consider the whole range of UN specialized agencies, programmes and funds (for instance, the World Health Organization (WHO) or the World Bank) as relatively autonomous task-specific organizations in their own right, because many have their own constitutional and institutional structures.

Apart from scope and membership, institutionalists point at *centralization* and *control* as two important features of institutional design (Koremenos, Lipson and Snidal 2001; Abbott et al. 2020). Centralization is about the extent to which policymaking takes place centrally in the international organizations or decentrally by the member states themselves (see also Chapter 1). In centralized international organizations, the member states may decide through majority voting and leave the implementation to the organization, whereas in decentralized international organizations, they decide by consensus and implement the decisions themselves. A core concept closely related to centralization is *delegation* (e.g. Abbott et al. 2000, 2020; Pollack 2003; Hawkins et al. 2006; Hooghe, Lenz and Marks 2019). Institutional theory seeks to explain why states delegate responsibilities and resources to third parties, such as executive boards, secretariats or adjudication bodies (see also Chapter 4), within international organizations. The institutionalist argument is that delegation allows international organizations to better address international or cross-border problems. For instance, member states may not always have all the relevant information and expertise at their disposal that are necessary to perform a certain task. They may thus establish an expert bureaucracy within an international organization (Hawkins et al. 2006: 13–15; Pollack 2003: 23, 28–9). Member states may also delegate agenda-setting competencies to an agenda-setting agent to 'avoid endless cycling among alternative policy proposals' (Pollack 2003: 24). Member states may furthermore not trust each other and anticipate free rider problems. As a solution they can decide to delegate (the monitoring of) implementation to independent third parties and/or establish an international court to adjudicate in case of disagreements. Through delegation, states can thus make cooperation within international organizations both more credible and more efficient (Keohane 1984; Hawkins et al. 2006).

The flipside of centralization and delegation is *control* (Abbott et al. 2020). While member states benefit from cooperation in international organizations by collectively addressing international problems, they want to ensure that their input is considered and that the benefits of cooperation are distributed fairly over the membership. They will therefore insist on strict control, yet there are various control mechanisms and they also differ across international organizations. A key control mechanism is the decision rule. While in some international organizations, member states take decisions by consensus, in others majority voting applies. Institutionalists point out that the decision rule often also depends on the type of international organization. Task-specific organizations with a large membership often have majority decision-making (Hooghe and Marks 2015), simply because it is difficult to come to consensus with 100+ member states. The UN General Assembly is an example in this respect. There are, however, many more control mechanisms that member states use. For instance, large parts of the budget of international organizations may be earmarked or consist of voluntary contributions by member states (Patz and Goetz 2019; Graham 2023). Member states also pay considerable attention when selecting the leaders of international organizations, judges on adjudication bodies, and many international organizations have rules on the appointment of staff members working in the secretariat. Variation in institutional design is once again important: the EU, for instance, appoints staff members on a permanent basis to ensure that they are independent from the member states, while in other organizations officials only work on temporary fixed-term contracts.

Delegation and control are combined in *principal-agency theory* which is a prominent variant of neo-institutionalist theory (Hawkins et al. 2006; Pollack 2003; Tallberg 2002a; Abbott et al. 2020; see also Abbott et al. 2015 on orchestration and indirect governance). According to principal-agent theory, the relationship between the member states of an international organization and its supranational bodies – that is, permanent secretariats, technical agencies and dispute settlement units – can be understood as the relationship between a principal and its agent. A principal–agent relationship is defined by a contractual arrangement which provides for the delegation of certain policy functions from a principal (e.g. the UN member states) to an agent (e.g. the UN Secretariat). This conditional and revocable grant of political authority empowers the agent to act on behalf of the principal in order to produce outcomes desired by the principal (Hawkins et al. 2006: 7; Tallberg 2002a: 25).

From the perspective of principal-agent theory, states create and sustain different kinds of international organizations with varying degrees of 'supranational' authority in accordance with the functions these agents are supposed to perform for the member states (Hawkins et al. 2006: 13–23; Pollack 2003: 20–4; Tallberg 2002a: 26). Yet despite all these advantages of delegation, member states will ensure they eventually keep control over their agents. Principal-agent theory underlines that member states need to control their agents through the use of material and immaterial incentives (carrots and sticks). This is necessary because supranational agents are actors that have preferences of their own, which may diverge from the preferences of their principals (the member states). As a result, supranational agents may behave opportunistically and minimize the effort they exert in the implementation of tasks on their principal's behalf. Or alternatively they may shift policy away from their principal's preferred outcome and towards their own preferences. In order to avoid a loss of agency, member states employ selection and control mechanisms and may sanction 'runaway bureaucracies' (Alter 2008: 34; see Pollack 2003: 39). However, control and sanctioning mechanisms are themselves costly, and too much control may undermine the very advantages of delegation (Kiewiet and McCubbins 1991: 27). Member states thus have to make trade-offs between efficient policymaking, the cost of exerting control and the potential loss of control (Dijkstra 2016; Abbott et al. 2020). They often prefer to err on the side of caution: they typically delegate too few tasks rather than risking a loss of control. While principal-agent theory puts forward an elegant model of the relationship between the member states and the supranational agents in international organizations, it is often also criticized for being simplistic.

Institutional theory thus argues that international organizations are created by states to address problems in international relations. It also argues that the type of problems affects how states design international organizations, while acknowledging the desire of member states to keep a significant degree of control over international organizations and supranational bodies. Institutionalists have furthermore studied in some detail the effectiveness of international organizations and whether international organizations mitigate anarchy in the international system. The effectiveness of international organizations will be discussed in Chapter 7, but it is important to note that institutional theory claims that effectiveness can be (partially) explained by institutional design. For instance, relatively autonomous international organizations may be better at addressing problems than international organizations which are tightly controlled by their member states (Lall 2017; Abbott et al. 2020; Sommerer et al. 2022b). Such institutional explanations of effectiveness differ from, for instance, realist theory which expects that international organizations can only be effective in the short term if the key member states agree.

Institutional theory thus does not simply assume that international institutions in general and international organizations more specifically are always effective. It rather holds that international organizations can effectively address a range of international problems, and it specifies the conditions under which international organizations are expected to be effective. Thereby, institutionalists also provide an explanation for why some international organizations are more effective than others. For example, its higher level of centralization may explain why the EU is in general more effective than, for instance, ASEAN or the AU.

Beyond effectiveness, institutionalist scholars also show that international organizations can take a life of their own. Institutionalist research has shown that international organizations' officials can develop their own preferences and that control by the member states is often incomplete. One branch of institutionalist theory (historical institutionalism) highlights that institutional choices that member states have made in the past now constrain them in the present (Fioretos 2011; Rixen, Viola and Zürn 2016). They note, for instance, that the current five permanent members of the UN Security Council were the winners of the Second World War, which ended eight decades ago. If the Security Council was to be designed today, the membership would surely look differently. Member states also do not always anticipate all the consequences of creating and designing international organizations. This implies that international organizations are often more than just what their founding member states intended them to be.

Constructivist theory

Different theories provide different explanations about international organizations, mainly because they have different views on how actors behave and the international system is structured. Realism and institutionalism generally agree that states are rational actors which make constant cost-benefit calculations. They merely draw different conclusions regarding the likelihood of cooperation between states and the usefulness of international organizations in strengthening such cooperation. Constructivist theory, however, differs fundamentally. It notes that key aspects of international relations, such as 'anarchy', which realists and institutionalists take for granted, are actually 'socially constructed' and can therefore be transformed

(Wendt 1992). In other words, the whole structure in which international relations take place is not a 'natural fact', such as gravity or the shape of the globe, but something resulting from social practice. The international system is made by people and can be changed by people. Constructivists thus claim that international organizations can help to transform, not just facilitate, relations between states.

The starting point of constructivism is the reflexive concept of action, according to which state and societal actors follow not only the rationalist 'logic of expected consequences' (Coleman 1990; North 1990; Shepsle 1997) but also the 'logic of appropriateness' (March and Olsen 1989). Actors try to pursue their interests, but they do so within the framework of existing norms and rules. For instance, as human beings we refrain from engaging in robbery not only because we fear the consequence of being caught but mainly because we have internalized the norms and rules that forbid engaging in robbery. In this view, norms and rules are not only part of institutional structures that constrain the action of actors, but they actually constitute and determine actors' interests and even their identities. Going beyond the purely anarchical understanding of the international system, by introducing an ideational concept of structure, has far-reaching consequences for the way in which international organizations are conceived.

Like other theories, constructivism has a longer historical tradition. For instance, the theories of normative idealism and transactionalism have long stressed that not states but societies – or people(s) – are the central actors of international politics (Kant 1991 [1795]; Wilson 1917/18). One key observation of idealist thought is that democratic societies, which share a number of ideals, rarely go to war with one another (e.g. Doyle 1986). Furthermore, intensive interstate and intersociety transactions and communications may lead to the creation of 'security communities' in which the threat or use of force between states becomes unthinkable (Deutsch et al. 1957). As states come to identify with one another and develop a sense of community, they develop 'dependable expectations of peaceful change' (Adler and Barnett 1998: 30). From that perspective, international organizations do not only facilitate cooperation but also contribute to socializing states into common values and norms which are constitutive for a collective identity.

The emphasis in this chapter is, however, on *social constructivism*, which has become one of the mainstream theories in international relations (Adler and Haas 1992; Wendt 1992, 1999; Risse 2000). Social constructivism stresses that the creation of international institutions in general, and of international organizations in particular, depends on whether there is a consensus over values and norms. International organizations are likely to emerge whenever the values and norms they represent are widely shared in the participating societies (Risse 2000). Furthermore, social constructivists draw attention to the importance of cognitive agreement when it comes to the creation of international organizations: different societies need to *perceive* cooperation problems in a similar manner. Indeed, constructivists argue that international or cross-border problems do not exist in themselves. The security dilemma, for instance, only becomes a 'problem' when states perceive military buildup as a security threat (e.g. Jervis 1976; Van Rythoven 2020). Migration becomes a 'problem' for states when it is framed as such (Huysmans 2000). Wherever there are fundamental differences in the perception of the problems at hand, it is particularly hard to set up a successful international organization. The creation of effective international organizations is therefore only likely when the participating societies share a basic perception of the problem (Haas 1990, 1992a; Parsons 2003: 1–33).

In contrast to realism and institutionalism, when analysing the creation of international organizations social constructivism focuses on the role of social groups (as well as individuals) that function as norm entrepreneurs seeking to persuade states to agree on and adhere to specific norms (Finnemore and Sikkink 1998). Out of altruism, empathy or ideational commitment, norm entrepreneurs call attention to political issues and try to convince states to embrace new norms within the context of international organizations. Thus, social constructivists attribute key roles to non-state actors in promoting social norms, as well as to epistemic communities and advocacy networks. Epistemic communities – transnational networks of recognized, issue-specific experts (for instance, environmental experts) – help in the formation of cognitive agreement (Haas 1992a: 3), whereas transnational social movements and advocacy networks are especially significant for the formation of consensual norms. Members of epistemic communities share causal beliefs and those of advocacy networks hold common principled beliefs (Keck and Sikkink 1998; Thakur, Cooper and English 2005; Oksamytna 2023). 'Principled beliefs' refer to ideas that express specific values on the basis of which individuals and collectives can differentiate between good and evil, just and unjust. 'Causal beliefs', by contrast, define ideas about the relations between cause and effect on the basis of which one can differentiate between true and false (Goldstein and Keohane 1993: 9–10).

From a social constructivist perspective consensual values and norms are not only important for the creation of international organizations but also for how international organizations are designed. Many constructivists argue, for instance, that there is a growing stock of global norms and blueprints of what 'proper' international organizations should look like (Archibugi, Held and Köhler 1998). For example, the increasing openness or even inclusiveness of international organizations towards civil society actors is seen as reflecting the diffusion of a global norm of democracy (Tallberg et al. 2013; Sommerer and Tallberg 2019). Similarly, accountability, transparency and legitimacy are increasingly demanded from international organizations (Grigorescu 2015). This ranges from accountability of peacekeeping funding in the UN to competitive elections for the European Parliament.

In terms of institutional design, social constructivism also claims that international organizations have their own bureaucratic authority. Theories of bureaucratic culture note that the power of international organizations is not only based on the functions delegated to them by states but derives also from their own expert or moral authority (Barnett and Finnemore 2004; Hurd 2007). Such authority allows international organizations to frame – for states and non-state actors – what are relevant political problems and propose appropriate solutions to these problems. International organizations develop a distinct life of their own. While not negative about international organizations' performance per se, theorists of bureaucratic culture do reject idealist notions of the effectiveness of international organizations and point to bureaucracies' dysfunctionalities and resistance to reform (Barnett and Finnemore 2004; Weaver 2008). They wonder how an international organization such as the IMF, created to help countries with failing economies, made recessions worse on a number of occasions. According to constructivists, one needs to account for the resilience of bureaucratic cultures to understand why international organizations sometimes do things contrary to what their founders had intended. For instance, in the IMF a bureaucratic culture exists that strongly prioritizes macroeconomic theory and models. This has persisted even in the face of unsatisfactory policy outcomes.

In the context of bureaucratic culture, scholars have also pointed at the different administrative styles, approaches to leadership and bureaucratic preferences across international organizations (e.g. Bayerlein, Knill and Steinebach 2020; Cox 1969; Schroeder 2014; Ege 2020). Even if organizations are fairly similar in terms of institutional design, staff members may still behave very differently based on the guiding organizational norms, socialization and individual preferences. Such a focus on what really goes on within international organizations also fits with practice theory, which is about how politics in international organizations is conducted, in practice, on an everyday basis (Adler and Pouliot 2011). Instead of being concerned with 'big things' such as anarchy and the nature of cooperation, it focuses on micro-level patterns in daily behaviour. As Adler-Nissen and Pouliot (2014) note, '[w]hile IR [international relations] theories may help identify *who* pulls the strings of multilateral diplomacy, they are less useful to understand *how* strings actually get pulled' (p. 890). Practice theory may thus reveal underlying patterns of power. Furthermore, despite formal rules on the equality of states within many international organizations, diplomats tend to be well aware of an informal 'pecking order' in international relations (Pouliot 2016). Diplomats from small states, such as Peru, will not claim a seat at the head of the table or repeatedly raise their voice in discussions, even if they are formally equal. This brings us back to the logic of appropriateness stressing appropriate behaviour.

In terms of the effect of international organizations on international relations, social constructivism underlines the dual role of international organizations. On the one hand, international organizations reflect the values and norms on which they are founded. On the other hand, they influence the values and norms of participating societies. As they influence the way in which state representatives and their societies think about the world, they – so the argument goes – do impact not only on their behaviour but also on their interests and identities. International organizations may shape the action of states depending on the configuration of their interests, but they can also, through the values and norms embedded in them, influence the interests and identities of states and thus, ultimately, the structure of the international system (Wendt 1999).

Three specific mechanisms can be distinguished through which international organizations may influence the values and norms of their members' societies. First, international organizations offer organizational platforms for NGOs that, as norm entrepreneurs, seek to persuade states to adhere to global norms such as human rights. If NGOs can argue that a state infringes norms to which it has committed itself through membership in the relevant international organization, it may be possible to mobilize social groups in support of these norms. The state is then compelled by internal forces to behave in a manner commensurate with the values and norms embedded in the relevant international organization (Klotz 1995; Katzenstein 1996). Second, international organizations can be seen as sites where persuasion and discourse within negotiations among states may lead to shifts in actors' interests. From this perspective, international organizations provide (or fail to provide) conditions under which, sometimes through the inclusion of NGOs, states can be convinced by the 'power of the better argument', even if it is advanced by traditionally weaker actors (Deitelhoff 2009). Third, the secretariats of international organizations themselves promote the respective values and norms by engaging in persuasive communicative action with member states and by supporting those NGOs, and the social groups represented by them, which espouse these values and norms. In this view, international organizations also act as 'teachers of norms' (Finnemore 1993).

One important critique of constructivism is that it implicitly assumes that international norms are becoming ever-more important. In particular, the idea of a 'norm life-cycle', where norms get slowly institutionalized but eventually internalized by actors (e.g. Finnemore and Sikkink 1998), has been challenged. Therefore, constructivist scholars now point out that many international norms, including well-established ones, have become contested (e.g. McKeown 2009; Wiener 2014, 2018; Panke and Petersohn 2016; Deitelhoff and Zimmermann 2020). Examples range from the ban against torture to the antimercenary norm or political human rights. This has implications for international organizations, which constructivists see as the institutional embodiment of relevant international norms. At the same time, if international organizations become contested and weakened, they will also have greater difficulty in serving as a platform for other actors such as NGOs in defending and promoting international norms. Some of these challenges are further discussed in the concluding Chapter 13.

Critical theories

We have discussed realist, institutionalist and constructivist theories of international organizations in quite some detail because these are well-established and widely applied theoretical approaches to international organizations. However, there are other theoretical perspectives on international organizations, several of which we discuss here under the broad label of critical theories. These approaches include, among others, Marxist, feminist, postcolonial and green theories of international organizations. Whereas realist and institutionalist theories, and constructivism to some extent as well, 'take the world as [they] find it' and try to make the best of a situation of anarchy and power rivalries, critical theories normatively call existing institutions and social power relations into question (Cox 2023: 169–70). Putting all these alternative theoretical approaches under the same label of critical theory does not do justice to the variety of arguments that these theories make. These theories may also not always provide comprehensive and precise explanations why international organizations are created, how they are designed and what their effects are. Critical theories rather critique the practices of many international organizations. This makes it unfair to compare their qualities to realism, institutionalism and constructivism, and many critical scholars would also vehemently oppose such an exercise. Nevertheless, these alternative critical theories do provide us with a different understanding about role of international organizations in international relations and point us at deeper, and often neglected, social power relations.

The various critical theories are, in their very own ways, concerned about power, inequality and hierarchy in international relations. They note that international organizations are an expression of hegemonic ideas, values and interests and reproduce inequalities and dominant norms and ideas at the expense of materially and discursively weaker actors. For some of these theoretical approaches, international organizations are established for this purpose (i.e. a cause), to maintain inequalities, while for most it is rather about the design and effects of international organizations. For Marxist theorists, including neo-Gramscian theorists, for instance, it is mainly transnational political-economic elites – including multinational cooperations such as 'Big Tech' – that use international organizations as vehicles for the reproduction and stabilization of a neoliberal world order (see Cox 1981, 1983; Strange 1996; van der Pijl 1998). From this perspective, international organizations are created if there is a transnational elite consensus that international organizations are conducive to the advancement of the neoliberal hegemonic project. Postcolonialists would equally point at international organizations as serving the interests of former colonial powers. The Non-Aligned Movement (NAM) and the New International Economic Order (NIEO) were, in this respect, attempts by the newly independent states to challenge existing inequality in international organizations during the Cold War (Adebajo 2023). Postcolonialists point these days at the double standards that international organizations apply when it comes to countries in the West and Global South.

Scholars coming from the different critical theories also point at the significant inequality in terms of the design of international organizations. This is particularly clear with regard to the underrepresentation of many states in international organizations. While realists would simply point out that powerful states also have powerful positions in international organizations and institutionalist scholars note that there is some historical path dependence in terms of representation, postcolonialist theory normatively challenges such inequalities. To them these persisting inequalities are wrong and need to be changed. It is, however, not just about state representation. Feminist theorists (see Tickner and Sjoberg 2010; True 2013) argue, for instance, that gender must be introduced as a category of analysis into the study of international organizations in order to shed light on how they deal with and are engaged in global gender politics. From a feminist perspective, the policy choices and activities of international organizations are often shaped by stereotypical ideas about gender and masculinity/femininity. International organizations produce gendered policy choices, which may harm women disproportionately, not least because women are underrepresented in international organizations' decision-making processes.

When it comes to the effects of international organizations on international relations, critical theories often point out that international organizations are a problematic part of hierarchy. For instance, since there can be no 'us' without a 'them', the potential of international organizations to contribute to the establishment of common identities beyond the state has an important (and inevitable) flipside: the social construction of 'an Other' that is excluded from the community (Linklater 1990, 1998; see also Neumann 1996). In this view, international organizations, just as with any social order, are based on, and inextricably involved in, mechanisms of inclusion and exclusion, differentiation between insiders ('good' members) and outsiders (non-members or 'bad' members), and resulting discriminatory treatment. Viola (2020), in this respect, points out that international organizations are part of, what she calls, the closure of the international system and help to keep various state and especially non-state actors out.

The effects of international organizations are also felt in terms of policy. From a Marxist perspective, the stabilization of a neoliberal world order as well as its concomitant negative effects on workers and politically and economically weak social actors are important problematic effects of international organizations. The neoliberal 'Washington consensus' of the World Bank and IMF is, in this respect, heavily criticized and critical scholars point at the negative societal and environmental externalities of their policies. Feminists stress that while international organizations can also promote gender-emancipatory discourses, norms and eventually laws, more often than not international organizations tend to reproduce prevailing gender images, for example, by reifying, in Security Council resolutions, gender-based expectations of women as 'passive victims' of violent conflict (Tickner and Sjoberg 2010: 202; see Shepherd 2008). Critical scholars furthermore give the example of the Non-Proliferation Treaty (NPT), which pits nuclear weapons states (which can keep their nuclear weapons) against non-nuclear weapons states (which are not allowed to acquire them) (e.g. Ritchie 2019). The NPT as such is an example of the institutionalization of inequality according to critical scholars, whereas institutionalists see the NPT as mitigating the potential risk of a destructive nuclear war.

Green theory approaches are a recent addition to the range of theoretical approaches to international relations and international organizations in particular. Critical of allegedly state-centric, rationalist and 'ecologically blind' mainstream realist and institutionalist approaches, green theorists, of both critical International Political Economy and normative cosmopolitan wings, analyse the role of international organizations in promoting or hindering global environmental justice and articulate alternative avenues for 'greening' international economic organizations such as the World Trade Organization (WTO) (Eckersley 2010: 265–73; Falkner 2012; see Paterson 2013). Scholars also discuss the implications of the Anthropocene era for international institutions (Biermann et al. 2012; Dryzek 2016; Young 2017). Overall, these scholars are critical of the attention paid to more traditional issues, such as peace and security, in international organization at the expense of what they consider really matters in international relations, namely the destruction of the environment and our habitat. As mentioned, each of these critical theories provides logically coherent perspectives on what international organizations are and should be. Yet it remains impossible to do justice to all of them in this book.

Conclusion

Each of the contemporary manifestations of the four theories of international organizations that we introduced in detail – realism, institutionalism, constructivism and critical theories – has something to say about the causes, design and effects of international organizations (see Table 2.2). In this respect, these theories compete with one another. At the same time, the creation of sustained patterns of cooperation in and through international organizations, such as the EU, the WTO and the IMF, but also the UN, International Organization for Migration (IOM) and NATO, provides a significant challenge to realist theoretical approaches. While realism can

TABLE 2.2 *Four contemporary theories of international organizations (IOs)*

	Neo-Realism	Neo-Institutionalism	Social Constructivism	Critical Theories
Structure	Material: anarchy	Material: anarchy and interdependence	Immaterial: distribution of ideas, values and norms	Material and immaterial: hierarchy
Actors	States	States, secretariats	States, secretariats, NGOs, individuals	Elites, multinational cooperations, states
Causes of IOs	Hegemon able to bear cooperation costs	Transnational problems require cooperation	Cognitive agreement; shared perception of problems	Ideologies and profit maximalization
Design of IOs	Procedures biased in favour of the most powerful states	Depends on cooperation problems; states delegate authority but ultimately remain in control	Shaped by global norms and bureaucratic cultures; high degree of bureaucratic authority	Procedures biased in favour of powerful private interests
Effects of IOs	No independent impact	Facilitating cooperation to reap joint gains	Change of political actors' identities, interests and policies	Reproduction of inequalities and dominant norms and ideas

undoubtedly explain 'a small number of big and important things' (Waltz 1986: 329) in international relations and urges us to take power seriously, it is not the strongest theory to analyse everyday developments in international organizations. It can explain why international organizations fail or why powerful states may ignore them but not necessarily why international organizations succeed and how they make policy. Likewise, while the critical theories importantly point at inequalities and normatively challenge how international organizations help to institutionalize hierarchies – including by providing powerful examples – they are less developed in terms of providing clear explanations about how international organization do operate on a daily basis. In this sense, much of the current scholarship on international organizations is largely informed by institutionalist and constructivist theories.

While it is attractive to compare theories and present alternative explanations, this assessment is, nevertheless, only partially justified because the theories operate on the basis of different assumptions. It is therefore necessary to contextualize each theory in order to evaluate its validity adequately. Realism may well help to explain security policy in the Middle East better than institutionalism or constructivism. In that particular region of the world, international politics does not yet appear to be marked by cooperation and compatible values. Instead it corresponds to a mainly anarchic self-help system so that international organizations such as the UN are only partially effective. Moreover, critical theories may be better equipped to analyse relations between the Global North and the Global South as they are characterized by the social hierarchies that critical theories are typically interested to uncover. These theories may thus be particularly suited to study the practices of international organizations such as the IMF and the World Bank for which these hierarchies seem to be constitutive. However, the EU's common policies or the WTO's international trade policy suggest a very different situation. In this case, realist explanations or critical theories can be expected to fare worse than those of institutionalism or social constructivism. For the EU with its largely compatible values, constructivism may offer the better explanation, whereas institutionalism is more suited to studying how the WTO facilitates global trading. As we noted at the beginning of this chapter, the purpose of theory is to structure and simplify the complexity of international relations, yet we should equally avoid making too simplistic claims about international organizations.

Discussion questions

1. Why do states create international organizations? Discuss the reasons from the perspectives of different theories of international organizations.

2. How autonomous are international organizations from their member states? Discuss this question with reference to different theoretical approaches.
3. How do the different theories, mentioned in this chapter, explain the design of international organizations?

Further reading

Barnett, Michael N. and Martha Finnemore (2004). *Rules for the World. International Organizations in Global Politics*, Ithaca, NY: Cornell University Press.

Hooghe, Liesbet, Tobias Lenz and Gary Marks (2019). *A Theory of International Organization*, Oxford: Oxford University Press.

Koremenos, Barbara, Charles Lipson and Duncan Snidal (2001). 'The Rational Design of International Institutions', *International Organization*, 55 (4); 761–800.

Mearsheimer, John J. (1995). 'The False Promise of International Institutions', *International Security*, 19 (3): 5–49.

3

History of international organizations

This chapter provides a historical perspective on how international organizations were created and how they developed over time. It starts with the Congress of Vienna of 1814–15 and ends with the Russian war against Ukraine. The chapter, however, does not provide a chronological list of events. Rather it seeks to explain where international organizations come from and how they change in response to important developments in world politics. It therefore uses the theories outlined in the previous chapter to give meaning to the history of international organizations.

Our starting point in this chapter is institutionalist theory. This approach notes that international organizations emerge when *international and cross-border problems* prod states into international cooperation to further common interests (the 'problem condition'). We have identified six important issue areas in international relations, which have caused problems for states over the past centuries. Indeed, in none of these six issue areas have individual states been able to address all challenges themselves. For instance, no individual state can solve the problem of climate change alone, thereby creating incentives for cooperation through the framework of international organizations. The six issue areas are:

1. War and power politics
2. International commerce
3. Global economic crises
4. Human rights violations
5. Developmental disparities
6. Environmental degradation

Institutionalist theory provides a strong answer to why we have seen increased cooperation among states. Yet the emergence of international organizations depends not only on the mere existence of international and cross-border problems but also on the *collective understanding* that these problems can be best overcome through cooperation. The constructivist theories, indeed, tell us that cooperation only occurs when international issues are perceived as problems, and it is recognized that international organizations can make a useful contribution (the 'cognitive condition'). From realist theory we know that the presence of a *powerful state*, willing to bear the costs of the creation of international organizations, is also often a requirement for cooperation (the 'hegemonic condition'). We therefore propose that international organizations are most likely to be created when each of the three conditions are met at the same time. Finally, we take from critical theories how various international organizations have been developed along (neoliberal) ideologies and privilege elites and other actors in *reproducing inequalities*.

War and power politics

The modern system of sovereign states dates back at least to the Peace of Westphalia of 1648. These treaties ended the Thirty Years War (1618–48), which was one of the most destructive wars in European history, between the Catholic Habsburg alliance and much of the rest of Europe. They marked the start of a new period in international relations characterized by the 'balance of power' between the great European powers. In this anarchic self-help system, where all states had to look after themselves, a 'security dilemma' was inherent: when one power became too dominant, it became a threat for the other powers. Some observers recognized – for instance, in the theoretical treatises of the Abbé de Saint-Pierre or Immanuel Kant – that this 'problem' could be addressed through international organizations standing above the states. Yet the idea that international organizations could contribute to stabilizing international relations by curbing the resort to violent means of self-help was insufficiently shared by states themselves. Moreover, no hegemonic power existed that could have helped to create such international organizations.

The situation changed after the Napoleonic Wars (1803–15) and the Congress of Vienna of 1814–15. The major European states assumed joint responsibility for securing peace and reducing prospects of conflict. They installed a consultation mechanism to facilitate peaceful conflict resolution, and they established a canon of clearly defined rules and customs for diplomatic intercourse. This consultation mechanism was called the 'Concert of Europe'. It is generally seen as an important forerunner of today's international organizations (Hinsley 1963; Armstrong, Lloyd and Redmond 1996: 4, 12–15). The Concert system was an inward-looking security institution (Wallander and Keohane 1999). Its task was not to deal with external threats but to guarantee security within the European system. With the exception of the Crimean War (1853–6), it contributed to the absence of continent-wide wars between the great powers for much of the nineteenth century. For instance, it helped to settle the Belgian, Greek and Italian revolutions that took place between 1821 and 1848. While it could not prevent the Franco-German War of 1870–1, the Berlin congresses of 1878 (convened to discuss the Balkan question) and 1884–5 (to settle the Congo question) were of particular significance. Afterwards, the system rapidly disintegrated and its fate was sealed with the outbreak of the First World War in 1914 (Osiander 1994).

The Concert of Europe was a consultative mechanism for states. During the nineteenth century, however, non-governmental actors also increasingly became involved in questions of war and peace. Most famously, the Swiss businessman Henry Dunant wrote about the horrors he had seen at Solferino in 1859, where wounded soldiers were left dying on the battlefield. He then lobbied Europe's leaders to promote the norm that wounded soldiers should be cared for. This resulted in the first Geneva Convention of 1864 and the creation of the International Committee of the Red Cross – a completely neutral international non-governmental organization (NGO) charged with taking care of the wounded regardless of the side they were fighting for. There were other attempts at international organizations. As the consultative Concert declined in importance, various NGOs lobbied for a 'world peace organization' (Chatfield 1997). While negotiations on arms control agreements and an all-encompassing international peace organization largely failed (Armstrong, Lloyd and Redmond 1996: 11–12), states created, as part of the Hague Peace Conferences of 1899 and 1907, the Permanent Court of Arbitration to resolve disputes arising from international agreements (Table 3.1).

The creation of international organizations became a significant topic of discussion after the First World War. The war had brutally exposed the problems of an anarchical international system (the problem condition). It was widely recognized that questions of war and peace could no longer be addressed in an ad hoc consultative mechanism such as the Concert of Europe. Instead, a more permanent and institutionalized solution in the format of an international organization was required (the cognitive condition). Furthermore, it was critically important that the United States intervened in the First World War as an outside power, albeit relatively late in 1917, thereby tilting the balance in favour of the Allied Powers. This gave the United States an aura of hegemony and considerable authority over how the post-war system would look (the hegemonic condition). The convergence of the problem, cognitive and hegemonic conditions resulted in the creation of the League of Nations as part of the Paris Peace Conference (1919–20).

As opposed to the Concert of Europe, the League of Nations was a fully developed international organization. Its main task was to strengthen

TABLE 3.1 *War and power politics as a stimulus for international organizations*

Security Threat	International Organizations (or Institutions)
Napoleonic Wars (1803–15)	Concert of Europe (1815–1914) The Hague Peace Conferences (1899/1907)
First World War (1914–18)	League of Nations (1919–46)
Second World War (1939–45)	United Nations (1945)
East–West confrontation (1947–89)	North Atlantic Treaty Organization (1949) Warsaw Treaty Organization (1955) Commission on Security and Cooperation in Europe (1975)
New wars and transnational terrorism (1990–present)	United Nations (since 1990) North Atlantic Treaty Organization (since 1991) Organization for Security and Co-operation in Europe (since 1994) African Union (since 2002) European Union (since 2003)
Collective defence (2014–present)	North Atlantic Treaty Organization (again since 2014)

international security worldwide, not just among the major powers in Europe (Walters 1952; Scott 1973; Gill 1996). For the first time, states pledged to ban the use of force in international politics with certain limitations. In order to implement this ban, which was further strengthened by the Kellogg–Briand Pact of 1928, systems for the peaceful settlement of disputes and for collective security were set up. In many ways, the League was a continuation of the Concert of Europe but now also included smaller states and had permanent institutions. Colonies remained excluded, apart from the colonial territories of the defeated Imperial Germany and the Ottoman Empire, which came under League oversight, and the United States refused to make racial equality one of the aims of the League (Acharya 2022). In seeking international stability, the League thus also institutionalized existing inequalities in international relations. The League's principal body was the Assembly, in which every member state had one vote. The Assembly met in Geneva once a year in September. In addition, the League of Nations had a Council composed of permanent members and non-permanent members elected by the Assembly. The permanent members were initially Britain, France, Italy and Japan and later also included Germany and the Soviet

Union. The idea was that the Council continued to uphold the tradition of the Concert's consultative system, thus maintaining its great power orientation. The Council met 107 times between 1920 and 1939. A final innovative element was the permanent secretariat in Geneva consisting of international experts, who were completely impartial with respect to the competing national interests. Their job was to prepare the agenda and keep the machinery running.

The League of Nations did not change the anarchical international structure, and it left states' sovereignty untouched. The organization was supposed to embody 'a world conscience' and help to strengthen the position of the 'general public' across all member states. According to US president Wilson, this would prevent the governments of member states from going to war, because governments were answerable to the people. Relying on this idealistic belief, the League stood by as Japan expanded aggressively in Asia (1931) and Italy in Abyssinia (1935). Most significantly, it did not respond to the aggression of Nazi Germany in the 1930s. The League also never had sufficient 'buy in' from its member states. While US president Wilson was a key proponent of the League, the United States did not join as a member state, after the US Senate failed to approve membership. Japan and Germany withdrew from the League in 1931 and 1933, respectively. The Soviet Union – founded in 1922 and suspicious of the League of Nations all along – joined only in 1934 after Germany's withdrawal. It was expelled in December 1939, as the Second World War was underway, for aggression against Finland (Scott 1973; Beck 1981).

After the Second World War, a new solution for the prevention of interstate war seemed imperative. The structural problem of sovereign states facing a security dilemma had persisted (the problem condition). There was a consensus that this structural problem was to be solved by the establishment of a new and strong international organization (the cognitive condition). Furthermore, the United States was deeply committed to stabilizing peace by means of international organizations (the hegemonic condition). Like its predecessors, the United Nations (UN) also emerged on the basis of a victorious war coalition (Goodrich 1947; Luard 1982; Osiander 1994). In 1945, the UN Charter was negotiated by fifty states in San Francisco. Today UN membership stands at 193 states.

The UN security system is based on a general ban on the use or threat of force among states as determined by Article 2(4) of the Charter with the exception of self-defence (Article 51). The member states undertake collective measures against any state that acts as an aggressor, and they further attempt to re-establish peace. The Security Council, as the principal security organ of the UN, bears primary responsibility for the maintenance of international peace. The Security Council determines the existence of any threats to, or breaches of, the peace and in addition, according to Chapter VII of the Charter, responds to acts of aggression with non-military or military enforcement measures (Malone 2007). Importantly, compared to the League of Nations, only the permanent members of the Security Council (China, France, Russia, the United Kingdom and the United States) have a veto over all substantive decisions. This ensures the 'buy in' of the great powers. Furthermore, the role of the UN secretary general was expanded beyond that of an impartial neutral civil servant: the secretary general needs to 'bring to the attention of the Security Council any matter which in [their] opinion may threaten the maintenance of international peace and security' (Article 99), even if this means confronting member states.

During much of the Cold War, the role of the UN in ensuring security remained effectively blocked. Within the Security Council, the United States and the Soviet Union used their veto to protect their own interests and allies (Malone 2007; Roberts 1996). As a result, the UN could often not directly act against aggressor states. Instead, it had to appeal to states to voluntarily renounce or terminate the threat or use of force. One of the innovations was the use of peacekeeping missions to facilitate ceasefire agreements. The UN would deploy 'blue helmets' to monitor whether conflicting parties were obeying their own agreements. Peacekeeping required the consent of all states involved. It was therefore different from peace enforcement, in which the UN would forcefully intervene into conflicts. secretary general Dag Hammarskjöld famously referred to peacekeeping as 'Chapter Six and a Half' of the Charter – a bit more than the pacific settlement of disputes (Chapter VI); a bit less than peace enforcement (Chapter VII). While UN peacekeeping was modest during the Cold War, it helped to stabilize regional disputes and to avoid escalation in which the two superpowers (United States and Soviet Union) would need to choose sides (UN 2004; Urquhart 1995: 575).

As the UN was gridlocked by the Cold War, two other international organizations dominated questions of peace and security: NATO (1949–present day) and the Warsaw Treaty Organization (usually referred to as the Warsaw Pact) (1955–91) (Wallander and Keohane 1999). The main responsibility of NATO was (and remains) the protection of all its member states against military aggression. NATO was founded by the United States, Canada and Western European countries in 1949 as an immediate response to the Berlin Blockade (1948–9) by the Soviet Union and the rigged elections in Central and Eastern Europe (late 1940s). Interestingly, NATO was originally a traditional alliance. It was not until 1951 – in response to the Korean War (1950–3) – that a secretary general was appointed, the International Staff was created and US general Eisenhower started to develop a permanent command structure (initially from Hôtel Astoria on the Avenue des Champs Elysées in Paris). The idea of a permanent and institutionalized alliance was certainly innovative. It was the result of a strong convergence of the problem condition (Soviet aggression), the cognitive condition (that bipolarity in a nuclear age required new forms of defence) and the hegemonic condition (the unquestionable role of the United States as a guarantor of Western Europe).

When mentioning NATO, it is important to also pay attention to the Warsaw Pact as an international organization. It was officially established in 1955 as a reaction to West Germany joining NATO. Yet it also served to buttress the Soviet Union's control within its sphere of influence, which shows both the importance of the hegemonic condition and the institutionalization of hierarchy stressed in the critical theories. It was meant to reinforce the signatories' military and foreign policy cooperation as well as their readiness for defence. In the case of an armed attack on any member state, an automatic duty of mutual assistance existed. Until 1975 this duty was geographically limited to Europe. In the course of the treaty's extension in 1975 the words 'in Europe' in Article 4 were deleted, thereby extending the treaty to the Asian part of the former Soviet Union. Besides the Warsaw Pact, various other bilateral agreements on assistance and the stationing of troops existed between its members. In the wake of rapprochement with the West at the end of the 1980s, the Soviet Union loosened its hold on its allies and, after the breakup of the local Communist parties' monopoly of political power, allowed the Eastern Bloc states to choose their own defence. As a consequence, the Warsaw Pact was disbanded on 1 July 1991.

The end of the Cold War in 1991 put renewed attention on the UN and its Security Council (see also Chapter 8). No longer gridlocked due to bipolarity, the UN became involved in a growing number of so-called 'new wars' such as those in Somalia (1992–5), Bosnia (1992–5), East Timor (1999) and Kosovo (1998–9), as well as in the global fight against 'new terrorism' (since 2001) (Kaldor 1999). During the 2000s, this resulted in a very significant increase of UN peacekeeping deployments to almost 100,000 blue helmets in 2018. Such 'twenty-first century peace operations' are driven by a strong convergence of the problem condition (many new (intrastate) wars), the cognitive condition (that UN peacekeeping is a (cost-)effective solution) and the hegemonic condition (the United States favouring robust missions). The UN Charter emphasizes also the importance of regional organizations in maintaining peace (Chapter VIII, and specifically Article 52) and the importance of regional organizations took after the end of the Cold War (see also Chapter 12). The African Union (AU) launched a large-scale operation in Somalia and a joint UN–AU peacekeeping mission in Darfur, Sudan. The European Union (EU) has also deployed various peacekeeping missions since 2003. And the Organization for Security and Co-operation in Europe (OSCE) became specialized in sending small-scale civilian peace support missions across Eastern Europe and Central Asia. NATO also adjusted to the new post-Cold War challenges with large-scale military operations in the Balkans and Afghanistan while simultaneously expanding the alliance to include many states from Central and Eastern Europe.

Throughout the centuries, we have thus witnessed an increasing institutionalization of how we organize collective security. Rather than organizing ad hoc peace conferences in the context of the Concert of Europe, we now have institutionalized forums such as the UN Security Council where ambassadors from conflicting parties can meet directly. At the same time, international cooperation in the peace and security has become increasingly contested. The reemergence of geopolitics, the Russian war against Ukraine (2022), the war in Gaza (2023) and the rise of China have made it much more difficult for several international organizations to operate (see also Chapter 13). The UN and its Security Council are under particular pressure with an increase in the number of vetoes. The OSCE, originally established to manage East–West relations during the Cold War and upgraded in the 1990s, is in a downwards spiral with a lack of consensus on its budget, leadership and future direction. At the same time, Russia's annexation of Crimea in 2014 and its full-fledged invasion of Ukraine in 2022 have created strong impetus for NATO and its collective defence mandate. Such recent developments to international organizations are discussed later in the book, but it is clear that international organizations are historically central to debates around international security.

International commerce

The Industrial Revolution, which started in the late eighteenth century, led to the creation of many international organizations in the nineteenth century. Due to the Industrial Revolution – resulting in increased production, better transport and multinational companies – the interdependencies between states increased dramatically. Global trade and commerce took off rapidly in what is often referred to as the 'first wave' of globalization. This created strong incentives to harmonize all sorts of standards for transport, communication, social regulation and intellectual property (the problem condition). These challenges were clearly recognized by contemporaries (the cognitive condition). The UK, as the most industrialized state at the time, was willing to sustain common standards (the hegemonic condition). The convergence of these conditions meant that a spectacular number of international organizations were created across different issue areas (Murphy 1994; Reinalda 2009) (see Table 3.2).

Transport

Early in the nineteenth century international organizations were set up to guarantee the freedom and security of international trade routes. For instance, river navigation still provided the most common means of transport for international trade. As trade volumes increased, this created an increasing demand for international standards of river navigation. One key example is the Rhine Navigation Act of 1815. In this treaty, the countries along the Rhine agreed to set up a special administration, the Central Commission for the Navigation of the Rhine, to develop navigation standards. The Rhine River

TABLE 3.2 *International commerce as a stimulus for international organizations*

Area of Expansion	International Organizations (One Example)
Standardization of transport regulations	
River navigation	Rhine River Commission (1815)
Railways	International Union of Railways (1922)
Maritime navigation	International Maritime Committee (1897)
Air transport	International Civil Aviation Organization (1944)
Weights and measures	International Bureau for Weights and Measures (1875)
Standardization of communications	
Telecommunication	International Telegraph Union (1865)
Post	Universal Postal Union (1878)
Internet	Internet Corporation for Assigned Names and Numbers (1998)
Standardization of social regulations	
Health	International Office for Public Hygiene (1907)
Food and agriculture	International Institute of Agriculture (1905)
Working conditions	International Social Conference (1890)

Commission, which still exists with its secretariat in Strasbourg consisting of a dozen civil servants, was one of the first international organizations as we define them today. It has more than three member states, meets on a regular basis and has a permanent secretariat (see also Chapter 1). The Rhine River Commission set the example for other river commissions, for instance, for the Elbe in 1821, the Weser in 1823, the Meuse in 1830, the Danube in 1856 and the Congo in 1885.

Maritime navigation further developed during the nineteenth century, which led to a standardized set of rules for international merchant shipping. The use of steamships, for instance, required clear rules for marine navigation to avoid collisions. The International Regulations for the Prevention of Collisions at Sea were therefore adopted in 1889, based on existing British maritime law (Luard 1977: 44–62). Throughout the twentieth century, the international maritime traffic regime and institutional arrangements had repeatedly been changed. Since 1982, the International Maritime Organization (IMO) has had responsibility for many aspect of maritime navigation.

Technological advances created a need for international regulation in other areas of transport too. The first international organizations for rail transport were founded in the mid-nineteenth century and for air transport in the early twentieth century. These were formalized in 1922 with the International Union of Railways (UIC) and in 1944 with the International Civil Aviation Organization (ICAO). Moreover, international organizations were established to standardize weights and measures, because international transport was handicapped by the multitude of national systems in existence. An example is the foundation of the International Bureau for Weights and Measures in Paris in 1875. This organization also acts as the keeper of two platinum standards for the metre and the kilogram.

Communication

Communication technology also went through a revolution in the nineteenth century – with the inventions of the telegraph, telephone and radio. These 'modern' means of communication required international regulation as well. For instance, through the telegraph, multinational companies could establish a quick line of communication, and major powers could communicate directly with their colonies. Interconnecting national telegraphic networks, however, required a set of common rules to standardize equipment uniform operating instructions and common tariff and accounting rules. After a multitude of conventions between different European states, the International Telegraph Union was founded in 1865. It finally became the International Telecommunication Union (ITU) after the Second World War. The ITU is responsible for the whole of the telecommunications spectrum: telegraph, telephone, radio, new information technologies, the allocation of frequencies and setting of fees. It enjoys universal membership (Lyall 2011).

Harmonizing the postal systems across countries proved more difficult. Individual states had fiscal interests, and the postal system represented a lucrative business. While there was a clear industrial and economic need for a faster, standardized, safer and cheaper cross-border postal system, it was not until 1874 that a treaty set up the General Postal Union (later the Universal Postal Union (UPU)). Significantly, the basic regulation of the UPU treats the territories of all member states as a single postal area, operating on the principle that the sender country's postal system determines and keeps the revenue. The treaty of the UPU has been extended several times in accordance with general technological advances. Today, the UPU is the world's largest international organization in terms of membership and geographical extent (ibid.).

Social regulation

The rapid increase in international transport and cross-border movement also resulted in international cooperation on public health. Starting with regular international sanitary conferences in the mid-nineteenth century, an International Sanitary Code was adopted in 1880 which called for the creation of health inspection commissions, especially at ports. In the Americas, a Pan American Sanitary Bureau was, furthermore, established in 1902, whereas in Europe an International Office for Public Hygiene (OIHP) was created in 1907. The OIHP, a direct forerunner of the World Health Organization (WHO), gathered and disseminated public health information. By comparison, WHO's activities today are far more comprehensive, covering the full gamut of public health activities such as the fight against epidemics, the establishment of hygiene guidelines to wipe out certain diseases (such as malaria and smallpox), vaccination and immunization and the training of medical personnel in developing countries (Lee 2009; Cueto, Brown and Fee 2019).

International commerce and the growing speed and safety of international transport also had consequences for food and agriculture. The development of sectoral world markets in agriculture had significant effects on traditionally influential producer groups as, for example, in the case of cereals. Continuous information about developments on world markets was required in order to manage suitable national protection mechanisms for domestic markets, producers and consumers. This was an essential precondition for the creation in 1905 of an early warning system in the form of the International Institute of Agriculture, a precursor of today's Food and Agriculture Organization (FAO). Created in 1945 as a UN Specialized Agency, the FAO attempts to improve world nutrition through increased production and improved distribution of food products (Marchisio and Di Blase 1991: 3–22). In addition, together with the WHO, in 1963 the FAO created the so-called Codex Alimentarius Commission (CAC), which defines international food standards to protect consumers from harmful food products (Hüller and Maier 2006).

In the late nineteenth century, the mitigation of the negative consequences of industrial expansion for the living and working conditions of industrial workers were also recognized as a public responsibility with an international dimension. As early as 1890, an international social conference was held in Berlin to discuss harmonizing national labour laws. The aim was to prevent and eliminate distortion of competition between countries because of different laws. A private initiative with official support led to the creation of an international bureau in 1901: the International Association for Labour

Legislation, based in Basel. It was responsible for providing information on new developments in national labour legislation and the elaboration of international treaty proposals for specific employment protection measures. For example, a convention was signed prohibiting night-time work by women.

The International Labour Organization (ILO), established in 1919, was an initiative by Western European trade union leaders which endeavoured to give legal force to stronger labour standards. The ILO features a tripartite representation of governments, employee and employer organizations in its decision-making bodies. After the Second World War, the ILO was incorporated into the UN system. Besides developing international standards in labour and social law, it has also implemented programmes to fight unemployment. Moreover, the ILO is heavily engaged in attempts to curb child labour, to fight forced labour, to battle against discrimination at work and to guarantee the freedom of association for trade unions, as well as employers' associations (Hughes and Haworth 2010).

Global economic crises

With the expansion of the world markets during the nineteenth century, a need emerged for international organizations to protect open markets and trade in times of economic crises (the problem condition). This need had been widely recognized as early as in the Long Depression of the 1870s and 1880s as well as in the Great Depression of the late 1920s and early 1930s (the cognitive condition). However, with the declining hegemony of Britain after the First World War, the structures of a liberal economic order collapsed. The world economic crisis which started in 1929 destroyed any hope of the order's resurrection. Led by Germany, almost all states turned to a policy of increasing tariff barriers, devaluing currencies and introducing non-tariff trade barriers. This led to an escalating spiral of protectionism. Between 1929 and 1932, the volume of world trade decreased by 30 per cent (Madsen 2001: 848). It was only after the Second World War that a liberal economic order could be re-established with the help of US hegemonic leadership (the hegemonic condition). This included the creation of various international organizations, such as the International Monetary Fund (IMF), the World Bank and the General Agreement on Tariffs and Trade (GATT)/ World Trade Organization (WTO). See Table 3.3.

Trade relations

In the spring of 1946, the UN Economic and Social Council convened a conference on a World Trade Charter, which concluded with the adoption of the Havana Charter. Its aim was to create an International Trade

TABLE 3.3 *Global economic crises as a stimulus for international organizations*

Crisis	International Organizations
Trade order	
Long Depression (1878–91)	British hegemonic power adopts the principle of free trade with limitations
Great Depression (1929–32)	General Agreement on Tariffs and Trade (1948)
Neo-protectionism (1970s and 1980s)	*Global* World Trade Organization (1995) *Regional* European Union (since 1987) Southern Common Market (MERCOSUR) (1991) Association of Southeast Asian Nations (since 1993)
Financial order	
Long Depression (1878–91)	Britain keeps the gold standard and free convertibility
Great Depression (1929–32)	International Monetary Fund (1944)
Collapse of the Bretton Woods system (1971–3)	Reformed International Monetary Fund (1978)
Great Recession (2007–12)	Reinvigorated International Monetary Fund (2010) Reformed European Union (2011)

Organization (ITO) that would guarantee free trade. However, the Havana Charter failed, as US president Truman never submitted the Charter to the US Senate for approval, fearing that the Senate would reject the proposals because of a perceived infringement on American sovereignty. Yet, in April 1947, at the same time as the deliberations for a World Trade Charter were taking place, the United States had begun to negotiate with twenty-three states in Geneva for the mutual dismantling of trade barriers. In a protocol, they agreed to a reduction of trade barriers and to the temporary coming into force of some parts of the Havana Charter on 1 January 1948. This was called the GATT. It would become the core of the international trade order.

The contracting parties committed to liberalizing trade relations by reducing trade barriers. They agreed to abolishing import quotas and to lowering import tariffs. Moreover, the GATT prohibited discriminatory treatment between trading partners. This would, for instance, avoid a situation in which the United States would apply different tariffs for New Zealand than for the Netherlands. Each state thus had to concede 'most favoured nation' status to all the other states. Only trading partners within a recognized free trade area or customs union, such as the EU, the Southern Common Market (MERCOSUR) or United States-Mexico-Canada Free Trade Agreement (USMCA, formerly NAFTA), could be given favourable treatment. During the existence of the GATT (1948–94), the contracting parties successfully reduced the average tariffs on goods from 40 per cent to 6.4 per cent (Senti 2000).

While the GATT was successful in targeting tariffs, many countries started to apply hidden forms of protectionism through what is called non-tariff trade barriers during the 1970s and 1980s. These range from product quotas to domestic subsidies (state aid) and anti-dumping measures (selling products under cost price) and bureaucratic customs and administrative entry procedures. Such non-tariff trade barriers were hardly regulated under the GATT, and they therefore presented a clear problem to global trade (the problem condition). When the United States, burdened in the 1980s by a growing trade deficit, recognized the problem (the cognitive condition), it took the initiative (the hegemonic condition) and put, among other things, the topic of non-tariff trade barriers on the agenda of the Uruguay Round of the GATT (1986–94). This major negotiation initiative, consisting of a series of high-level conferences, eventually gave rise to a new international trade organization: the WTO (Hoekman and Mavroidis 2016; Van den Bossche and Zdouc 2021).

With the creation of the WTO, international trade regulations were transformed insofar as they now covered not only trade in industrial product (as under the GATT), but also trade in services (the General Agreement on Trade in Services, or GATS) and the protection of intellectual property (TRIPS). This wider coverage of regulations is reflected in the institutional structure of the WTO. Beneath the highest decision-making body of the Ministerial Conference (formerly the Assembly of the contracting parties), there is the General Council which presides over three other councils: the Council for Trade in Goods (formerly the GATT Council), the Council for Trade in Services (GATS Council) and the Council for Trade-Related Aspects of Intellectual Property Rights (TRIPS Council). As an organization the WTO also has a secretariat and a Director-General, both of which already existed prior to 1995 under the old GATT. A Trade Policy Review Mechanism was furthermore established, and the existing Dispute Settlement Procedures were strengthened considerably (Zangl 2008).

Whereas the WTO is the main international organization for trade at the global level, there are also a multitude of regional free trade areas and customs unions organized through regional organizations. The EU is perhaps the most famous example. The six original member states (Belgium, France,

Germany, Italy, Luxembourg and the Netherlands) formed a customs union in which all internal tariffs were removed and replaced by a common external tariff. While the customs union was completed by 1968, the global neo-protectionism and non-tariff barriers gave rise to the ambition in the 1980s to establish a genuine EU single market. In North America, South America and Southeast Asia regional trade organizations have also been created. Through NAFTA (now USMCA), the United States, Canada and Mexico formed a free trade area in 1994. The member states of the Association of Southeast Asian Nations (ASEAN) have also formed such a free trade zone, and four states in South America (Argentina, Brazil, Paraguay and Uruguay) also established a common market (MERCOSUR). While the EU has abolished all internal tariffs, agreed on common external tariffs and made great strides towards eliminating non-tariff barriers to trade, other regional organizations are still stuck at a lower stage of integration (see also Chapter 12).

While states have tried to liberalize their trade relations through the reduction of tariffs and quotas in the context of the WTO as well as regional free trade agreements, during the last decade we have witnessed the return of mercantilism in what is often called geoeconomics (e.g. Blackwill 2016; Roberts, Moraes and Ferguson 2019). Particularly the United States and China have used trade policy, such as imposing tariffs on each other, as a means to fight out their geopolitical rivalry. Such bilateral disputes have also had a serious effect on the WTO which is now caught up in geopolitics and finds itself often gridlocked. Geoeconomics also includes states negotiating bilateral trade agreements with strategic partners and an effort on the side of the EU – one of the world's largest trading blocs – to consider the geopolitical consequences of its extensive trading and reliance on other states (Meunier and Nicolaidis 2019; Herranz-Surrallés, Damro and Eckert 2024). Overall, it seems that the era of expanding trade and trade programmes is over.

Monetary relations

Following US leadership after the Second World War, a new monetary order was also established based on the Bretton Woods Agreement of 1944 (Helleiner 1994). The Bretton Woods Agreement required states to guarantee the free convertibility of their currencies and to maintain a stable exchange rate with the US dollar. It was the responsibility of the IMF – one of the key Bretton Woods institutions together with the World Bank (see below) – to oversee the implementation of this monetary regime. In addition, the IMF was meant to be a 'currency buffer' by granting loans to states with temporary balance-of-payments deficits.

After a difficult start, the Bretton Woods system began to function in the late 1950s. Yet in the late 1960s the first crisis symptoms appeared. The unexpected growth in international trade and the increased private and public demand for money raised questions about the gold standard – that is the arrangement whereby central banks across the world could exchange their dollar holdings for gold (at a fixed rate of US$35 per ounce). At first, the IMF tried to stabilize the liquidity of global markets, yet in 1971 US president Nixon removed the gold backing of the dollar and thereby destroyed the system of fixed exchange rates (in the words of US Treasury Secretary John Connally: 'The dollar is our currency, but it's your problem'). A reform of the IMF statute in 1978 took account of the new realities and accepted exchange rate fluctuations. However, the IMF membership remained committed to avoiding erratic fluctuations of exchange rates. The IMF was therefore given the task of supervising exchange rate policies. In addition, 'special drawing rights' (SDRs) were introduced as a new reserve currency, but they have failed to challenge the continued dominance of the US dollar (Braithwaite and Drhos 2000: 115).

A new challenge for the IMF came as a result of the debt crises of many developing countries in the 1980s, such as the Latin America debt crisis. The IMF sustained debtor countries in order to keep them creditworthy, thereby averting a possible collapse of global financial markets (Helleiner 1994: 175–83). The IMF became a crisis manager. It provided not only financial but also political support while insisting that debtor countries comply with their loan conditions. While the IMF's political and market power was increasingly questioned, especially after the Asian financial crisis of the 1990s, the IMF once again played a key role during the most recent 2007/8 global financial crisis. Together with the EU, the IMF also helped bail out Eurozone countries, such as Greece, Ireland and Portugal. This resulted in a reinvigoration of the IMF whose borrowing capacity was increased tenfold in 2010. For the EU it resulted in an extensive package of Eurozone reforms aimed at reducing the future risk of sovereign debt crises.

Human rights violations

By the second half of the nineteenth century the idea of a democratic constitutional state began to assert itself in Western Europe and North America. This gave rise to the consensus that sovereignty and internationally supervised human rights protection were not mutually exclusive. However, despite the noteworthy advocacy activities of early transnational antislavery and women's rights movements in the late nineteenth century (Keck and Sikkink 1998: Chapter 2), and the Geneva Convention of 1864, human rights (for civilians) remained mostly an issue of domestic politics. The situation changed after the Second World War. The enormities of the Nazi crimes demonstrated the 'moral interdependence' between states and societies (the problem condition). They also led to the recognition that some international guarantees for the protection of human rights were needed (the cognitive condition). In addition, the United States, as the most powerful state, was willing to convince the community of states to accept such international guarantees for the protection of human rights (the hegemonic condition).

Protection of universal human rights

In 1941, British prime minister Churchill and US president Roosevelt adopted the Atlantic Charter, which included Roosevelt's doctrine of the four basic freedoms: freedom from want, freedom from fear, freedom of expression and freedom of religion. The Preamble of the UN Charter adopted in 1945 similarly emphasized the importance of human rights. In 1948, the international community took this commitment further, adopting the Universal Declaration of Human Rights which called for civil, political, economic, social and cultural rights. Subsequently, the UN Commission on Human Rights, which was established in 1946, was tasked to codify the rights enshrined in the Universal Declaration into international law. This led to tough negotiations, as the member states of the liberal West, the Communist East and the growing number of developing countries from the South held conflicting understandings of human rights. It finally resulted in the adoption of the International Covenant on Civil and Political Rights (the Civil Pact) and the International Covenant on Economic, Social and Cultural Rights (the Social Pact) (Donnelly 2006) in 1966. It took another decade before the Covenants came into force.

Through the Civil Pact, the UN provides individuals with many liberal rights against abuse of power by the state. They include the right to life, liberty and security of the person, to protection against discrimination, to protection from torture and slavery, to equality before the law, to the protection of privacy, to freedom of thought, conscience and religion, to freedom of expression, to the protection of the family and to vote in elections based on universal and equal suffrage. The rights embraced by the Social Pact include the right to be free from hunger and to an adequate standard of living, to work and to enjoy just and favourable conditions of work, to leisure, holidays and social security and to education. Despite their significance, the mere codification of human rights in the Civil and Social Pacts was not going to lead automatically to compliance. Therefore, committees of experts were established to check the reports that states have periodically to submit regarding human rights. A similar practice is in place for the various other UN Human Rights Conventions negotiated since the 1960s. The Commission on Human Rights and its Sub-Commission on the Promotion and Protection of Human Rights were empowered in 1967 and 1970 to undertake specific investigations of a state's human rights practices, with or without the permission of the state concerned.

Since the end of the Cold War, various additional institutions have been established to address human rights violations. For instance, the Office of the UN High Commissioner for Human Rights (OHCHR) was established following the World Conference on Human Rights in Vienna in 1993. The Human Rights Council (HRC), a standing committee of forty-seven member states, was furthermore set up in 2006. It uses three procedures to monitor states' human rights policies, including Universal Periodic Review (UPR), Special Procedures and a complaints mechanism. It can also launch investigations and appoint experts. This work is strongly supported by human rights NGOs, especially Amnesty International and Human Rights Watch. These NGOs, along with many others, have been granted consultative status which gives them the right officially to take part in meetings of the HRC.

These human rights developments have taken place outside the realm of the UN Security Council. Yet, since human rights questions are often related to issues of war and peace, the Security Council has also carved out a role for itself. In the 1960s and 1970s, it had already interpreted massive human rights violations of the apartheid regimes in Rhodesia (now Zimbabwe) and South Africa as threats to international peace and security and decided to impose sanctions. Following the end of the Cold War, the Security Council started more actively intervening in states' domestic affairs if they committed massive human rights violations (Chayes and Chayes 1995: 47). The UN peace missions to Somalia, Cambodia and Haiti in the 1990s were justified by such violations. In the 2000s, these practices gave rise to the norm of a responsibility to protect (R2P). The norm holds that sovereign states have a responsibility to protect their own citizens. Yet when they are unwilling or unable to do so, it becomes the role of the 'international community of states', that is, of the Security Council, to take over this responsibility (International Commission on Intervention and State Sovereignty (ICISS) 2001; United Nations General Assembly 2005). While the Security Council made implicit reference to R2P in 2011 when it authorized member states 'to protect civilians and civilian populated areas under threat of attack in [Libya]' (Resolution 1973), the norm of R2P has also become very contested as it may imply foreign intervention.

In addition, in the 1990s the Security Council introduced the practice of setting up war crimes tribunals following the outbreak of brutal ethnopolitical conflict in the former Yugoslavia and Rwanda (see below). These tribunals, in turn, provided the blueprint for the international community to set up an International Criminal Court (ICC) with the authority to bring alleged war criminals to justice. The Rome Statute, setting up the ICC, was signed by 120 state representatives in 1998. The Court itself is based in The Hague and began functioning in 2002. In addition to examining possible instances of war crimes, the ICC has indicted various high-level individuals, including the Sudanese president Omar al-Bashir, the Russian president Vladimir Putin and the Israeli prime minister Benjamin Netanyahu. While various indicted individuals remain at large, almost two dozen have been detained with some awaiting trial while others have been acquitted, are serving their sentence or have already completed their sentences.

Regional protection of human rights

While human rights are often said to have universal character, they are also addressed at a regional level. Especially in Europe, a remarkable set of institutions for the protection of human rights has emerged. The European Movement, consisting of important politicians and civil society actors, born at The Hague Congress of 1948, drafted a European human rights charter and demanded oversight by European courts. It thus contributed decisively to the foundation of the Council of Europe in 1949 and the signing of the European Convention on Human Rights (ECHR) in 1950 (Grabenwarter 2005; Keller and Stone Sweet 2008). Civil society actors were also decisive in the elaboration of the European Social Charter of 1961 and the negotiation of numerous additional protocols to the ECHR.

The main difference between the global human rights institutions and the regional human rights regime in Europe is not the interpretation of human rights norms but the institutionalized procedures for implementing them (Moravcsik 1995). Monitoring in the European human rights system is based on three routes similar to those of the UN: the states' duty to report, complaints by states and complaints by individuals. The striking feature of the European human rights regime is, however, that ordinary citizens have direct access to the European Court of Human Rights in Strasbourg. Once all national legal instruments have been exhausted, individual citizens can launch a complaint with the European Court. While compliance with the court judgements remains a challenge (particularly in those countries), it is extraordinary for ordinary citizens to have access to an international court. At the regional level, several international courts have also been set up to deal with human rights violations. Examples are the African Court on Human and Peoples' Rights as well as the Inter-American Human Rights Court (Table 3.4).

Developmental disparities

Decolonization in the 1940–60s led to a further demand for international organizations. Despite their newfound political independence, economic dependencies of decolonized states on their former colonial powers persisted. These dependencies of developing countries in Africa and Asia went hand in hand with global socio-economic disparities. This North–South divide had the potential to undermine the world economic order, which created an incentive to reduce these disparities with a view to stabilizing the global economic order (the problem condition). In the Cold War context, demands from the South could not be easily rejected either. As a result, as soon as the international community grasped these disparities (the cognitive condition), under the leadership of the United States (the hegemonic condition), it took

TABLE 3.4 *Human rights violations as a stimulus for international organizations*

Violations	International Organizations
Second World War: human rights violations during Nazi and fascist reign in Europe	*Global* United Nations Commission on Human Rights (1946) United Nations Universal Declaration of Human Rights (1948) *Regional* Council of Europe (1949) European Convention on Human Rights (1950) European Court of Human Rights (1959)
After the end of the East–West conflict: continuing human rights violations	*Global* United Nations High Commissioner for Human Rights (1993) International Criminal Court (1998) Human Rights Council (2006) *Regional* Reformed European Court of Human Rights (1998) Inter-American Human Rights Court (1979) African Court on Human and Peoples' Rights (2004)

the initiative in building international organizations that could reconcile the South with the existing economic order. Two types of international organizations emerged: those to administer funds for financing development and those to sustain economically fair structures favourable to developing countries. See Table 3.5.

Financing development

The most significant international organizations to address disparities in economic development between the South and the North belong to the World Bank Group, comprising the International Bank for Reconstruction and Development (IBRD), the International Finance Corporation (IFC) and the International Development Association (IDA) (Marshall 2008). The IBRD

TABLE 3.5 *Developmental disparities as a stimulus for international organizations*

Disparity	Organization
Shortage of available resources in developing countries	World Bank Group: International Bank for Reconstruction and Development (1944); International Finance Corporation (1955); International Development Association (1960); United Nations Development Programme (1966)
Structural dependence of developing countries	United Nations Conference on Trade and Development (1964) United Nations Industrial Development Organization (1966)

makes loans at market rates to governments, their subordinate authorities and, exceptionally, to private enterprises. These loans are always linked to a specific project agreed to by the Bank and intended to stimulate private, and especially foreign, direct investment. The Bank gives technical assistance to recipients on the preparation, running and implementation of the project. A small part of the Bank's financial resources comes from the member states. For the rest the Bank taps the world's capital markets. The contributions of the 189 member states are based on their economic capacities and determine their number of votes in the main decision-making bodies of the Bank. The Bank makes loans to the tune of almost US$40 billion each year.

Compared to the IBRD, the IFC and the IDA have a somewhat different lending profile. The IFC only provides loans to the private sector in less developed countries for projects aimed at raising the productivity of the borrowing country. As with the World Bank, these loans are made available at market rates. Approximately 80 per cent of the IFC's resources come from the international capital markets. The remaining 20 per cent are borrowed from the World Bank. The activities of the IDA are more oriented towards comprehensive economic and social development goals. It provides concessional assistance to the poorer developing countries, generally in the form of interest-free long-term loans, with repayment periods of thirty-five to fifty years being quite common. Its contributions can truly be called development aid. The IDA is thus more of a fund administrator than a bank, in contrast to the IBRD and the IFC. Its resources have to be replenished repeatedly to make approximately US$35 billion worth of loans a year.

Beyond the World Bank institutions, the UN Development Programme (UNDP) is also engaged in financing development. Compared to the World Bank institutions its agenda is more strongly influenced by the interests of the developing countries, which form the vast majority of UN members. The main activity of UNDP is technical assistance, including the financing of pre-investment activities. In contrast to financial assistance by the World Bank institutions, technical assistance generally means sending experts, granting scholarships for training or further education and sending equipment or other forms of aid in support of these objectives. UNDP's financing of development projects takes the form of non-repayable grants. In total, UNDP had a budget of about US$7.0 billion in 2024.

Development and trade

In the wake of decolonization, the developing countries brought their own political agenda to the UN system. They insisted on creating international organizations within the UN system to change global economic structures, allowing them to catch up with developed countries. The most important of these is the UN Conference on Trade and Development (UNCTAD), a subsidiary organ of the UN General Assembly, created in 1964. While Western industrialized countries saw the GATT as the institutional centre for international trade policy, developing countries were determined to discuss trade policy in the context of UNCTAD. Following the successful conclusion of the Uruguay Round and the establishment of the WTO, the rationale of UNCTAD has repeatedly been questioned. Many developing countries have joined the WTO.

The UN Industrial Development Organization (UNIDO) also came into being at the insistence of developing countries. Formed in 1966, it became a UN Specialized Agency in 1986. This means that within the UN it has sector-specific competencies in the area of industrial development for developing countries. During the early 1990s, UNIDO entered a serious crisis. Leading member states questioned not only the effectiveness of the organization but also its right to exist. In 1996 the United States withdrew from the organization, resulting in a decrease of the budget by US$60 million. In response to this crisis, UNIDO went through a successful reform process, streamlining its programmatic focus and increasing its overall effectiveness. In 2004, the British Department for International Development (DFID) ranked UNIDO the most effective specialized agency in the UN system.

Environmental degradation

Environmental problems, such as air and water pollution, have always been side effects of industrial production. The state, however, was at least in principle capable of dealing with these problems by introducing and enforcing legislation on environmental protection. But in the age of nuclear power plants, the diminishing ozone layer and global warming many of these environmental problems transcend national borders and can therefore not be resolved by one state alone. In order to mitigate these cross-border problems, the international community of states must act collectively (the problem condition). The resulting demand for international organizations led to their creation mainly in issue areas in which public awareness was bolstered by non-governmental environmental organizations (the cognitive condition), with hegemonic leadership provided by the United States (the hegemonic condition). See Table 3.6.

To facilitate cross-border environmental protection, states have created a number of international regimes. They have passed the responsibility for ensuring compliance either to existing international organizations or to new organizations created for the purpose (Biermann, Siebenhüner and Schreyögg 2009). This has therefore resulted in an expanded scope of the mandates of several international organizations to cover environmental protection activities. The World Meteorological Organization (WMO), for instance, went beyond its initial concerns with meteorology and data exchange to also take environmental questions into its purview after the hole in the ozone layer and global warming had been discovered (Newell and Bulkeley 2010; Parson 1993). Similarly, the IMO was given the task of sustaining efforts at reducing pollution of the high seas (Mitchell 1994). Since 1959 various conventions have been concluded to ban, for example, the dumping of substances such as radioactive waste in the high seas. The UN Economic Commission for Europe (ECE) has achieved impressive results in the formation and implementation of the acid rain regime in Europe (Levy 1993). The EU was given competencies for the protection of the environment in 1987 (Lenshow 2010).

Beyond the establishment of specific international regimes for the protection of the environment, states were willing to confront international

TABLE 3.6 *Environmental problems as a stimulus for international organizations*

Problem	International Organizations
Cross-border environmental degradation	*Creation of new organizations*: United Nations Environment Programme (1972) International Renewable Energy Agency (2009)
	Extension of international organizations' mandate: International Maritime Organization World Meteorological Organization United Nations Economic Commission for Europe European Union (since 1987)

environmental problems within the more encompassing context of the UN, which in turn has increasingly shaped domestic environmental agendas. Meeting in Stockholm in 1972, the UN Conference on the Human Environment led to the establishment of the UN Environment Programme (UNEP), providing the UN with a special organ to deal with environmental questions. UNEP consists of a Governing Council of fifty-eight state representatives elected by the UN General Assembly and a small secretariat with its seat in Nairobi (Chasek, Downie and Brown 2010). UNEP is responsible for coordinating the environmental activities of states and international organizations to promote better regional and global environmental protection. In the beginning, its role was more that of a coordinator and catalyst; more recently it has evolved into an actor with its own programmes.

UNEP has made an impact. International negotiations, under UNEP, have not only shaped domestic environmental agendas and promoted the establishment of national ministries for the environment (Buzan, Waever and de Wilde 1998: Chapter 4; De Wilde 2008): UNEP also made a substantial contribution to, for instance, the Vienna Convention for the Protection of the Ozone Layer in 1985 and its formalization in the Montreal Protocol of 1987. UNEP played a key role in preparing the Rio UN Conference on Environment and Development in 1992 and the Johannesburg Earth Summit in 2002. In addition, UNEP developed important activities to combat climate change caused by the greenhouse effect. A landmark success was the signing of the UN Framework Convention on Climate Change (UNFCCC) in 1992 and its elaboration in the Kyoto Protocol in December 1997. Under the framework of the UNFCCC, states also negotiated the Paris Agreement on climate change signed in 2016. The Paris Agreement was interesting not just for the clear presence of the problem and cognitive conditions but particularly for its American and Chinese leadership. An important question is whether the hegemonic condition will continue. The United States under the Trump administration has been sceptical of international cooperation in the field of climate change. In January 2025, President Trump announced the US withdrawal from the Paris Agreement for the second time.

Conclusion

How can we make sense of this historical account of international organizations? In this chapter, three relevant conditions have been identified, which help to explain why states create international organizations. First of all, states need to encounter a cooperation *problem* (problem condition). Second, they need to *recognize* that they cannot address this problem alone, bilaterally or in an ad hoc manner: they need to recognize that they can most effectively address it through the creation of international organizations (cognitive condition). Third, since international negotiations are complex and involve many competing interests, the creation of international organizations is most likely if a *powerful state* is truly committed and nudges the other states into international cooperation (hegemonic condition). When all the three conditions are present, the creation of international organizations may prevail.

This chapter has provided many examples of the creation and development of international organizations across different policy areas. It has shown that industrialization and globalization since the nineteenth century have posed many cross-border *problems*, which states have addressed through international organizations: from the Rhine River Commission (addressing cross-border transport) to the GATT (lowering tariffs) and UNEP (dealing with pollution). It is important, too, that certain problems, such as human rights violations and poverty, are no longer *recognized* as purely domestic affairs but, indeed, also as international problems which need to be addressed through international organizations: from the ICC (addressing war crimes) to the World Bank and UNDP (providing funds for development). Finally, the chapter has made clear that the commitment and 'buy in' of the United States and its post-war Western *hegemony*, in particular, have been critical: from the UN Security Council (as the main forum for questions of peace and security) to the promotion of liberal values in the areas of trade, human rights and development. We have also seen that *inequalities* play a key role with regard to international organizations. While some have institutionalized historical privileges, others have actually been established to address international inequalities.

These developments across the six policy areas, discussed in this chapter, are also reflected in the total number of international organizations as they have developed since the early nineteenth century. In the introduction of this book, we have provided a graph that shows how the total number of international organizations has dramatically increased over time (Figure 1.1). In particular, we saw sharp increases after the Second World War ended in 1945. The post-war period can be characterized as an era of growing institutionalization of interstate relations. Apart from a whole range of *new problems* that states needed to address (decolonization; environment; 'new wars'), there was also strong *cognitive support* that international organizations provided the answer. Indeed, it was often understood that problems were previously not effectively addressed as a result of weak forms of international cooperation. Especially in the years following the Second World War, this resulted in strong international organizations, such as the UN, the Bretton Woods institutions and NATO. This institutionalization of cooperation was not only supported by the United States as a *hegemon* willing to incur some cooperation costs; indeed, intensive Western cooperation was seen as the best remedy to keep the Soviet Union at bay.

While the extent of international cooperation has increased dramatically during the post-Cold War era – inspired by continuous US leadership – it is also remarkable that the total number of international organizations has stabilized in more recent years (Pevehouse et al. 2020). It is worth reconsidering the conditions, in this respect, to see whether they can also explain why we have not seen the creation of more international organizations in the past two decades. In terms of the *problem condition*, we would expect that once cooperation problems have been solved, states will disband the international organization. Examples include the war crimes tribunals for the former Yugoslavia and Rwanda. At the same time, there are also currently so many international organizations that we can wonder whether we have reached a maximum. Creating new international organizations tends to be expensive. Increasing the scope of existing international organizations may therefore be a better way of addressing new problems that arrive on the international agenda (Jupille, Mattli and Snidal 2013). We have also seen the creation of many other types of international institutions, including informal institutions, public-private partnerships, ad hoc coalitions and networks. In the concluding chapter of this book, we return to such innovative types of institutions.

In terms of the *cognitive condition*, the trust in the ability of international organizations to actually address problems has also decreased. Whereas in previous decades increased institutionalization and the creation of more international organizations was seen as the solution to cooperation problems, currently international organizations face a lot of criticism in terms of their effectiveness and legitimacy. In some cases, such criticism has resulted in member states leaving international organizations, including the EU, ICC and UNIDO. International organizations are also increasingly criticized by emerging powers for sustaining historical *inequalities* and insufficiently reforming to reflect the current balance of power in international relations. Finally, in terms of the *hegemonic condition*, it is clear that the United States is no longer willing to bear a disproportionate amount of the costs of sustaining a liberal system of global governance. Part of the success of many international organizations is that they have expanded their membership. The flip side of the coin is that with more members, the ability of the United States to control international organizations diminishes, which results in less 'buy in'. Two centuries of international organizations have, however, shown us that their development does not necessarily follow a predictable path. We should, therefore, be cautious in making predictions about how international organization will develop in the future (see further Chapter 13).

Discussion questions

1. What conditions explain the development of international organizations in the last two centuries? Choose a specific issue area to illustrate your argument.

2. To what extent does the creation of international organizations differ per policy area? Are international organizations used similarly in the area of security as in trade?
3. How will international organizations develop without the strong support of a hegemon, such as the United States? Give examples of different policy areas.

Further reading

Clavin, Patricia (2013). *Securing the World Economy: The Reinvention of the League of Nations, 1920–1946*, Oxford: Oxford University Press.

Kott, Sandrine (2024). *A World More Equal: An Internationalist Perspective on the Cold War*, New York, NY: Columbia University Press.

Mazower, Mark (2009). *No Enchanted Palace: The End of Empire and the Ideological Origins of the United Nations*, Princeton, NJ: Princeton University Press.

Reinalda, Bob (2009). *History of International Organizations. From 1815 to the Present Day*, London: Routledge.

PART II

Policymaking in international organizations

4

International organizations as political systems

We conceive of international organizations as political systems. Political systems convert inputs into outputs (Easton 1965). Based on developments in the international environment, political actors formulate demands and provide support for international organizations (inputs). International organizations convert these inputs into decisions and activities (outputs) directed towards the international environment. For instance, following the attack against Israel in October 2023 and the subsequent war in Gaza, many states demanded a response from the United Nations (UN) Security Council (input), which eventually adopted Resolution 2735 in June 2024 supporting a ceasefire proposal (output) even if it did not have an immediate impact on the war. When the Covid-19 virus started to spread around the world, the international community looked to the World Health Organization (WHO) (input), which declared a global health emergency and facilitated consultations between medical experts (output). Meanwhile, heavily hit Italy put public pressure on the European Union (EU) to respond as well to the pandemic (input). The EU adopted various Covid-19 policies including financial support for its member states and joint vaccine procurement (output). International organizations, such as the UN, WHO and EU, thus convert inputs into outputs. Such outputs are sometimes effective in addressing international and cross-border problems. In other cases, they may have limited impact. This, in turn, may result in renewed input for international organizations. See Figure 4.1.

In this book we argue that *the process* through which international organizations convert inputs into outputs significantly affects what outputs eventually look like. In other words, what happens *inside* international organizations matters (the grey box in Figure 4.1). By acting through international organizations, member states can therefore expect different outputs than when they act outside the framework of international organizations. Yet the argument goes further. The way international

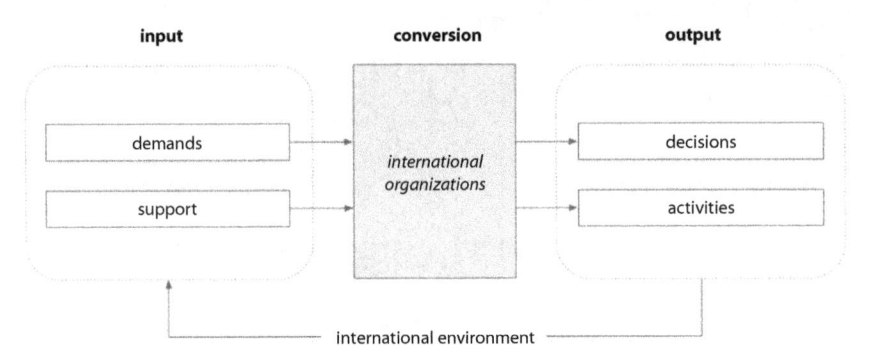

FIGURE 4.1 *The political system of international organizations.*

organizations are designed, in terms of rules, scope, membership and so on, also affects what outputs eventually look like. The reality that the UN Security Council has five permanent members with veto powers significantly affects the number and substance of its resolutions. The fact that states have delegated tasks in many policy areas to the experts of the World Bank makes a difference in terms of development loans. If two international organizations are designed differently, they will convert the same inputs into different outputs.

This chapter and the next three chapters discuss the different aspects of the political system. This chapter focuses on the *constitutional structure* and *institutional structure* of international organizations. Just as in sports the size of the field greatly affects the players' tactics, the same can be said about international organizations. The structure of international organizations determines how states negotiate and make policy within them. Therefore, we should first analyse the structure ('the box' itself) before we can study how states and other actors pursue their interests within international organizations. While the constitutional and institutional structure determine the venue and set the fundamental rules of the game, it is important to understand that they themselves have also been subject to intensive negotiations by the member states. Yet once the constitutional and institutional structure are agreed, they provide the overall framework for policymaking. After this chapter about the structure of the political system of international organizations, Chapters 5, 6 and 7 focus, respectively, on the input dimension, conversion process and output dimension.

The constitutional structure of international organizations

Despite the anarchical structure of the international system, international politics is not devoid of legal rules and norms. Besides the general principles of international law (e.g. *pacta sunt servanda* (agreements must be kept)), there are two primary sources of international law: international treaty law and customary international law. International treaty law is of great importance for the creation of international organizations. In general, international organizations are set up by a treaty between three or more states. Such treaties are frequently negotiated at diplomatic conferences before being signed and ratified. For example, the founding treaty of the UN (the UN Charter) was drawn up and signed in 1945 by representatives of fifty countries who had convened in San Francisco for the UN Conference. However, international organizations can also be established by the decision of an existing international organization if this right was granted in its founding treaty. For example, the UN can create new subsidiary organs through resolutions of the General Assembly (Johnson 2014). The UN Conference on Trade and Development (UNCTAD) (1964), United Nations Industrial Development Organization (UNIDO) (1966) and UN Entity for Gender Equality and the Empowerment of Women (UN WOMEN) (2010) are examples of organizations established in this way within the UN system.

A founding treaty normally outlines the organization's mission and membership, establishes its various organs and determines the allocation of competencies between these organs. It thus acts as a sort of 'constitution'. While international organizations do not fully compare to sovereign states, they are clearly 'constituted' through their founding treaties. These founding treaties vary considerably in terms of their ambition and precision. For example, the EU treaties are very detailed and ambitious and cover almost 400 pages (consolidated version of Treaty on European Union (TEU) and Treaty on the Functioning of the European Union (TFEU)). Besides general statements about the EU's mission and institutional structure they also contain policy programmes (such as the freedom of movement of persons, services and capital, Articles 45–66 TFEU) and clauses authorizing the formulation of further policy programmes. The UN Charter, by contrast, is both less detailed and less ambitious. It is only twenty pages (excluding the Statute of the International Court of Justice (ICJ)). Although the Charter contains statements about the UN's general mission and its organizational structure, it hardly defines any policy programme which could be implemented without further elaboration. The same goes for the founding treaties of the North Atlantic Treaty Organization (NATO), the African Union (AU) and the Association of Southeast Asian Nations (ASEAN) all of which are concise.

Constitutions of international organizations are subject to formal and informal change. Formal changes can occur either through a procedure prescribed in the constitution itself or through a new (complementary) treaty signed by the member states. Informal changes occur on the basis of customary international law. Yet, just like constitutions of countries, the founding treaties of international organizations tend to be hard to amend. For example, the UN Charter requires that amendments (1) are adopted by two-thirds of the members of the General Assembly and (2) are ratified by two-thirds of the members of the General Assembly, including all permanent members of the Security Council (UN Charter, Article 108). There have only been five amendments to the Charter in 1965, 1968 and 1973. These amendments were about increasing the membership of the Security Council and Economic and Social Council (ECOSOC) as a result of the increased overall UN membership after the period of decolonization.

Often, formal constitutional changes in international organizations have to do with the expanded scope or membership of the organization. The founding treaties of the EU, for instance, have been amended through, among others, the Single European Act (1987) and the Treaties of Maastricht (1993), Amsterdam (1999), Nice (2003) and Lisbon (2009). All of these changes had to do with further European integration, strengthening the EU institutions and creating more flexible decision rules (Christiansen and Reh 2009). In addition, the EU has amended its founding treaties to allow for the accession of twenty-two countries between 1973 and 2013. The 2000 Constitutive Act of the AU that replaced the 1963 Charter of the Organization of Africa Unity, on the other hand, was not the result of an increase in membership. Rather it had to do with the changing and more ambitious scope of the newly established AU compared to its predecessor. Interesting, the 1951 Refugee Convention which sets out the policy programme for the UNHCR originally only applied to events in Europe that had taken place before 1951. The 1967 Protocol removed these restrictions after which the Convention became applicable to refugee crises worldwide. Just as the constitutional structure of international organizations can change due to new member states, many treaties also include procedures for the withdrawal of states.

Since formal changes to constitutions of international organizations are difficult to achieve – often requiring supermajorities, consensus and domestic ratification – informal constitutional changes play an important role (Gray 2024). The legal source of such informal changes is not the international law of treaties but rather customary international law. It can be defined as 'general practices' in international relations which are accepted by states as law (Statute of the ICJ, Article 38(1)(b)). It thus consists of two elements. First, many states, including ideally major powers, should engage in the practice. Second, states should consider that they are bound by this practice as if they are obliged by law (*opinio juris*). Customary international law can result, in some cases, in change. States can, for instance, adopt certain working methods within the international organizations, which get reinforced over time and therefore become a 'practice'. In some cases, this can go against the letter of the treaty. For instance, the UN Charter states that '[d]ecisions of the Security Council . . . shall be made by an affirmative vote of nine members *including the concurring votes of the permanent members*'

(Article 27(3), emphasis added). This implies that the five permanent members cannot abstain. After all, an abstention is not a concurring vote and therefore formally equals a veto. The five permanent members, however, quickly decided among themselves that they should have the possibility to abstain. They did not decide to formally amend the UN Charter but rather created a new informal practice. Following decades of precedent, it is now customary international law that the permanent members can also abstain.

It is not just that it is difficult to formally change treaties because of supermajorities, consensus and domestic ratification in an increasingly large number of member states. Scholars have also argued that due to an increasing politicization of international organizations in various countries around the world, formal treaty change has become virtually impossible. They have nonetheless witnessed that the constitutional structure of international organizations has expanded (and in some cases contracted) in the absence of formal treaty change (Kreuder-Sonnen 2019; Kreuder-Sonnen and Zangl 2024). The most significant operational activity of the UN, for instance, is peacekeeping even if the Charter does not mention it (see Chapter 8). Another interesting example is the Covid-19 pandemic, which resulted in various international organizations taking on a public health function even if they did not have a treaty-based mandate (Debre and Dijkstra 2021b). The argument, however, goes further. Because of the politicization of international cooperation, many states no longer develop treaty-based cooperation. The Paris Agreement on Climate Change is a prime example here. Because binding treaties require a two-third majority in the US Senate, the United States has become very reluctant to negotiate treaties. The Paris Agreement was therefore negotiated as a non-binding agreement instead. More generally, we have seen more informal institutions in recent decades (see further Chapter 13).

International organizations can also be dissolved, replaced or merged with other institutions. This can happen for a variety of reasons (e.g. Debre and Dijkstra 2021a; Eilstrup-Sangiovanni 2021). Sometimes, the international and cross-border problems which led to the creation of an international organization may disappear. As discussed in the previous chapter, for instance, the International Telegraph Union evolved into the International Telecommunications Union. In other cases, international organizations break down due to conflict between the member states. In the 1930s, for instance, various member states withdrew from the League of Nations, which eventually could not prevent the Second World War from breaking out. The dissolution of international organizations can, however, be a lengthy and difficult legal process because the member states still need to agree on what to do with the assets and liabilities of the organization, such as buildings, pension plans for staff as well as funds and debts (Klabbers 2022; Mumby 2023; Dijkstra, Debre and Heinkelmann-Wild 2024).

The institutional structure of international organizations

The description of the institutional structure is often an important part of the founding treaties. About half of the chapters and articles of the UN Charter deal with the six UN organs (Chapters III–V, X, XIII–XV). In the 2007 ASEAN Charter, around three-fourth of the articles are about the different institutions and how they operate. Even if the institutional structure features prominently in most founding treaties, international organizations vary widely in terms of how their institutions look. As noted in Chapter 1, international organizations should have, at the minimum, a plenary meeting of three member states at least every ten years as well as a permanent secretariat and correspondence address. Many international organizations, however, have a much more elaborate structure. To allow for the comparison between international organizations, this chapter discusses six different types of 'organs' (Amerasinghe 2005; Klabbers 2022). While a few international organizations have all six organs, many international organizations possess only two (plenary meeting and a permanent secretariat). The six different types of organs are:

1. A plenary organ representing all state (and, if applicable, non-state) members – for example, a general conference, a general assembly or a council of ministers. The plenary organ is normally the international organization's highest authority.

2. An executive council or board to manage and supervise day-to-day business. The executive council usually consists of a limited number of state (and, if applicable, non-state) members elected by the plenary organ.

3. A permanent secretariat with administrative staff led by a secretary general, a director-general or a commissioner responsible for expert advice, implementation and external representation as well as administrative tasks such as conference management.

4. A court-like body or a court of arbitration in cases of disputes among members or between the administrative body and another organ or a member.

5. A parliamentary assembly of elected representatives or delegates from national parliaments that debates, reviews and, in certain cases, approves of the organization's policies.

6. An organ representing civil society organizations and/or other private actors or subnational, regional or local administrative bodies.

Plenary organs

The plenary organs of international organizations are based on the principle of member states' sovereignty. All states therefore have their own representatives within the plenary organs. They act according to their governments' instructions. Despite the increasing role that non-state actors play within international organizations, in most plenary organs, such as the UN General Assembly or the International Monetary Fund's (IMF's) Board of Governors, only governments are represented. A long list of 'non-member states, entities and organizations' has a standing invitation to participate, for instance, in the UN General Assembly as observers, but they are not formal members and do not have voting rights. The plenary organs are frequently at the centre of international organizations' decision-making. They are normally the international organizations' highest authorities (Figure 4.2).

The policymaking procedures in plenary organs vary considerably. While in some international organizations the plenary organs take decisions by consensus (e.g. the Ministerial Council of the Organization for Security and Co-operation in Europe (OSCE)), other international organizations have majority voting (e.g. UN General Assembly). Yet even when it comes to majority voting, there is a wide variety among the plenary organs in terms of the number of votes required for reaching a decision and the weighting given to the votes of different members. The number of votes required can be situated on a continuum ranging from the principle of near unanimity to that of a simple majority (50 per cent + 1). The closer the procedure in the plenary organ is to the principle of unanimity, the more arduous and time-consuming it is to reach decisions (Tsebelis 2002). Sometimes decisions cannot be reached at all. It is also important how many votes each member state has. While in the UN General Assembly each state has one vote, in the plenary organs of the EU, IMF and World Bank votes are weighted. In giving powerful states more voting power, chances are smaller that powerful states

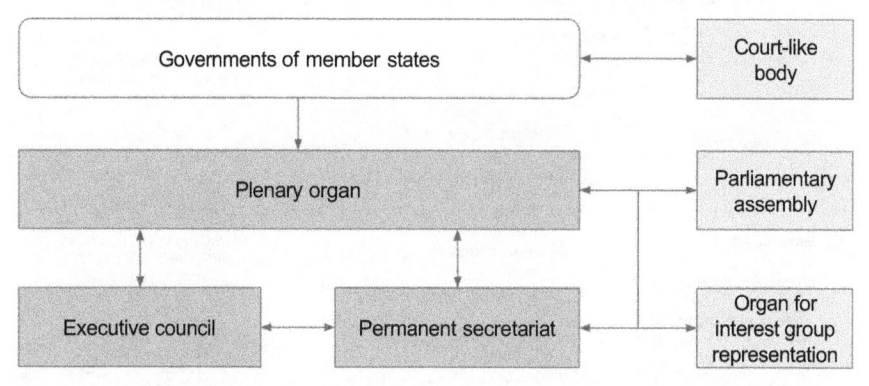

FIGURE 4.2 *The institutional structure of international organizations.* Arrows indicate interactions between the different organs.

will simply disregard decisions made by a majority of smaller states. The weighting of votes can be based on the population of member states or their economic power.

When it comes to policymaking procedures in plenary organs, there is an important balance between the efficiency and legitimacy of decision-making. In the EU, for instance, for reasons of quick and efficient decision-making, member states have over time moved away from consensus decision-making towards qualified majority voting in most policy areas. At the same time, there is the risk that states which are outvoted do not consider the decision legitimate and will not implement it domestically. In many international organizations, states will therefore negotiate until they have a consensus even if the formal rule is majority voting. A good example is the UN General Assembly: while decisions can be taken by 'two-thirds majority of the members present and voting' (UN Charter, Article 18(2)), most decisions are actually taken by unanimity. If there is no unanimity, implementation and compliance with the decisions of the General Assembly becomes a real issue of concern. For instance, the General Assembly regularly votes on resolutions sponsored by Arab countries aimed against Israel. While such resolutions get adopted, because they have a two-thirds majority, they also get ignored by Israel, the United States and other countries voting against.

As noted, the plenary organ of the UN is the General Assembly (Figure 4.3). It convenes at least once a year from September to December for a regular session. All member states are represented, with one vote each.

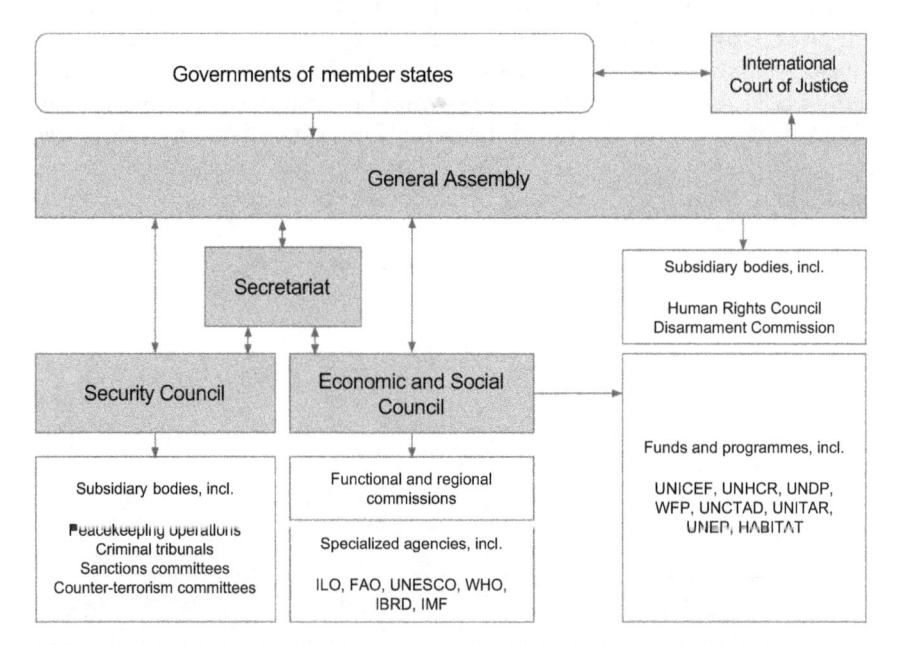

FIGURE 4.3 *The institutional structure of the United Nations (UN)*. Arrows indicate interactions between the different organs.

The General Assembly starts off with a high-level 'General Debate' which involves a week of speeches by national leaders and their foreign ministers. In the months after, much of the work gets done in the six committees of the General Assembly in which all states are represented. The General Assembly is chaired by a president, who is elected every year. The General Assembly examines and approves the organization's budget, determines the members' contributions and elects, in conjunction with the Security Council, the UN secretary general and the judges of the ICJ. Furthermore, it can voice an opinion on practically all problems of international politics in the form of legally non-binding resolutions. As every state has one vote in the General Assembly, it is politically the domain of 'the Global South'. For instance, the Group of 77 (G77), which is the main coalition of 130+ developing countries, already has a two-thirds majority and is therefore a key actor in the General Assembly.

When reviewing plenary organs we also need to mention the Board of Governors of the IMF and the World Bank. The Board of Governors includes a representative from each member state, typically the minister of finance or head of the central bank. The Board of Governors of the IMF and World Bank hold one joint Annual Meeting once a year. The decisions are based upon weighted voting and are taken with a qualified majority. In both international organizations, approximately 5.5 per cent of the votes are distributed equally among the member states (so-called basic votes). The remaining 94.5 per cent of the votes are distributed based on the contribution that member states make to these organizations. IMF members get one vote for each quota of 100,000 Special Drawing Rights (SDRs), whereas votes in the case of the World Bank are calculated on the amount of share capital. This weighted voting right gives Western industrialized countries, and especially the United States, a decisive influence. In the case of decisions such as the replenishment of capital and change of quotas, which require a qualified majority vote (85 per cent), the United States and the member states of the EU (acting collectively) have de facto veto rights. For instance, the United States had respectively 16.49 per cent and 15.84 per cent of the votes in the IMF and World Bank in 2024.

In regional organizations, we also find a range of plenary organs (see also Chapter 12). The plenary organ of the EU is the Council of the EU (often referred to as the Council of Ministers). It consists of the member states' ministers and meets in ten different configurations, such as the Foreign Affairs Council, the Agriculture and Fisheries Council and the Economic and Financial Affairs Council. The Foreign Affairs Council consists of the foreign ministers, whereas the Agriculture and Fisheries Council consists of agriculture ministers. While the Council of the EU is the formal plenary organ and the EU highest law-making authority, it operates under the European Council. The European Council, consisting of national leaders, defines 'the general political directions and priorities' of the EU (Article 15 TEU). As such, it is critically important (and has become even more important over the past decade) but it does not engage in actual EU law-making. Decision-making procedures in the Council of the EU vary widely across policy areas. In most of the cases, it takes decisions with qualified majority, but in some policy areas consensus decision-making remains the rule.

In other regional organizations, we also find plenary organs consisting of summits by heads of state and government as well as ministerial councils. The AU has an Assembly of the heads of state and government of the member states. Similarly, ASEAN has a Summit of the national leaders even if it has a Coordinating Council, Community Councils and Sectoral Ministerial Bodies as well. All of these could be counted as part of the plenary organs, just as ministerial councils in the EU constitute the plenary. The Southern Common Market (MERCOSUR) simply has a Council as a plenary organ. In each of these of the regional organizations, consensus decision-making remains the rule, even if the AU allows for voting in case consensus cannot be reached. This also reflects the fact that ASEAN and MERCOSUR have a lot less member states, as regional organizations, than universal organizations such as the UN. Theoretically it is easier to take decisions in such a smaller group, even if in practice reaching consensus can be quite the challenge.

Executive councils

Executive councils of international organizations meet more frequently than the plenary organs. Indeed, some meet in permanent session. Their main task is to supervise the permanent secretariat of the organization and to take on the implementation of policy programmes decided by the plenary organ. Executive councils are often smaller than plenary organs. Many executive councils are composed of a limited number of member states' representatives elected by the plenary organ. In some inclusive organizations such as the Global Fund to Fight AIDS, Tuberculosis and Malaria, the executive council (or rather the 'board') is formed by representatives of state and non-state (civil society and/or business) constituencies. Moreover, some executive councils have a mixture of permanent and non-permanent members. The UN Security Council, for instance, has five permanent members and ten non-permanent members. In the Governing Body of the International Labour Organization (ILO) the ten major industrial countries are similarly permanently represented. Where members are elected, often the larger, politically and economically important countries are more regularly chosen, for instance, in the Executive Board of the UN Development Programme (UNDP). In addition, the allocation of seats on governing bodies or executive councils often has to satisfy principles of fair regional representation. For instance, this holds for the election of the members of the Security Council and of ECOSOC.

The division of competencies between the plenary organ and the executive council is of major importance for the decision-making process of international organizations. Sometimes, the executive council is given important competencies. This makes decision-making quicker and more efficient, because the number of participants is limited. Yet it makes compliance by the members of the organization not represented on the executive council more difficult. The effects of keeping the major decision-making competencies within the plenary organ are the reverse: decisions may be easier to implement, but reaching them is often much more arduous. Also, when the plenary organ fails to take a decision, further negotiations may have to wait for the next session (which could be in twelve months). Hence the question of a sound distribution of competencies between the plenary organ and the executive council is a key topic of debate.

The system of governing bodies and executive councils in the UN system follows a functional differentiation. The Security Council, for instance, is responsible for all questions pertaining to international peace and security. ECOSOC, on the other hand, deals with economic, social and cultural problems of international politics. Yet the competencies of ECOSOC, which can only make legally non-binding decisions by simple majority, are rather modest. It functions mainly as a coordinating body for different UN Special Organs and Specialized Agencies. The fifty-four members, eighteen of whom are elected annually by the General Assembly for a three-year period, meet two to three times a year.

The UN Security Council, by contrast, has far-reaching competencies. It can, according to Chapter VII of the UN Charter, pass legally binding resolutions, including resolutions about military operations and sanctions. Such resolutions are binding not only on UN member states but also on non-members and even on individuals. Terrorist groups such as Al-Qaida or private companies such as North Korean banks can be the targets of legally binding Security Council resolutions, as can be individuals such as state or rebel leaders indicted by the International Criminal Court (ICC) or leaders of terrorist groups who have been violating UN Charter principles. Of the Security Council's ten non-permanent members, five are elected each year by the General Assembly for a two-year term. The election follows a geographical distribution: three states from Africa, two from Asia, two from Latin America and the Caribbean, two from the 'Western Europe and Others' group and one from Eastern Europe. Decision-making in the Security Council depends partly on the issue under consideration. While decisions on procedural matters require a majority of nine of the total of fifteen permanent and non-permanent members (Article 27, paragraph 2 of the Charter), decisions on all other matters require the same majority but can, in addition, be vetoed by any one of the five permanent members (Article 27, paragraph 3). Since, in practice, most matters the Security Council has to deal with are not considered 'procedural' but rather 'other matters', this extends the right of veto to each of the permanent members on nearly all questions (Malone 2007).

Some international organizations can do without executive councils. For example, the Council of Europe does not have an executive council in addition to its plenary organ, the Committee of Ministers. The EU, on the other hand, does have executive councils. The range of its tasks cannot be managed by the Council of Ministers alone. Thus the Committee of Permanent Representatives (COREPER) assumes the responsibilities of an executive council and deals with day-to-day business. It meets at least once a week in order to coordinate relevant policies and to prepare the agenda for Council meetings. In addition, the EU has a number of other executive councils, including the Political and Security Committee for foreign and security issues, the Special Committee on Agriculture, the Economic and Financial Committee and the Trade Policy Committee. These committees are formally different from the Council of Ministers and have their own set of competencies defined in the Treaties. This makes the EU different from, for instance, NATO's North Atlantic Council which is a single body that can meet at different levels (ministers and ambassadors).

Permanent secretariats

A permanent secretariat with administrative staff is a necessary part of the institutional structure of any international organization (as per the definition of international organizations, see Chapter 1). Since the secretariat, also called 'bureau' or 'commission', often has a building, a figurehead, a press department and serves as the main contact point, it is frequently mistaken for the international organization as a whole. This is not the case: the UN Secretariat is not the same as 'the UN', and the IMF staff is not the same as 'the IMF' (e.g. Claude 1996; Weiss, Carayannis and Jolly 2009). Also, in some international organizations, there is a permanent secretariat as well as a separate secretariat for the plenary organs and executive councils. In the EU, for instance, the European Commission is considered the main secretariat, even if the Council of the EU has its own sizeable secretariat (Council Secretariat) to facilitate all the meetings between the ministers and diplomats. Unlike the members of the plenary organs or executive councils, the secretariat staff are normally not representatives of member states' governments. They are therefore independent of instructions from the governments of their countries of origin (in small international organizations, one of the member states may provide secretarial services which are then often based in the ministry of foreign affairs). Some permanent secretariats only provide technical services in the preparation for meetings of the plenary organs or executive councils. However, in many of the larger international organizations, permanent secretariats have become large bureaucracies that frequently exert independent influence on policymaking in international organizations (Barnett and Finnemore 2004).

The UN Secretariat's staff members are recruited on the basis of ability and suitability as well as political-geographical distribution. UN personnel constitute an international civil service and are not allowed to follow instructions from their countries of origin or other member states. That said, officials from high- and low-income countries are overrepresented across the UN system, while officials of middle-income countries are underrepresented (Parízek 2017). The secretary general presides over the Secretariat and is elected by the General Assembly for a period of generally five years on the recommendation of the Security Council. The secretary general can exert influence on decision-making in the General Assembly and the Security Council. Formally, the secretary general has the duty to bring to the attention of the Security Council all matters affecting peace and security (Article 99 of UN Charter). The secretary general, with support of the Secretariat, does so by writing formal reports on a daily basis. These reports contain concrete policy options for the Security Council and the General Assembly. They have also a considerable media profile and can draw attention of the international community to certain conflicts simply by visiting a country or holding a press conference (Chesterman 2007).

The European Commission, the administrative staff of the EU, is one of the largest and strongest permanent secretariats. It has extraordinarily wide competencies. Across most policy areas, the European Commission is the only body that can submit draft proposals for legislative acts to the Council. Therefore, the Commission is the engine of law-making in the EU. Besides its involvement in law-making, the Commission also monitors the application of European laws in member states and can, in case of their non-compliance, file lawsuits before the European Court of Justice (ECJ) (Jönsson and Tallberg 1998; Wallace 2010: 70–5). The head of the Commission is the president, who is nominated by the national leaders and approved by the European Parliament, subject to hearings, for a five-year term. The same goes for the other commissioners, one for each member state. It is important to note that members of the Commission are independent from the governments of their state of origin. The commissioners are supported by more than 30,000 officials who run the EU on a day-to-day basis. They get recruited through an open competition (concours) and are formally independent from the member states. Beyond the EU, there are other international organizations with large secretariats, including the World Bank, UNHCR and NATO all of which employ thousands of employees.

Courts of justice

Some international organizations have courts of justice or court-like bodies as part of their institutional structure. Their task is to decide on disputes between the members of the organization, between the organization and its members or between organs of the organization. Sometimes they can even decide on disputes between individuals, the organization and/or its member states. In some international organizations these bodies function as supranational courts in which independent judges exercise compulsory jurisdiction. This means that the court has automatic authority to deal with a dispute: the disputant states do not have to first accept the court's authority. The Appellate Body of the World Trade Organization (WTO) is a case in point. In other organizations, however, these bodies can hardly be regarded as standing above the parties; they may not be able to exercise compulsory jurisdiction, and the judges may be politically dependent state representatives. Usually these bodies are meant to support intergovernmental efforts at dispute settlement through political compromise rather than to adjudicate disputes and appoint a 'winner' and a 'loser' (Keohane, Moravcsik and Slaughter 2000; Zangl 2008).

The ICJ in The Hague is the relevant body for the UN, and the ECJ in Luxembourg settles disputes for the EU. While the fifteen judges of the ICJ are elected separately by the UN Security Council and the General Assembly, with an absolute majority required in both organs, the judges and advocates general of the ECJ are appointed unanimously by the EU member states. In practice, each EU member state proposes one judge of its nationality. The political independence of the judges is guaranteed in both courts. However, the ICJ's capacity to decide in cases of a legal dispute between states is rather limited, because the court does not have compulsory jurisdiction. The ECJ, by contrast, can exercise compulsory jurisdiction. Hence, no member state that has been charged with violating its commitments under EU law can prevent the court from ruling. Through binding rulings the ECJ asserts the supremacy of EU law over national law and implements it in conjunction with the courts of the member states. The ECJ thus has competencies that are comparable to those of national administrative and constitutional courts (Alter 2001). The AU has also established an African Court of Justice and Human Rights, even though this African Court largely deals with human rights cases rather than disagreements between the member states.

Parliamentary assemblies

Some international organizations, such as the EU, the AU, the Council of Europe, the Organization for Security and Co-operation in Europe (OSCE) and NATO, have parliamentary assemblies. Their function is to provide legitimacy for the intergovernmental organization's decision-making process. Parliamentarians represent the input of citizens. However, the competencies of, as well as the representation in, these assemblies vary considerably. While since 1979 the members of the European Parliament have been elected directly, the members of most other parliamentary assemblies are delegated by member states' national parliaments – that is, a select group of parliamentarians from each national parliament meet as part of the parliamentary assembly of the international organization. The European Parliament has generally accrued major rights (Rittberger 2005). It is now the co-legislator on most EU policy areas and has the right to appoint and dismiss European Commissioners. The parliamentary assemblies of most international organizations play a much more modest role.

Since the European Parliament has such exceptional powers for a parliamentary assembly, it is important to elaborate further to put them in context. The role of the European Parliament has gradually developed over time, partially due to a general understanding that the EU has a 'democratic deficit' and partially through precedent. The introduction of the co-decision procedure in the Treaty of Maastricht (1993) was important. The role of the Parliament as the 'second legislative organ' beside the Council was further affirmed by the Treaty of Amsterdam (1999), the Treaty of Nice (2003) and the Treaty of Lisbon (2009). These treaties allowed the European Parliament to exert influence through the ordinary legislative procedure, which is used in the large majority of policy dossiers. In addition, the European Parliament has used its various competencies to further increase its power. For instance, it threatened to exceptionally use its power to dismiss the full Santer Commission in 1999 following a corruption scandal involving one of the commissioners, after which the full Commission resigned. Since this 'triumph' of the Parliament, it has used this precedent to hold tough hearings with all commissioners prior to the appointment of the full Commission. These hearings regularly lead to individual commissioners getting blocked. The European Parliament has also used its budgetary powers to further increase its profile.

Representation of non-governmental actors

So far, we have mainly focused on the institutional structure of what can be called traditional international organizations. Many of the relevant international organizations such as the UN, the WTO or NATO are still relatively closed organizations that cater for their governmental member states. However, the representation of non-governmental actors in international organizations has significantly increased since the end of the Cold War (Tallberg et al. 2013). Inclusive organizations such as the Global Fund have been created in which state and non-state actors are members of the plenary organ and/or the executive council (usually called 'board'). In addition, most international organizations have tried to increase their legitimacy by opening up for a more or less formalized participation of non-state actors. For that purpose, they allow for non-governmental actors' consultative status and have created organs and procedures for the representation of civil society groups, business actors or regional and local administrative bodies. However, the opportunities that these organs and procedures offer to non-state actors in terms of effective participation in decision-making vary considerably (Tallberg et al. 2013).

Within the UN, ECOSOC is an open intergovernmental body that provides formal access for NGOs. According to Article 71 of the UN Charter and ECOSOC resolutions 1296 (1968) and 1996/13 (1996), NGOs can be granted consultative status (Alger 2002). The Committee on Non-Governmental Organizations of ECOSOC examines NGOs' applications.

Currently, more than 4,000 NGOs, such as Amnesty International, Greenpeace and Transparency International, enjoy consultative status in ECOSOC. They are allowed to make oral or written statements in ECOSOC sessions and to submit proposals for the agenda of ECOSOC sessions and its subsidiary organs (Schulze 2002). Besides participating in ECOSOC meetings, NGOs can also take part in global conferences convened by the UN. This enables the UN to take the interests articulated by non-governmental actors into consideration. In the area of protection of the environment and of human rights, NGOs have become remarkably influential participants in global conferences held under the auspices of the UN.

Within the political system of the EU, the European Economic and Social Committee (EESC) is the main organ in which NGOs can formally present their concerns in hearings before the Commission, Council and Parliament. Such formal representation comes in addition to the informal lobbying of the other EU institutions by NGOs and business associations. In addition, the Committee of the Regions established in 1993 by the Treaty of Maastricht gives regional and local authorities some access to decision-making in the EU. Its members aim to aggregate regional and local concerns at the European level and to channel these into EU decision-making. The EESC and Committee of the Regions must be consulted by the Commission, the Council and the Parliament in areas such as education, employment and the environment. Despite their formal position in EU policymaking, neither the EESC nor the Committee of Regions has really been able to significantly influence policy output.

Conclusion

This is the first of four chapters that analyse international organizations as political systems. Political systems convert inputs into outputs. This is also a useful conceptual approach to understand policymaking by international organizations. The argument in this book is that *the process* through which international organizations convert inputs into outputs matters. Different international organizations may convert the same inputs into different outcomes. This chapter has focused on the constitutional and institutional structures of international organizations. Picking up again on the sports analogy referred to at the start of this chapter, the constitutional and institutional structures of international organizations can be compared to the field and the fundamental rules of the game. They provide the setting for actors to make policy within international organizations. If different international organizations have different constitutional and institutional structures, they are also likely to convert inputs differently into outputs. The founding treaties or 'constitutions' shape policymaking by outlining the organization's mission, establishing its organs and determining the allocation of competencies between them. Focusing on institutional structure, we have introduced six typical organs of international organizations and how they shape the process of policymaking.

This chapter has largely focused on the political systems of international organizations as more or less fixed entities. This makes sense: if today a certain input reaches an international organization – for instance, a recent conflict is brought to the attention of the UN Security Council by the member states or the secretary general – such input is converted into an output on the basis of the constitutional and institutional structure as it is in place at this time. In other words, at least in the short term, the constitutional and institutional structure is fixed and stable. Through various examples, this chapter has, however, also hinted at the fact that the constitutional and institutional structures of international organizations develop over time and are subject to change. Indeed, states put in a great deal of attention when they design the constitutional and institutional structures (Abbott et al. 2000; Koremenos, Lipson and Snidal 2001; Hooghe, Lenz and Marks 2019). They make careful trade-offs, for instance, in voting rights between the sovereign equality of the member states on the one hand and the need to recognize the special role of the great powers within international organizations.

Because the design of the constitutional and institutional structures is often a matter of compromise between the founding states, the constitutional and institutional structures tend to be hard to change. It is therefore not a surprise that the five permanent members of the Security Council are still the same ones as when the UN Charter was negotiated in 1944–5. It is also not a surprise that the leadership positions in the IMF and World Bank are always divided between Europe and the United States. At the same time, there have been several changes in the constitutional and institutional structures of international organizations over the past decades. China, India and some of the other emerging countries have lobbied hard, with some success, for more representation in the international organizations (Zangl et al. 2016; Lipscy 2017). Furthermore, while NGOs were largely excluded from policymaking during the Cold War, many international organizations now formally consult them and in several instances they have become formal power holders of their own.

The perspective of political systems assumes that international organizations are the 'focal institutions' (Jupille, Mattli and Snidal 2013) where international problems get addressed. In other words, when states and other international actors face certain problems, they turn to the relevant international organization. This perspective is not concerned with international cooperation and conflict outside the framework of international organizations. It can thus not explain why international actors may sometimes act 'through' international organizations and at other times address their problems in an informal ad hoc manner (Abbott and Snidal 1998; Vabulas and Snidal 2013; see further Chapter 13). Furthermore, while this perspective is very helpful to understand how states fight out their conflicts, and how dissatisfied states change their support and demands of international organizations, it is less appropriate to explain why states challenge the political system as such. For the hostility of the Trump administration towards international organizations or the British decision to withdraw from the EU (challenges to the political system of international organizations), we need to return to the three conditions why states create (and join) international organizations in the first place (see Chapter 3). In other words, the political system perspective is most effective in explaining how international organizations address problems as they come along on a day-to-day basis.

Discussion questions

1. How are constitutional and institutional structures of international organizations created and how can they be changed?
2. Why is it problematic if people argue that 'the UN often fails to act'? Please refer to the six different organs of international organizations.
3. Can the political systems of international organizations be compared to the political systems of countries? Argue in favour or against.

Further reading

Easton, David (1965). *A Framework for Political Analysis,* Englewood Cliffs, NJ: Prentice Hall.

Hix, Simon and Bjørn Høyland (2022). *The Political System of the European Union,* 4th edn, London: Bloomsbury.

Tallberg, Jonas, Thomas Sommerer, Theresa Squatrito and Christer Jönsson (2013). *The Opening Up of International Organizations: Transnational Access in Global Governance,* Cambridge: Cambridge University Press.

United Nations (1945). *United Nations Charter* (full text). Online available: https://www.un.org/en/about-us/un-charter/full-text

Weiss, Thomas G. and Sam Daws, eds (2018). *The Oxford Handbook on the United Nations,* 2nd edn, Oxford: Oxford University Press.

5

Input

Actors' demands and support

In the previous chapter, we discussed the constitutional and institutional structure of the political system of international organizations – the venue and the rules of the game. In this chapter, we focus on the actors by discussing the input dimension. While the venue and rules affect how the actors play the game, and can put certain actors at a disadvantage, they do not determine the ultimate score. We therefore also need to analyse the actors' motivation, commitment and behaviour. Following the discussion of the constitutional and institutional structures, we therefore focus in this chapter on the actors relevant to international organizations. On the basis of their interests and values, actors formulate their preferences towards international organizations and they provide support (input) (see Figure 5.1). For instance, when scientific research showed in the 1970s that certain greenhouse gases had a negative effect on the ozone layer, most states developed preferences on how quickly they wanted to reduce those greenhouse gases (input). The administrative staff of the United Nations Environment Programme (UNEP) with support of environmental non-governmental organizations (NGOs) pushed for a policy programme for the protection of the ozone layer (input). Communities of experts furthermore made additional scientific evidence available (input). All these inputs were converted through negotiations into output: the adoption of the Montreal Protocol on Substances that Deplete the Ozone Layer in 1987 (see Chapter 10).

In this chapter, the main focus is therefore on five different types of political actors active within international organizations. We discuss who they are, what they want and their resources to achieve their preferences. It is important, in this respect, to distinguish the political actors from the institutional structures they have at their disposal. For instance, a founding treaty (constitution) may establish a permanent secretariat (institutional

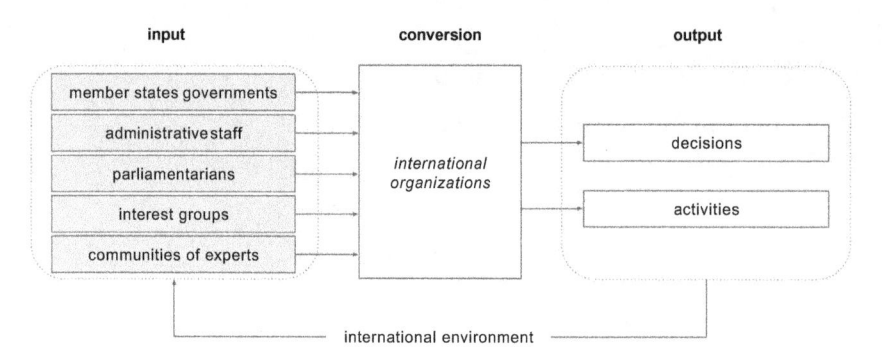

FIGURE 5.1 *The political system of international organizations (input).*

organ), but this does not automatically determine whether the administrative staff within the secretariat will behave as a political actor, on the basis of which interests and values and how it will leverage its resources to exert political influence over the output. Similarly, international organizations may have a formal platform (institutional organ) for NGOs and other interest groups to provide their input, but this does not determine what the actual input from NGOs looks like. In this chapter, we therefore study five different groups of political actors:

1. Member states' governments
2. Administrative staff
3. Parliamentarians
4. Interest groups
5. Communities of experts

Governments of member states

The member states in most international organizations are represented by their governments, either through ministers in the plenary organ or ambassadors and diplomats in the executive councils. Most of the inputs in international organizations – and often the most important inputs – therefore come from the governments of the individual member states. It is critical to stress the word 'government', because the interests and values of governments do not necessarily align with the interests and values of the *entire* member state. For instance, the inputs of the United States to international organizations over the past two decades have differed considerably depending on whether the Republican or Democratic Party held the presidency: the Bush and Trump administrations have been much more sceptical of global environmental cooperation than the Clinton, Obama and Biden administrations. The preferences pursued by member states may therefore be affected by elections and the composition of the government. That being said, the United States remains an exception. The input provided by most member states is more stable and less affected by the government composition. Yet it still matters whether member states have left-wing or right-wing governments for issues such as trade, development cooperation or counterterrorism.

Because the United States has played such an important role, as a hegemon, in establishing international organizations (see Chapter 3), it is important to discuss its foreign policy traditions. When it comes to international cooperation, liberal internationalism or 'Wilsonianism' immediately comes to mind. According to this foreign policy tradition, the pursuit of liberalism abroad, including the promotion of democracy, human rights and free trade, is the best guarantee for world peace. For US president Woodrow Wilson the origins of the First World War could be traced to the oppression of nations in the Austrian-Hungarian Empire and the secrecy with which states negotiated international treaties and military alliances. Wilsonianism in US foreign policy has had its ups and downs but has left a strong mark on international organizations, including through the creation of the United Nations (UN), the Bretton Woods institutions, US support for European integration after 1945 and the promotion of global human rights norms, as well as environmental cooperation (Ikenberry 2020).

While liberal internationalism has been a significant tradition in US foreign policy, it stands in contrast to equally important traditions of isolationism and non-interventionism (Wertheim 2020). The Monroe Doctrine of 1823, for instance, stated that the United States would not interfere in Europe's wars while demanding at the same time that the European states would stay out of North and South America. It may seem odd to associate the United States with non-interventionism, with its recent military adventures in Afghanistan, Bosnia, Iraq, Kosovo, Libya and Somalia, but the US public traditionally remains rather sceptical of liberal interventionist examples (Jentleson and Britton 1998). And the fact that the United States acts internationally does not mean that it acts through international organizations. Both US presidents Bush and Trump have been sceptical of international cooperation, from questions of international security to support for the climate change regime, or diplomacy with Iran, North Korea and Cuba.

US input for international organizations has therefore fluctuated from general support for the overall system of global governance (in the Wilsonian tradition) to specific support for issues that benefit the United States in particular (Mead 2002). In general, however, international organizations are regarded by the United States as a means to an end rather than an end in itself. They can help the United States achieve its interests and values, but the United States does not hesitate to go unilateral whenever it believes this is required. It is also significant that the United States goes to great lengths not to be bound by international organizations. It did not join the League of Nations as a member, it does not deploy its own troops in UN peacekeeping missions and it withdrew its signature from the Rome

Statute of the International Criminal Court (ICC) in 2002 exactly to avoid that its leaders and soldiers would be tried for war crimes. The United States also does not hesitate to withdraw its support for international organizations, through cutting funding and even leaving, if it disagrees with the adopted policies. Under the first term of President Trump, for instance, it left UNESCO (2018), withdrew from the Paris Agreement (2020) and cut funding for the World Health Organization (2020). Such 'America First' policies have been repeated during his second term with US withdrawal from the Paris Agreement and the World Health Organization announced on Inaugural Day in January 2025. Because the United States is the largest donor in many international organizations, paying sometimes as much as a quarter of the budget, it can use its resources to support or undermine international organizations.

Europe's three largest states – France, Germany and the UK – traditionally put stronger emphasis on multilateralism and international organizations than the United States. For them, global governance can be an end in itself. France and the UK jealously guard their permanent membership of the UN Security Council and take a particularly active role in supporting the work of the Security Council. Interestingly, both have not used their vetoes in the Security Council since 1989, which indicates that they see their input differently from the other three permanent members which do resort to vetoes. This is also a clear example where we need to distinguish between the institutional structure (a Security Council with five permanent members with veto power) and the actual behaviour of the actors within that institutional structure. At the same time, France and the UK consider themselves major powers by the virtue of their nuclear weapons; this is formally recognized under the Non-Proliferation Treaty (NPT). While Brexit presented a challenge to the EU, the UK has not reduced its support for other international organizations. Germany traditionally has a strong attachment to international organizations as part of its post-war legacy. This includes strong support for international organizations, such as the UN and the EU. At the same time, being one of the principal donors of many international organizations, Germany has also been keen to increase its influence. Furthermore, it actively uses its financial power within international organizations, including by insisting on zero or limited budgetary growth.

Russia has long been sceptical of the independent role of international organizations in world politics. For Russia, international organizations are foremost venues where national interests are defended and power politics is played out. Ever since Joseph Stalin demanded a veto in the Security Council in 1945, Russia has keenly used this institutional power to block all sorts of undesired resolutions. Russia has, in this respect, an ambiguous attitude with regard to international law. During the post-Cold War period, it has insisted on the UN Charter stipulating that questions of peace and security need to be addressed in the Security Council (where it has a veto). In New York, it has also upheld the non-interference norm including, for instance, by vetoing more than half a dozen Western-sponsored resolutions on the civil war in Syria since 2011. At the same time, Russia has not shied away from breaking international law when it comes to conflicts in its own neighbourhood. Its invasion of Georgia in 2008, annexation of Crimea in 2014 and fully fledged invasion of Ukraine in 2022 are unprecedented in the post-Cold War era and a very blatant disregard for international law. Indeed, such actions call the rules-based international order, of which international organizations are a critical part, into question (see further concluding Chapter 13).

While China regularly sides with Russia in the UN Security Council, particularly when it comes to non-interference in the domestic affairs of other UN member states, the preferences of China towards international organizations are actually quite different. The People's Republic of China was originally deeply sceptical of international organizations. In 1945, China had been granted a permanent seat on the Security Council, but the seat was occupied by Taiwan for two decades (1949–71) following the Chinese civil war. China has also long opposed international human rights regimes that affect its internal policies, including after the Tiananmen Square protests of 1989. In more recent decades, however, China has largely turned into a supporter of international organizations (Johnston 2007). Importantly, it became a member of the World Trade Organization (WTO) in 2001. Its membership has contributed to tremendous economic growth in China, and China was initially seen as a moderate voice in this organization (Hopewell 2015), even if the WTO is currently severely strained due to bilateral trading conflicts between China and the United States. China has furthermore become a key player in the climate change negotiations. It is also the only permanent member of the Security Council that regularly contributes troops to UN peacekeeping missions. China has thus discovered that global governance can be greatly beneficial (Ikenberry 2008, 2011). At the same time, during the past decade, China has also pursued a more assertive position trying to impose its own world view on international organizations, demanding stronger representation and contesting existing institutions and practices (Weiss and Wallace 2021; Haug, Foot and Baumann 2024).

While the permanent five members of the Security Council are actors of their own, many countries actually try to act within international organizations through regional groupings or special coalitions. The EU itself is a prime example. On many dossiers within international organizations, the member states of the EU vote as a bloc or even speak with one voice through representatives from the European Commission and the European External Action Service (Jørgensen 2009). Yet there are many more regional groups. The Group of 77 (G77) of 130+ developing member states is a critical group when addressing economic and social issues. Through its sheer size, it can determine the outcome of UN General Assembly resolutions. Similar things can be said about the Non-Aligned Movement (NAM) or the Organization of Islamic Cooperation (OIC). In the field of climate change, the unlikely alliance of thirty-nine small island developing countries, many of which are at serious risk of flooding, has become a relevant political actor. One of the main challenges, however, for regional groups and special coalitions is their internal coherence. Sometimes it can be more difficult for them to agree internally than it is for them to subsequently agree with other groups.

A final set of states are the emerging countries and particularly the BRICS (Brazil, Russia, India, China and South Africa). Emerging countries have long tried to increase their weight in international organizations. For instance, Brazil and India have been key political actors in the WTO ever since the start of the Doha Round in 2003 (Narlikar 2004; Narlikar and Tussie 2003; Odell 2006). And, in several areas, China and Russia are not even emerging countries but rather established powers with a permanent Security Council seat and nuclear weapons. Yet in Durban, South Africa, in 2013, the BRICS made a powerful collective statement demanding a larger say in international organizations. The summit declaration was a *tour d'horizon* with input for many of the world's international organizations. It notably called 'for the reform of International Financial Institutions to make them more representative and to reflect the growing weight of BRICS and other developing countries' (paragraph 13). What made, however, this BRICS statement stand out was the establishment of a 'New Development Bank' (paragraph 9), a parallel institution to the World Bank and Asian Development Bank, run entirely by the BRICS. It was a clear signal to the existing, Western-dominated international organizations: if you do not take our demands seriously, we will create new institutions. The BRICS have remained a powerful force in international relations, despite their tremendous differences, and even expanded: Egypt, Ethiopia, Indonesia, Iran and the United Arab Emirates joined in 2024 and 2025.

The governments of the different member states thus have varying interests and values (Figure 5.1). And depending on the issue, preferences can differ tremendously. The United States, France and the UK were keen to establish UN peacekeeping missions around the world during the 2000s and 2010s but have been reluctant to make their own soldiers available for such missions. The BRICS may want a larger say in policymaking in international organizations, but they generally oppose international organizations infringing on the sovereignty of their members. It is therefore difficult to make general statements about what each state precisely wants in each area of global governance. Furthermore, governments change in countries and many governments make up their mind only once faced with developments in the international environment. Yet once governments have defined their preferences on an issue, the question is how they go about achieving them. They have various resources to influence and support the policymaking process in international organizations.

A first resource is material power. Countries around the world pay attention to the United States simply by virtue of its hegemonic military and economic power. This extends to its role in international organizations.

For all the sovereign equality of international organizations, ultimately some states are more equal than others, and this particularly goes for the major powers. In crisis situations and moments where policymaking within the international organizations really matters, all eyes turn to the major powers (Stone 2011), whether the United States in the UN Security Council, France and Germany in the EU or China and the United States when it concerns climate change. The major powers are also often able to exert influence in areas where they may not have obvious resources. For instance, while American fishing companies are not engaged in whaling, the United States can nevertheless be regarded as one of the most influential members of the International Whaling Commission (IWC) (Zangl 1999). And many non-permanent members of the Security Council vote along with the United States, because they know this may result in more development aid and more favourable treatment at the International Monetary Fund (IMF) and World Bank (Kuziemko and Werker 2006; Dreher, Sturm and Vreeland 2009a, 2009b). The United States has indeed control over issue-transcending resources and can link negotiations across several international organizations (Keohane and Nye 1977: 3–47).

A second resource is the expertise and administrative capacity that states have. This is often issue-specific. Due to its expertise in nuclear technology, for instance, France is a major actor in the issue area of nuclear reactor safety. In deliberations about international standards of reactor safety within the International Atomic Energy Agency (IAEA), French diplomats are therefore particularly influential. The importance of expertise and administrative capacity cannot be overstated. With so much going on in all international organizations across the world, it is hard for most member states to keep up. The ten elected members of the Security Council are not necessarily able to assess the exact consequences of a specific clause in a resolution authorizing a peacekeeping mission in, for instance, Haiti; and yet, they are expected to vote on exactly such resolutions. This strengthens the position of those Security Council members that do have country or issue expertise or the capacity to find out (Dijkstra 2015a).

A third resource is the support (or 'buy in') of member states in international organizations. Through their financial contributions and their supply of information and personnel they provide the support which enables international organizations to carry out their tasks. The dependence of international organizations on the financial contributions from member states is especially obvious because hardly any international organization has its own financial resources (see Patz and Goetz 2019). In the case of the UN system, the financial resources are divided into 'assessed' (i.e. compulsory) and voluntary contributions (Graham 2023). In some international organizations – such as inclusive organizations – member states are less dominant in terms of providing inputs. The Gates Foundation, for instance, also makes a contribution to the Global Fund. Yet states are usually the key political actors formulating demands on, and offering support to, the organization. It is important to elaborate on the support of member states as it provides a concrete input to international organizations.

In most international organizations the size of national contributions reflects the 'ability to pay' based on the wealth of each of the respective countries. Accordingly, the United States, Japan and China provide the biggest financial contributions to the UN. The US contribution to the UN's regular budget for 2024 amounted to US$790 million (22.0 per cent of the total of US$3.59 billion) in addition to US$1.5 billion for the UN peacekeeping budget (27 per cent of the total of US$5.59 billion). The Japanese regular contribution was US$287 million and its peacekeeping contribution was US$447 million. The Chinese regular contribution was US$548 million, and its peacekeeping contribution was $US1 billion.

It goes without saying that the size of member states' financial contributions can have a crucial effect on their influence within international organizations. In other words, states try to use their financial support as a source of influence. This has been evident, for instance, in the IMF and the World Bank, where the major Western donors have largely shaped policy programmes in the post-war era. On the other hand, when major contributors turn their backs on international organizations, these organizations get into major financial trouble. The United States, for instance, withdrew from UNESCO in 1984, accusing it of excessive politicization and lack of budgetary restraint, and again in 2018 as a result of Palestinian accession to UNESCO. Similarly, it withdrew from the United Nations Industrial Development Organization (UNIDO) in 1996 because it dismissed this organization as ineffective and viewed its advocacy of public sector responsibility for industrial development with suspicion. In both cases, the United States deprived these organizations of its contributions, which made up sizeable proportions of their overall resources. In a similar way, since 2002 the United States has refrained from providing financial contributions to the UN Population Fund (UNFPA) in protest over UNFPA's endorsement of China's population policies. This has severely compromised the viability of UNFPA's projects. The UN is currently facing a considerably liquidity crisis, as various member states are failing to pay their contributions on time. The Trump administration, in particular, is withholding funding for much of the UN system, which implies that the various UN departments, agencies and programmes are forced to seriously reorganize their activities.

It is also important to note that, in many international organizations, a large part of funding is voluntary contributions by states. Various international organizations, for instance, have taken on more tasks and projects over time. To find money for such activities, interested states donate extra funding on top of their assessed contributions, particularly in international organizations where it may be difficult to find consensus among states on significant increases in the regular budget (e.g. Graham 2023; Reinsberg, Heinzel and Siauwijaya 2024). States may co-fund projects or international organizations may set up trust funds for which states can chip in. Such voluntary contributions are also often referred to as earmarked funding. They come with a number of complications for international organizations. After all, international organizations are much more constrained in how they can spend such earmarked funds, as the funds tend to be allocated for specific projects, in specific countries, in specific sectors, for a specific amount of time. States may also decide unilaterally to reduce or stop voluntary funding which, in turn, leaves international organizations in budgetary trouble. Voluntary contributions, even more so than assessed contributions, are thus an important lever for states' input into international organizations (Heinzel, Cormier and Reinsberg 2023).

Although states adjust their support according to whether their demands are met, withdrawing from an international organization or holding back 'assessed' (compulsory) financial contributions is not how states usually behave. Normally, states make their demands through their delegations or permanent representatives to the organization. In most cases such demands are voiced in the plenary organ or executive councils, since that is where the member states' representatives have the right to speak and vote. This holds especially for far-reaching demands: nothing beats making a big statement during the UN General Assembly's General Debate in September. For the less important demands of day-to-day politics, it is unlikely that member states' concerns will be addressed by delegations or permanent representatives to the plenary organ. In such situations, matters are raised in committees, working parties or with the relevant department of the permanent secretariat. States may also adjust their support for international organizations through their voluntary contributions on a case-by-case basis.

Administrative staff

While most inputs to international organizations come from representatives of the member states, there are several other political actors that provide considerable input to policymaking as well. It is important to pay particular attention to the administrative staffs of the permanent secretariats. Although their power is formally quite small, their contributions are nevertheless very real (Barnett and Finnemore 2004; Biermann and Siebenhüner 2009; Jacobson 1984: 118–23; Eckhard and Ege 2016; Ege et al. 2023). Secretariats provide planning documents for military operations in the UN, EU and NATO (Dijkstra 2016). IMF officials visit indebted countries to verify whether policy is properly implemented. The officials of the UN Framework Convention on Climate Change (UNFCCC) keep track of Nationally Determined Contributions (NDCs) for climate action. States have also recognized that the administrative staff of international organizations can be an important ally when developing policy (Manulak 2017; Dijkstra 2017). Member states are thus keen to invest in the administrative staff and to make sure that their nationals are well represented (Parízek 2017). They also lobby the administrative staff heavily (Urpelainen 2012; Panke 2012).

The influence of international organizations' administrative staffs, especially their executive heads, stems mainly from their location at the centre of the policymaking process. As a result, administrative staffs often have an information advantage over member states. This information advantage can come from studies, reports and proposals that members of administrative staff are asked to prepare, or which they themselves initiate, to inform policymaking within the organization. In addition, their central position lends a secretariat's leadership a remarkable influence as an agenda setter. Frequently, the administrative staffs of international organizations (co-)determine the agendas, thus influencing the decisions to be taken. Where member states' interests are not clear, the administrative staff's influence on policymaking can grow very rapidly to the point where it is not only playing the role of agenda setter but also that of policy entrepreneur (Pollack 2003).

The extent to which tasks are delegated to the administrative staff varies significantly across international organizations (Hooghe, Lenz and Marks 2019). In the UN, a considerable agenda-setting power can be ascribed to the administrative staff, with the secretary general at its apex. Under Article 99 of the UN Charter, the secretary general is tasked to bring all matters to the Security Council that affect questions of peace and security. Successive secretary generals have interpreted this function as a right to travel around the globe and engage in mediation and conflict prevention. The administrative staff in the UN Secretariat has also played a critical role in developing peacekeeping doctrine: from Dag Hammarskjöld's original focus on peacekeeping to the 1992 Agenda for Peace and the Pact for the Future in 2024 (Weinlich 2014). Even when the member states decide on policy, the officials in the UN Secretariat can give it extra spin. For instance, the administrative staff turned the lengthy and dry Millennium Declaration of 2000 into seven concrete Millennium Development Goals (MDGs) with clear targets and started communicating these MDGs. This logic was then also followed with the Sustainable Development Goals (SDGs) adopted in 2015.

Also beyond the UN, we see a significant footprint left by the administrative staffs of international organizations. In the IMF, for instance, the administrative staff has considerable expert authority in the area of macroeconomics. While the Executive Board formally can amend staff proposals, for instance, on loans with borrowing countries, in practice this almost never happens (e.g. Martin 2006: 143). The Executive Board relies, in this respect, heavily on the expertise of the IMF staff. NATO provides another example, where the secretary general actually chairs the North Atlantic Council. As such, the secretary general can determine the agenda and the procedure with which NATO takes decisions. In the World Health Organization (WHO), the administrative staff has been able to play member states from the North out against member states from the South, thereby furthering its agenda (Chorev 2012).

Given their rational-legal, delegated, moral and expert authority (Barnett and Finnemore 2004), an important question is what the preferences of administrative staffs are. While there is almost always some sort of goal conflict between some of the member states and the administrative staffs of secretariats, it is more difficult to make general statements on what administrative staffs actually want (Ege 2020). In the literature on bureaucratic politics, many scholars make relatively simple assumptions about motivations of administrative staffs of international organizations, such as their desire to maximize their budget or institutional power (Vaubel 1996; Vaubel, Dreher and Soylu 2007; Pollack 2003). The reality is more complicated (Trondal et al. 2010). For instance, high-level officials may focus on increasing operational budgets, as it gives their organization more relevance in the outside world, rather than fighting for the administrative budgets that actually pay for staff (Dunleavy 1985). While many officials in the secretariats will undoubtedly prefer to expand their own bureaucracies, in reality the administrative staffs of international organizations are still relatively small. For instance, only around 500 officials in the UN Secretariat are responsible for the deployment of around 60,000 peacekeepers (Dijkstra 2016). Secretariat staff in different international organizations also can adopt different administrative styles in terms of how they approach policymaking: Some will proactively pursue the goals of their organization, such as creating peace or mitigating climate change, while others consider themselves impartial brokers whose job it is to seek consensus among the member states (Bayerlein, Knill and Steinebach 2020).

Apart from budget maximization, we can identify three goals which are shared across most administrative staffs. First, the administrative staff tends to be pro-cooperation, wanting member states to reach viable agreements that benefit the international organization as a whole (Beach 2004). Officials in UNEP, for instance, are keen to see more cooperation on environmental protection. Second, the administrative staff tends to value policy effectiveness based on its technical expertise. They tend to depoliticize issues (Louis and Maertens 2021). The IMF staff has a preference for economic considerations (Martin 2006: 142), and the WHO staff focuses on medical and scientific evidence (Cortell and Peterson 2006: 266–7). Finally, the administrative staff is, like most political actors, guided by a desire to avoid uncertainty. Officials in the administrative staff know very well that in case their international organization fails, they are first in line to receive the blame. They will be cautious in the risks they take on and insist on achievable policies and adequate resources to fulfil the delegated functions (e.g. Barnett and Finnemore 2004: 130–5). This can put secretariats on a collision course with the member states, which may demand as much value possible for money or are looking for a convenient scapegoat.

The initiatives – the demands of the administrative staffs of international organizations – are for the most part addressed to the member states of the organization or the plenary organ in which they take decisions. Thus the agenda-setting phase of the policymaking process can be described as the interplay of initiatives between the member states and the administrative staff. While the administrative staff represents the collective interest of the organization, each member state mainly looks after its individual interest. The initiatives of the administrative staff of an international organization will mostly be directed towards strengthening the authority of the organization, while those of member states are of various kinds.

Parliamentarians

Although generally less effective than representatives of member states' governments and the administrative staff, parliamentarians can also formulate demands for or lend some support to the policymaking processes within international organizations. Apart from the democratic control of their governments through their own national parliaments, their main forums for influence are the parliamentary assemblies that some international organizations have. Their most important input, within these parliamentary assemblies, is to increase the legitimacy of policymaking. In fact, parliamentary assemblies are often created in order to reduce the so-called 'democratic deficit' of international organizations, which is considered a consequence of policymaking being dominated by government representatives (Zürn 2000; Schimmelfennig et al. 2020). Indeed, sometimes governments actually use their privileged position in international organizations to insulate themselves from national parliaments. Governments benefit from the fact that policymaking procedures in international organizations are complex and not very transparent. Also national parliaments are confronted with policies made in international organizations on a 'take it or leave it' basis. In such circumstances national parliaments are unable to provide democratic legitimacy. To compensate for this gap, international parliamentary assemblies are created to provide additional legitimacy (Rittberger 2005).

While it is not always obvious that parliamentarians in parliamentary assemblies are actually able to provide additional legitimacy, the perception that they represent the 'voice of the people' makes it hard for the member states and administrative staffs of international organizations to completely ignore their demands. In other words, their perceived legitimacy is the main source of influence. The European Parliament, in particular, has repeatedly been successful in bringing its concerns onto the agenda of the EU (Corbett 2002; Sandholtz and Zysman 1989). The European Parliament can also rely on power resources other than its perceived legitimacy to influence EU policymaking. Over the decades, it has increased its legislative powers. Hence, it has become an indispensable player in EU policymaking, and neither the national ministers in the Council nor the Commission can ignore the Parliament's concerns. While the role of the European Parliament is exceptional in terms of parliamentary assemblies within international organizations, it does serve as a model for democratic input.

If we accept that parliamentarians in political assemblies provide relevant input to the work of international organizations, it is important to ask what parliamentarians actually want. Beyond generic interests, such as more influence for their political assembly and to be taken seriously by the government representatives and administrative staff, it is difficult to pinpoint precise preferences. The European Parliament has traditionally been largely pro-European integration even though there is some left-right politics ongoing during the debates in Brussels and Strasbourg (Hix, Noury and Roland 2006). In recent years, Eurosceptics parties have also gained a much stronger position. The European Parliament has also given several national politicians a platform and resources. For instance, the National Rally of Marine Le Pen has had great difficulty in getting elected in the French presidential system and has used instead the European Parliament as its base. Yet the European Parliament is and remains an exception. In many parliamentary assemblies, such as the ones of NATO, the Organization for Security and Co-operation in Europe (OSCE) and the Council of Europe, one only finds supporters of the specific international organization. For instance, parliamentarians in the NATO political assembly tend to serve in foreign affairs and defence committees in their own national parliaments. They are largely pro-NATO. Most often, national parliamentarians critical of NATO do not bother to go to the parliamentary assembly. This, in turn, seriously affects the legitimacy and seriousness of political assemblies.

Interest groups

Interest groups, such as civil society actors and private businesses, are also a source of inputs in the form of both demands and support. They can use either formal or informal channels, depending on the institutional structure and the inclusiveness of the international organization (see Chapter 4). There is a mutual benefit. Non-governmental actors frequently have an interest in gaining access to policymaking processes. At the same time, international organizations also need access to the information, expertise and legitimacy of non-governmental actors (Brühl 2003). As already mentioned, the extent of, and the institutional channels for, non-governmental actors' inputs varies considerably. In inclusive organizations such as the Global Fund, non-governmental actors are allowed to participate in the decision-making process of the organization with a vote. This is also the case with the International Labour Organization (ILO), in whose tripartite decision-making organs, state representatives vote alongside employer and trade union representatives.

More frequently, however, non-governmental actors do not have a (formal) right to vote but can, more or less effectively, take part in policy deliberations (Steffek, Kissling and Nanz 2008). Two channels of input can be distinguished: first, non-governmental actors can act through an institutionalized procedure, which gives them the opportunity to raise their concerns. As mentioned, according to Article 71 of the UN Charter and ECOSOC Resolutions 1296 (XLIV) of 1968 and 1996/31, civil society actors can obtain consultative status in ECOSOC and consequently participate in its meetings or those of its committees as well as submit oral or written opinions and agenda proposals. Second, non-governmental actors can act through their own representative organs within the institutional structure of an international organization. The European Economic and Social Committee (EESC) of the EU is an example of such an organ, consisting of approximately 350 representatives ranging from employers to trade unions, as well as other interest groups such as consumer organizations. Of course, the expression of preferences does not always take the form of formal input channels. In many international organizations informal input channels are at least as important as, or complement, formal input channels.

The demands of non-governmental actors and their support for policymaking – no matter whether through formal or informal channels – rely on various material and immaterial resources. These include providing information, expertise and legitimacy, which they offer and which are essential for international organizations' goal achievement. In addition, interest groups can gain influence by mobilizing public opinion in favour of their own concerns. For example, Greenpeace was quite successful in mobilizing global public opinion against whaling, thereby forcing the IWC to agree on an international moratorium on major whaling operations (1982). With respect to the humanitarian catastrophe caused by the civil war in Somalia in the early 1990s, various aid organizations were able to activate public opinion in the United States to support a humanitarian intervention authorized by the UN Security Council (Hasenclever 2001). NGOs and grassroots movement have also contributed to the establishment of the ICC (Bosco 2014). More recently, many NGOs provide support to the international community in its efforts to reduce global warming (Keohane and Victor 2011; von Allwörden 2025).

Transnational advocacy networks and transnational social movements are particularly successful in mobilizing public opinion (Keck and Sikkink 1998; Smith, Chatfield and Pagnucco 1997). Such advocacy networks and social movements do not represent particular material interests but claim to act in the global interest in supporting international organizations in their policymaking efforts. However, there are also transnational advocacy networks and transnational social movements that criticize the policies of major international organizations. For example, ATTAC, a global network linking groups that criticize economic globalization for its negative social and ecological effects, was able to mobilize public opinion against the World

Bank, the IMF and the WTO through media campaigns (Green and Griffith 2002; Waters 2004).

Communities of experts

Some inputs to the political system of international organizations come from outside experts giving advice on policymaking. As the policies of international organizations have to respond to increasingly complex problems, the knowledge resources and advice of (frequently non-state) experts have a growing importance for their policymaking. The UN makes frequent use of committees of outside experts or consultants that are often chosen according to the usual geographic distribution criteria and provide the expertise the UN administrative staff cannot provide. Therefore, the administrative staff often has an interest in bringing outside experts into the policymaking processes, while the experts themselves have an interest in being incorporated because this gives them influence on policymaking within the organization. It is therefore not always easy to clearly distinguish between the administrative staff (members of which are often experts themselves) and outside experts brought in to provide expertise for policymaking.

Experts' influence depends, among other things, on whether they agree or disagree on the advice that should be given for policymaking within the organization (Haas 1989, 1992a, 1992b). If all or most relevant experts agree on the causes and consequences of a given problem and how to deal with it – and therefore form an 'epistemic community' – the likelihood that their advice will have an impact is quite high because the member states find it more difficult to ignore that advice. If, however, these experts disagree on how to cope with a specific problem their advice will be taken less seriously. Moreover, member states can point to the disagreement among experts in order to justify why their advice does not have to be taken up. And member states with conflicting interests can justify their positions by relying on those experts whose advice is most in line with their own interests, which then can easily lead to an impasse in the policymaking process.

To illustrate the influence which experts, and in particular epistemic communities, can exert, let us look at the policymaking activities of various international organizations in relation to protection of the environment. Some of these activities came about in part on the initiative of experts within international organizations' administrative staffs. Thus we owe the activities of the UNEP and the World Meteorological Organization (WMO) for the protection of the stratospheric ozone layer to the efforts of committed experts (Breitmeier 1996; Haas 1992b). Almost all experts on the Intergovernmental Panel on Climate Change (IPCC), founded in 1988 under the patronage of UNEP and the WMO, agreed on the causes as well as the consequences of climate change. Thus, the experts of the IPCC were able to play a prominent role in the preparation of the UN Framework

Convention on Climate Change, which was ready for signature at the UN Conference on Environment and Development in 1992, as well as of the Kyoto Protocol agreed to by the Conference of the Parties (COP) in 1997. However, the difficulties in agreeing on a stricter successor agreement to the Kyoto Protocol, initially during the COP meeting in Copenhagen in 2009 and later in Paris in 2015, also show the limits of the influence of expert knowledge when this conflicts with major states' vital economic interests.

The input of experts and the use of outside expertise have also become contested with regard to policymaking in international organizations. There is considerable politics around expertise, and various actors within international organizations, such as the administrative staff but also parliamentarians, NGOs or state representatives, may selectively use outside experts and their expertise to advance their political projects. It is, in this respect, important to emphasize that the science, methods and evidence that experts bring as input to international organizations are rarely neutral and often for some purpose (e.g. Littoz-Monnet 2017; Littoz-Monnet and Uribe 2023). That is why we also consider experts, in this book, as actors in the political system of international organizations. A climate expert, for instance, may favour more climate action, while a public health expert might point at the need to address malaria. Both experts may provide high-quality scientific recommendations, and climate and public health are undoubtedly important societal causes, but international organizations as political systems need to make difficult choices on how to use their scarce resources.

Conclusion

This chapter has focused on the political actors within international organizations. Based on the broader developments in the international environment, political actors provide the inputs to international organizations through their demands and support. For instance, if human rights violations take place in a particular country (international environment), different political actors (from governments of member states to human rights advocates) may bring their concerns (input) to the relevant forums in international organizations. The chapter has, in this respect, identified a set of relevant political actors. These include member state governments, the administrative staffs of permanent secretariats, parliamentarians meeting in the parliamentary assemblies, interest groups, and communities of experts. In this chapter, we have analysed each group's contribution to the policymaking process of international organizations. In Chapter 6 we turn to the conversion of inputs into outputs and in Chapter 7 to the outputs themselves.

In terms of inputs, it is worth thinking both about the preferences of actors and their 'buy in' (support) in international organizations. Actors typically have a relatively fixed set of interests and values. Once an international problem comes on the agenda, they develop their preferences on the basis of those interests and values. We have seen that such preferences differ significantly not only across political actors but also across policy areas. While most of the members of administrative staff of international organizations often have pro-cooperation preferences, it is difficult to determine a priori what, for instance, UN officials may want on any given policy area. Similarly, while the majority of members of the European Parliament are pro-European integration, they also have political left-right positions to defend. The representatives of member states may not even have their mindset on their final objectives. As part of regular negotiations, they may develop a clearer sense of their priorities.

In this chapter, however, we have not only focused on the preferences of political actors and the channels they use to achieve them; we have also discussed the support that the political actors provide for the work of international organizations. Member states can provide financial resources for international organizations. In addition to the assessed resources, they often have the ability to make unilateral voluntary contributions to specific projects of international organizations they support. Members of administrative staff often provide expertise to international organizations as well as continuity. They also facilitate the policymaking process and may be delegated implementation tasks. Parliamentary assemblies lend international organizations additional legitimacy, whereas the involvement of civil society, business and NGOs may provide international organizations with more information and societal support. External experts can also help to increase the knowledge base of international organizations. To conclude, international organizations are no longer neutral forums where major powers fight their battles. Indeed, much goes into international organizations. In the next chapter, we focus on the conversion process.

Discussion questions

1. How do powerful states differ in their demands and support for international organizations?
2. To what extent do the administrative staffs of international organizations have their own preferences and how do they go about making an autonomous impact on policymaking?
3. Through which channels can non-governmental actors formulate demands on, and lend support to, international organizations? Give a concrete example for each channel of input.

Further reading

Eckhard, Steffen and Jörn Ege (2016). 'International Bureaucracies and Their Influence on Policy-making: A Review of Empirical Evidence', *Journal of European Public Policy,* 23 (7): 960–78.

Graham, Erin R. (2023). *Transforming International Institutions: How Money Quietly Sidelined Multilateralism at the United Nations,* Oxford: Oxford University Press.

Haas, Peter M. (1992). 'Introduction: Epistemic Communities and International Policy Coordination', *International Organization,* 46 (1): 1–35.

Keck, Margaret E. and Kathryn Sikkink (2014). *Activists Beyond Borders: Advocacy Networks in International Politics,* Ithaca, NY: Cornell University Press.

Papa, Mihaela, Zhen Han and Frank O'Donnell (2023). 'The Dynamics of Informal Institutions and Counter-hegemony: Introducing a BRICS Convergence Index', *European Journal of International Relations,* 29 (4): 960–89.

6

Conversion

Decision-making in international organizations

International organizations convert inputs into outputs. In this book, we argue that the conversion process is vitally important: two different international organizations may convert similar inputs into different outputs. So what does this conversion process look like? And what is so special about it? In this chapter, we discuss how inputs are transformed into outputs in international organizations. It is important to differentiate, in this respect, between two types of decisions: programme decisions and operational decisions. *Programme decisions* are decisions about a set of norms and rules aimed at directing the behaviour of actors. Examples include the obligation of states to protect refugees under the United Nations (UN) Refugee Convention or the ban to discriminate among the member states of the World Trade Organization (WTO). The programme decisions of international organizations mostly set normative standards for the behaviour of their member states and are comparable to law-making at the state level. International organizations that mainly take programme decisions have been defined as programme international organizations (see Chapter 1). Operational international organizations, by contrast, mainly take *operational decisions*. These decisions relate to the implementation of the norms and rules of existing programmes. An example includes decisions on whether to open a refugee camp and how to administer them. Operational decisions also include activities such as monitoring member states' compliance with normative standards and enforcing those standards in case of non-compliance, for instance, through the WTO dispute settlement process. Distinguishing between programme decisions and operational

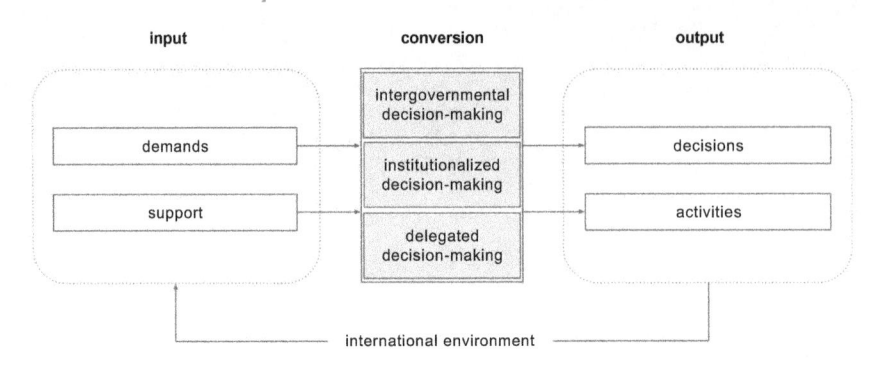

FIGURE 6.1 *The political system of international organizations (conversion).*

decisions is important, because the decision-making processes frequently differ.

For both programme decisions and operational decisions, we identify the prominent modes of decision-making (Figure 6.1). The 'big' programme decisions are often made in the intergovernmental conferences that establish or amend the constitutional structure of international organizations. In those conferences, the member states dominate and normally have vetoes. Programme decisions are also made after international organizations have been established. The plenary organs and executive councils are, in this respect, the main bodies for programme decisions. In these bodies, government representatives from the member states take the lead, but the institutionalized nature of many plenary organs and executive councils also gives a role to officials from the permanent secretariats and occasionally access to non-state actors. Operational decisions, which implement programme decisions, can occasionally be political sensitive but they are taken within the confines set out by programme decisions. While in many international organizations operational decisions are also subject to input by the member states, a substantial number of international organizations work with delegated decision-making: the member states have delegated the authority to make operational decisions to the permanent secretariat or another implementing agency. To interpret programme decisions, they may also grant international courts the authority to make operational decisions. Subsequently, the member states control how the secretariat implements and the court interprets the programme decisions.

Programme decisions

The programme decisions of international organizations directly affect the autonomy of member states, since they require the member states to submit to international norms and rules. As states are generally zealous to preserve their autonomy, they usually insist that they dominate and control the decision-making process for 'big' decisions leading to the making of such norms and rules. As such, programme decisions are normally taken at the intergovernmental conferences where treaties are negotiated or in the plenary organs and executive councils of international organizations. These are the organs where the member states dominate.

Intergovernmental decision-making: Conferences

Many of the 'big' programme decisions of international organizations are actually already included in the founding treaties. For instance, the UN Charter states that '[a]ll Members shall refrain in their international relations from the threat or use of force against the territorial integrity or political independence of any state' (Article 2(4)). The North Atlantic Treaty, which established NATO, notes that '[t]he Parties agree that an armed attack against one or more of them in Europe or North America shall be considered an attack against them all' (Article 5). One of the purposes of the Treaty of Rome, which established the European Economic Community (EEC) – the frontrunner of the European Union (EU) – was to ensure 'the elimination, as between Member States, of customs duties and of quantitative restrictions on the import and export of goods, and of all other measures having equivalent effect' (Article 3(a)). The Bretton Woods Agreement made clear that the International Monetary Fund (IMF) should 'promote exchange stability, to maintain orderly exchange arrangements among members, and to avoid competitive exchange depreciation' (Article 1(3)). The 1991 Treaty of Asunción aimed to establish a Southern Common Market (MERCOSUR) by the end of 1994. The founding treaties of international organizations therefore include ambitious policy programmes.

The policy programmes included in the founding treaties often seriously impinge on the autonomy and sovereignty of the member states. For instance, the UN Charter limits a member state's sovereignty to use military force against other states (and also to pre-emptively protect itself). In the North Atlantic Treaty, member states commit to the collective defence of their allies. While Article 5 includes some qualifications, there normally is no 'opting out' in case of war. The Treaty of Rome not only meant that European states no longer could set their own tariffs, but it also meant a common customs tariff and a common commercial policy towards third countries (Article 3(b)) – in other words, it meant the end of unilateral trade policy. If states require bailout funds from the IMF, they will be subjected to (often harsh) economic conditionality. These treaties thus seriously reduced the autonomy of the member states in what they can do with their armed forces, their trade policy and their budget.

Given the important consequences for sovereignty, it is therefore not a surprise that the 'big' programme decisions at the level of founding or amending treaties tend to be taken by consensus during intergovernmental conferences which are dominated by the representatives from the governments of member states. Because of their significance, it is worth elaborating on this process. The UN Charter was negotiated at the San Francisco conference, for instance, where 850 national delegates met for two months in 1945. They were supported by another 2,500 advisers and staff, and also 2,500 journalists and observers joined the conference. Eventually fifty states signed the UN Charter on the last day of the conference. While the conference in San Francisco was an important happening, the foundations for the UN had been laid earlier. For instance, in January 1942, while the Second World War was not nearly over, twenty-six states signed the Declaration by United Nations. Several conferences then followed including in Moscow (1943), Tehran (1943), Dumbarton Oaks (1944) and Yalta (1945) where representatives of China, the Soviet Union, the United Kingdom and the United States met. Such meetings and conferences were purely intergovernmental affairs compared to the much larger San Francisco conference. The Yalta conference of 11 February 1945 is a good example. Here, Prime Minister Winston Churchill, President Franklin D. Roosevelt and General Secretary Joseph Stalin famously met in person and agreed on the rules and composition of the UN Security Council as we know it today. Yalta is, in this respect, a case in point of an intergovernmental negotiation directly between the leaders of major powers. The San Francisco conference was already a bit less intergovernmental – due to the presence of staffers, observers and journalists – even if state delegates were clearly the main negotiators.

Within the UN system, the mode of intergovernmental decision-making remains relevant. The UN regularly initiates international conferences that are intended to give rise to decisions binding on all participating states (e.g. international treaties). Since UN conferences can only make binding decisions when all states agree, it is primarily the states and their interests which dominate the decision-making process. Yet, non-state actors are now regularly involved in major UN treaty conferences, and transgovernmental networks channel and substantively shape final decision-making through crucial preparatory work on treaties. The relevance of intergovernmental state-centred decision-making was very evident at the Third UN Law of the Sea Conference from 1973 until 1982. In the course of a lengthy and at times complicated negotiating process to reformulate the law of the sea, it was a question of harmonizing the differing interests in maritime issues of over 150 states. The result, a colossal achievement, is a negotiating package which mainly reflects the interests of states with long coastlines as well as the interests of the great military powers. The extension of coastal waters, exclusive economic zones and the continental shelf met the interests of states with long coastlines, while the unimpeded transit of shipping through these zones corresponded to the commercial and military interests of the great powers. The agreement of states with short coastlines and of landlocked states, as well as of producers of certain minerals, was assured through various concessions. This comprehensive package illustrates how, in intergovernmental negotiations, the interests of all states have to be respected. But it also shows that states which have issue-specific power resources at their disposal – maritime powers and states with long coastlines – can influence the final decision to a larger extent than states that do not have equally effective resources (Talmon 2000; Wolf 1981: 76–273).

A large intergovernmental conference also underpins the IMF and the World Bank. In a holiday resort, outside of the town Bretton Woods in New Hampshire, more than 700 delegates met in July 1944 to develop multilateral economic cooperation for the post-war era. The final Bretton Woods Agreement resulted in the creation of both international economic organizations. Bretton Woods can, in this respect, be compared to San Francisco. Large conferences are, however, not always how the intergovernmental decision-making process functions. The EU's Treaty of Rome (1957) can be traced back to a three-day conference in Messina (1955) attended by the six foreign ministers of the EU's founding member states. Much of the work on the Treaty was then done at the offices of the Belgian foreign ministry under the leadership of Paul-Henri Spaak. Interestingly, when the EU decades later embarked on negotiating a Constitution for Europe (2004), it put together a two-year long Convention with 102 members led by the former French president Valéry Giscard d'Estaing. Their Constitution was however rejected in popular referendums, even if much of the substance was used for the Lisbon Treaty (2007). The BRICS also provides an interesting example of intergovernmental programme decision-making. Even if the BRICS is not an international organization, at their summit in 2013, the leaders of Brazil, Russia, India, China and South Africa decided to establish a BRICS development bank. This materialized when during their next summit in 2014, they signed the agreement on the New Development Bank (NDB). China furthermore initiated the Asian Infrastructure Investment Bank (AIIB) in 2014 and its Articles of Agreement were negotiated during several rounds of Chief Negotiators Meetings until the end of 2015.

While 'big' programme decisions are often taken at intergovernmental conferences, it is worth reiterating that such conferences are not purely intergovernmental affairs. Various new international organizations in the UN system have been negotiated with the support of the existing UN bodies and secretariat officials. This has affected how they have been designed (Johnson 2014). More generally, new international organizations tend to be inspired by past organizations. When the national delegates met in San Francisco in 1945 to negotiate the UN, they were clearly aware of the experiences of the League of Nations system during the interbellum. What is more, important staff members of the League of Nations worked during the Second World War on the design of the post-war institutions and ultimately around 200 staff members of the League started working for the

UN (e.g. Pedersen 2007; Clavin 2013). So, while 'big' programme decisions are normally taken by states and their representatives, it is also important to acknowledge the context in which they take such decisions as well as their cognitive understanding of international cooperation as experienced in the previous existing institutions.

Programme decisions made at intergovernmental conferences are often subject to domestic ratification procedures. This means that while representatives of state governments negotiate and sign treaties establishing or amending international organizations, each state subsequently needs to ratify the agreement and the programme decisions following its own domestic constitutional procedures. Ratification is all but guaranteed. For instance, the US constitution stipulates that the US Senate needs to approve international treaties with a two-thirds majority vote. Such a high threshold implies, in practice, that both political parties in the US Senate need to support a treaty. While the Senate has approved many more treaties than it has rejected, the US president frequently decides not to forward a treaty to the Senate when unsure about the vote. For instance, the United States is the only state in the world that has signed but not ratified the UN Convention on the Rights of the Child. Ratification is, however, not only a challenge in the United States. Scholars find an increasing number of 'no' votes in national parliaments in international treaty ratification processes across a range of countries (Ostermann and Wagner 2023). When a decision made at an intergovernmental conference enters into force is mentioned in the decision itself. For instance, the Paris Agreement on Climate Change entered into force once at least fifty-five countries that produce at least 55 per cent of the world's greenhouse gas emissions had ratified the agreement.

Institutionalized decision-making: Plenary organs and executive councils

While 'big' programme decisions are made at the level of founding and amending treaties normally in the context of intergovernmental conferences, most programme decisions are actually taken within the international organizations themselves. The plenary organs and executive councils (and their committees) are, in this respect, the principal venues where programme decisions are taken. All member states have a seat in the plenary organs. For the executive councils and the committees, member states representation varies. In the UN Security Council, only a fraction of the member states are present. In the committees of the UN General Assembly, all member states have a seat. The Board of Governors of the IMF and the World Bank include all members, whereas only a limited number of member states are on the IMF Executive Board and World Bank Board of Directors. In the EU, all member states are present in the Council of Ministers, the Committee of Permanent Representatives (COREPER), and the large number of working groups. Participation in the executive councils and committees therefore varies across international organizations.

While the plenary organs and executive councils are often referred to as the 'intergovernmental organs' of international organizations (as opposed to the permanent secretariat which is the 'supranational organ'), the reality is more nuanced. The term 'intergovernmental' refers to relations solely between governments – normally at the ministerial level or higher – taking place on a largely ad hoc, non-institutionalized, basis. The intergovernmental conferences described above are normally ad hoc and dominated by states. International organizations, in contrast, are by definition permanent and have some degree of institutionalization (see Chapters 1 and 4). Therefore, the decision-making in the plenary organs, executive councils and committees is never truly 'intergovernmental'. It always takes place within a constitutional and institutional structure, so the venue is determined and some fundamental rules are set. We therefore use the concept of *institutionalized decision-making* to describe the mode of decision-making within the plenary organs and executive councils.

Particularly in the EU, scholars have questioned the intergovernmental nature of decision-making in the Council of the EU, COREPER and the working groups. Some suggest that EU decision-making processes are better understood as 'intensive transgovernmentalism' (Wallace 2010: 100–2) or 'new intergovernmentalism' (Puetter 2014; Bickerton, Hodson and Puetter 2015). The concepts are, however, not only applicable to the EU. They are relevant for many of the prominent international organizations. Interactions between member states in the plenary organs, executive councils and committees of international organizations take place on a daily basis and are no longer irregular events. Discussions are also no longer solely at the political level between ministers, but civil servants from different member states also contact each other directly. Furthermore, member states are no longer the only ones present in the plenary organs and executive councils; indeed, significant input comes from permanent secretariats and even non-governmental organizations (NGOs) and experts. Meetings are run in a business-like fashion according to clear rules of procedure and established practices.

Apart from the very significant degree of institutionalization in international organizations, such as the EU, IMF and UN, we can also witness a process of 'elite socialization' (Checkel 2005; Lewis 1998, 2005). Contrary to, for instance, the one-off meeting of Roosevelt, Stalin and Churchill at Yalta in 1945, where they decided on the future of the world, ambassadors and diplomats may meet each other every single day in international organizations. This creates a social dynamic which affects actual negotiating behaviour. It is not just that diplomats need to be friendly with one another because they meet each other again the next day or because they get invited to the same receptions and barbecues. Socialization goes deeper. As a result of the intensive interactions, they learn to appreciate the interests of the other parties and the difficulties that other member states may have with certain decisions. Regularly, diplomats also need to convince their own ministries about the need to compromise with international organizations. Indeed, a long-standing risk in diplomacy is that diplomats 'go native': They may show more appreciation for the demands from their international organizations than their instructions from their own ministries.

Actors in plenary organs and executive councils

While member states are clearly the key actors in the plenary organs, executive councils and the committees, they are not the only ones. These meetings are run by a chairperson or presidency. They also include representatives from the permanent secretariat. Various NGOs and other actors may participate as well, either as observers or occasionally as full members themselves. The constitutional and institutional structures of international organizations often determine which actors can participate and contribute to the work of the plenary organs, executive councils and committees (see Chapters 4 and 5). The founding treaties provide, in this respect, the fundamental rules. Yet these are then often complemented by more detailed rules of procedure.

It is difficult to run any meeting without a *chairperson*. The same goes for the meetings of the plenary organs, executive councils and their committees. There are three different ways to appoint a chairperson (Tallberg 2010). First, these organs can have a permanent chairperson. The typical case is NATO, where the secretary general chairs the North Atlantic Council. Second, these organs can have an elected chairperson. An example is the UN General Assembly, which elects its president each year. Still, custom dictates that the UN General Assembly member states elect a president each year from a different region, that all countries should ultimately have the chance to hold the presidency once and that the five permanent members of the Security Council do not also take the presidency of the General Assembly. Third, the chairperson rotates among the member states. An example is the yearly rotating chair of the Association of Southeast Asian Nations (ASEAN). Another example is the monthly rotating presidency of the Security Council. While in international organizations with a relatively small membership there is often a rotating chairperson, this option is suboptimal for international organizations with a larger membership.

Being the chairperson of plenary organs, executive councils or committees is of significant symbolic value and brings prestige. In most international organizations, however, the chairpersons also have a substantive role and can exert influence on decisions: it matters who chairs the meetings and negotiations in international organizations. The starting point for discussing chairpersons is, however, their formal impartiality. Chairpersons are not supposed to promote the national interests from their home country. Instead, they should act as an 'honest broker' trying to find compromise between the member states and, where necessary, defend the interest of the organ they represent towards other organs and the outside world. For instance, the rotating presidency of the Council of the EU defends the collective interests of the member states in their negotiations with the European Parliament. If chairpersons appear biased towards the national interests from their home countries, they may lose the confidence of the other member states.

While impartiality is critical, and many chairpersons take it seriously, being at the helm of decision-making offers significant opportunities to shape the actual decisions (Tallberg 2006). First, the chairperson often has a role in managing the agenda. They may prioritize or exclude certain topics on the agenda. The chairperson also typically decides on the order of the agenda and the time allocated to certain issues. Furthermore, in some international organizations, the chairperson may decide on the timing of meetings. For instance, the NATO secretary general has the procedural power to call for an emergency meeting of the North Atlantic Council. Second, the chairperson is often closely involved in brokering deals. Through informal bilateral negotiations with the relevant member states, the chairperson may get insider knowledge of bottom lines and therefore the 'zone of possible agreement' (ZOPA). Within the ZOPA, the chairperson can propose compromises that benefit their home country most. Finally, as noted above, the chairperson may represent their organ to the outside world and sometimes even negotiate on behalf of their organ. Such an external context allows the chairperson some discretion as well.

In addition to the chairperson, the administrative staff from the *permanent secretariat* is almost always present during decision-making. Members of staff from the secretariat take on different functions. A key function is to provide elaborate conference services, such as booking rooms, distributing documents, providing translation and security and ordering coffee. In addition, in many international organizations, the secretariat contains legal experts or even a legal service to advise the member states on legal and institutional questions. Yet another function is support for the chairperson. Especially when the chairperson is elected or rotating, it is important to have a set of more permanent assistants that can help the chair to run the meetings. They may take minutes, keep an eye on the speaking order, administer the votes and even provide the chairperson with procedural and political advice on negotiations. Because the members of staff of the permanent secretariat are also supposed to be impartial, they too may act as the honest brokers seeking compromise for the member states. An important part of the role of secretariats is thus to 'oil the wheel of compromise' (Beach 2004) in plenary organs and executive councils.

Particularly in the larger international organizations, the permanent secretariats have also been delegated a function as expert bureaucracy. In the UN General Assembly and the Security Council, negotiations often start off by the secretary general (or the Under-secretary generals) presenting a formal report with their views. The same can be said about other international organizations. In the EU, for instance, the European Commission presents and defends its proposals in the Council and the underlying committees. In the IMF, the staff from the various functional and area departments prepare documents for decision-making. In NATO, experts from the International Staff and the International Military Staff provide much of the input for negotiations in the North Atlantic Council.

The rules of procedure often dictate how *the representatives of the member states* can participate in the formal meetings. For instance, the rules of procedure of the UN General Assembly note that the chairperson shall give the floor to speakers 'in the order in which they signify their desire to speak' (Rule 68). It is therefore 'first come, first served', and representatives from larger states are not privileged in line with the emphasis on sovereign equality in the General Assembly. The same rules stipulate that for formal meetings interpretation will be provided for the six working languages of the General Assembly (Arabic, Chinese, English, French, Russian and Spanish) (Rule 51). Speakers are allowed to speak in their own language, but then they need to provide interpretation in one of the six working languages themselves (Rule 52). So when the German Chancellor wants to address the General Debate in German – not one of the working languages – the German delegation has to provide and pay for interpretation. Based on the rules of procedure, the chairperson may also put time limits on interventions or cut national representatives off. In the EU, for instance, it used to be custom to start discussions with a *tour de table*, in which every minister got a say. Following the 2004 enlargement round, which resulted in many more ministers around the table, it was decided to stop with this practice: if the representatives of all the member states got two minutes each, the *tour de table* would take a full hour.

Also important is the seating order (see Chadwick 2014). In the UN General Assembly, the secretary general each year randomly selects a member state to sit in the first seat. The rest of the member states then follow in English alphabetic order. This is significant, because it means that like-minded countries or regional groups do not sit together. In the EU, seats are allocated in the order that member states have the rotating presidency. So if the rotating presidency is coming up soon for a member state, it sits at the beginning. If a member state has just concluded the presidency, it sits at the end. The order of the presidencies is also strategically determined so that there is a good mix between large and small member states as well as member states from the North, South, East and West. For instance, Germany normally sits between Croatia and Portugal. The other institutional actors are typically strategically located: the UN secretary general sits next to the president of the General Assembly and the president of the Security Council, whereas the European Commission has a prominent position with multiple seats at the table of the Council of the EU.

Non-member states, other international organizations and NGOs – including civil society actors and business representatives – often have access to plenary organs and executive councils. In some international organizations they are formal members (with voting rights) and sit at the same table. In many international organizations, they are observers of associate members and typically sit in the back or have to be invited to the table. In the UN General Assembly, the Holy See and the State of Palestine are non-member state observers. They have far-reaching participation rights but cannot vote even if the representatives of Palestine now sit among the other member states in the Assembly hall. The EU as an international organization has also been granted exceptional rights to participate in the UN General Assembly. A whole range of other international organizations participate in the General Assembly as well. NGOs have less access but can instead provide their input to the UN Economic and Social Committee (ECOSOC).

Negotiations in plenary organs and executive councils

The plenary organs, executive councils and committees provide a formal setting for negotiations and decision-making among member states. It is the place where member states present their views and provide official statements. This formal setting has a number of advantages. It guarantees access and equal participation for all member states and other actors. It ensures that minutes are made and an official record of discussions is kept. Many plenary organs and executive councils are currently open to the public and interested parties or are streamed online. This creates considerable openness and transparency. At the same time, these formalized meetings are not necessarily the most effective way of coming to decisions. Ministers or ambassadors may not make concessions when they are in public. Furthermore, having a negotiation where one needs to go back and forward via the chair is not necessarily a speedy process. Therefore, informal negotiations are often organized and complement formal negotiations.

The UN, in particular, has set up an elaborate network of informal meetings. First of all, the work of the General Assembly is divided over six subcommittees, in which all member states have a seat. The committees organize informal consultations ('formal informals') which still have a strong formal nature: each committee has a chairperson, and all member states sit in the same order as the UN General Assembly proper. Therefore, work on UN resolutions is mostly done in the so-called informal informal consultations ('informal informals'). These meetings are still published in the daily UN journal, so all interested member states can attend, but normally they only involve the main negotiating parties. The constellation of the main negotiating parties varies from issue to issue. In the Second Committee dealing with economic and development cooperation, the main negotiating parties could include the United States, the EU, Russia, Japan and the G77 representing 130+ developing countries. There is one further level of informality: ironing out a deal over a coffee in the Café Austria

('Vienna Café') or a drink in the Delegates Lounge Bar, both located within the UN building.

The situation is slightly different with the UN Security Council. It can meet formally in open and closed sessions. Closed meetings are obviously not open to the public (nor accessible for the rest of the UN membership); there is no live streaming and no verbatim record of statements is kept, but these are formal meetings. The Security Council also regularly holds informal consultations and also informal meetings that only include the five permanent members. For instance, it can hold 'Arria-formula' meetings behind closed doors with high-level UN officials or representatives from selected member states to discuss sensitive issues. These working methods of the Security Council are a matter of regular criticism – so much so that the Security Council has so far failed to adopt rules of procedure (it still operates under 'provisional rules of procedure'). On the one hand, the secretive nature of Security Council dealings provides the great powers with an opportunity to 'blow off steam'. It also provides them opportunities to offer concessions and craft deals without the risk that these get undermined by external exposure. On the other hand, this secretive, informal process allows for very little accountability of the permanent members.

While the UN members have formalized 'the informal' into the working methods, in the EU there is a stronger emphasis on formal meetings. If deadlocks appear during formal meetings, the chairman can call for a break and address the issue informally with the relevant parties. For instance, during high-level EU summits, national leaders can be summoned to the office of the President of the European Council for informal consultations. Within the EU, deals are also often precooked prior to formal meetings. Leaders of Germany and France may be directly in contact in advance of a meeting to discuss their differences and then present a common front to the other member states. What is clear, both in the EU and the UN, is that informal negotiations benefit the powerful member states. They have the administrative capacity to attend all informal meetings, and they are no longer constrained by the rules of formal negotiations.

It is not only important whether the mode of negotiations is formal or informal. It is also important to pay attention to negotiation styles. It is conventional to distinguish, in this respect, hard bargaining from problem-solving (Hopmann 1995; Elgström and Jönsson 2000; Odell 2010). The logic of hard bargaining resembles a zero-sum game: if one party wins something, the other parties lose. Despite the generally cooperative atmosphere in international organizations, and the polite language used by diplomats, one should not be mistaken. There is a lot of hard bargaining going on in international organizations: from the redistributive negotiations over the budget to whether the UN Security Council authorizes the use of force. At the same time, many observers note that the dominant negotiation style resembles problem-solving. Generally, member states establish international organizations to address problems (see Chapters 2 and 3), so it is logical that many of the negotiations on the programme decisions within international organizations also concentrate on solving problems. For instance, in the UN Security Council, diplomats may work hard on finding 'language' for resolutions that is acceptable to all permanent members.

Voting procedures in plenary organs and executive councils

The negotiation process ends with the adoption (or not) of a decision. Depending on the constitutional and institutional structure of a particular international organization, decisions in the plenary organs and executive councils can be taken by consensus or majority voting (see Chapter 4). The consensus rule applies in many international organizations. This means that member states need to negotiate as long as it takes to get everyone on board. While most smaller member states may not want to 'block the consensus' all the time, they will ensure that they get heard on topics they care deeply about. While a consensus rule potentially makes negotiations more difficult, it does not mean that international organizations are weak or permanently gridlocked. NATO, for instance, famously has a consensus rule, but most observers would still rank it among the strongest international organizations.

As a rule of thumb, the more a programme decision of an international organization impinges on member states' autonomy, the more decision-making can be expected to require the consensus of all member states. States show little readiness to submit to a majority vote if their fundamental autonomy is at stake. But the more a programme decision leaves member states' autonomy untouched, the more likely the decision-making mode is majority voting. Therefore, legally binding programme decisions of international organizations are usually (though not exclusively) made through intergovernmental negotiations, while legally non-binding programme decisions can be taken through majority voting. However, this distinction reflects a rule of thumb rather than an empirical law. There are legally binding programme decisions that are taken by majority vote, and they seem to be on the rise (Hooghe et al. 2017; Zürn, Binder and Ecker-Ehrhardt 2012). Examples are UN Security Council resolutions in the issue area of anti-terrorism policies that impose legislative and administrative obligations on all UN member states or the expansion of (qualified) majority voting in the Council of the EU (Johnstone 2008; Hix and Høyland 2022).

Because programme decisions are so important, member states often have a veto. Yet at the same time, such decisions can hardly be said to satisfy strict criteria of fairness: the more powerful states have greater influence on the decisions made than less powerful states (Krasner 1991; Steinberg 2002). Nevertheless, making decisions in an international organizational framework can be fairer than making decisions outside such a framework where the more powerful states can, to a large extent, make their own decisions while simply ignoring the interests of less powerful states. The decision-making procedures of international organizations help less powerful states (or non-state actors) to get their interests heard (the so-called 'voice' function of international organizations) and give them the opportunity to demand compensation from more powerful states in return for their support of decisions favoured by major powers. This holds especially true where less powerful actors form coalitions among themselves or join a coalition led by a powerful state which then has to take their interests into consideration (Voeten 2000).

Also, when the number of member states increases, reaching consensus becomes more difficult (all other things being equal). It is thus not a surprise that, particularly in international organizations with a large membership, states have adopted majority voting rules (Hooghe and Marks 2015). Voting in plenary organs and executive councils should be seen as separate from negotiations. Essentially, when a plenary organ or executive council puts a decision to a (majority) vote, it means that negotiations have failed to reach a consensus. It is useful to think of voting as 'negotiation failure', because for the implementation of decisions, international organizations are often dependent on the goodwill of the member states. There thus exists a strong risk that states may 'win' the vote, but that it ultimately results in little as the outvoted states fail to comply. As a result, there is a strong commitment in most international organizations to continue negotiations – even on dossiers where voting is an option – until a consensus is finally reached. In the EU, the estimate is that about 80 per cent of decisions are taken by consensus even though majority voting would be possible (Häge 2013).

It is important to note that voting is not always for the purpose of adopting decisions. In the UN Security Council and General Assembly, for instance, votes are also occasionally orchestrated for symbolic reasons. Because of intensive informal negotiations in the UN Security Council, the use of vetoes normally does not come as a surprise. Indeed, when it becomes clear that one of the five permanent members will veto a resolution, the resolution is often not put to a vote. The five permanent members, particularly since the end of the Cold War, normally do not want to put each other on the spot and prefer a cooperative working relationship. For instance, between 1990 and 2014, only thirty-five vetoes were cast in total (Wallensteen and Johansson 2016: Table 2.1). This comes down to about half a veto per permanent member per year. The situation has however changed. For symbolic reasons, the Western powers have started to regularly put resolutions to a vote on, for instance, the use of chemical weapons in Syria. Indeed, around two-thirds of the approximately forty vetoes cast between 2011 and 2024 are about security issues in the Middle East. In the UN General Assembly, it has also been a long practice to vote on symbolic resolutions, such as on Israeli aggression. The purpose of such resolutions is not to have a direct impact on Israeli behaviour but rather to send a signal. When voting takes place, in many international organizations, member states often are able to give an explanation of their vote – before and/or after the actual vote. These statements become a formal part of the record.

Operational decisions

Operational decisions are about the implementation of the norms and rules of programme decisions. Because the programme decisions often infringe on the sovereignty of states, states have to give up some of their autonomy. Operational decisions of international organizations, on the other hand, do not affect member states' autonomy to the same degree as programme decisions do. While they may be important and occasionally politically sensitive, operational decisions normally take place in the framework set by programme decisions. The UN Security Council, for instance, may adopt a resolution authorizing a peacekeeping mission (programme decision), in which context the UN secretary general appoints a Force Commander (operational decision) who decides when and where the blue helmets go on a patrol (operational decision). As a result, states are typically less eager to dominate the decision-making process for operational decisions and it is easier for the permanent secretariats of international organizations to act in a relatively independent manner. States may also grant international courts to interpret the programme decisions. Operational decisions are therefore also not necessarily made in the plenary organs and executive councils. Even though in many international organizations states remain in charge of operational decisions, in some international organizations states may instead opt for a system of delegated decision-making where they grant decision-making authority to a permanent secretariat, an international court or another implementing agency.

Delegated decision-making: Secretariats and agencies

Under the model of delegated decision-making, the secretariat has the discretion to make decisions in the scope of its competencies. This can include simple, everyday decisions, such as making travel arrangements for the secretary general to visit one of the member states or ordering catering for the annual plenary meeting. Yet in various international organizations, delegated decision-making goes much further. In the EU, the European Commission, for instance, has the power to adopt 'delegated acts' and 'implementing acts'. These often deal with technical issues, such as food safety standards, agriculture or the customs union and its tariffs, but with significant consequences. For instance, the energy labels put on electrical appliances in Europe are designed by Commission experts. The Commission also made decisions with regard to body scanners at airports across Europe. In the UN system, decision-making is also often delegated. The formal command of peacekeeping operations has been delegated to the Special Representative of the secretary general. They decide – and not the Security Council – whether blue helmets go out on mission patrol and can intervene in conflicts (within the overall mandate set by the Security Council).

Delegated decision-making is nothing exceptional. In the national context, we are used to the fact that most decisions are taken by the executive rather than the legislative branch of government. The advantages of delegated decision-making is that decisions can be made more swiftly and that the executive branch has much more expertise and administrative capacity. Indeed, we do not expect parliamentarians making laws in the national parliaments to also be involved in the implementation of those laws. They do not have the expertise, time or interest to make, for instance, decisions in individual asylum cases, about whether tax forms have been filled out properly or which garbage collecting company needs to be hired. At the same time, national parliamentarians do make sure that they set up a range of control mechanisms to ensure that the executive does its work properly: the delegation of tasks can be precise, leaving little scope for interpretation; the executive can be given incentives to do its job properly; parliamentarians can do some random checks or can rely on citizens to notify them in case of bad behaviour on the side of the executive (e.g. McCubbins and Schwartz 1984; McCubbins, Noll and Weingast 1987). While the comparison with the national context is fitting, delegated decision-making in international organizations tends to be more limited, because it is more difficult to control international organizations (Dijkstra 2016).

It is difficult to say which operational decisions in which international organizations fall under a mode of delegated decision-making. A large number of factors (both on the side of the permanent secretariats and on the side of member states) affect the competencies of the permanent secretariats so that it is hard to make tenable and generalizable predictions. Nevertheless, one can claim that, all other things being equal, the more the programmes of international organizations affect member states' autonomy, the less states are prepared to transfer control over operational decisions – through which these programmes are implemented – to an international bureaucracy. And conversely, the less the programmes impinge on their autonomy, the more the states are willing to transfer authority over operational decisions to the bureaucracy. At the same time, the stronger the competencies of the permanent secretariats, the more control we can also expect from the side of the member states (Hawkins et al. 2006; Dijkstra 2016). In the EU, for instance, the member states have set up a rather elaborate system of 'comitology', consisting of around 250 member states committees where the Commission officials need to explain the contents of delegated implementing acts (Brandsma and Blom-Hansen 2017).

Also the fact that the member states may delegate their decisions to a permanent secretariat does not mean they leave the secretariat alone. States tend to continuously meddle in the affairs of the permanent secretariat (Urpelainen 2012). Powerful member states generally exert a large influence on appointments of the heads of international organizations' secretariats. For instance, the permanent five members of the Security Council have a veto right over who gets to be the UN secretary general. Yet the interference goes further. High-level positions within permanent secretariats (for instance, the UN Under-Secretaries-General or Directorate-Generals in the European Commission) are often informally given to the major powers which then use these positions to affect decisions (Kleine 2013). Indeed, in recent years, we have seen serious disputes between Western states and China and Russia over the appointment of high-level positions in UN agencies. Yet even at the level of regular staff, we can witness the prominence of the major powers and donor countries, which are overrepresented (Parízek 2017). Still, empirical research on international bureaucracies has shown that the capacities of even the most powerful states to control, rein in and reform bureaucracies are frequently limited (Barnett and Finnemore 2004; Nielson et al. 2006; Weaver 2008).

How operational decision-making works in practice can be illustrated by looking at the EU as well as the UN. Within the EU, for instance, the European Central Bank (ECB) takes important operational decisions regarding European monetary policy such as setting the interest rate. Decisions are made by the Governing Council, which consists of the six members of the Executive Board and the governors of the national central banks. Another example of delegated decision-making in the EU concerns the establishment of more than forty agencies located throughout Europe (Majone 1997; Keleman 2002; Wonka and Rittberger 2010). Many of these agencies have important implementing functions. For instance, the European Border and Coast Guard Agency (also known as Frontex) can deploy border guards to EU and non-EU countries to strengthen national capacities. It is also deployed in the Mediterranean Sea to guard against irregular migration.

In the UN we can also find operational decisions made according to delegated decision-making. The decisions of the UN Special Commissions that had to verify the dismantling of weapons of mass destruction in Iraq after the Gulf War of 1991 are an example. These Special Commissions were established by the Security Council as a result of Resolution 687 (1991). In order to track down and eliminate all the components of the weapons of mass destruction programme, the Special Commissions – first the United Nations Special Commission (UNSCOM) (1991–7) and later the United Nations Monitoring, Verification and Inspection Commission (UNMOVIC) (1999–2007) – had to take many decisions. For example, they had to determine how to inspect Iraqi installations suspected of storing weapons of mass destruction, how to react to Iraq's refusal to allow the inspection commission access to certain installations and how to guarantee that Iraq would be permanently unable to manufacture or acquire new weapons of mass destruction. The necessary operational decisions were taken by the Special Commissions in close cooperation with the UN secretary general. Furthermore, the chairpersons of the Special Commissions were obliged to report regularly to the Security Council through the secretary general on the implementation of their mandate. Thus, the Special Commissions were not entirely free in their decisions yet were not totally constrained in reaching decisions either by the Security Council or by the secretary general. Rather, decisions occurred by means of bureaucratic politics between the Special Commissions and especially its chairpersons, the secretary general, the Security Council and, in particular, the representatives of the latter's permanent members.

The overview of operational decisions in the context of the UN would be incomplete without referring to the important work of development and humanitarian agencies 'on the ground' (Kortendiek 2024). From the work of the UN Development Programme (UNDP) in 170 countries around the world, where it seeks to implement the Sustainable Development Goals (SDGs), to the food assistance and emergency relief provided by the World Food Programme (WFP), the UN Refugee Agency (UNHCR) and the UN Office for the Coordination of Humanitarian Affairs (OCHA), officials of the UN and affiliated organizations take decisions every day. These include operational decisions on whether to declare an emergency as a result of conflict or natural disasters, where to set up refugee camps and when to deploy helicopters to monitor crises and provide help. In many such cases, the trained professionals of the UN have to take difficult decisions within the scope of the broader mandates and resources allocated to them. They are, in this sense, reliant on what the international organization's membership provides in terms of support, but they can have considerable autonomy when it comes to operational decisions on the ground.

Delegated decision-making: Courts

Delegated decision-making also takes place through international courts. In various international organizations states have delegated the role to interpret programme decisions to courts. As such, the judgements of international courts are also operational decisions. After all, through their judgements courts help to implement the norms and rules of programme decisions (see Chapter 7). There are different sorts of international courts. The most frequent are arbitration tribunals that aim to settle conflicts between member states by providing relatively neutral third-party interpretation of the norms and rules that member states have set themselves. The EU provides a clear example. In the original treaties, for instance, the EU member states adopted a policy programme on the freedom of movement of workers. Yet an important question was how to define a 'worker'. Would freedom of movement also extent to part-time workers, interns or even unemployed job seekers? It was also up to the European Court of Justice (ECJ) to make operational decisions. It eventually came up with a rather expansive interpretation of the freedom of movement. Other types of courts are the international criminal courts and war crimes tribunals. They too make operational decisions through their judgements, for instance, by deciding whether individuals are guilty of war crimes.

One of the key debates among academics and observers is the politics of international courts. Precisely because arbitration courts need to settle conflicts between the member states, they need to maintain some distance and stand above the parties. Similarly, the main reason to have war crimes tribunals is their moral authority to interpret the law. The control of member states over delegated decision-making by international courts is therefore more limited than their control over secretariats (Tallberg 2000). This raises the question of whether international courts may use their considerable authority to pursue a political agenda. For instance, the ECJ is often said to push for more European integration (Alter 2001). The member states nevertheless exert still some control over courts. For instance, they often nominate the judges to be appointed to international courts (Elsig and Pollack 2014). International courts are also aware that they cannot make member states comply with their judgements, so they will have to take political sensitivities into account (see Chapter 7). There has nonetheless been a considerable backlash against international courts in the past decade. The United States, for instance, has criticized the WTO Appellate Body of judicial overreach and favouring China too much in rulings. As such, the Trump administration has blocked the appointment of judges rendering the Appellate Body inoperable in 2019. Burundi and the Philippines have similarly withdrawn from the International Criminal Court (ICC).

Conclusion

International organizations produce many decisions every day. And how international organizations convert inputs into outputs matters. International organizations are more than the simple sum of their member states. Based on an elaborate constitutional and institutional structure, member states and other actors have to follow a set of rules and procedures in order to arrive at a final decision. How international organizations convert inputs into outputs depends on the institutional particularities of the individual international organizations: the UN Security Council votes over questions of war and peace, whereas the North Atlantic Council (NAC) takes decisions by consensus. To explain such an important difference, we need to know the historical context and understand how the constitutional and institutional structure of both international organizations came about (Chapters 3 and 4). That said, this chapter has outlined two general models of decision-making, based on whether the relevant decision concerns a programme or operational decision.

Programme decisions involve the generation of norms and rules that apply to the member states (and occasionally even non-member states and other actors). Member states are therefore reluctant to grant permanent secretariats substantial decision-making authority over programme decisions.

Indeed the 'big' programme decisions are often made at intergovernmental conferences with limited input by the permanent secretariats. More day-to-day programme decisions within the context of international organizations often require consensus of the member states even if the mode of decision-making is institutionalized. Operational decisions, on the other hand, relate to the implementation of these norms and rules. This allows for delegated decision-making by the secretariat or other implementing agencies. It does not apply that operational decisions do not matter. Indeed, operational decisions may have actual concrete consequences. While secretariats can have considerable decision-making authority over operational decisions, their authority is not absolute. Normally, delegated decision-making comes with fine-grained control by the member states. The important point is to distinguish different types of decisions taken in international organizations and to offer a heuristic device to analytically simplify the ever-growing complexity of international organizations' decision-making.

Discussion questions

1. What are the main differences between programme decisions and operational decisions? Illustrate your answer with specific examples of decision-making in international organizations.
2. If you compare programme decisions with operational decisions, which have the greatest potential to infringe on the autonomy of member states? How is this reflected in the decision-making processes?
3. What is potentially more significant: the provision in the UN Charter that states shall refrain from the use of force or the delegation of decision-making authority to a UN peacekeeping commander who has to make life/death decisions? Provide arguments for both.

Further reading

Dimitrov, Rado S. (2016). 'The Paris Agreement on Climate Change: Behind Closed Doors', *Global Environmental Politics*, 16 (3): 1–11.
Hawkins, Darren, David A. Lake, Daniel L. Nielson and Michael J. Tierney, eds (2006). *Delegation and Agency in International Organizations*, Cambridge: Cambridge University Press.
Sommerer, Thomas, Theresa Squatrito, Jonas Tallberg and Magnus Lundgren (2022). 'Decision-making in International Organizations: Institutional Design and Performance', *The Review of International Organizations* 17(4): 815–45.
United Nations (2020). *The United Nations Guide to Model UN*, New York: United Nations.

7

Output

What international organizations produce

International organizations convert inputs into outputs. In the preceding chapters, we have focused on the inputs as well as the structures, actors and processes that shape decision-making in international organizations. But arguably, what matters most is what comes out of international organizations: the policies that international organizations produce. In this chapter we take a systematic look at the main outputs of international organizations. We differentiate between *policy programmes* and *operational activities* (see Figure 7.1).

Policy programmes are the result of programme decisions and set norms and rules for the member states of international organizations and occasionally also non-member states and private actors. We can distinguish between regulatory policy programmes that aim at directing the behaviour of social actors and redistributive policy programmes that aim at redistributing rights and duties among the member states of international organizations. Apart from the objectives of policy programmes, it is also important to distinguish between binding and non-binding policy programmes. Through operational activities, international organizations implement policy programmes. While in many international organizations implementation is done by the member states themselves, various international organizations do perform a number of operational tasks. They can, for instance, further specify the policy programme or implement a policy programme. In addition, operational activities may include the monitoring of implementation by the member states, adjudicating between the member states in case of conflicts or imposing sanctions for non-compliance. As part of the operational

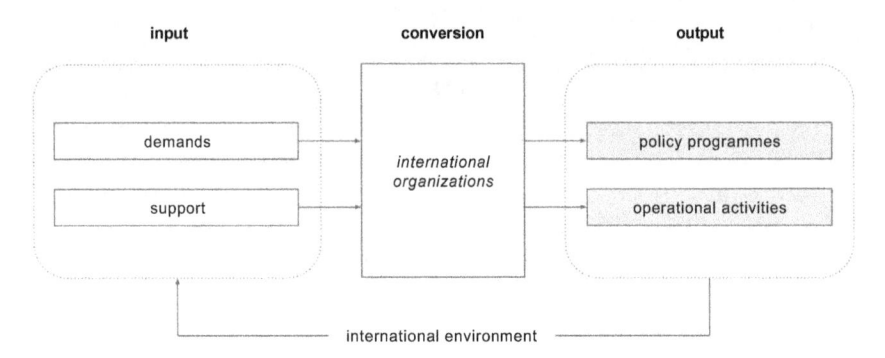

FIGURE 7.1 *The political system of international organizations (output).*

activities, international organizations take operational decisions, often through delegated decision-making procedures (see Chapter 6).

After discussing different kinds of outputs, this chapter addresses the effectiveness of outputs produced by international organizations. While international organizations can adopt a variety of outputs, such as policies, laws, statements and declarations, and launch all kinds of operational activities, such as development programmes or peacekeeping missions, this still tells us little about the outcomes of such outputs. The fact that the United Nations (UN) Security Council puts something in a resolution does not mean that it will ultimately happen on the ground in a peacekeeping mission in Africa. Furthermore, even if the outcomes are broadly in line with the intended goals of an international organization, it is not yet guaranteed that the intended outcomes also have the intended impact. Peacekeeping missions, for instance, can be very effective in bringing security and safety on the ground, but it does not mean that they provide a durable solution to an ongoing conflict.

Policy programmes

Policy programmes are sets of norms and rules aimed at directing the behaviour of social actors. While they usually set normative standards for the behaviour of their members, they can also touch upon the interaction between the members and the international organization itself. Sometimes international organizations also formulate norms and rules that directly address non-state actors that are not members of the international organization. Policy programmes are the result of programme decisions of international organizations. Policy programmes can be differentiated, first, according to the objectives their norms and rules are intended to reach and, second, according to the degree to which their norms and rules are legally binding.

Objectives

Policy programmes in general, and not just in international organizations, are intended to have diverse effects, depending on whether they are regulatory programmes or redistributive programmes (Lowi 1964). *Regulatory programmes* aim to direct the behaviour of social actors in order to achieve desirable interactions. To this end, norms and rules of behaviour are set that prescribe or proscribe certain behaviour in specified circumstances. They act as guidelines for actors (Lowi 1964: 694). National examples of regulatory programmes whose norms and rules regulate interactions are criminal law, environmental law, human rights law and consumer protection law. At the international level, regulatory policy programmes help states to avoid undesirable interactions such as wars or to achieve desirable interactions such as peace. Hence the UN Charter's ban on the threat or use of force is an example of a regulatory programme. Other examples are the Nuclear Non-Proliferation Treaty (NPT), proscribing the acquisition of nuclear weapons for all states apart from China, France, Russia, the United Kingdom and the United States; the General Agreement on Tariffs and Trade (GATT), prescribing that all World Trade Organization (WTO) member states have to grant most favoured nation treatment to all other member states; or the Montreal Protocol on Substances that Deplete the Ozone Layer to the Vienna Convention on the Protection of the Ozone Layer, prescribing that all states have to ban the use of chemicals such as chlorofluorocarbons (CFCs) which contribute to the depletion of the ozone layer.

The European Union (EU) is perhaps the international organization with the most elaborate regulatory programmes. It has been compared to a regulatory state (Majone 1994). In support of its internal market, the EU has vigorously tried to take away all possible obstacles to the freedom of goods and services as well as capital and labour. It has done so partially through 'mutual recognition' – that is, the principle that goods, which are legally brought to the market in one member state, should be allowed automatic market access in all member states. For instance, if a product is considered safe in one member state (and does not cause a health risk), it should be considered safe in all the member states (and cannot be excluded from the market on health grounds). While this simple rule is attractive and has resulted in considerable market integration in the EU, it has also been criticized: it results, almost by default, in deregulation, social dumping and a 'race to the bottom'. After all, companies may move production to member states with business-friendly rules. This market-making approach has therefore been complemented by additional programmes that focus on the harmonization of regulation across the EU. For instance, the EU has adopted a rule on the maximum energy that vacuum cleaners can use. Rather than having separate rules in every member state and a potential race to the bottom, the EU considers that such harmonization results in a stronger internal market.

Redistributive programmes are directed towards social actors' behaviour in order to change the distribution of goods and services among them. They benefit some actors while others are burdened with additional costs (Lowi 1964: 711). The best-known examples of redistributive programmes at the national level are welfare state policies of providing housing, education, unemployment benefits or health care. Many of these programmes are subsidized by the state, which collects taxes on income, sales, wealth and property among others. Hence, costs are concentrated on certain social groups to reallocate them as benefits to other groups. At the international level, within international organizations, there are also examples of redistributive programmes. For instance, much of the UN system is concerned with development assistance and the EU has its Cohesion Funds which redistribute money to the poorer member states and regions. At the same time, member states of international organizations are not necessarily keen to redistribute a lot of funding. International solidarity tends to be lower than national solidarity. While taxpayers may be willing to make money available for citizens in a different country struck by humanitarian disaster, they may not be willing to hand out unemployment benefits or pay for social housing in other countries. In the UN, donor countries have committed to spend 0.7 per cent of their gross domestic product (GDP) on development assistance (yet very few donor countries meet this target).

We find a large number of redistributive programmes run by international organizations such as the UN Development Programme (UNDP), World Food Programme (WFP) or the UN Industrial Development Organization (UNIDO). Their principal concern is the transfer of resources from developed to developing countries (Marshall 2008; Murphy 2006). The Bretton Woods institutions, such as the World Bank and the International Monetary Fund (IMF), can also be said to engage in redistributive programmes. That said, the World Bank provides loans and thus eventually wants its money back. It does not provide a blank cheque. The same goes for the IMF, which provides bridging loans for member states unable to get money from the financial markets. It is also important to note that in the case of both international organizations, the 'donor' countries benefit as well. As a result of the support of the IMF, borrowing member states may not have to default on their loans.

Binding nature

In addition to the differentiation based on the objectives that norms and rules of policy programmes may have, one can also distinguish them according to whether their norms and rules are legally binding (Abbott et al. 2000; Abbott and Snidal 2000). The degree of legal obligation does not necessarily correlate with the level of member states' compliance. Nonetheless, it certainly remains an important characteristic of the programmes, whether they contain legally binding obligations or are simply political recommendations. It is not unusual to find within one and the same international organization the coexistence of both legally binding and non-binding programmes.

The EU is one of the few international organizations that has the authority to make programmes directly binding not only on member states but also on private actors within member states. In particular, in matters pertaining to the internal market the EU has long used regulations and directives as part of its policy programme. Regulations are legally binding and applicable from the moment they have been enacted by the EU, without the need for national authorities to implement them through domestic law. Directives, although binding, give member states' authorities some discretion in how to make them applicable by implementation through domestic law. In addition, there are also EU programmes which are not legally binding, embodying recommendations or opinions which express political objectives rather than legal obligations.

In the UN, many policy programmes have no legally binding effect. With the exception of decisions on budgetary questions or the UN's internal organization, resolutions and declarations of the UN General Assembly merely have the character of recommendations. If repeated frequently the programmes contained in such resolutions may become legally binding as international customary law but only if most UN member states agree (in their practice and their legal opinions) to that effect. By contrast, resolutions of the UN Security Council made under Chapter VII of the UN Charter are immediately binding. Conventions, agreements or treaties negotiated within the framework of the UN or its Specialized Agencies can also become legally binding on member states. But this usually requires their ratification by the states that are party to the relevant treaty, agreement or convention (see Chapter 6). In the case of many treaties, agreements and conventions the UN General Assembly avails itself of the possibility of recommending an early signature and ratification in a resolution to the member states.

Operational activities

In addition to policy programmes, a large part of the output of the work of international organizations takes an operational form. Operational activities of international organizations are the result of operational decisions which relate to the implementation of policy programmes. We can differentiate five types of operations:

1. Specification of the norms and rules of policy programmes
2. Implementation of (specified) norms and rules
3. Monitoring of the implementation of policy programmes
4. Adjudication in cases of alleged non-compliance
5. Imposition of sanctions in cases of non-compliance

Specification

The norms and rules of policy programmes generally require further specification in order to implement them. This specification is often done by member states' authorities. Member states' parliaments, governments or bureaucracies select the means and measures to fulfil the commitments laid down in international organizations' policy programmes. Yet in numerous international organizations such as the EU, the IMF, the World Bank and also the UN, the specification of programmes has become the responsibility of the organizations themselves. For example, as noted above, the EU internal market programme requires the harmonization of technical and legal standards. But rather than defining these standards in the member states, the programme provides that the specification of the actual standards be made by the organs of the EU themselves. Similarly, the World Bank draws up detailed conditions for projects in developing countries. And several measures taken by the UN Security Council should be interpreted as operational decisions specifying its programme of maintaining international peace and security.

Sometimes, international organizations do not conduct the specification of general policy programmes themselves but either explicitly transfer this task to transnational expert bodies or endorse the activities of private bodies for that purpose. For example, the EU only defines broad minimum requirements in technical product standards and mandates private standard-setting bodies to specify which conditions must be met for these broad requirements to be fulfilled (Abbott et al. 2000). In a similar way, the EU decided that stock market-listed European companies should use uniform international accounting standards. Rather than defining these standards itself, the EU endorsed the standards developed by the private International Accounting Standards Board. Another example is the WTO's practice of referring to decisions of the Codex Alimentarius Commission in regulations on food safety.

Implementation

Through the specification of programmes international organizations not only help states to implement norms and rules but also sometimes provide a starting point for international organizations to implement the norms and rules directly themselves. Oftentimes the implementation of internationally agreed programmes remains the prerogative of member states' authorities, their parliaments, governments and bureaucracies. Thus the standards for the quality of drinking water, for instance, are set for all member states by the EU, but the measures necessary for their implementation, such as the construction of water purification plants, are taken by the relevant authorities within EU member states. Yet when international organizations implement the norms and rules themselves, they are typically very visible. This holds, for instance, for the World Food Programme (WFP) when it delivers food assistance during emergency or the UN Refugee Agency (UNHCR) when it sets up refugee camps. The general public, and particularly the recipients of such support, therefore tend to identity international organizations at least as much with their operational activities 'on the ground' as with the policy programmes set by the member states in the headquarters of the international organizations (Kortendiek 2024).

The direct implementation of policy programmes through international organizations occurs whenever those organizations, on the basis of their informational, financial and personnel resources, can provide support for the activities desired by member states. The EU, for instance, directly administered the fixed price system for European agricultural markets while the UN, along with many of its Specialized Agencies, is heavily engaged in providing humanitarian aid for war-torn countries, managing technical assistance for developing countries, administering funds for development and keeping up research institutions. Examples of direct implementation by the UN can also be found with respect to its many peacekeeping missions. In 2024, it had 60,000 blue helmets under its command spread over eleven missions on different continents. Through its peacekeeping activities the UN even assumed full administrative responsibilities in Kosovo and East Timor for a limited period of time under the Security Council Resolutions 1244 (Kosovo) and 1272 (East Timor) (both 1999) (Schmitt 2009).

It is also important here to point at the various programmes, funds and specialized agencies in the broader 'UN family'. The principal organs of the UN have been discussed in Chapter 5, but 'the UN' also includes a variety of UN programmes and funds, such the UN Development Programme (UNDP), the United Nations Children's Fund (UNICEF), WFP and UNHCR. These programmes and funds are at the heart of the operational activities of the UN in implementing the UN economic and social policy programmes, such as the Sustainable Development Goals (SDGs). The UN family also includes several specialized agencies, some of which are programme organizations but others also have considerable operational activities including notably the World Health Organization (WHO), the World Bank and the IMF. The precise operational activities of several of these international organizations are discussed in the following chapters.

International organizations may also transfer the implementation of policy programmes to non-state actors which then act on behalf of the international organization. For example, the UN and several of its Specialized Agencies have for a long time relied on humanitarian non-governmental organizations (NGOs) in the implementation of development assistance, humanitarian relief and disaster response programmes. The Basel Committee on Banking Supervision (BCBS) heavily relies on private actors (banks and credit rating agencies) in the implementation of international capital reserve standards. The BCBS requires banks to fulfil certain minimum capital reserve requirements. These capital reserve requirements are based on banks' credit risk exposure: the more risky banks' investments are, the higher their capital reserve requirements will be. But the BCBS does not measure banks' credit risk itself. Instead, it relies, among others, on banks' and private credit rating agencies' risk assessments (see Kruck 2011). These examples illustrate that international organizations do not necessarily implement their policy programmes themselves, even if they have the authority to do so. They increasingly opt for transferring or outsourcing the implementation of policy programmes to non-state actors whom they endorse, support, coordinate and/or monitor (see Abbott et al. 2015). This is particularly likely when the international organization lacks time, knowledge and/or material resources to implement the programmes themselves.

Monitoring

Since the implementation of norms and rules is, in many cases, undertaken by member states rather than by the international organization itself or its agents, monitoring of implementation is required. Without monitoring, member states might feel tempted to disregard the policy programmes of international organizations, because they expect that this would go unnoticed or that other states could disregard these programmes without being caught. In order to mitigate this temptation, many international organizations are given the task of monitoring member states' compliance with agreed policy programmes (Chayes and Chayes 1995; Moravcsik 1998; Underdal 1998).

A good example is the International Atomic Energy Agency (IAEA), which monitors member states' compliance with the NPT of 1968. Its safeguard system allows the IAEA to request reports about civilian nuclear activities from the signatory states. More remarkably, it also has the right to undertake on-site inspections of civilian nuclear facilities. Through these inspections the IAEA is able to sustain the expectation among most signatory states that none of them could divert nuclear material from civilian to military uses. This expectation was not only the precondition for signatory states to comply with the NPT but was also for many states a precondition for renouncing nuclear weapons by signing the treaty in the first place.

The far-reaching monitoring activities by the IAEA are certainly an exception. Even the European Commission's abilities to monitor member states' compliance with EU norms and rules are more limited. This is illustrated, for example, by the Commission's inability to get a clear picture of Greece's fiscal policies that ultimately led to a severe debt crisis and a massive EU/IMF bailout package in 2010. Greece had actually broken EU debt ceilings for years before its financial collapse. As a result, the EU has introduced a stronger monitoring mechanism within the context of the so-called European Semester. Nonetheless, many international organizations responsible for the implementation of international environmental agreements have noteworthy monitoring options. For instance, if the International Whaling Commission (IWC) allows the resumption of commercial whaling, it will have the right to place international observers on whaling vessels in order to monitor whalers' compliance with IWC regulations. Moreover, many of today's arms control treaties provide for far-reaching 'verification' activities.

Again, international organizations do not only pursue monitoring on their own. They also lend support to, and draw on, the contributions of non-state actors to the monitoring of compliance with international norms and rules. This is particularly salient in the issue area of human rights protection. On the one hand, international organizations provide human rights NGOs with information, an organizational platform for action and internationally agreed human rights instruments that serve as authoritative standards and benchmarks against which states' human rights records can be measured. On the other hand, due to time, resource and political constraints, international organizations such as the UN Office of the High Commissioner for Human Rights (OHCHR) are heavily dependent on human rights NGOs such as Amnesty International or Human Rights Watch for monitoring and information provision. Therefore, organizations such as OHCHR have created institutionalized channels of access through which NGOs can pass on information on human rights abuses (Sweeney and Saito 2009). International organizations thus coordinate, actively support and make use of NGOs' monitoring activities.

Adjudication

Monitoring alone cannot reliably guarantee the compliance of member states. A serious source of non-compliance is that, in doubtful cases, the member states concerned can often claim that they are in compliance while other member states may accuse them of violating the organization's programmes. If no third party is allowed to adjudicate such disputes and provide authoritative interpretations of the relevant policy programmes, the door is wide open to violations of the organization's policy programme. Member states' compliance can only reasonably be expected if they cannot effectively ignore programme requirements through arbitrary interpretation. For this reason, many international organizations are given the task of adjudicating disputes about member states' compliance. They can thereby contribute to a relatively unbiased interpretation of their policy programmes. This is particularly the case for those organizations which do not only sustain member states' efforts to settle disputes by diplomatic means but also have their own courts or court-like bodies able to adjudicate disputes about legal claims and obligations independently of member states (Keohane, Moravcsik and Slaughter 2000; Zangl 2008).

In the UN, the International Court of Justice (ICJ) is generally responsible for the adjudication of disputes about member states' compliance. Its competencies are, however, very limited since it can only become involved if the disputing states accept its jurisdiction. In fact, the Security Council and the Human Rights Council are more important with respect to the adjudication of disputes about member states' non-compliance with UN programmes. Under Article 39 of the UN Charter the Security Council can ascertain breaches of the ban on the use of force and condemn such violations of the UN Charter (Mondré 2009). Likewise, one of the Human Rights Council's tasks is to decide in disputes about member states' alleged violations of human rights obligations. That is to say, both the Security Council and the Human Rights Council are authorized to condemn member states that are violating fundamental legal obligations (Cronin 2008).

Various other international organizations have established courts. The European Court of Justice (ECJ) is generally responsible for the adjudication of disputes about member states' compliance (Alter 2001). The ECJ, unlike the Security Council and the Commission on Human Rights but similarly to the ICJ, is politically independent. Unlike the ICJ, and similarly in this regard to the Security Council and the Human Rights Council, it can examine breaches of binding policy programmes without being dependent on special authorization by the parties in dispute. The African Union (AU) has also established an African Court of Justice and Human Rights. This African Court is, however, more concerned with human rights cases than with disputes between the member states. In the area of human rights, we also find the International Criminal Court (ICC), which addresses crimes of aggression, war crimes, crimes against humanity and the crime of genocide in line with the Rome Statute of 1998. Many international organizations do not have standing courts but do include dispute settlement mechanisms and arbitration procedures in case of disagreements between states. ASEAN and MERCOSUR are two such examples. The World Trade Organization (WTO) does have a standing Appellate Body for trade disputes even if it has not been operational since 2019 due to the unwillingness of the United States to confirm its judges.

Sanctions

Adjudication by international organizations may help to bring about member states' compliance with the norms and rules of their policy programmes. If, however, a member state is not prepared to abide by the ruling handed down by a court or a court-like body, sanctions may be needed. In fact, international organizations can sometimes help efforts to employ sanctions against states that continuously disregard their international commitments. Nevertheless, international organizations should in most cases not be regarded as central authorities entrusted with the capacities to employ sanctions against states violating their policy programmes. Rather, they serve as agents that help to coordinate member states' efforts to impose sanctions against cheats.

In many international organizations, sanctions are limited to the publication – and possible condemnation – of a member state's violation of international commitments. Nevertheless, these sanctions, albeit moderate, expose the relevant state to moral pressure, internationally by other states and domestically by concerned groups (Risse-Kappen 1995). In addition, this might damage the state's reputation as a trustworthy partner that respects the principle of *pacta sunt servanda* (agreements must be kept), grounded in international law. Losing this reputation can create marked negotiating disadvantages within and outside international organizations (Guzman 2008). It might, for instance, have the effect that other states make reliable monitoring activities of international organizations henceforth a precondition for negotiated agreements with the disreputable state (Keohane 1984; Young 1979: 19). Overall, it might make striking a deal that benefits the disreputable state more costly for this state.

Some international organizations can go beyond mere moral sanctions. They can exclude member states that continuously violate their obligations. This option is enshrined in the foundation treaties of many international organizations. In the UN the General Assembly can, on the recommendation of the Security Council, exclude members who have persistently acted against the Charter. The Statute of the Council of Europe provides for states violating the principles of the organization to be asked to resign. However, the exclusion of members from international organizations has proved to be a double-edged sword. On the one hand, the organization can punish violators through their exclusion, but, on the other hand, it thereby loses the possibility of further influencing these states. For instance, the League of Nations voted to expel Russia in 1939 due to its war in Finland, but this helped Finland barely during this Winter War (1939–40). Similarly, the Council of Europe expelled Russia in 2022 after its invasion of Ukraine. While symbolically important, it also meant that Russia would no longer have to observe the European Convention on Human Rights in spite of more than 17,000 human rights cases against Russia still pending before the European Court of Human Rights.

In the UN, the Security Council can impose non-military sanctions on states to counter a breach of, or threat to, the peace or an act of aggression. However, to be able to effectively impose sanctions such as an arms, air or trade embargo, it has to rely on the support of other member states to implement the sanctions decided by the Council. Yet even in cases where member states actually impose sanctions the effectiveness of such measures cannot be taken for granted. For example, the 1977 arms embargo against South Africa did not lead to a behavioural adjustment by the castigated state. The poor effectiveness of sanctions has led some authors to question whether they can be an effective instrument to secure member states' compliance with international obligations (Chayes and Chayes 1995).

Other authors have studied 'smart sanctions', which states have increasingly used, like financial sanctions, boycotts on specific commodities (diamonds, oil, timber products), travel sanctions and arms embargoes targeting specific persons and areas of an economy (Drezner 2011).

If the UN Security Council deems it necessary it can go beyond embargoes and impose military enforcement measures. To do so, however, it again depends in fact, if not strictly speaking in law, on member states being ready to supply troops and to deploy them under UN tactical and operational command. In authorizing military enforcement measures the Security Council is thus in practice limited by states' willingness to engage in enforcement actions. In the 1990s the Security Council authorized some member states to intervene with force in the humanitarian catastrophes in Somalia (1992), Bosnia (1992), Rwanda (1994) and Haiti (1994) which it determined to be threats to peace (Abiew 1999; Pape 1997). In September 2001, the Security Council authorized military measures to combat international terrorism particularly (though not exclusively) in Afghanistan, and in 2011 it authorized its member to take 'all necessary measures' to protect the Libyan population from the Gaddafi regime.

Policy effectiveness

International organizations convert inputs into outputs. Some international organizations are good at performing this function and produce a lot of outputs. Other international organizations are less successful in turning input into output (Tallberg et al. 2016; Lundgren et al. 2024). Member states may veto decisions, insufficient expertise may be available in the permanent secretariat or mechanisms for monitoring, adjudication or sanctions may be absent. Yet even when an international organization produces output, it is not guaranteed that the output will ultimately have the intended effect. It is therefore important to take one additional step: to evaluate the effectiveness of the output.

Scholars usually discuss the effectiveness of policy in terms of (1) output, (2) outcome and (3) impact (Easton 1965; Underdal 1992, 2004; Gutner and Thompson 2010; Tallberg et al. 2016). Much of this chapter has already discussed output. When the permanent members of the UN Security Council reacted to member states' concerns about the aggression of the Gaddafi regime against the Libyan people in 2011 (input) by adopting within days a resolution (output), the Security Council showed a remarkable *output* effectiveness: the resolution was adopted quickly, had substance and was legally binding. The adoption of this resolution, in turn, resulted in the NATO military intervention establishing a no-fly zone and taking out convoys of Gaddafi forces (outcome). In this sense, *outcome* effectiveness was also high: the outcome was broadly in line with the objectives set by the

Security Council. The immediate effect of the NATO military intervention was the security and protection of the Libyan population (impact). This impact was in line with the logic of the resolution and the Security Council's general mandate in peace and security: therefore *impact* effectiveness was also high. At the same time, when looking back at this episode in 2011, we can also conclude that the death of Gaddafi (which was an outcome) has resulted in enduring civil unrest in Libya, instability and a lack of security and ultimately led to the death of thousands of civilians (impact). The longer-term impact was therefore not very effective.

The effectiveness of an international organization therefore depends on whether the international organization 'solves the problem that motivated its establishment' (Underdal 2002: 11; cf. Young 1999: jacket). The UN Framework Convention on Climate Change (UNFCCC) is therefore effective to the extent that it reduces climate change. The WTO is effective when it reduces trade barriers and increases trade volumes among the membership. And since the goal of a UN peacekeeping mission is to 'keep the peace', it makes sense to measure whether the peace was kept after a (civil) war (Doyle and Sambanis 2000; Fortna 2004a, 2008). While international policy can thus be measured against the status quo and the optimal policy outcome (Underdal 1992; Sprinz and Helm 1999; Helm and Sprinz 2000), optimal policy outcomes are not necessarily realistic. The optimal policy outcome in global warming may be to bring the average global temperature back to pre-industrial levels, but this will not be possible. Therefore, the Paris Agreement negotiated under the framework of the UNFCCC set the benchmark to keep the global temperature rise below 2 degrees Celsius above pre-industrial levels. Its effectiveness should therefore be judged against this 2 degrees target.

While such a conceptual approach seems straightforward, there are several complications in evaluating effectiveness. International organizations, for instance, may set themselves modest goals: in the UN it has become established doctrine not to send blue helmets to places that are too dangerous where there is 'no peace to keep' (see Panel on United Nations Peace Operations 2000). While there is good reason for this choice – following the disasters of UN peacekeeping in Bosnia, Rwanda and Somalia in the mid-1990s – it does create a selection bias which affects our understanding of effectiveness. As Page Fortna and Lise Howard (2008: 290) note, a critical question is 'whether peacekeepers tend to undertake easier cases or harder ones'. It is also often quite difficult to establish a causal relationship between the intervention of the international organizations and the final outcome. For instance, if advances in technology help us to further develop renewable energy sources that lead to less global warming, is it then fair to conclude that the UNFCCC has been effective? Perhaps member states and private industry have been inspired by the various climate change agreements to invest in research and development, but establishing a direct causal link is difficult.

Conclusion

The output of international organizations is a crucial component of contemporary global governance. International organizations are involved both in the establishment of norms and rules and in their implementation. They perform actions which, in the absence of a central authority such as a global state, might make it easier for states and non-state actors to regulate their social relations in a predictable manner. Output of international organization is also important as it is a precondition for international organizations to be effective and have an actual impact. Even if effectiveness is difficult to measure, when international organizations are criticized it is often for their perceived lack of effectiveness. Academic research however shows that effectiveness tends to vary across the various international organizations (Gutner and Thompson 2010; Lall 2017) and even across individual country projects by international organizations.

In this chapter and the preceding chapters, we have analysed international organizations as political systems that convert inputs into outputs. We have discussed inputs, outputs and the conversion process. In doing so, we have provided examples from different relevant international organizations. However, so far we have not investigated whether their policy programmes and their operational activities do actually support global governance in various issue areas. In Part 3 we shall therefore examine whether the outputs of international organizations really enhance cooperative outcomes between states (and non-state actors). We shall also consider the extent to which these programmes and operational activities of different international organizations contribute to global governance particularly in the fields of security, development and economic relations, the environment and human rights.

Discussion questions

1. How are policy programmes different from operational activities?
2. To what extent do international organizations have to rely on, and partner with, non-state actors to effectively fulfil crucial operational tasks?
3. Why is it so difficult to evaluate the effectiveness of international organizations?

Further reading

Abbott, Kenneth W. and Duncan Snidal (2000). 'Hard and Soft Law in International Governance', *International Organization*, 54 (3): 421–56.

Gutner, Tamar and Alexander Thompson (2010). 'The Politics of IO Performance: A Framework', *The Review of International Organizations*, 5: 227–48.

Lall, Ranjit (2017). 'Beyond Institutional Design: Explaining the Performance of International Organizations', *International Organization*, 71 (2): 245–80.

Lundgren, Magnus, Theresa Squatrito, Thomas Sommerer and Jonas Tallberg (2024). 'Introducing the Intergovernmental Policy Output Dataset (IPOD)', *Review of International Organizations*, 19 (1): 117–46.

PART III

Activities of international organizations

8

Peace, security and war

International cooperation in the area of security has traditionally been difficult to achieve. Because today's allies can turn into tomorrow's enemies, states try to avoid relying on others for their own security and survival. Furthermore, the efforts of states to enhance security by enlarging power (through increasing military capabilities) are frequently perceived by other states as threatening. This results in a vicious circle of mutual distrust, security competition and strife for power. Pervasive distrust lies at the heart of this security dilemma (Herz 1950; Jervis 1983). Such mistrust is regarded, by realists, as the most fundamental obstacle to international cooperation in the field of security. In addition, states caught in the security dilemma tend to focus not on the absolute gains from cooperation but mostly on their gains relative to others. Even when a state gains from security cooperation in absolute terms, a relative loss compared to others equals a relative decrease in power. This often makes security cooperation a zero-sum game: it is not possible for all states to gain in relative terms.

Yet against these odds, states have tried time and again to establish cooperation in the area of security. Perhaps because the potential benefits of cooperation are so large, and the prospects of war so frightening, they have created a wide range of security institutions from the Concert of Europe to the League of Nations and the United Nations (UN) (see Chapter 3). They have also relied for their survival on other states by forming alliances. According to institutionalist and constructivist theories, international organizations can help to facilitate cooperation, also in the field of security and defence. While they may not be able to overcome the security dilemma or international anarchy, they can at least provide some norms, a forum for diplomacy and some transparency among the member states. This, in turn, can foster a degree of trust.

In this first chapter on the policies of international organizations in the security realm, we focus on the policy programmes and operational activities of the UN and the North Atlantic Treaty Organization (NATO). UN policy programmes have been developed to deal with the use of force, and the UN has a range of operational activities to promote peace and security. NATO does not just give collective defence guarantees to its members but has also developed an extensive institutional structure and a variety of operational activities including military operations and deterrence. While the UN and NATO are not the only international organizations with a mandate in peace and security, we focus in this chapter on both examples to better understand precisely how international organizations establish and implement norms and rules in this policy area.

Banning force and keeping peace

Inherent in the security dilemma is the danger of the threat or use of force by states, independently of their good or bad intentions. Even states that prefer mutual non-aggressive behaviour can be tempted to threaten or use force to guarantee their own security. The fundamental security problem is therefore about stabilizing states' expectations about the non-violent behaviour of others to make it possible for them to reciprocate and refrain from the threat or use of force as well. International organizations can contribute to stabilizing such expectations through their policy programmes as well as operational activities. We focus, in this chapter, on the UN as the most significant international security organization. It has a policy programme that puts restrictions on the use of force and operational activities aimed at keeping the peace. It is nevertheless important to note that the UN policy programme and activities are complemented by other international organizations, notably regional organizations, such as the African Union (AU), which are discussed in Chapter 12.

Policy programme of the UN

The principal aim of the UN is 'to maintain international peace and security' (Article 1 of UN Charter). To achieve this end, the UN Charter contains a policy programme. This has since been complemented by detailed acts, such as resolutions of the General Assembly and the Security Council, and also agreements reached by international conferences organized by the UN. The result is a regulative programme which attempts to curb the threat and use of force. In fact, the Charter lays down, for the first time in history, a general ban on the threat or use of force between states. Article 2(4) states that 'all Members shall refrain in their international relations from the threat or use of force against the territorial integrity or political independence of any state, or in any other manner inconsistent with the purposes of the United Nations'. This general ban on the threat or use of force is complemented by Article 2(3) according to which 'all Members shall settle their international disputes by peaceful means in such a manner that international peace and security, and justice, are not endangered'.

The UN Charter provides only for two exceptions from the general ban on the use of force. First, Article 51 confirms the right of states to individual and collective self-defence in case of aggression by others. Second, Chapter VII of the UN Charter gives the Security Council the right to authorize military enforcement to maintain peace and security. Since the UN Charter recognizes the 'inherent right of individual or collective self-defence' (Article 51), the use of military force by states is justified if it is an act of self-defence. Yet the right to self-defence could also provide a potential cover for states that want to engage in aggressive warfare. To reduce the risk of such an abuse of the right to self-defence, the UN General Assembly was tasked to define the concept of aggression. This proved difficult: the General Assembly only decided on a definition in 1974 after lengthy and tough negotiations (Resolution 3314 (XXIX)). On a basic level, one could say that an act of aggression is committed when a state uses military force first. But as states may engage in pre-emptive actions (to get a 'first-mover advantage' and to strategically use the element of surprise) when an act of aggression by another state is imminent, things are more complicated.

The Resolution 3314 (XXIX) defines a whole range of state actions which can be considered as acts of aggression. These include an invasion or an attack, a blockade of ports and coasts and the deployment of armed groups, irregulars or mercenaries by a state (Article 3). This resolution has thus contributed to specifying which actions amount to an act of aggression, even though international legal discussions on the precise definition of aggression and also the declaration of victimhood continue to the present day. For instance, the United States and its coalition partners have used Article 51 to justify their intervention in Syria since 2014 against the terrorist organization the Islamic State. Israel has also used Article 51 for its war in Gaza and Lebanon and to attack targets in Iran since 2023. Russia and Georgia have long quarrelled over which side started their war in 2008. In other words, while it is now well-accepted that unilateral interventions are unlawful, Article 51 on self-defence still leaves some room for manoeuvre.

Military enforcement measures are also legitimate when they are authorized by the Security Council under Chapter VII as a response to acts of aggression, threats and breaches to the peace. The definition of what constitutes a threat to peace has expanded significantly over time. Originally only threats of *interstate* warfare were considered as threats to peace. Nowadays *internal* wars and internal massive human suffering are also regarded as threats to peace (Pape 1997). The first time that the Security Council declared an internal conflict as a threat to peace was in 1991 (Resolution 688). In the aftermath of the Gulf War, Iraqi military forces took action against the Kurdish and Shiite populations within Iraq. Even though it was an internal conflict, these actions resulted in a massive outflow of refugees, which created cross-border problems. In 1993, the

Security Council went a step further. It determined the civil war in Angola as a threat to peace without mentioning any interstate problems (Resolution 864) (Chesterman 2003: 137–8). The Security Council has since considered the internal wars in, for instance, Somalia, Bosnia, Kosovo, East Timor, the Democratic Republic of the Congo, Sudan, Libya and Syria as threats to peace.

Apart from internal violent conflict between government and rebel forces, the Security Council can also consider serious human rights violations within states as a threat to international peace and security (for more details see Chapter 11). This may also result in military intervention. Since the late 1990s, the norm of the Responsibility to Protect (R2P) has emerged (International Commission on Intervention and State Sovereignty 2001) which entails that while the primary responsibility for the protection of civilians lies with the state, the international community needs to step in if the responsible state fails to fulfil its duty. The Security Council has, nonetheless, been keen to point out that only the Security Council can determine whether a state has failed in its duty. It has done so on one occasion: by adopting Resolution 1973, it authorized military enforcement measures against the Libyan regime of Muammar Gaddafi in 2011. The impact of this resolution is, however, contested. China and Russia underline that the resolution authorized the international community to protect civilians, but that it did not include a mandate for the killing of Gaddafi. China and Russia have therefore reconsidered their stance on R2P (Morris 2013). They are currently much more sceptical and put again strong emphasis on non-interference.

Beyond the two above-named exceptions – self-defence and Security Council resolutions – the Charter does not foresee any further exceptions from the general ban on the threat or use of force. However, the Charter does not explicitly ban the intervention by one state at the request of the government of another state. This provides a loophole to circumvent the general ban on the threat or use of force. For instance, the Iraqi government invited the United States and the other states to fight the Islamic State on Iraqi territory in 2014. The Malian government invited Russian mercenaries in 2021 to provide security. The Somali government has invited the EU to attack pirates within Somali territorial waters. While such invitations are justified in purely legal terms, it is often not clear in many internal conflicts which political group has legitimate state power and is therefore entitled to request intervention by another state.

Operations of the UN

The operational activities of the UN can be analysed on the basis of the different elements of the political system of international organizations (see Chapters 4–7). The sequence is often as follows. First, a dispute between states or within states breaks out. This is brought to the attention of the

Security Council either by the secretary general or an interested member state (input). Second, consultations are held within the Security Council (conversion). This may include the conflicting parties. Furthermore, the secretary general and UN Secretariat officials may be asked for advice or a formal report. Third, the UN Security Council can adopt a resolution (output) launching operational activities such as (1) the peaceful settlement of disputes, (2) peace enforcement or (3) peacekeeping. The Security Council decides by an affirmative vote of nine of its fifteen members including the concurring votes of the five permanent members (China, France, Russia, the United Kingdom and the United States). Some of these operations are carried out by the UN itself. For other operations, the UN can rely on its member states or a regional organizations. Fourth, if the UN output does not have the satisfactory outcome or impact – such as ending the dispute – the process starts again: negative outcomes/impact may provoke new input. The UN Security Council may then, for instance, decide to scale up its decisions.

Peaceful settlement of disputes

The first operational activity of the UN, as defined by Chapter VI of the Charter, concerns the peaceful settlement of disputes. This is about 'consensual security': measures undertaken always require a consensus of all the parties involved. While the peaceful settlement of disputes is, first and foremost, a question for the conflicting parties themselves (Article 33 of UN Charter), the UN supports peaceful settlement. Its most obvious institution is the Security Council (and the General Assembly). The Security Council provides a forum for diplomacy and is the principal venue where matters of peace and security are discussed. The UN Charter indeed makes clear, under Chapter VI, that any UN member state 'may bring any dispute . . . to the attention of the Security Council or of the General Assembly' (Article 35(1)). The Security Council also has a task to 'call upon the parties to settle their dispute by [peaceful] means' (Article 33(2)). The Charter thus makes clear to conflicting parties that they have to try to settle disputes through peaceful means and that the UN organs provide the principal forums to turn to.

The UN's role, however, goes further. It also has a set of formal and informal instruments at its disposal. One formal instrument of peaceful dispute settlement is the conduct of investigations by the UN Security Council. If the UN uses investigations as a means of peaceful dispute settlement it sets up a commission which is given the task of clarifying the facts behind a dispute. This provides the disputing parties with reliable information through a neutral third party. Although the disputing parties are not bound by these findings, such information can be helpful in reaching a settlement. Article 34 of the Charter specifically authorizes the Security Council to establish commissions of inquiry. It has used this possibility in a few situations (e.g. Greece in 1946; Kashmir in 1948; Western Sahara in 1975) with explicit reference to Article 34. In various other cases, the Security Council has ordered investigations but has not made explicit reference to Article 34. For instance, in 2014, it stressed the need for an international investigation into the downing of Malaysia Airlines flight MH17 above Ukraine (Tanaka 2018: 79–80).

In addition to the Security Council, the UN secretary general (or an appointed envoy) can play a key role in peaceful settlement through 'good offices'. When engaging in good offices, the secretary general offers indirect communication channels to the disputing parties that are unwilling to directly communicate with each other (Whitfield 2007). The parties concerned, for instance, can make use of the good offices of the secretary general to agree on conditions for starting negotiations. They can communicate in this way without officially entering into negotiations, that is, without recognizing the other side as a negotiating partner. The good offices of the secretary general may contribute to the initiation of negotiations which may then lead to the peaceful settlement of the dispute. And, when tensions between parties run high, the good offices of the secretary general can keep a (indirect) dialogue going. Secretaries-General have repeatedly offered their good offices (and the prestige of their office) to conflicting parties.

Related to good offices is the role of the UN as a mediator. Mediation goes beyond good offices and investigation since it is concerned with procedures, factual information and the specific content of a peaceful settlement (Bercovitch 2007; Wallensteen and Svensson 2014). As a mediator the UN plays an active role in the negotiations and can contribute to a negotiated settlement by suggesting solutions. The secretary general has repeatedly been appointed by the Security Council to mediate in conflicts between states or asked to name a UN envoy as mediator. UN mediation activities currently spread out over all continents. Within the UN Secretariat, a Mediation Support Unit was, furthermore, set up in 2006. This Mediation Support Unit has its standby team of experts who can deploy within seventy-two hours, allowing for immediate mediation if tensions between different parties suddenly emerge. Between 2015 and 2023, the UN Standby Team of Senior Mediation Advisers had on average 130 mediation support assignments per year. In 2023, it worked in twenty-eight countries.

Going yet one step further, the UN has established a whole range of special political missions in conflict countries and regions. These missions are civilian in nature but perform a wide variety of functions: from electoral observation to political support for a peace process to civilian capacity building. Many of them are relatively small missions and consist of several dozen officials around a UN envoy. Some are, however, larger in scale. The UN Assistance Mission in Iraq (UNAMI), for instance, was established by the Security Council through Resolution 1500 (2003). It employed more than 600 officials (of which 250 international officials) in 2024. Its mandate includes supporting the Iraqi government in elections, humanitarian tasks, the return of internally displaced persons, the promotion of human rights as well as the coordination of international organizations active in Iraq. Such special political missions are often difficult to distinguish from peacekeeping missions (see below). For instance, the UN Mission in Kosovo (UNMIK), which is the only civilian peacekeeping mission, could have well been a special political mission.

A final way for conflicting parties to peacefully settle their disputes is through adjudication. They can bring their conflicts to international courts, of which the International Court of Justice (ICJ) is the most prominent (Kolb 2013; Hernández 2014). Going to the Court, whose Statute is part of the UN Charter, can be an effective means of peaceful settlement of a dispute, since its judgements are binding on all parties. The problem with the ICJ is that it is not automatically competent to take on a dispute. The ICJ distinguishes between two types of cases: states can themselves decide to put forward their legal dispute to the ICJ or agree to the potential of ICJ referral in agreements among themselves (contentious cases) and UN organs and specialized agencies may request non-binding advisory opinions on legal questions by the ICJ (advisory proceedings). Because states or the UN organs and specialized agencies need to agree among themselves refer a case, many disputes do not reach the ICJ. Between 1946 and 2024, the ICJ has taken on about 200 cases. In the last decade, the ICJ handles around two to three cases per year. Even if such numbers remain small, the ICJ has been involved in some key disputes notably in the conflict between Israel and Palestine. South Africa, for instance, used Article IX of the 1951 Genocide Convention (to which Israel is also a state party) to start a case at the ICJ in December 2023 to invoke Israel's obligation to prevent genocide in Gaza. In parallel, the UN General Assembly requested an ICJ advisory opinion in December 2022 concerning Israel's practices with regard to human rights in Palestine. Both cases have resulted in landmark judgements in 2024 even if the conflicting parties did not implement them.

Peace enforcement

The UN has also devoted parts of its operations to peace enforcement. This falls under the rubric of collective security. The UN Charter allocates far-reaching competencies to the Security Council to implement collective security (Thompson 2006; Voeten 2005). The Security Council can authorize collective enforcement measures in the event of a breach of, or acute threat to, international peace. Only the Security Council can determine whether an infringement of the ban on the threat or use of force has occurred. Threatened or attacked states may themselves inform the Security Council of any aggression against their territorial integrity or political independence. In addition, other states or the UN secretary general may bring to the attention of the Security Council any matter which in their opinion may threaten international peace and security (Article 99). The Security Council has to determine 'the existence of any threat to the peace, breach of the peace or act of aggression' (Article 39). Only such a conclusion by the Security Council allows for further measures of collective enforcement within the framework of the UN system of collective security.

The number of breaches of the peace or acts of aggression determined by the Security Council has been modest. During the Cold War, the Security Council was hamstrung by a veto of one or the other of the main contenders in the East–West conflict. As a result, it only determined that there was a breach of, or threat to, the peace or an act of aggression in the case of pariahs like South Africa and the former Rhodesia. The Security Council also exceptionally took action against North Korea for its attack on South Korea in 1950. Another example was Resolution 502 (1982) which allowed the UK to claim self-defence in its military action against Argentina following the occupation of the Falkland Islands. Another explanation for the limited number of breaches of the peace or acts of aggression is the fact that during the Cold War period, the Security Council focused largely on international wars and not on civil wars.

Since 1990, however, the number of condemnations by the Security Council acting under Chapter VII has increased considerably (Human Security Project 2010: Chapter 4). The end of bipolarity after the Cold War accounts for much of this development. It also facilitated the above-mentioned broadening of the concept of a threat to peace. In the cases of Somalia (Resolution 746 (1992)) and Rwanda (Resolution 918 (1994)), for instance, the Security Council saw the threat to peace in humanitarian crises resulting from internal armed struggles. Over time, the Security Council has increasingly condemned internal conflicts as threats to peace (see, for instance, Resolution 1272 (East Timor, 1999); Resolution 1925 (DR Congo, 2010); Resolution 1973 (Libya, 2011)). Moreover, the Security Council no longer reserves condemnations of threats or breaches of peace exclusively to states' actions. The Security Council has also determined activities of non-state actors such as the Taliban, al-Qaeda and pirates to be threats to peace. The Security Council has even determined that the destruction of cultural heritage can constitute a war crime (Resolution 2347 (2017)). Since 2005, the Security Council has adopted some thirty resolutions under Chapter VII every year, compared to on average one resolution every two years during the Cold War (Wallensteen and Johansson 2016: 29–31; UN n.d.).

Once the Security Council has determined the existence of a breach, it can impose legally binding obligations onto states. The Security Council can demand cessation of military action and human rights violations, withdrawal from occupied territories, respect for the sovereignty and territorial integrity of a state or the destruction of chemical and nuclear weapons. The Security Council thus imposes clear limits to the freedom of action of the parties concerned and prescribes specific behavioural guidelines aimed at maintaining or restoring international peace and security. If actors ignore these demands, the Security Council can decide what measures of collective enforcement 'are to be employed to give effect to its decisions'

(Article 41). This includes a range of both non-military and military enforcement measures. The first step is usually non-military enforcement, such as sanctions. Since 1990, the Security Council has imposed sanctions in numerous instances: Afghanistan, Angola, the Democratic Republic of the Congo, Ethiopia and Eritrea, Haiti, Iran, Iraq, Ivory Coast, Liberia, Libya, Rwanda, Sierra Leone, Somalia, Sudan and the former Yugoslavia.

The Security Council has also increasingly relied on so-called 'smart sanctions'. These are not directed at states but rather at individuals who are seen as being a threat to peace. Such sanctions often include a travel ban and the freezing of assets (Cortright and Lopez 2002; Drezner 2011). Sanctions may also be imposed against governmental leaders or military officers accused of war crimes. The trend to directly target individuals through non-military enforcement actions goes, however, further. For instance, the Security Council decided in its Resolution 1593 (2005) and Resolution 1970 (2011) to refer 'the situation' in, respectively, Darfur and Libya to the International Criminal Court. This has resulted in indictments for key individuals, such as the Sudanese president Omar al-Bashir as well as members of the Gaddafi family. Compliance with sanctions and other non-military enforcement actions against states and individuals, however, can be a challenge. While the United States and EU member states will normally automatically try to enforce travel bans on their territory and instruct their banks to freeze assets, compliance elsewhere in the world is not guaranteed. It can also be difficult in practice to link assets to sanctioned individuals, who may use shell corporations to hide their assets. To increase compliance, the Security Council can ask its member states to help with the implementation of enforcement. This can also happen through military means. Warships of NATO have enforced arms embargoes against the former Yugoslavia in the 1990s and Libya in 2011. This included inspecting and verifying the cargo of maritime vessels sailing into the territorial waters of those countries. Furthermore, even if compliance is not watertight, it may put severe restrictions on the behaviour of those targeted by the non-military enforcement actions. Since the ICC, for instance, issued arrest warrants against the Russian president Vladimir Putin and Israeli prime minister Benjamin Netanyahu, they can no longer travel around the world freely. Any time they step on a plane to a different country, they run the risk of getting arrested.

When the effect of non-military enforcement measures is inadequate, the Security Council can resort to measures of military enforcement. According to the Charter it can take 'such action by air, sea, or land forces as may be necessary to maintain or restore international peace and security' (Article 42). During the Cold War, the Security Council never agreed on measures of military enforcement. The measures decided in relation to the Korean War in 1950 came close to enforcement as stipulated by the UN Charter. In accordance with Article 48, the Security Council recommended UN members to provide assistance to the Republic of Korea. The United States was asked to lead this effort (as 'framework nation'). The military deployment therefore had the character of an authorized US-led operation rather than that of a UN deployment. Since the end of the Cold War, measures of military enforcement by the Security Council have become (slightly) more common. The Security Council has authorized peace enforcement missions in Iraq in 1991, Somalia in 1992, Bosnia in 1992–3, Haiti and Rwanda in 1994, Afghanistan in 2001 and Libya in 2011. In all of these cases, member states and regional organizations, rather than the UN itself, implemented the military actions.

In addition to the UN-authorized peace enforcement operations, there are two notable cases where intervention took place in the absence of a UN Security Council mandate. The NATO mission 'Allied Force' in the Kosovo conflict in the spring of 1999 was carried out without the approval of the Security Council. Despite Resolution 1244 (1999), passed by the Security Council *after* the cessation of military hostilities, NATO strikes against the former Federal Republic of Yugoslavia were not authorized according to the UN Charter. NATO, under leadership of the United States, argued that it could not stand by while war – and likely war crimes and crimes against humanity – would take place in the Western Balkans. This unauthorized intervention resulted eventually in negotiations over a new R2P policy programme. Neither did the Security Council authorize the invasion of Iraq in 2003 by a US-led multinational 'coalition of the willing'. The United States and the United Kingdom had argued that the possibility of Iraq possessing and employing weapons of mass destruction posed a threat to international peace and security.

Peacekeeping

Peacekeeping is not mentioned in the UN Charter but it has become the major UN operational activity in the field of security (Koops et al. 2015). The repeated recourse to peacekeeping and its recognition by the community of states have become part of customary international law. Peacekeeping activities were first developed at the time of the Cold War and required the consensus of all the parties involved. Since the classic form of peacekeeping is based on the agreement of the parties to the dispute to deploy UN observers or a UN force ('blue helmets'), it mostly falls under the peaceful settlement of dispute (Chapter VI) rather than peace enforcement (Chapter VII). However, peacekeeping missions normally involve the deployment of military personnel. This is why peacekeeping has also been called 'Chapter Six and a Half' (Dag Hammarskjold, cited in Weiss et al. 2007: 39). Moreover, more recent 'robust' peacekeeping missions have been mandated under Chapter VII to restore a 'secure environment', if necessary by force, and are no longer contingent upon the consent of all parties.

The Security Council authorizes all peacekeeping operations through its resolutions. These resolutions are normally quite precise in terms of specifying the mandate, the area of operations and the material conditions for deployment. The Security Council is, however, not the only relevant actor. Peacekeeping missions are planned by the UN Secretariat. Based on this planning, the secretary general advises a mandate and implementation plan to the Security Council. The Security Council is free to ignore the planning of the UN Secretariat – and does so regularly (Dijkstra 2015a; Oksamytna and Lundgren 2021) – but it also ultimately relies on the secretary general and the UN Secretariat to implement the mission. After the adoption of a Security Council resolution, the Secretary-General appoints a Special Representative of the secretary general (SRSG) who commands the operation on the ground. The UN Secretariat also liaises with Troop Contributing Countries, which provide the actual soldiers. In other words, there are multiple actors involved in peacekeeping operations.

Peacekeeping operations have had a variety of functions. These have expanded progressively over time (Di Salvatore et al. 2022). Traditionally, such operations dealt with the monitoring of ceasefire agreements. The UN would send observers or a relatively small peacekeeping force to a border region with the aim of observing and supervising adherence to a ceasefire. The 400-strong UN Iran–Iraq Military Observer Group (UNIIMOG) was charged with supervising the ceasefire between Iraq and Iran (1988–91). It was a classic example of an observer mission. Traditional peacekeeping was therefore not about forcefully separating conflicting parties but rather about helping to create a minimum level of trust in a ceasefire situation (Fortna 2004a). More encompassing, 'multidimensional' peacekeeping operations have been established since the 2000s. The basic idea is that ensuring a ceasefire is not sufficient to establish a durable peace. The UN Peacekeeping Force in Cyprus (UNFICYP), for instance, has maintained the military status quo but has not brought a durable solution to the island. Peacekeeping (and peacebuilding), many argue, should therefore also be concerned with continued political mediation, providing rule of law and humanitarian assistance, ensuring human rights, democratization, good governance, gender equality and other things. As such, the scope of the peacekeeping mandates has increased dramatically and is occasionally likened to a 'Christmas tree': just as Christmas trees are full of ornaments, the mandates of peacekeeping missions get overloaded as well. Such 'multidimensional' peacekeeping has put tremendous demands on the UN as an international organization. New tasks not only require funding and manpower but also expertise. The UN had to learn how to do all these new tasks, and this has taken considerable time (Benner, Mergenthaler and Rotmann 2011).

However, multidimensional peacekeeping mandates are not the only challenge. Compared to traditional peacekeeping, the UN has had to face another challenge. Traditional peacekeeping normally involved the monitoring of peace agreements between two states. Current-day peacekeeping operations are deployed, however, in areas of civil war. The fact that the government of the host country gives consent to such peacekeeping operations does not necessarily mean that all the rebel groups do as well. Peacekeeping missions are now often authorized under Chapter VII of the UN Charter and involve a task to create a secure environment – if necessary by force – to enable them to fulfil their mandate. Examples of 'robust peacekeeping' include missions in Congo and Mali (Karlsrud 2015). In such missions there have been hundreds of fatalities among the peacekeepers. Because of the difficulty of multidimensional and robust peacekeeping as well as the costs involved, and the interference in domestic affairs of states, UN members have gradually reduced such missions in recent years. While there were more than 100,000 peacekeepers deployed in 2018, total deployments are 60,000 peacekeepers in 2024. The UN has also closed several peacekeeping operations and has not started new ones since 2014 (with the exception of the new but modest mission in Haiti). Therefore, the UN has clearly reduced this operational activity.

Evaluation of the organization's effectiveness

One of the most important questions in the study of international organizations relates to the issue of whether international organizations are effective. Do their outputs (policy programmes and operational activities) have the desired outcomes in line with organizations' self-set objectives, and do they help to resolve international problems individual states are unable to tackle (effectiveness on the impact level) (see Underdal 2002, 2004)? In

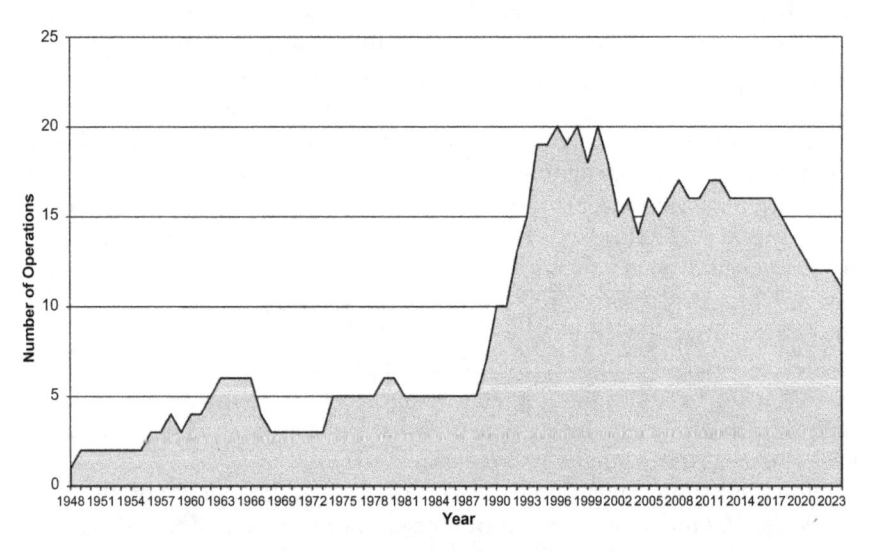

FIGURE 8.1 *Number of UN peacekeeping operations, 1948–2024*. Source: Based on data from the UN Department of Peacekeeping Operations.

this section, we draw on empirical studies to assess the UN's effectiveness in preventing, mitigating and ending violent conflict. We look at both the outcomes (in terms of modifying the behaviour of actors) and the impacts (in terms of resolving the political problem of violent self-help) that the UN's activities generate. We will offer parallel assessments of international organizations' effectiveness in all the issue areas we cover in Chapters 8–12.

Does the UN make a relevant contribution to overcoming the threat or use of force in international relations and to stabilizing the peace? Simply by prohibiting the use or threat of force between member states, the UN already makes an important contribution to international peace. Since 1945, we have witnessed a decreasing number of interstate armed conflicts. While this is not definite proof of the UN's effectiveness, as this may have causes unrelated to the UN ban on the use of force, it may be seen as one indication of this effect (see Figure 8.2).

With regard to the UN's operational activities, peacekeeping has attracted most scholarly attention. Measuring the effectiveness of UN peacekeeping is, however, not straightforward. For instance, scholars wonder what the actual goal of peacekeeping is: Do we measure UN peacekeeping by the mere absence of war (negative peace) or should we be interested in 'positive peace' or a sustainable peace (Galtung 1969) whereby conflicting parties truly make peace? This is a relevant question, because in early quantitative studies of UN peacekeeping effectiveness, scholars would often measure how many years after a war the peace was kept. The mentioned Cyprus peacekeeping operation is, in this respect, very effective with more than fifty years of peace kept, yet it has not resolved the conflict. Importantly, peacekeepers are not sent to every conflict: Because they are a scarce resource, one can expect that they are only sent to the more difficult cases, rather than to ones in which peace will likely last in any case (Fortna 2004b: 491, 499). When one takes this into account, Fortna (2004b: 517) finds that 'peace lasts substantially longer when international personnel deploy than when states are left to maintain peace on their own'.

The bulk of empirical studies on the effectiveness of peacekeeping focus on civil wars. As is the case with interstate wars, peacekeepers tend to be sent to more difficult cases of civil conflict (Ruggeri et al. 2018). If this is taken into account, peacekeeping has a large and statistically significant effect on the duration of peace after civil wars (Fortna 2004a; Fortna and Howard 2008: 290). The deployment of peacekeeping missions also results in fewer battle deaths in civil wars (Hultman, Kathman and Shannon 2014). It is less clear which types of missions are most effective. Doyle and Sambanis (2000) argue that multidimensional peacekeeping missions significantly improve the chances of success (defined as absence of violent conflict two years after the end of a war). Yet Fortna (2008) finds that relatively small and militarily weak consent-based peacekeeping operations are often just as effective as larger, more robust enforcement missions. Yet she finds no strong difference between the effects of Chapter VI and Chapter VII missions. A

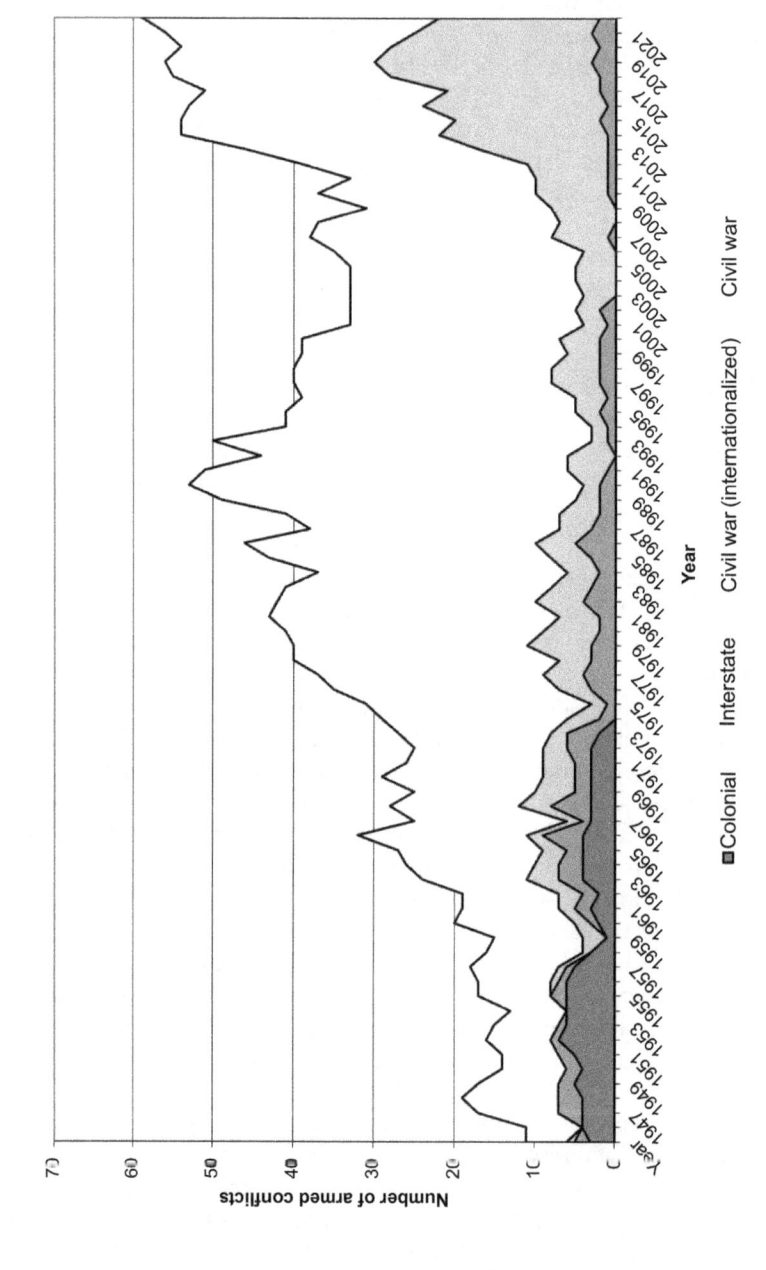

FIGURE 8.2 Number of global armed conflicts, 1946–2022. Source: UCPD/PRIO (2024) – processed by Our World in Data.

comprehensive qualitative analysis of peacekeeping operations also shows that the overall score is positive (Koops et al. 2015). Indeed, reviews of the academic literature on peacekeeping highlight that the question is not so much whether UN missions are effective but 'how, when and why' (Walter et al. 2021: abstract; see also Di Salvatore and Ruggeri 2017).

That said, UN peacekeeping missions have also included major failures, particularly in the 1990s in Bosnia, Rwanda and Somalia, where peacekeepers were unable to prevent genocide from taking place (Barnett and Finnemore 2004: 121–55). Regular human rights abuses, including sexual abuses, by peacekeepers against the most vulnerable continue to occur, and the UN leadership has been insufficiently capable of addressing this major problem. Furthermore, in 2010, UN peacekeepers unintentionally brought cholera to Haiti. This caused an epidemic resulting in nearly a million sick local people and 8,500 deaths (Pillinger, Hurd and Barnett 2016). Importantly, the UN often takes a critical approach to itself. It has launched frank and transparent investigations into its own role in the Rwanda and Srebrenica genocides. Furthermore, it has established several high-level panels to evaluate the practice of peacekeeping. This has resulted in a number of landmark documents that have helped the UN to further establish a peacekeeping doctrine, develop its own organization and address some of its shortcomings.

Alliances and collective defence

Collective security provided by the UN and regional organizations is important, yet its efficacy is limited. Throughout history, states have thus also established military alliances. Such alliances have varied in design. While the Delian League, under the hegemony of Athens, perhaps included as many as 150–300 city states in the fifth century BCE, the Treaty of Mutual Cooperation and Security between the United States and Japan of 1960 only has two signatories. Many current-day alliances remain bilateral, are occasionally trilateral and are only institutionalized to a limited degree. Furthermore, several regional organizations, such as the EU, include defence provisions (see Chapter 12). One key multilateral alliance which stands out is NATO. The North Atlantic Alliance, founded in 1949, is not just an alliance but also an international organization (Sperling and Webber 2025). Based on its treaty, NATO has established a considerable organizational structure consisting of political and policy departments in Brussels as well as an elaborate military command structure to implement the policy programme. Indeed, NATO is one of the largest international organizations in terms of staff numbers. Because of the central role that NATO plays in collective defence and because it can be considered an actual international organization, this chapter will study NATO further as an example of international cooperation in the field of security and defence.

Policy programme of NATO

The North Atlantic Treaty was signed by twelve states from Europe and North America (Canada and the United States) in April 1949. The Treaty was a response to the beginning of the Cold War following rigged elections in Central and Eastern Europe and the expansion of Soviet influence. During the Cold War, NATO expanded with Greece, Türkiye, West Germany and Spain, and since the end of the Cold War another seven accession rounds have taken place with states from Central and Eastern Europe, the Western Balkans and Scandinavia. Currently, NATO has thirty-two member states. Interestingly, we consider NATO as an international organization in this book, but initially it resembled more a traditional alliance. Only in response to the Korean War, which started in June 1950, did the NATO allies appoint US general Dwight Eisenhower as a military commander. He initially set up shop in the Hôtel Astoria in Paris in January 1951, since NATO did not have a headquarters. The first secretary general, Lord Ismay, arrived a year later as the permanent chair of the North Atlantic Council. NATO member states are therefore still often referred to as 'allies' and NATO itself as an 'alliance' even though it fulfils the criteria of our definition of international organizations, including having three or more states as members, regular meetings and a secretariat and correspondence address (see Chapter 1).

While NATO has significantly developed since 1949, the North Atlantic Treaty remains critical in terms of defining the policy programme. The Treaty is actually succinct with only fourteen articles but at the same time rather precise and far-reaching. It recognizes the UN Charter in terms of promoting peace and security (Article 1); encourages economic cooperation, free institutions, stability and well-being between the allies (Article 2); and notes that the allies will maintain their capacities to resist armed attack (Article 3). What follows is the core of NATO's policy programme in Articles 4–6 about collective defence. Article 4 foresees consultations between the allies when 'the territorial integrity, political independence or security of any of the Parties is threatened'. In many ways, this article seems straightforward: the members of an alliance are, and should be, in constant contact with one another on security matters. Yet 'the Article 4 procedure' has also become a process in itself for NATO members to highlight key security concerns. Article 4 has been explicitly invoked by allies seven times between 2003 and 2022. Türkiye has requested five times consultations because of instability on its borders with Iraq and Syria as well as terrorist attacks. Poland and other allies have invoked the article in 2014 and 2022 following Russian military aggression in Ukraine. An Article 4 consultation may lead to a NATO decision or action but it is mostly symbolically important for allies to put certain concerns on the agenda. Interestingly, Article 4 has never been invoked during the Cold War. It has become a post-Cold War practice for allies to signal issues of national security.

NATO's Article 5 is of course well known and reads that

> The Parties agree that an armed attack against one or more of them in Europe or North America shall be considered an attack against them all and consequently they agree that, if such an armed attack occurs, each of them, in exercise of the right of individual or collective self-defence recognised by Article 51 of the Charter of the United Nations, will assist the Party or Parties so attacked by taking forthwith, individually and in concert with the other Parties, such action as it deems necessary, including the use of armed force, to restore and maintain the security of the North Atlantic area.

In other words, the allies come to each other's rescue in case of an armed attack. What is less well known is that Article 5 is qualified by what the individual allies deem 'necessary' and by the phrase 'including the use of armed force'. This implies that all allies can decide for themselves how they want to respond and that non-military means can also be part of that response. Particularly for the United States it was important, when negotiating the North Atlantic Treaty, that it would not be automatically dragged into each and every conflict that European states might get themselves involved in. In practice, the North Atlantic Council has to decide by consensus that Article 5 applies. This has happened once following the terrorist attacks against the United States on 11 September 2001. The next day, the NATO Council met and invoked Article 5.

Important as well is that Article 5 is geographically restricted. Article 6 details that an armed attack under Article 5 needs to take place 'on the 'territory' or against the 'forces, vessels, or aircraft' in the 'North Atlantic area north of the Tropic of Cancer'. This excludes for instance an armed attack on the islands of Hawaii or a potential naval war between China and the United States over Taiwan. While Article 6 is specifically about the geographical dimension of Article 5, the Treaty is generally about the 'North Atlantic area' which gets mentioned six times. In spite of this geographical restriction, there have been serious debates among allies on whether NATO can go 'out of area' and cover also the Mediterranean and can send operations to the Western Balkans and Afghanistan. These points will be further discussed below. Through its operations, NATO has currently also a significant focus on China and the Indo-Pacific which is, at least in spirit, a departure from the 75-year-old Treaty.

While NATO has not seriously revised its Treaty over all these decades, it has clearly developed its policy programme (Rynning 2024). In the post-Cold War period, it has adopted five so-called Strategic Concepts, which are complemented by lengthy declarations at the end of NATO summits, which take place almost every year. The 1991 Strategic Concept noted, for instance, that while collective defence remains important to the Alliance, despite the end of the Cold War, there was also a need for partnerships with the former adversaries in Central and Eastern Europe. This led to operational activities in the field of cooperative security (see below). The 1999 Strategic Concept highlighted a role for NATO in new security risks such as counterterrorism, political instability and the spread of nuclear, biological and chemical weapons. It also noted that in addition to collective defence and partnership, NATO has a task in crisis management (Article 10). The 2010 and 2022 Strategic Concept equally highlighted that NATO's three core tasks are collective defence, crisis management and cooperative security, even if the latter put a strong emphasis on the Russian war against Ukraine. In other words, through successive Strategic Concepts, NATO has developed its policy programme over time and particularly in the post-Cold War period.

Operations of NATO

The operational activities of NATO can be analysed on the basis of the different elements of the political system of international organizations (see Chapters 4–7). The sequence is often as follows. First, one or several of the allies feel threatened or are victims of an armed attack (input). Second, consultations are normally held within the North Atlantic Council (NAC) (conversion). The NAC is chaired by the secretary general and gets political and military advice from the International Staff and the NATO Military Committee consisting of generals from all allies. Third, following the decision-making process, which always takes place on the basis of consensus, the NAC can launch operational activities (output) such as (1) collective defence and deterrence, (2) crisis prevention and management or (3) cooperative security with partner countries around the world. NATO carries out many of these operational activities itself – including through its formidable military command structure – even if the member states always deliver the soldiers and equipment (there is no 'NATO army'). Fourth, if the output does not achieve the objectives, the process starts again.

Collective defence and deterrence

NATO's core task is arguably collective defence. The first secretary general, Lord Ismay, famously quipped that it was NATO's purpose to 'keep the Soviet Union out, the Americans in, and the Germans down'. The challenge was thus not just Soviet expansion and potential aggression but also how to manage a demilitarized Germany after the Second World War and ensure the continued American interest in European security. To achieve these objectives, NATO developed during the Cold War an institutional structure for political consultations and military command as well as operational activities in terms of providing credible (nuclear) deterrence, scenario planning, military exercises and training. During the Cold War, NATO held the assumption that Soviet conventional forces would be superior in terms of numbers of soldiers, tanks and fighter jets. This meant that NATO would not only need to be a well-coordinated machinery but also possess access to (American) nuclear weapons and have the willingness to use them in case of an armed attack. Around the NATO framework, allies also developed a thick network of a defence industry providing allies with state-of-the-art weaponry. While NATO has significantly developed and reformed since the end of the Cold War, the military command structure as well as its operational activities and plans are still a core part of collective defence and deterrence.

As mentioned above, the Treaty established the NAC, which became a permanent forum for consultation under the chairmanship of the secretary general in 1952. The NAC not only meets in Brussels every week at the level of ambassadors but also meets regularly in the format of foreign and defence ministers and in the summit format with the heads of state and government. In the event of an armed attack, or a looming threat, the allies can thus convene within hours to discuss the collective response. The secretary general furthermore heads a sizeable International Staff of NATO civil servants and also has an International Military Staff of advisers at his disposal (Dijkstra 2015b). The secretary general and the ambassadors in the NAC are furthermore supported by the Military Committee of generals from all allies. Importantly, these institutions located at the NATO headquarters in Brussels are complemented with an operational military command structure. The Supreme Headquarters Allied Powers Europe (SHAPE) in Mons, Belgium, is the most well known. It leads all military operations of NATO under the command of an American general. NATO, however, also has three joint force headquarters in Brunssum, the Netherlands, Naples, Italy, and Norfolk, United States, dealing, respectively, with NATO operational activities on the eastern border of NATO, the Mediterranean and the Atlantic Ocean. Furthermore, NATO has separate operational commands for the land, air and maritime forces. In all these commands, military officers are not only working on active operational activities, but they also engage in contingency planning for potential future armed attacks.

A prerequisite for collective defence and deterrence is that all the allies have high-quality armed forces. As a response to the Russian annexation of Crimea in 2014, the NATO members agreed therefore to work towards spending 2 per cent of gross domestic product (GDP) on defence. This was considered necessary, because after the economic and financial crisis of 2008–12, many European allies had cut defence expenditure. In 2023, following the full Russian invasion of Ukraine, NATO members agreed that 2 per cent should be an absolute minimum and, in 2025, under pressure from US president Trump, allies agreed to a future target of 3.5 per cent defence spending (see Box 8.1). While NATO cannot provide binding spending targets, it has developed a series of operational activities to increase defence spending by its allies. First of all, it publishes every year figures on which allies achieve their targets and which fall behind. This creates peer pressure. Yet allies have also established the NATO Defence Planning Process (NDPP), which requires all allies to submit defence spending plans, which are subsequently discussed with NATO officials. This ensures that the different allies buy the right military capabilities and make sensible defence investments in research and development. Nevertheless, 'burden sharing' between the NATO allies remains heavily debated, since not all allies fulfil the commitments in terms of defence spending.

In addition to keeping the military forces of allies strong, NATO has also established eight multinational battlegroups in Bulgaria, Estonia, Hungary, Latvia, Lithuania, Poland, Romania and Slovakia to defend the so-called eastern flank. This concerns, in total, around 10,000 soldiers from all the allies. Indeed, within each multinational battlegroup, soldiers from different allies work together. These battlegroups together are called 'NATO's Forward Presence'. While these battlegroups in themselves might not be enough in case of a full-scale invasion, they provide a clear signal that NATO is committed to collective defence and Article 5. For instance, if Russia were to attack Estonia, it would encounter not only Estonian soldiers but also British soldiers who are part of NATO battlegroup in Estonia. Having such battlegroups already in place would also allow NATO to scale up more rapidly in case of increased threats. The main purpose of these operational activities is, however, deterrence.

Apart from conventional forces, NATO also draws on nuclear deterrence. The United States, France and the UK are the three allies with nuclear forces, but all allies benefit from these weapons in terms of what is called 'extended' deterrence. The United States has also stationed nuclear weapons at selected European army bases, and several European allies possess aircraft that can carry these US nuclear weapons. To ensure credibility, NATO organizes each year also a nuclear exercise. The purpose of such military exercises – with conventional and nuclear weapons – is for NATO allies to test interoperability (i.e. troops from different allies working together), get familiar with geographical terrain of the NATO allies, but once again also deterrence. Finally, NATO and the United States have also established a range of military colleges where officers from all the allies are trained together. This not just strengthens the skills of individual officers but also allows them to better operate in a NATO context. In other words, NATO has developed a considerable range of operational activities to make its collective defence more credible.

BOX 8.1 NATO AND THE WAR IN UKRAINE

The Russian war against Ukraine since 2022 is very important for NATO, yet NATO itself is not a party to this war. Ukraine is not a NATO member state, which means that Article 5 on collective defence does not apply. NATO has also avoided direct confrontation with Russia, as this would put nuclear powers at a collision course. NATO allies nevertheless discuss the war every single day, and NATO has also taken several key steps in response to the war.

- NATO allies have significantly increased their defence budgets. While prior to war, they had agreed to move towards 2 per cent defence spending, they made the 'enduring commitment to invest *at least* 2% of our Gross Domestic Product (GDP) annually on defence' in Vilnius in July 2023 (Article 27, emphasis added). Only seven allies were meeting the 2 per cent target in 2022, yet no less than twenty-three allies did so in 2024. During the summit in The Hague in June 2025, NATO agreed to a future target of 3.5 per cent defence spending by 2035.
- NATO welcomed Finland and Sweden – previously neutral states – into the alliance, thereby providing both countries with collective defence as well.
- NATO established four new battlegroups in Bulgaria, Hungary, Romania and Slovakia, thereby doubling its military presence in Eastern Europe to almost 10,000 soldiers.
- NATO has made a commitment that Ukraine will become a member in the future when the allies 'agree and conditions are met'; it coordinates training and equipment for Ukraine and has pledged long-term financial assistance of minimally 40 billion euros. NATO also facilitates and participates in the Ukraine Defense Contact Group, which coordinates the donation of military equipment (e.g. artillery and tanks) to Ukraine.

The war in Ukraine has therefore highlighted once more the relevance of NATO for the collective defence of its allies.

Crisis prevention and management

Following Russia's invasion of Ukraine, much of NATO attention is on collective defence and deterrence. Yet for most of the post-Cold War era, so-called crisis management operations in the Western Balkans and Afghanistan were NATO's main purpose. With the dissolution of the Soviet Union in

1991, NATO no longer had an obvious enemy, which raised questions about NATO's future. Yet, as noted above, NATO is much more than a traditional alliance. In addition to its extensive institutional structure, including its military command, NATO was a cornerstone of the transatlantic security establishment. This kept it going (Wallander 2000). There were also new security issues. The civil war in former Yugoslavia, accumulating in the genocide in Srebrenica, Bosnia, resulted in NATO airstrikes against Bosnian-Serbian targets. NATO then deployed 60,000 troops to implement the Dayton Peace Agreement of 1995. The pattern repeated itself when NATO intervened in Kosovo in 1999, without a UN Security Council resolution, and subsequently deployed 50,000 ground troops as part of its Kosovo Force (KFOR), a military operation that continues to date albeit with a much smaller military presence. In both cases, NATO was leading military operations – something it had never done during the Cold War – and the enemy was not a rival military power posing a clear threat to the allies.

NATO's military operation in Afghanistan from 2003 to 2014 deserves specific attention (Rynning 2012; Auerswald and Saideman 2014). Following the 11 September 2001 terrorist attacks, NATO allies invoked Article 5. This did not, however, immediately lead to extensive operational activities. The United States, with the help of some of its allies, essentially went into Afghanistan alone to go after Al-Qaeda, the terrorist organization responsible for the attacks, and the enabling Taliban regime. It then established, through a UN Security Council resolution, the International Security Assistance Force (ISAF), which would help secure the capital city of Kabul. Only two years later did NATO take over the military command of the ISAF mission with the ambition to gradually expand and provide security over the whole country. This became a massive undertaking resulting ultimately, at its height in 2011–12, in a 130,000 troops strong military operation drawing on the contributions of fifty-one NATO allies and partner countries. While the ISAF mission was to provide security and stability, it involved considerable combat with Al-Qaeda and Taliban forces. More than 3,000 soldiers died during the ISAF deployment. This death toll in Afghanistan is not far from the number of UN casualties in all peacekeeping missions combined since 1948. As this operation was not sustainable, NATO started focusing on training the Afghan national army and police with the view that they should be able to take full responsibility for Afghan security by the end of 2014. NATO allies also worked on the reconstruction and development of Afghanistan through provincial reconstruction teams to build local Afghan capacity.

After the ISAF mission, NATO launched a follow up Resolute Support Mission. Contrary to ISAF, this was not a combat mission. It operated from Kabul with several regional hubs in support of the Afghan government. It was also much smaller than ISAF with around 17,000 troops, which was soon reduced to 10,000 troops. NATO announced in the spring of 2021 that it would terminate the Resolute Support Mission and bring all soldiers home. While NATO had hoped that the local Afghan government would be able to continue to provide some security in Afghanistan, following all the training efforts, this turned out to be wishful thinking. In May 2021, the Taliban started a widespread military offense taking over rapidly the territory that the United States and NATO allies were leaving. The Afghan government collapsed and by 15 August the Taliban forces reached the gates of Kabul. What followed was a massive scramble by the United States and its allies to evacuate more than 100,000 people, including many (Western) civilians who had been working with the Afghan government, via Kabul airport within the space of two weeks. On 31 August 2021, the Taliban marched into Kabul and took over the country once again. The United States and NATO allies were defeated.

While NATO's military operations in Afghanistan have dominated the Alliance for nearly two decades, it is worth to point at the other operational activities in the area of crisis prevention and management. NATO intervened militarily in Libya to protect civilians from the Gaddafi regime in 2011. The mentioned KFOR operation continues to date with around 4,500 soldiers. NATO also has a non-combat advisory and capacity-building mission since 2018 that assists Iraq in the fight against the Islamic State. It has naval operations in the Mediterranean providing situational awareness and counter terrorist activities and human smuggling. NATO cooperates with the African Union (AU) and occasionally provides strategic airlifts and training for the military missions of the AU. NATO also provides round-the-clock air policing supporting civilian aircrafts in distress as well as interceptions in case of airspace violations. It has furthermore provided assistance following earthquakes in Pakistan and Türkiye and has provided the United States with support after Hurricane Katrina in 2005. While some of these operational activities are more prominent than others, it is clear that NATO possesses a set of military assets that can be deployed for a variety of tasks. Military operations are not as prominent at NATO anymore today as they were in the 1990s and 2000s, but these remain relevant operational activities.

Cooperative security

The final operational activity of NATO concerns cooperative security. This operational activity started shortly after the end of the Cold War with NATO reaching out to the Central and Eastern European countries to help them with their security. In 1994, it established the Partnership for Peace (PfP) programme which currently covers eighteen countries (with relations with Belarus and Russia being suspended). The PfP programme is not about collective defence but rather seeks to address common security threats and helps countries develop defence capabilities. PfP countries differ. They include, for instance, not only neutral European states, such as Austria,

Ireland, Malta and Switzerland (not Cyprus because of its fraught relations with NATO ally Türkiye), but also countries in the Western Balkans which are not (yet) members of NATO, such as Bosnia and Serbia (but not Kosovo which is not yet recognized as a state by various NATO allies). They furthermore include Moldova and Ukraine, the three Caucasus countries and several countries in Central Asia. Because of the wide variety of countries in the PfP programme, NATO engages with them individually. It develops together with these countries collaboration objectives and activities.

The PfP programme is clearly not a pre-accession trajectory for all partners. It is unlikely, for instance, that neutral Switzerland will become a NATO member any time soon. At the same time, the PfP programme has often prepared the ground for states becoming NATO members. Various PfP countries have become NATO members in the past, including the Czech Republic, Hungary and Poland in 1999. It is, in this respect, worth remembering that Article 10 of the North Atlantic Treaty stipulates that 'any other European state' may join the Alliance. For many Central and Eastern European countries this has been a prize worth pursuing. NATO membership, after all, guarantees security and the military backing of the United States. NATO itself is also keen to stress its 'open door policy': European countries are free to choose whether they want to join NATO. At the same time, NATO has a number of membership criteria. Applicants need to subscribe to the principles and commitments of the Treaty. They should also be democracies, respect minority populations and make a military contribution to the Alliance. Perhaps, most importantly, however, they should not be part of an active military war or conflict, because that would immediately drag NATO into such a war as well by virtue of Article 5. This makes it also difficult to envision Ukraine joining NATO in the short term. As long as the Russian war is continuing, NATO is unlikely to welcome Ukraine in the Alliance. Decisions over admitting new members, as with all decisions in NATO, are ultimately made by consensus.

Beyond the PfP programme, originally set up to engage with the immediate neighbouring states, NATO has developed partnerships with countries around the Mediterranean Sea, countries in the Gulf region and also partners around the globe. The latter include notably allies in the Pacific region, such as Australia, New Zealand, Japan and South Korea. This is an important development, as it implies that NATO is going 'out of area'. At the same time, it also indicates that Euro-Atlantic security is no longer confined to the geographical European continent. China and Russia have, for instance, deepened their strategic partnership and China has also become a rival with respect to cyber, critical infrastructure, strategic materials and supply chains. Countries such as North Korea, Iran and Syria are of relevance when it comes to arm's control and proliferation risks. The 2022 NATO Strategic Concept, in this respect, notes that '[t]he Indo-Pacific is important for NATO, given that developments in that region can directly affect Euro-Atlantic security' (paragraph 45). While various allies remain hesitant about a 'global NATO', particularly when it comes to collective defence, it is clear that NATO does need to sustain global partnerships to fulfil its mission.

Evaluation of the organization's effectiveness

NATO was established for the purpose of collective defence, and it has kept its allies safe for more than seventy-five years. In many ways, NATO has thus been a highly effective international organization. Some even claim that NATO 'won' the Cold War. Important, in this regard, is not only the continuing leadership of the United States over the decades but also the significant institutional structure of the Alliance. Ultimately, Article 5 is a political commitment: the allies have promised that they will help each other out in case of a future armed attack, but there are no actual guarantees. For NATO, it has therefore been important to develop credible deterrence so that no adversary would dare to attempt an armed attack in the first place. As this chapter has shown, the development of NATO's formidable command structure along with a range of operational activities and the forging of a Euro-Atlantic security establishment have been important in this regard. The fact that Article 5 has only been invoked once (symbolically on 12 September 2001) is a testament that NATO has achieved its original goals.

NATO has also survived the end of the Cold War. In fact, NATO has almost been as long a post-Cold War military alliance (thirty-six years) as it has been a Cold War alliance (forty years). The agility of the organization should be noted in this respect. NATO has been able to transform itself to deal with the civil wars in the Western Balkans in the 1990s, the new threats of the 2000s and again the collective defence imperative in the 2010s and 2020s. While some argue that NATO enlargement since the 1990s has posed a threat to Russia and has contributed to the wars in Georgia and Ukraine (Mearsheimer 2014), it has also brought stability and security to Central and Eastern European countries as well as the Western Balkans. By bringing former adversaries – including from the Balkans – into the Alliance, NATO has also been a pacifying force among its own member states. Poland is, for instance, no longer threatened by German defence spending as it has historically been; quite the contrary: Poland indeed wants Germany to spend more on defence with a view to the Russian war in Ukraine. NATO has, in this sense, been very effective.

Defence spending and the burden sharing among allies remain indeed enduring challenges for NATO and major points of frustration for US president Trump. Despite decades-long pressure, various European countries continue to freeride under the American security umbrella. At the same time, NATO allies have significantly increased their defence spending since they made a commitment at the Wales Summit in 2014 (see Figure 8.3). It remains, however, difficult to assess whether NATO allies have started

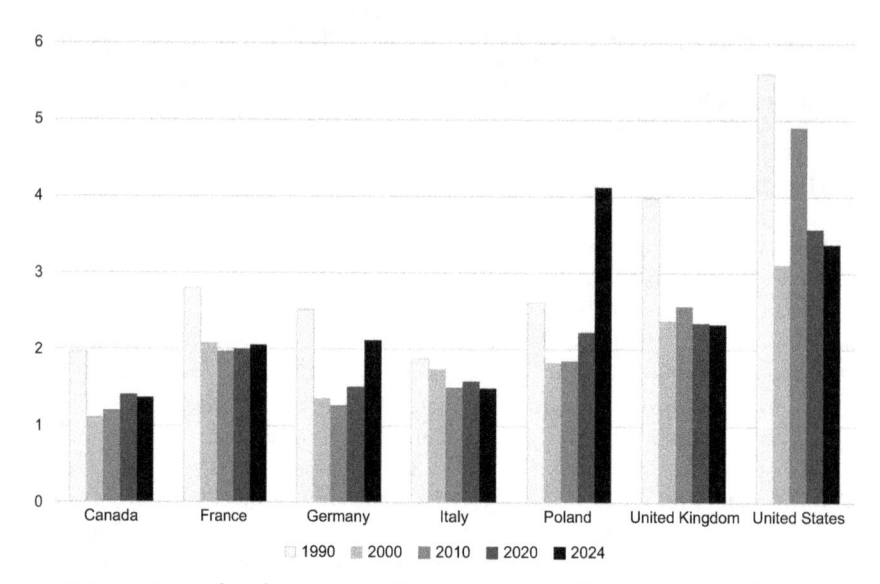

FIGURE 8.3 *Burden sharing in NATO: defence spending by selected allies (% of GDP). Source: SIPRI data until 2013 (processing by Our World in Data); NATO data since 2014.*

to spend more on defence due to NATO, the Russian threat or pressure by American presidents such as Donald Trump. Recent academic research shows that the 'public shaming' of European allies by American presidents does not have the desired effect and that the 'Wales pledge' seems to have driven some of the increased burden sharing (Becker et al. 2024; Becker 2024). The NDPP whereby NATO officials discuss with the different member states their defence plans seems in this respect a partially effective operational activity.

NATO's major failures are to be found in the area of crisis management operations. While NATO has been highly effective with regard to peace enforcement in the early stages of military operations, it has disappointed in creating safe and secure environments through the deployment of ground troops. It is, in this respect, worth noting that NATO's (heavily US-led) military intervention in Bosnia created the conditions for the Dayton Peace Agreement, that NATO suffered no casualties when it intervened in Kosovo in 1999 and that it very effectively toppled the Gaddafi regime in Libya in 2011. The trouble for NATO has been the follow up. While Bosnia and Kosovo remain relatively safe, it is already three decades since Dayton and these military operations have failed to bring a sustainable peace. Security in Libya has collapsed. But clearly Afghanistan has been NATO's largest failure. For all NATO efforts and the deployment of around 130,000 troops have not nearly brought the outcomes and impact envisioned.

Conclusion

Following the horrors of the Second World War, the UN member states have set up an elaborate policy programme which bans the use of force. While this policy programme is not entirely complete, leaving exceptions for cases of self-defence, it provides an important set of norms and rules that constrain states in questions of peace and security. This UN policy programme is complemented by a plethora of operational activities. The UN is at the forefront of providing a peaceful settlement of disputes, it has launched many peacekeeping missions and the Security Council occasionally authorizes peace enforcement. The chapter has also discussed questions of collective defence. It has analysed NATO as an example of an international organization which provides its allies with self-defence. Article 5 is, in this respect, at the heart of NATO's policy programme, but the Alliance has also developed important operational activities over time in terms of a military command structure, credible deterrence, military operations and cooperative security partnerships.

It is important to recognize that the need for cooperation resulted from pressures from the international environment. While the UN policy programme initially focused on interstate wars, the changing nature of war over the past three decades has resulted in a situation where the UN also gets involved in civil wars. Something similar can be said about NATO, which focused during the Cold War on collective defence but has involved itself in the post-Cold War period in crisis management, for instance, in the Western Balkans, Afghanistan and Libya. As a result of such developments in the international environment, states and other political actors have formulated their preferences and demands for international cooperation (input). For instance, the United States and other Western states have become supportive of UN-authorized action to protect human rights, whereas China and Russia have insisted on non-interference. In the context of NATO, the United States has long demanded that European states share a larger part of the burden. How all these inputs are channelled through the decision-making processes of the UN and NATO (conversion) is also critically important. The UN Security Council falls and stands with its permanent members, while NATO formally operates by consensus even if the voice of the United States is often decisive.

The UN and NATO provide a wide range of outputs in the area of peace and security. The UN Security Council has, for instance, adopted more than 2,750 resolutions (per 2024). Some of these Security Council resolutions are legally binding and can be used to authorize the use of force, establish a peacekeeping mission or put in place economic sanctions. These are significant outcomes. For instance, in 2024, the UN had more than 60,000 blue helmets under its command based on those Security Council resolutions. When it comes to collective defence, we similarly see important outputs. NATO has established eight battlegroups along its eastern flank, provides maritime security in the Mediterranean sea, organizes large-scale military exercises and has deployed large military operations to different countries. While the UN and NATO thus provide considerable output and often achieve the intended outcomes (such as the instalment of economic sanctions or keeping allies safe), both organizations are still often criticized over their impact. UN peacekeeping has not been entirely successful, and NATO has failed miserably in Afghanistan when considering eventual impact. Overall, however, we can conclude that even in the area of peace, security and war, international organizations play a key role.

Discussion questions

1. Has the UN Security Council succeeded in establishing itself as the prime guardian of international peace and security after the Cold War? Justify your position with the appropriate empirical evidence.
2. How have UN peacekeeping operations evolved in the past few decades? To what extent do UN peacekeeping operations succeed in creating and/or keeping the peace?
3. Why is NATO considered an international organization instead of a traditional military alliance and how does this matter?

Further reading

Auerswald, David P. and Stephen M. Saideman (2014). *NATO in Afghanistan: Fighting Together, Fighting Alone*, Princeton, NJ: Princeton University Press.
Autesserre, Séverine (2014). *Peaceland: Conflict Resolution and the Everyday Politics of International Intervention*, Cambridge: Cambridge University Press.
Koops, Joachim, Norrie MacQueen, Thierry Tardy and Williams Paul D., eds (2015). *The Oxford Handbook of United Nations Peacekeeping Operations*, Oxford: Oxford University Press.
Rynning, Sten (2024). *NATO: From Cold War to Ukraine, a History of the World's Most Powerful Alliance*, New Haven, CT: Yale University Press.
Sperling, James, and Mark Webber, eds (2025). *The Oxford Handbook of NATO*, Oxford: Oxford University Press.
Walter, Barbara F., Lise M. Howard and Virginia P. Fortna (2021). 'The Extraordinary Relationship between Peacekeeping and Peace', *British Journal of Political Science*, 51 (4): 1705–22.

9

Trade, development and finance

In the area of trade, development and finance – as in security – there is a dilemma which sets the parameters for international cooperation. The starting point is that free trade tends to be good for economic growth and development. It allows countries to specialize in industries where they have a comparative advantage and larger international markets allow for economies of scale. Yet without a central authority, each state can decide its own trade policies. Thus, each state may be tempted to raise tariffs, impose import restrictions or provide state aid. This is known as mercantilism: the policy of maximizing trade and accumulating wealth *at the expense of other states*. It may result in short-term economic gain or provide a lifeline for struggling domestic industries. If, however, all states engage in such opportunistic behaviour, it comes at the expense of overall growth. The economic dilemma thus describes a trap in which trade policies aimed at increasing wealth for individual states place the community of states, and ultimately also each state individually, in a worse situation than would have been the case with effective cooperation. This economic dilemma therefore resembles the Prisoner's Dilemma (see Chapter 2). An open international economy may furthermore result in greater economic disparities between richer and poorer countries. For instance, if poorer countries specialize in labour-intensive industries (as they have the comparative advantage of lower wages), it will be difficult for them to 'upgrade' their economy (Lin and Chang 2009). There is thus a need to provide assistance or flexibility to developing countries to allow them to compete in the international economy. Finally, there is also a risk that economic crises in other countries spill over. In an open global economy, governments that can no longer service their foreign debts or core financial companies going bankrupt will likely result in ripple effects and cross-border problems.

The creation of strong international treaties and organizations is the classic solution to this economic dilemma. They allow states to credibly commit to free trade. States can, for instance, rely on international organizations to monitor the implementation of trade agreements and to adjudicate in case of trade disputes. This significantly increases the chance of compliance and reduces the risk of cheating. Given the obvious direct benefits, economic cooperation is often more extensive than security cooperation (Lipson 1984). Furthermore, international organizations have become central players when it comes to development assistance and providing loans to poorer countries. Through international organizations, the donor countries can pool their development assistance and as such provide more effective support than through bilateral development channels. States have also set up international organizations with a mandate for monetary affairs to ensure financial stability. While there are many international organizations dealing with economic relations, we shall limit our discussion to a few that deal with global trade, development and finance. In this chapter, we take a detailed look at the policy programmes and operational activities of the World Trade Organization (WTO). We also focus on the World Bank Group and its extensive loans to developing countries as well as the International Monetary Fund (IMF) as a key finance organization. In Chapter 12, we discuss in detail regional cooperation, such as the Southern Common Market (MERCOSUR) or the free trade areas on the African continent.

Global trade relations

The economic dilemma can lead to undesirable results in international trade relations if states try to increase their own share of global trade at the expense of others through tariffs and non-tariff barriers. To counter such mercantilist trade policies, states can benefit from economic cooperation and international organizations. States need to, in this respect, first agree on policy programmes. At least as important, however, is that states agree to a variety of operational activities by international organizations: policy programmes need to be specified and it is critical that they get uniformly interpreted and implemented. The activities of the WTO serve as examples of institutionalized attempts to overcome barriers to cooperation in global trade relations.

Policy programme of the WTO

The General Agreement on Tariffs and Trade (GATT) of 1947 was provisionally established in the form of a governmental agreement regulating international trade relations (see Chapter 3). Since 1995, the revised GATT has formed the programmatic core of the newly created WTO (Cohn 2002: 216–18; Wilkinson 2000: 11–30). Thus, the WTO sets norms and rules aimed at the realization of liberal trade relations. Yet neither the GATT nor the WTO has established a world trade order based entirely on free trade (or 'pure liberalism'). They are committed to 'embedded liberalism' (Ruggie 1982). They strive for liberal trade relations while at the same time allowing states to shield their national markets from the global market to the extent necessary for the pursuit of domestic economic steering and social policy measures. However, the creation of the WTO also brought along a softening of the principle of 'embedded liberalism' in favour of 'pure liberalism' (Ruggie 1994).

The regulatory programme of the WTO is only to a small extent the result of programme decisions of the international organization itself. The original GATT (and later extensions and alterations) already contained the constitutive norms and rules which still govern international trade relations today under the WTO (Matsushita, Schoenbaum and Mavroidis 2004). At the heart of the WTO programme is the norm of non-discrimination. This consists of two elements. First, this norm prohibits the 166 member states (as of 2024) to discriminate between the other WTO member states (Wilkinson 2000: 80–4). The so-called 'most-favoured-nation' principle requires that:

> any advantage, favour, privilege or immunity granted by any contracting party to any product originating in or destined for any other country shall be accorded immediately and unconditionally to the like product originating in or destined for the territories of all other contracting parties. (Article 1, GATT 1947)

In other words, the United States cannot treat China and Germany differently, as both are WTO members. If the United States reduces its tariffs for German products, it also needs to reduce its tariffs for Chinese products. This rule is fundamentally important and increasingly so in an era of growing geopolitics. States can no longer, under WTO rules, treat their friends and rivals differently. The 'reciprocal tariffs', which US president Trump proposed in 2025 with varying rates for different countries, are therefore a blatant violation of the WTO Agreement. There is, however, an important exception. If several members of the WTO establish among themselves a customs union or free trade agreement, they are allowed to give preferential treatment to their trade partners (Article 24, GATT 1947; see also Chapter 12). To give an example, member states of the EU (a customs union) can make better trade deals within their own internal market than with the other WTO members. The same goes for members of MERCOSUR. The assumption is that, on the whole, the effect of customs unions and free trade agreements is to create trade rather than merely to divert it (Wilkinson 2000: 93–5).

The second part of the non-discrimination norm obliges WTO member states to treat products of foreign origin – once they have cleared customs – the same as domestic products. More precisely, national treatment is defined as follows:

> The products of the territory of any contracting party imported into the territory of any other contracting party shall be accorded treatment no

less favourable than that accorded to like products of national origin in respect of all laws, regulations and requirements affecting their internal sale, offering for sale, purchase, transportation, distribution or use. (Article 3, paragraph 4, GATT 1947)

For instance, a member state is not allowed to impose a sales tax of 15 per cent on domestic products and a sales tax of 20 per cent on similar foreign products. It is also not allowed to have different health or safety standards or labelling requirements for foreign products. National treatment only applies after the products have been imported and does not affect what happens at the border: member states are still allowed to impose tariffs on foreign goods. Also member states remain perfectly in their right to impose taxes or to stipulate product requirements, as long as they do not discriminate between domestic and foreign products. So member states can still insist on product labelling in their local language, because such a law applies to both domestic and foreign products equally.

In addition to these norms, the GATT and WTO have a progressive policy programme: they oblige member states to go beyond mere non-discrimination by limiting tariff and non-tariff trade barriers. In particular, restrictions in the form of import quotas are prohibited (Article 11, GATT 1947). Other non-tariff barriers as well as tariff barriers in the form of duties are tolerated in principle, but member states are obliged to strive for their reduction in recurring rounds of trade negotiations, convened by the Ministerial Conference of the WTO, on the principle of reciprocity (Wilkinson 2000: 109–11). The Ministerial Conference, the highest decision-making organ of the WTO, meets at least every two years and all member states are represented. Although majority decisions are possible, decisions are normally reached by consensus.

The WTO has substantially widened the scope of its policy programmes when compared with the original GATT (Cohn 2002: 235). This expansion has gradually evolved through several GATT negotiating rounds. The scope has also considerably increased with the transition from GATT to the WTO: in the Uruguay Round (1986–94), for example, agriculture, textiles and trade in services were integrated into the WTO framework. This was a significant first step towards liberalization of trade in products other than manufactured goods. This is important because agricultural goods and textiles are especially significant for developing countries, whereas trade in services is more advantageous for industrialized countries where the services sector contributes up to 50 per cent or more to the economy. However, after the programmatic expansion at the inception of the WTO, attempts to increase the scope further through intergovernmental negotiations in the Doha Development Round (launched in 2001) have largely stalled since the late 2000s. Growing conflicts of interest between developed countries, led by the EU and the United States, and emerging economies, such as Brazil, China and India, have blocked further programmatic progress on vital issues like agricultural trade or trade in services (Jones 2009; Hopewell 2015).

The WTO policy programme allows for waivers to WTO rules. The impact of such waivers should not be underestimated. One such waiver refers to the grave distortion of domestic markets as a result of superior foreign competition (the norm of market security). It allows states temporarily to protect one of their industrial sectors if they find themselves exposed to a considerable increase in imports from a specific foreign industrial sector (Article 19, GATT 1947). It enables member states to reduce social hardships resulting from the liberalization of trade. Another exception concerns preferential treatment for developing, and in particular least developed, countries (the development norm). The norm allows developing countries to suspend or at least reduce the obligation of reciprocity. This should help to improve export opportunities for developing countries without forcing them to immediately open their own markets to imports from industrialized states. Indeed, the ban on discrimination and the requirement of most favoured nation status is partially lifted for trade between industrialized countries and developing countries. Such rules have, however, also become more contested in recent years. Despite its economic growth and being a major trading bloc, China still claims to be a developing country at the WTO, for instance, which greatly angers the United States and others (Schöfer and Weinhardt 2022).

Operations of the WTO

Making sure that the policy programme gets properly implemented can be very difficult, as states have incentives to cheat in the area of trade. The operational activities, for which international organizations are responsible, are therefore critically important. Specifying the norms and rules set in the WTO's policy programmes is an important operational activity. The WTO programmes determine which trade barriers have to be removed and in which sector but do not provide concrete prescriptions by which states must abide. The specification of existing programmes and the development of new ones within the WTO is the task of the recurring negotiating rounds (Cohn 2002: 231–75). The decision-making process in these negotiating rounds remains dominated by the member states, but officials from the WTO staff provide input. Particularly, the high-level negotiating rounds aimed at furthering the trade programme of the WTO are dominated by the interests of the large trading countries or blocs such as the United States and the EU. More recently, emerging economies, such as China and India, increasingly take the lead in the formation of developing countries' coalitions. These emerging economies take a hard bargaining stance towards developed states (Hopewell 2022; Zangl et al. 2016). The preferences of the member states indeed vary (input): while the United States and the EU are keen on liberalization in the area of services, including e-commerce, the emerging countries focus on liberalization in the area of agricultural and industrial products.

Three high-level negotiation rounds in the GATT are viewed as particularly successful: the Kennedy Round (1964–7), the Tokyo Round (1973–9) and the Uruguay Round (1986–94) brought about a reduction of tariffs for manufactured goods of one-third each time. In other words, average tariffs, which in 1947 made up over 40 per cent of the import value of goods, were reduced by the year 2000 to approximately 3 per cent. Thus, tariffs as trade barriers were largely eliminated from international trade in industrial goods, after decades of multilateral negotiations (Hauser and Schanz 1995: 63–70). Furthermore, in the Tokyo Round and especially in the Uruguay Round, the member states reached agreements to push back non-tariff trade barriers, by adopting anti-subsidy and anti-dumping rules (Kahler 1995: 29–47). Thus, it is no longer in the purview of states to simply determine dumping, subsidies or market distortions. The Tokyo and Uruguay Rounds also reduced considerably the trade barriers set up through national regulations to protect public health, consumers and the environment. The original GATT had stipulated that such regulations must not be applied in a discriminatory fashion (Article 20, GATT 1947). However, this agreement was so vague that the definition of these regulations was left to individual states, which were able to exploit them as trade barriers. The new and much more precise rules of the current WTO largely limit this abuse by prescribing that technical regulations must not be more restrictive than necessary to satisfy public health, consumer and environmental concerns.

Even though states have worked towards closing trade loopholes under the WTO, the stalemate of the Doha Round since the late 2000s also points to the limits to cooperation. Negotiations in the Doha Round between developed economies and developing as well as emerging economies have stalled over divisions on a number of substantive issues, including agricultural trade liberalization, liberalization of trade in services and manufactured products. While some states, such as India, want to uphold the Doha development agenda, others want to move on to address new trade issues that have emerged since, such as e-commerce. Within the WTO context, states have not been able to reconcile their conflicting inputs. Indeed, the preferences of the membership have diverged. Emerging economies are pursuing their interests more assertively as their economic and political weight has grown. Developed countries, on the other hand, no longer want emerging economies, such as China and India, to free ride on trade liberalization and claim differentiated treatment. This conflict makes progress on substantive issues and thus further specification of the WTO's policy programme difficult to achieve. The WTO is ultimately a member states-driven organization whose capacity for programme development and specification largely depends on member states' willingness and ability to strike mutually beneficial deals (Steinberg 2002).

The decisions taken in high-level negotiating rounds are often further specified within the member states' bureaucracies and the WTO's executive councils and committees. For this purpose, a multitude of thematic councils, committees and working parties exist within the framework of the WTO. There are three thematic councils: the Council for Trade in Goods; the Council for Trade in Services; and the Council for Trade-Related Aspects of Intellectual Property Rights. These councils consist of all WTO members and are responsible for the more specific workings of the WTO agreements dealing with their respective areas of trade. These councils have subsidiary bodies where trade diplomats from the member states discuss the specification and the 'nitty-gritty' application of the still rather abstract trade rules that are agreed upon in the negotiating rounds. For example the Goods Council has twelve committees dealing with specific subjects (such as agriculture, market access, subsidies, anti-dumping measures, etc.).

Agreeing on international trade rules is one thing; adhering to them is another. States may often be tempted to ignore or contravene agreed rules in order to obtain additional advantages for themselves. Thus, monitoring, adjudication and (to a lesser extent) sanctioning are important operational activities undertaken by the WTO. While the GATT limited itself mainly to obliging its member states to report regularly upon the implementation of norms and rules, the WTO has more far-reaching powers of supervision at its disposal. In particular, the large trading states and blocs must submit to regular supervision of their trade policies. On these occasions each member state, as well as the secretariat of the WTO, has to present a report on the implementation of existing norms and rules. Both reports are then submitted to a body specifically charged with supervising trade policies, the Trade Policy Review Body (TPRB), where the two reports are compared (Van den Bossche and Zdouc 2021). States practices are therefore monitored. It renders the supervision of practices by states within the WTO much more reliable than was the case for GATT. Since WTO dispute settlement is currently under pressure (see below), member states have taken a renewed interest in the function of monitoring of compliance and using the WTO also as a forum for exchange about how they can implement standards.

Nevertheless, the WTO policy programme requires compliance to be effective and the organization provides an answer to this cooperation problem with its Dispute Settlement Understanding (DSU) (Jackson 2004; Merrills 2017). The DSU represents an agreement to adjudicate cases of a dispute through a judicialized, court-like, dispute settlement procedure (Zangl 2008). It is unique compared to many other international organizations since it is binding and includes an enforcement mechanism. The procedure can be activated by any member state being affected by another state's breach of norms and rules laid down in the WTO agreements. The complaining state can request scrutiny by a panel consisting of three to five neutral trade experts. The panel investigates the case and hears complainants and defendants. It examines the norms and rules which apply to the case and assesses whether these have been violated. It thus establishes what speaks in favour of and what against the complaint. The panel finally draws up a report in which it describes and assesses the dispute from its point of view and gives its verdict. Panel reports become automatically binding unless they are rejected by consensus by the Dispute Settlement Body (DSB).

Yet, before panel reports are accepted by the DSB both defendants and complainants may file an appeal with the Appellate Body. The Appellate Body consists of seven independent experts in trade law who are elected for four years. Appellate Body reports cannot be blocked by individual member states. They also become binding unless all members of the DSB reject them (Zangl 2008). Meanwhile, the WTO has made it possible for parties other than member states, such as non-governmental organizations (NGOs), to participate in a dispute settlement procedure. Although they cannot be a party to a dispute, they can nevertheless forward information to the panel in the form of an '*amicus curiae* brief' which provides information and thereby exerts influence on the dispute settlement outcome. Because of its prominence, the Appellate Body has also been heavily criticized, notably by the United States which has accused the Body of judicial overreach. In particular, the United States claims that the WTO rules favour China's state-led capitalist system (with China winning trade cases against the United States), which is problematic as the rules were meant to apply to market economies. These challenges escalated when the first Trump administration decided to block the appointment and renewal of all judges on the Appellate Body. As of December 2019, therefore, the Appellate Body no longer has a sufficient number of judges to make rulings. It has thus become defunct. While other WTO members hoped that this crisis would be temporary, the Biden administration did not resume the process of appointing judges and the second Trump administration is unlikely to do so. The WTO thus operates without an Appellate Body.

If a state fails to implement a panel or Appellate Body report, it ultimately faces trade sanctions. These sanctions are implemented by the complainant state ('countermeasures') rather than the WTO itself. However, complainant states cannot resort to any sanctions. They must wait for the DSB to approve specific sanctions (formally: the suspension of trade concessions that had previously been granted to the losing defendant). These sanctions are approved unless they are opposed by all DSB member states, making it considerably easier to act in the event of norm and rule infringements in the WTO than used to be the case under GATT (Bown and Pauwelyn 2010: 2; Zangl 2008). Thus, while sanctioning still occurs in a decentralized manner, the fact that sanctions must be authorized gives the WTO an operational role in sanctioning which aims at preventing escalation to 'trade wars'. Yet since the Appellate Body no longer functions, the whole dispute settlement procedure has been weakened and this also makes the authorized countermeasures more difficult. Rather, major trading blocs such as China, the EU and the United States have resorted to unilateral tit-for-tat strategies instead of acting through the WTO process. The EU has led the establishment of the Multi-Party Interim Appeal Arbitration Arrangement (MPIA) in 2020. This panel is outside but based on the WTO system and acts as a temporary solution as long as the Appellate Body does not function. China joined the MPIA but the United States has stayed out of it.

Evaluation of the organization's effectiveness

Since the 1970s the trade ratios of major economies, that is, the ratio of their exports and imports to their gross domestic product (GDP), have increased substantially (see Figure 9.1). For the EU member states (both intra-EU and extra-EU trade), the United States, China and the world in general, the trade ratios have more than doubled over the decades. We have, however, witnessed a new development since the mid-2000s. While the ratios of the EU member states continue to grow, those of the United States have stabilized and those of China have very clearly declined. In the case of China, this is the result of the deliberate stimulation of the domestic economy after the major trade gains in the early 2000s following China's entry into the WTO. To put it differently, China benefited dramatically from the WTO in terms of trade but has been trying to absorb this (positive) shock. Also, when we exclude intra-EU trade (trade between the member states of the EU), we find that extra-EU trade was comparable in terms of trade ratio with that of China in 2023. In other words, EU member states have increased the trade among themselves a lot more than trade with the rest of the world. In conclusion, the trade ratios of the three major trading

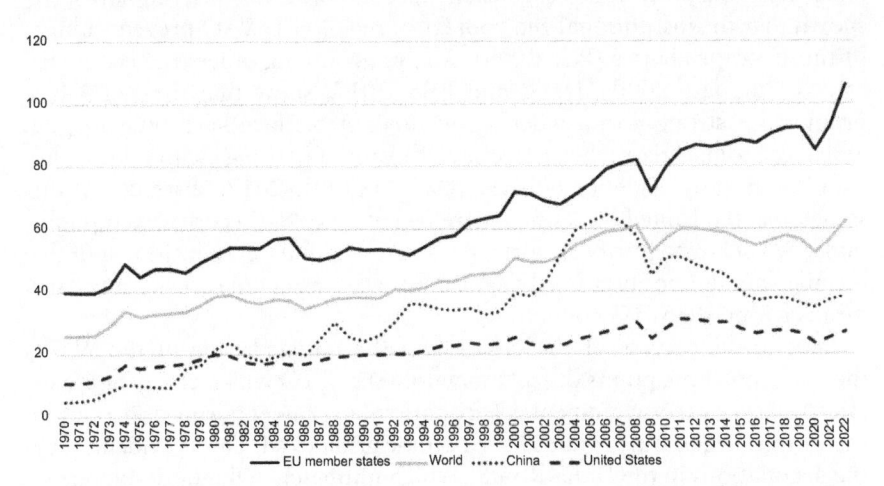

FIGURE 9.1 *Trade ratios of major economies and the world, 1970–2022* (ratio of imports + exports of goods and services to GDP, %). *Source: Based on data from the World Bank.*

blocs have significantly increased since the 1970s, but they have stabilized or even declined since the mid-2000s.

There is a growing scientific consensus that the GATT/WTO can be credited with this rise of world trade. In fact, the GATT/WTO has long been cited as one of the most successful international institutions. Membership of the GATT/WTO has expanded dramatically since 1947, and international trade has grown in tandem. Many observers have assumed that these trends are linked. Goldstein, Rivers and Tomz (2007) demonstrate that, over the decades, the GATT/WTO has indeed substantially increased trade among its member states. The benefits of the GATT/WTO in terms of increased trade have not been limited to developed economies but have extended also to developing countries (Goldstein, Rivers and Tomz 2007: 63–4). A positive assessment of the GATT/WTO's effectiveness in enhancing trade is supported by a number of further studies. For example, Mansfield and Reinhardt (2008) find that the GATT/WTO has served to reduce volatility in trade policy and trade flows. In so doing, these institutions have increased long-term global trade levels (see also Ingram, Robinson and Busch 2005).

Empirical evidence also suggests that the weavers in the WTO's policy programme have done more good than harm. Opportunities to temporarily suspend or circumvent trade-liberalizing provisions increase states' readiness to both conclude trade agreements in the framework of the WTO and make deeper concessions when doing so. States able to take advantage of these flexibility provisions are significantly more likely to agree to more ambitious tariff reduction commitments and to implement lower applied tariffs as well (Kucik and Reinhardt 2008; see also Rosendorf and Milner 2001: 832). Even though the GATT and WTO have escape clauses for countries to temporarily suspend trade rules when an economic crisis hits, scholars have shown that the institutionalized context of the GATT/WTO prevents abuse of those escape clauses (Pelc 2009). Analysing among others the economic crisis of the late 2000s, Davis and Pelc (2017) show that the WTO has promoted a strong norm: when all member states face hard times (e.g. a global economic crisis), they exercise self-restraint in using escape clauses 'to avoid beggar-thy-neighbor policies' (Davis and Pelc 2017: abstract). At the same time, the United States has more recently evoked security exemptions under WTO law to justify all sorts of trade restrictions, even if the rest of the membership did not necessarily agreed on what 'essential security interests' means within the WTO context.

Despite the success of the GATT and the initial decade of the WTO, there are, however, points of friction within the WTO which compromise its effectiveness. Intergovernmental negotiations over new norms and rules in the various negotiating rounds have become gridlocked. This is evidenced by the negotiations in the Doha Round, which ultimately fell into desuetude in the mid-2000s. Restrictions to market access are still a main impediment to trade in agriculture, and there is still a shortage of multilateral rules on trade in services. The industrialized states frequently insist on trade liberalization while protecting or subsidizing sectors of their own economies in which developing countries have a comparative advantage, as in the agricultural and textile sectors. Moreover, the economic rise and growing political assertiveness of states such as Brazil, China and India (besides the traditional trading powers, the EU, the United States and Japan) has hardly facilitated progress on further trade liberalization. Since the failed Doha Round, the bilateral conflicts between the United States and China have become more prominent with disagreements over state-owned enterprises and subsidies as well as the development status of China within the WTO.

Indeed, as a result of the stalled Doha Round in the WTO, states are moving away from the negotiation of multilateral trade agreements in favour of comprehensive bilateral trade agreements. The EU has been at the forefront of negotiating bilateral free trade agreements with countries such as South Korea, Canada, Japan and New Zealand as well as a range of neighbouring countries. It has started negotiations with Australia, India and Indonesia and is modernizing a series of existing agreements. Perhaps most relevant of all, the EU and the United States started negotiations, in 2013, on a Transatlantic Trade and Investment Partnership (TTIP), thereby signalling that the Doha Round had failed. At the same time, the negotiations on TTIP themselves also failed. The EU did conclude a free trade agreement with MERCOSUR, but this agreement has not entered into force due to political opposition from countries such as France. The United States has similarly tried to negotiate bilateral free trade agreements but with little success. President Trump, for instance, withdrew the US signature from the not-yet-ratified Trans-Pacific Partnership (TPP), a major trade deal between the United States and various Pacific countries, such as Australia, Canada, Chile, Japan, Singapore and Vietnam. While we have thus seen a move towards new bilateral free trade agreements, rather than further WTO negotiations, the record of bilateral free trade negotiations is mixed. The EU has been much more successful than the United States in this respect, even if some major EU free trade agreements are stalled.

The deficit in policy programme development of the WTO, which has not significantly advanced since the Doha Round, could long be contrasted with a high degree of effectiveness in the adjudication of trade disputes (Davey 2014). States demonstrably act more in accordance with the judicialized WTO dispute settlement *procedures* than with the previous diplomatic GATT procedures: in the case of trade disputes states tend to follow, rather than avoid, manipulate or openly disregard WTO dispute settlement procedures (Zangl 2008; see also Jackson 1999). The dispute settlement system has also improved compliance with the substantive outcomes, that is, the *decisions* of the DSB (Iida 2004; Leitner and Lester 2005). The effectiveness of the WTO in these operational activities, however, also did not last. Particularly the Appellate Body has been criticized for judicial overreach in the context of adverse trading relations between China and the United States. This started already with the Obama administration in the United States (2009–17), which began to scrutinize and block the appointment of individual judges. Under the first Trump administration (2017–21), however, the United States began to block the appointments of all the judges, which eventually resulted, in 2019, in the Appellate Body no longer being able to function. With the second Trump administration, the Appellate Body remains defunct and the WTO as a whole stands by as several of the major trading blocs return to mercantilist trading policies and tariff wars.

While we measure effectiveness of international organizations ultimately against the goals in the policy programmes of those organizations (see Chapter 7), it is also important to mention that those goals were set by the Western and richer countries that founded the GATT and WTO. Much of the criticism in the Global South towards the WTO, in this respect, stems from the fact that the organization has been institutionalizing the Western free trade paradigm, thereby paying insufficient attention to the economic needs of the rest of the world. Chimni (2006), for instance, states that the WTO 'has emerged as a key institution to sustain the global capitalist order to the advantage of an emerging transnational capitalist class (TCC) whose interests are articulated by powerful states' (p. 5) and makes a case for more attention to democracy and development within the WTO. Equally, scholars highlight hierarchies between states when it comes to WTO negotiations even if all members formally have an equal say (e.g. Kwa 2003; Geck 2024). Such perspectives on the WTO fit well with the critical theories identified in Chapter 2. The question here is not so much how to problem-solve trade dilemmas through international organizations but rather whether the preference for free trade and the goals set for the WTO are just in the first place.

Disparities in development

International organizations in the field of trade, such as the WTO, facilitate mutually beneficial solutions of the economic dilemma: to avoid countries engaging in mercantilism at the expense of overall growth. However, simultaneously, they may give rise to or exacerbate disparities in development as critical theories have also highlighted (see Chapter 2). Since the end of the Second World War and, particularly, following the period of decolonialization from the mid-1940s until the 1970s, we therefore see an increased emphasis on policy programmes and operational activities to rectify trading inequalities, to continue relations with former colonies and assist newly established states in their economic development. These days development cooperation includes a wide range of assistance ranging from food security to pandemic prevention, climate mitigation and security projects. Such development cooperation is frequently channelled through international organizations. The programmes and operational activities of the relevant organizations are often criticized by critical scholars and observers as forms of neocolonialism (e.g. Escobar 1995). The argument is that the various international organizations in the area of development cooperation keep historical legacies in place rather than fostering genuinely mutual cooperation between states on the basis of sovereign equality. In this section, we do not take sides in this debate but rather want to shed light on what international organizations do in the field of development. We focus on development assistance and loans by the World Bank Group, which is a premier international organization in the area of development.

Policy programme of the World Bank Group

The policy programme of the World Bank Group is mainly redistributive, which sets it apart from the regulatory programmes of the international organizations discussed so far. It is the mandate of the World Bank Group to support the development of its less developed member states in 'the South' and, also, following the end of the Cold War, the countries in transition in 'the East'. Its main task is to provide these countries with loans, some at the usual market rates and some under preferential conditions, grants as well as offering technical assistance. The loans, grants and technical assistance are allocated for specific projects for which private finance is not available or which could not be implemented independently without technical assistance from outside (Gilbert and Vines 2000; Marshall 2008). The World Bank Group consists of the International Bank for Reconstruction and Development (IBRD), which was already conceived at Bretton Woods in 1944. The World Bank's affiliate organizations, the International Finance Corporation (IFC), the International Development Association (IDA) and the Multilateral Investment Guarantee Agency (MIGA) were established in 1956, 1960 and 1988, respectively. Although the IBRD, IDA, IFC and MIGA are formally independent organizations with different sources of finance and loan conditions they are de facto so much intertwined organizationally that they can be seen as a single organization, the World Bank Group.

Originally the World Bank concentrated almost exclusively on rebuilding the war-ravaged areas of Europe. This changed following the process of decolonization in the 1960s and 1970s. The growing number of developing countries turned developmental disparities into a problem for developed countries; in particular their greater voting power in the UN compelled the developed countries to take into account the developing countries' request for a more equitable distribution of welfare (Krasner 1985: 141–51). They had to react to protect the stability of the liberal world economic order against the challenge of a 'new international economic order' (NIEO) demanded not only by the 'Third World' but also by public opinion in their own societies. Developments in the international environment thus resulted in clear input for the World Bank and its member states. To prevent an NIEO the developed world accepted the expansion of the multilateral financing of development through, inter alia, the institutions of the World Bank Group (Marshall 2008).

The financial basis of the IBRD is its share capital subscribed by member states which the Bank uses to sell bonds on international financial markets. The subscriptions are based on a state's relative weight in the world economy, which also determines its voting share in the Board of Governors and the Board of Directors. However, the IBRD only has a small amount of this share capital directly at its disposal. In 2023, for instance, the IBRD had a total subscribed capital of US$318 billion, of which only US$22 billion was 'paid in capital' (7 per cent) and US$296 billion was 'callable capital' (93 per cent) (World Bank Group 2024), even if the policy is to have a 20–80 per cent ratio. The access to 'callable capital' makes the World Bank creditworthy on private capital markets and thus it can borrow to make capital available to its loan recipients.

The Board of Governors of the World Bank, on which member states are typically represented by their finance and development aid ministers or central bank governors, has raised the share capital of the World Bank step by step. The IBRD uses this capital to sell (top-rated) bonds on international financial markets which in turn finance lending to developing countries. Its capacity for making loans has broadened substantially, mainly by borrowing on the international capital markets and through repayments of earlier loans. Since 1964 net gains from financial transactions are no longer used to provide loans from the IBRD but are mostly passed to the IDA. IBRD loans are almost exclusively granted to states. Loans to private investors are exceptional and must be backed by a repayment guarantee from a sovereign government (of the investor or of the country where the investment is to take place). Loans are normally granted for several decades and at a more favourable rate of interest than commercial market rates.

IDA loans are 'soft loans'. They run for several decades and are de facto interest free with merely an administrative fee of 0.75 per cent. Repayments are made after a grace period of five to ten years. Because of these very favourable terms, only the poorer member states of the World Bank which lack the financial ability to borrow from IBRD can request these loans. In 2024, some seventy-five states had the right to such loans. Unlike the IBRD, which operates almost like a conventional bank, the IDA is more of a fund administration. To be able to provide such favourable loan conditions it requires regular restocking of its financial means and relies on repayments of IDA loans from recipient countries and interest-free contributions from member states, as well as allocation of IBRD resources. The financially strong members of the World Bank Group meet every three years to determine the extent of replenishment. The financial sources of the IFC are practically identical to those of the IBRD but states must pay their contributions to the share capital in full. Just as with the IBRD, the IFC's share capital has been raised repeatedly by decisions of the Board of Governors. Repayable external means are only sought from the IBRD and not on the private capital markets. The decisive difference between this organization and the IBRD and the IDA lies in the fact that loans can be allocated to private investors in developing countries without a sovereign government's repayment guarantee. Furthermore, the IFC can become an equity partner in a business for a limited period.

The MIGA aims at promoting foreign direct investment in developing countries through investor insurances. The MIGA insures investors against political risks such as currency transfer restrictions, expropriation, internal violent conflict or breach of investment contracts by governments. Corporations or financial institutions are eligible for coverage if they are either incorporated in, or have their principal place of business in, a member country. The MIGA prices its guarantee premiums based on a calculation of both country and project risk. Since its inception, MIGA has issued hundreds of guarantees for projects in more than 100 developing countries. The MIGA also advises governments on attracting investment and mediates disputes between investors and governments.

Operations of the World Bank Group

Since redistributive programmes like those of the World Bank Group are particularly difficult to implement, its operational activities are of considerable significance. These programmes, within which resources are transferred to specific projects, require specification, formulated in two stages. In the first stage, the Group presents a global development strategy, giving first clues to the nature of the project or the countries deemed worthy of support. In the second stage, countries make proposals and the World Bank Group negotiates with recipient countries specific development projects.

Formally, it is the responsibility of the Board of Directors of the Bank to determine the basic features of project financing. The Board consists of twenty-five Executive Directors and 25 Alternate Executive Directors representing the member states. In reality, the president and the bureaucratic apparatus determine the development strategy and the guidelines for the allocation of loans, though, of course, they cannot ignore donor states' interests in loan allocations. On the whole, the Board of Directors merely approves or rejects the development strategies and guidelines worked out by the bureaucratic apparatus. Thus, while both NGOs and large donor states are trying to influence decisions and Bank staff is building coalitions with these actors, the World Bank Group, through its president and administration, is still enjoying a relatively high degree of autonomy in designing development projects (Woods 2000: 137–47).

The development strategy, as specified by the World Bank Group, has gone through different phases. The changes from phase to phase mainly reflect new research findings, some by the Group itself, as well as a reaction to the dynamics of the world economy (Kanbur and Vines 2000). In the first phase of 'modernization without worry' (Tetzlaff 1996: 73), it mainly supported large infrastructure projects in transport, energy, telecommunications and the like. The development strategy of the 1970s saw a significant shift in emphasis. Robert McNamara, as president (1968–81), promoted financing of projects of various sizes in agriculture and rural development. The new key concepts were basic needs orientation, investment in the poor and redistribution with growth. The sobering effect of the growing debt crisis of many developing countries from the start of the 1980s, and the change in paradigm to a neoliberal monetary economic policy in the United States and the United Kingdom (Higgott 2001), forced the World Bank Group to respecify its programme for the gradual removal of developmental disparities. In this third phase, in conjunction with the IMF, the strategy of structural adjustment was developed. With the help of Structural Adjustment Programmes (SAPs) the creditworthiness of developing countries was to be re-established as quickly as possible in order to focus once again on the fight against poverty. The Group and the IMF linked the allocation of loans initially to macroeconomic conditions and later even to political conditions (Barnett and Finnemore 2004). The application of neoclassical economics to the area of development assistance led to a ten-point catalogue of measures which the Group and the IMF made the benchmark for their policies in relation to countries receiving loans (known informally as the 'Washington Consensus', see Box 9.1; Higgott 2001; Williamson 1990).

BOX 9.1 THE TEN-POINT CATALOGUE OF THE WASHINGTON CONSENSUS

1. fiscal discipline
2. redirection of public expenditures (from subsidies to investment in education and infrastructure)
3. tax reform (combining a broad tax base with moderate marginal tax rates)
4. liberalization of interest rates (market-determined interest rates)
5. competitive exchange rates
6. trade liberalization
7. liberalization of inward foreign direct investment
8. privatization (of state enterprises)
9. deregulation (of business activities)
10. guarantee of effective property rights

In early 1999, the then president, James D. Wolfensohn, submitted a plan for a new, fourth development strategy, that of a Comprehensive Development Framework (CDF) which, in many points, is also reflected in the UN Millennium Development Goals. For the first time, the Group set itself concrete targets. Thus, in conjunction with the Organisation for Economic Co-operation and Development (OECD), the IMF and the UN, six key targets were to be met by 2015. Among these were halving the number of people living in absolute poverty, the reduction of child mortality by two-thirds and the achievement of primary education for all. In 2013, the Board of Governors of the World Bank Group adopted a new strategy that focused on ending extreme poverty and promoting shared prosperity in correspondence with Sustainable Development Goals (SDGs) 1 and 10 agreed in the framework of the UN. As such the World Bank Group makes a concrete contribution to the global development agenda. At the same time, with only the two key targets, the World Bank Group's development strategy is much more focused than the overall SDGs agenda of the UN. While not formal targets, the World Bank Group furthermore stresses the need for sustainable development that will secure 'the future of the planet and its resources, promote social inclusion, and limit the economic burdens that future generations inherit' (World Bank Group 2014: 1).

For individual countries, the World Bank Group has developed the 'Country Engagement Model'. This is a four- to six-year cycle of four steps. It starts with a Systematic Country Diagnostic which is a research report that sets out key development challenges and priorities. It is followed by a Country Partnership Framework which details the World Bank's involvement in around twenty-five pages. This document considers the country context, the country's development strategy and is based on extensive consultations with the local government, other international organizations and stakeholders. The next step is a Performance and Learning Review, which is done at mid-term, to inform the World Bank Board about possible adjustments and developments. The cycle is then concluded with the Completion and Learning Report, which evaluates the country engagement. Through this framework, the World Bank Group also considers its loans and projects. At the level of individual projects, there is also a cycle starting with the identification and preparation of projects, followed by negotiations and decision-making in the World Bank Board, implementation and evaluation.

Evaluation of the organization's effectiveness

An assessment of the World Bank's effectiveness can be made at several levels. In general, there can be little doubt that the World Bank Group is relatively effective in achieving the transfer of sizeable resources to developing countries through projects (Einhorn 2001). However, the real question is whether World Bank grants and loans contribute to improving the socio-economic conditions of living in developing countries. Thus, a

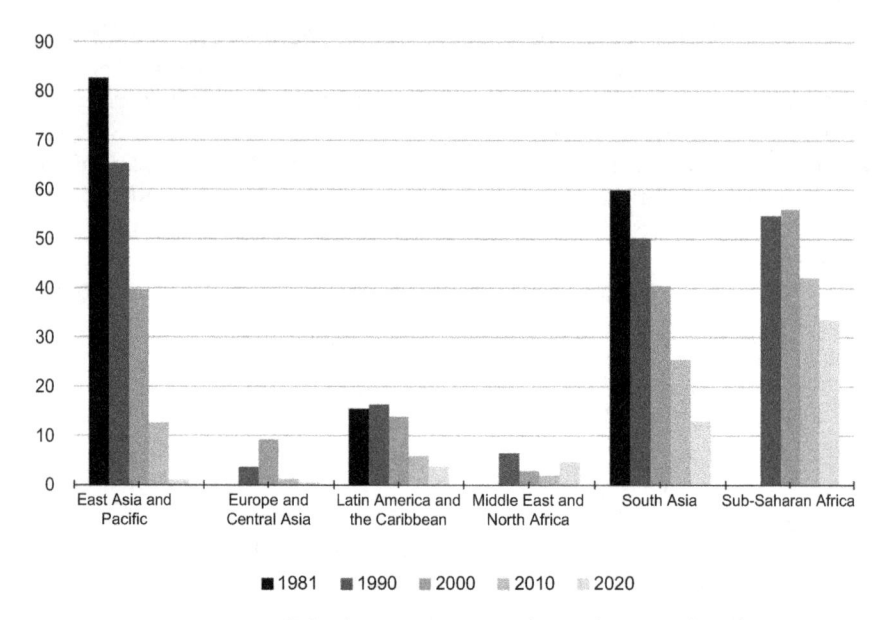

FIGURE 9.2 *Decrease of absolute poverty: population living on less than US$2.15 per day, 1981–2022 (%). Sources: Based on data from the World Bank.*

look at global trends in the prevalence of absolute poverty provides a first, albeit very broad, clue as to whether the World Bank's activities have had a positive impact (see Figure 9.2). Within the period from 1981 to 2022 the share of people living in absolute poverty (i.e. on less than US$2.15 a day) has decreased on the global scale. However, a closer examination of regional trends casts some doubts on the proposition that the World Bank has played a major role in this positive development. The largest decrease of poverty has occurred in Eastern Asia, first of all in China, where World Bank lending has been limited. On the other hand, in Latin America and especially in sub-Saharan Africa, where the World Bank has been much more involved in funding development projects, the reduction of absolute poverty is much smaller – though by no means negligible (see Figure 9.2). Whereas these broad macro indicators certainly do not prove the uselessness of World Bank development assistance, they do suggest that the World Bank's impact is limited: large-scale multilateral lending seems to be neither a necessary nor a sufficient condition for lifting countries and people out of poverty.

On a somewhat more specific level, scholars have investigated whether World Bank lending promotes (sustainable) economic growth in developing countries. A recent extensive review of the academic literature shows that development assistance has a positive but small effect on economic development at best (Dreher, Lang and Reinsberg 2024), though some studies remain inconclusive. In contrast, development assistance has been effective in achieving many of the other objectives of aid donors. Assistance, for instance, can mitigate conflict or reduce migration flows (ibid.). Apart from these somewhat disappointing results concerning the impact of World Bank programmes on growth and poverty alleviation, the World Bank's effectiveness in addressing global disparities in development is hampered by the prevalence of organized hypocrisy in and around the Bank (Weaver 2008). The World Bank faces ever-increasing and at least in part conflicting demands from donor countries, recipients, NGOs and private investors, which are very hard to satisfy at the same time, especially in an organization with an entrenched bureaucratic culture that makes fundamental reform difficult.

Much of recent scholarship on the effectiveness of the World Bank focuses on the individual projects of the Bank in various countries (Kilby 2000). The Independent Evaluation Group, which is a research unit within the World Bank, evaluates individual projects at the end of the project based on a predefined set of criteria and makes such data publicly available. Scholars have used these data on more than 10,000 projects to study with quantitative methods which factors explain effectiveness (e.g. Denizer, Kaufman and Kraay 2013; Girod and Tobin 2016; Heinzel 2022). They find that the effectiveness of World Bank projects varies not only across countries (with projects in country A being more effective than in country B) but also within countries. Relevant variables are, in this respect, not only project specifics such as project size and duration but also project supervision and the autonomy and involvement of the relevant World Bank officials (Honig 2019; Heinzel, Cormier and Reinsberg 2023). Such project-level evidence is excellent for international organizations such as the World Bank to improve their performance, but it also shows that it is difficult to make more generalized statements about the effectiveness of the World Bank as a whole.

Global financial relations

The limitation of convertibility and the devaluation of currencies are instruments that states can use to achieve similar effects to the setting of tariffs. If several states make use of these options for their own short-term gain, international exchange relations suffer lasting damage, to the detriment of all in the long term. In the long term all states are worse off, both collectively and individually, if they do not cooperate to eliminate such financial practices. The IMF serves as an example of how international organizations can contribute to international cooperation in finance. The IMF has, furthermore, become the lender of last resort for heavily indebted countries, which is currently its core business. As such, it is a crisis manager that can safeguard global financial stability and prevent that economic and financial crises spill across borders.

Policy programme of the IMF

After the Second World War, the IMF's policy programme (see Chapter 3) created a limited liberal financial order corresponding to the world trade order of the time. The 1944 intergovernmental negotiating process at Bretton Woods, which also set up the World Bank, established norms and rules for the IMF which were intended to strengthen the envisaged liberal trade relations eventually agreed under GATT (1947) while simultaneously leaving states some leeway for national economic steering and welfare state policies (Gilpin 2000: 57–68; Helleiner 1994: 25–72). The norms and rules obliging states to establish the free convertibility of their currencies were particularly aimed at promoting liberal trade relations. The logic was that the smooth payment transactions necessary for international trade can only take place if the free exchange of one currency for another is guaranteed (in the absence of a world currency).

Furthermore, the original norms and rules of the IMF committed the member states to fixed, but adaptable, exchange rates for their currencies (Kahler 1995: 48–64; Spero and Hart 2003). This solution tried to combine the advantages of a system of fixed exchange rates with those of flexible rates without burdening member states with the disadvantages of either. In the case of both fixed and flexible exchange rates, supply and demand on international financial markets determine the value of a currency because of its free convertibility. However, while with flexible exchange rates demand and supply are not influenced by states (allowing for relatively free fluctuation), in the case of fixed exchange rates national central banks influence supply and demand on international financial markets so that the exchange rate remains stable at the agreed level. This means that international business can take place without the constant fear of fluctuations in the currencies in which the value of services or goods is calculated. However, in order to keep the value of their currencies constant, states must orientate their entire economic and financial policy towards maintenance of international equilibrium. Unlike in the case of flexible exchange rates, they largely lose the scope for using domestic measures in areas which affect competitiveness, like social and environmental policies.

Within the IMF's system of fixed but adaptable exchange rates all currencies were linked to the US dollar acting as a currency anchor. The dollar was itself protected through its gold parity of US$35 to one ounce of gold (the 'gold standard'). However, the various currencies were allowed to deviate from the rate fixed in relation to the US dollar by up to 1 per cent up or down, which means that in relation to other currencies there could be deviations of up to 2 per cent. Furthermore, it was possible to adapt the exchange rate of a national currency in cases of severe balance-of-payments imbalances, which continuously threatened the agreed fixed exchange rates. This possibility gave states the leeway to take, for instance, social policy measures or measures of economic steering that otherwise would have accentuated balance-of-payments imbalances (Helleiner 1994: 25–50; Spero and Hart 2003).

To enhance the domestic leeway for economic steering and social policy measures independently of potential exchange rate adaptations, each member state transferred currency reserves, called 'quotas', to the IMF which were then available as temporary foreign currency loans to be drawn on by individual states in times of balance-of-payments deficits. Such a fund was to enable states to finance interventions on financial markets in favour of their currencies. The amount of the loan, called 'drawing rights', was calculated in relation to the amount of currency reserves which the state concerned had put at the IMF's disposal. Thus states with high quotas disposed of a higher amount of credit than states with lower quotas. In case of balance-of-payments problems states were allowed to borrow up to 100 per cent of their quotas without having to fulfil certain conditions. If they wanted to borrow up to 125 per cent of their quotas certain conditions were set. This loan facility created a currency buffer which enabled states to maintain liberal trade relations despite a system of fixed exchange rates, even when they got into balance-of-payments difficulties (Gilpin 2000: 59–62; Helleiner 1994: 25–50).

In the spirit of a limited liberal financial order, the norms and rules of the IMF did not oblige member states to renounce controls over capital movements. States were able to use controls over capital movements to finance domestic measures through their taxation system or debt policy without fear of a flight of capital (Gilpin 2000: 139–40). In addition, it was hoped that a restricted movement of capital would strengthen the system of fixed exchange rates because it limited the possibility of speculative foreign exchange movements and the resulting attacks on one or the other currency (Helleiner 1994: 25–72; Pauly 1997: 79–97).

The Bretton Woods system embedded in the IMF became operative in the 1950s and 1960s but was only effective as long as the movement of capital could really be limited. Yet this became less and less feasible with the creation of the 'eurodollar markets' that arose in the late 1950s and early 1960s: British and US banks in London attempted to circumvent existing controls on the movement of capital for their international financial business. While British banks began to conduct their international financial affairs in US dollars, American banks transferred their international financial affairs to London. Since British controls on the movement of capital only applied to deals in pounds sterling and American controls applied only to deals in the United States, this created a financial centre in London allowing for a largely unregulated movement of capital (Eichengreen 1996: 93–152; Helleiner 1994: 81–122).

The rapidly growing Eurodollar market put pressure on the Bretton Woods system because the freer movement of capital enabled speculative attacks on individual currencies, making it more and more difficult to maintain the fixed exchange rate parities. The IMF's loans were insufficient to counter these attacks effectively, especially as speculation was directed at the dollar as well. The United States faced a dilemma and could do little about it. If it reduced its balance-of-payments deficits, which began to show up in the 1950s, international trade relations would have suffered lasting damage since international trade would have lost the liquidity the deficits provided. But by continuing its policy of balance-of-payments deficits the US dollar lost its gold standard parity credibility. It was impossible to maintain the dollar–gold parity in the long term since the policy resulted in a loss of gold reserves (Helleiner 1994: 81–122). To defuse this dilemma the IMF created Special Drawing Rights (SDRs) in 1969 as an additional means of payment which were to supply the liquidity necessary for international trade. But since this did not provide a way out of the dilemma the United States finally gave up gold parity with the dollar in 1971 and the fixed rates became untenable. After a futile attempt to revive the fixed rates in the Smithsonian Agreement of 1971, with revised exchange rates and revised fluctuation bands of up to 4.5 per cent, exchange rates were finally set free in 1973 (Gilpin 2000: 124–5; Spero and Hart 2003).

The passage from fixed to flexible exchange rates fundamentally altered the function of the IMF's loans allocation. In the 1970s, the IMF had become superfluous as a currency buffer and, since the 1980s, it has been operating as a lender of last resort in the framework of a liberal financial and currency order largely without controls on capital movements. Through its allocation of loans, the IMF is supposed to ensure that national or regional financial crises, such as those in Asia and Russia in 1997 or debt crises like the Mexican one of 1982 and the Brazilian one of 1987, do not spread or possibly threaten the entire global financial and currency system (Helleiner 1994: 169–91). Nevertheless, the IMF (with 191 member states in 2025) could not prevent the US financial (mortgage) crisis of 2007 from escalating to the most severe global financial and economic crisis after the Second World War.

In the case of debt and/or financial crises, the IMF's mandate is to help the states concerned, which would otherwise be unable to pay for imports or service their debts. However, recipients must agree to certain structural adaptations. These should ensure that the recipient will be able to service its debts. In other words, these loans come with conditions: the IMF requires the state concerned to alter its domestic and foreign economic policies if it wants to avail itself of the loan. To be able to respond to the demand for loans and fulfil its role as lender of last resort, the IMF has had to restock its quotas several times, with the latest increase in quotas being in 2023 when the Board of Governors decided to raise quotas to about US$960 billion.

Operations of the IMF

The granting of loans forms the major part of the IMF's operations. Specification of the norms and rules for the allocation of loans is of special significance. The IMF determines the size and conditions of the loan to be granted to a state with balance-of-payments problems. States can get loans to a maximum of 600 per cent of their quota and they need to submit a proposal to the IMF giving details of how they intend to solve their problems. A state can submit such a proposal in the form of a 'letter of intent' whose implementation should help to overcome its balance-of-payments problems and guarantee repayment of the loan to the IMF. The IMF lays down conditions for budgetary, financial, market and labour policies, often with far-reaching consequences for the society of the state requesting the loan (Barnett and Finnemore 2004; Martin 2006). The state's policies must be approved by the Executive Board of the IMF before the loan requested can be granted. The loan is usually released in instalments, with later instalments dependent upon the state adhering to its commitments (Driscoll 1998: 19–24).

The IMF disposes of a number of loan instruments, or 'facilities', tailored to different types of countries and the specific nature of the most common problems (see IMF n.d.), such as Stand-By Arrangements (SBA), the Extended Fund Facility (EFF), the Rapid Financing Instrument (RFI) and the Flexible Credit Line (FCL). Under the SBA the IMF gives loans to help states deal with short-term balance-of-payments problems. The loan will be paid in instalments over normally one to two years provided that the state keeps to its promised reforms. Repayments are expected within three to five years. The EFF is generally used for structural difficulties in the balance of payments, which is why instalments are phased over a period of three to four years with repayment within four to ten years. The RFI allows for outright purchase in case of urgent balance-of-payment problems, while the FCL is intended as an instrument for countries with strong economic fundamentals facing current balance-of-payment pressures. It is meant to serve crisis prevention and crisis mitigation purposes. The length of the FCL is one or two years and the repayment period the same as for the SBA.

In addition, low-income countries may borrow on concessional terms through a number of short-term and long-term facilities. In 1996, the IMF launched the Heavily Indebted Poor Countries (HIPC) initiative to provide rapid debt relief for such countries. In 1999, the HIPC initiative was modified to improve debt relief and to strengthen the links between debt relief, poverty reduction and social policies. The enhanced HIPC initiative foresaw macroeconomic adjustment and structural and social policy reforms including higher spending on basic health and education. In 2010, during the economic crisis, the IMF again reformed its system of support to low-income countries and established three new concessional facilities: the Extended Credit Facility (ECF), the Standby Credit Facility (SCF) and the Rapid Credit Facility (RCF). Financing under the ECF carries a zero interest rate, with a grace period of five and a half years and a final maturity of ten years. The SCF provides financial assistance to low-income countries with short-term balance-of-payments needs. It can be used in a wide range of circumstances, including on a precautionary basis. It comes with a zero interest rate, with a grace period of four years and a final maturity of eight years. The RCF provides rapid financial assistance with limited conditionality to low-income countries facing an urgent balance-of-payments shortfall. With a zero interest rate, it has a grace period of five and a half years and a final maturity of ten years.

The IMF's operational activities refer not only to the provision of loans but also to their financing. The main sources of finance are the quotas which member states pay on joining the organization, based broadly on each country's relative weight in the world economy. Up to a quarter is paid in a widely accepted foreign currency and three quarters in the state's own currency. This represents the maximum financial contribution which a state must put at the IMF's disposal. However, given constant change in the overall world economy and in that of individual states resulting in a growing need for loans, the quotas need to be regularly adapted to new circumstances. Accordingly, the Executive Board reviews the quotas at least every five years to recommend a possible increase, which requires the approval of at least 85 per cent of member states' votes in the Board of Governors. For example, in December 2023 the IMF's Board of Governors approved to conclude a review of quotas that foresees an increase in total quotas (up to more than US$960 billion) and a realignment of quota shares to better reflect the changing relative weights of the IMF's member states in the global economy. This subsequently needed to be approved by the member states in 2024.

The IMF not only approves loans but also actively implements the disbursement – and repayment – of loans. After agreeing to such a loan, the IMF disburses it itself by making available, to the state concerned, funds in widely accepted foreign currencies obtained from other states either as quotas or as a loan. The borrowing state 'purchases' these foreign currencies with its own currency. When repaying, the state in question will repurchase its own currency with the foreign currency. Loans are provided under an arrangement which stipulates in advance the performance criteria for success or failure of the recipient's agreed reform plan. This reduces the need to supervise how the plan is implemented and concentrates on verifying whether the agreed targets have been reached. Nevertheless, the IMF continues to rely heavily on conditionality (Kentikelenis, Stubbs and King 2016). If, in the light of these criteria, a reform plan is deemed not to have been implemented successfully, the IMF can withhold further instalments or tie their continuation to new reform efforts to be negotiated.

The IMF does not limit its monitoring to reform plans agreed as part of a loan but extends this to the entire economic, currency, financial and monetary policies of its member states. In essence, this is done through annual consultations with each member state, when four or five members of the IMF staff visit a country for about two weeks to collect and sift through data about growth, foreign trade, unemployment, inflation, interest rates, salaries, money supply, investments and public expenditure. Furthermore, they hold intensive discussions with government representatives to establish whether the economic policy being pursued is successful or whether, and if so how, it should be changed. Thereafter, the IMF representatives write a detailed report which is submitted to the Executive Board. Since 1997 these reports have been published along with the Executive Board's assessment. With this monitoring system the IMF aims at recognizing potential financial crises in advance and at being able to prevent them (Schirm 2007: 267–73). In the wake of the global economic crisis of 2007–8, the IMF has reasserted its roles not only as lender of last resort but also as monitoring guardian of global financial stability through strengthened surveillance of financial markets at the national, regional and global level.

Evaluation of the organization's effectiveness

The record of the IMF in contributing to a stable global financial and monetary order is mixed. It was unable to prevent the debt crises of developing countries in Latin America in the 1980s as well as the financial crises in Asia or Russia in the 1990s. Nonetheless, until the most recent economic crisis (the global financial and economic crisis 2008), it did manage to prevent national or regional financial crises from escalating into global ones. This crisis has unveiled the serious limits to the IMF's capacity in crisis prevention. In that sense, the IMF, just like many other national and international financial supervisors, has failed seriously. Serious deficiencies in the IMF's capacity to predict and prevent financial crises have even been pointed out by the Independent Evaluation Office (IEO) of the IMF. In the run-up to the recent crisis a high degree of organizational groupthink within the IMF's staff, intellectual capture by the transnational financial industry as well as supervisory authorities in the most advanced economies and inadequate analytical approaches undermined the IMF's ability to detect important risks and to alert the membership to these risks (IEO 2011: v). Moreover, the IMF's effectiveness in monitoring member states' financial policies and consulting with them is limited in that multilateral surveillance fails to be organized in a way that promotes institutional learning. Multilateral surveillance is further constrained by the fact that a greater delegation of authority by member states to the organization is missing (Lombardi and Woods 2008).

Paradoxically, the crisis in the late 2000s and early 2010s has reinvigorated the IMF, for its function as international public lender of last resort has been underlined in the rescue of Greece, Hungary, Iceland, Romania, Ukraine and other economies after a decade in which states had increasingly turned to private capital markets for borrowing (Moschella 2010: 148–51; Underhill, Blom and Mügge 2010: 4). However, the empirical record of IMF lending in terms of promoting financial stability and economic growth is subject to controversial scientific debate. A number of studies find no significant effect of IMF lending on economic growth, and some even argue that IMF programmes have had a negative effect on growth (Steinwand and Stone 2008: 124, 141–3; Vreeland 2007: 89–90). In fact, little is known with certainty about the effects of IMF lending on economic growth. However, it does seem that IMF programmes can indeed contribute to containing budget deficits, lowering inflation levels and improving the balance of payments in recipient states (Steinwand and Stone 2008: 141–3; Vreeland 2007: 89–90). At the same time, the academic literature points at the adverse effects of IMF programmes for inequality, healthcare, education, bureaucratic capacity and human rights (Abouharb and Cingranelli 2009; Reinsberg et al. 2019; Foster et al. 2019, 2020; Stubbs et al. 2020). The success of these kinds of financial stabilization policies can be undermined by the politicization of loan decisions and conditions along the economic and political interests of the most powerful shareholder states (as well as of IMF bureaucrats), which can be at odds with the objective of promoting country-level and, even more so, global systemic stability (Copelovitch 2010: 6; Momani 2004).

One further criticism directed at the IMF is that it has been preoccupied mainly with the developed countries' interest in financial stability while neglecting the specific interests of developing countries and countries in transition (Stiglitz 2002). Thus, it has not dealt with the crises of developing countries unless they threatened to unleash chain reactions liable to affect developed countries as well. The IMF has equally been criticized because loan conditions imposed on developing countries have made it more difficult for them to combat poverty effectively. The IMF has reacted to this criticism by altering its loans programmes in such a way as to focus more on the fight against poverty and to assist developing countries in escaping from the debt trap, though preliminary empirical evidence does not look too promising.

Conclusion

International organizations make a significant contribution to cooperation in the areas of trade, development and finance. Within the context of the WTO, the member states have established an ambitious regulatory policy programme on global trade, whereas the World Bank Group and IMF have become key institutions with regard to development and finance. These policy programmes have been complemented with extensive operational activities. The WTO has a dispute settlement mechanism, whereas the World Bank Group and the IMF focus on redistributive policies through their loans and funds. Through the operational activities, these international organizations operate quite autonomously from direct member state interference, though they are by no means devoid of deficiencies in effectiveness. At the same time, it is also clear that even in the area of economic cooperation, the member states still play a key role. It is the conflict between the member states that prevents progress in the WTO development round, while member states also remain at odds over the representation and distribution of votes at the World Bank and IMF.

When thinking about international organizations as political systems, it is worth pointing out some of the key developments in the international environment that led to further cooperation. For the WTO, the stalemates of the 1970s and 1980s and the increasing prominence of non-tariff barriers made member states reconsider their inputs. The emergence of new 'problems' (from intellectual property rights to new communication and digital technology) also resulted in further input for cooperation. In terms of the conversion process, the GATT/WTO has seen repeated negotiation rounds. Despite the member states' dominance in these conferences, it also needs to be said that these were not one-off ad hoc events. High-level negotiations also took place in an institutionalized context. When focusing on the operational activities, we see the prominence of the plenary organs and executive councils as well as delegated decision-making. The plenary organs and executive councils in the WTO have been critical in terms of specifying the norms and rules. Through delegated decision-making, the WTO members settle their trade disputes through the DSU, though this has been compromised by the inoperability of the WTO Appellate Body since 2019. As a result of these policy programmes and operational activities (output), we have seen a significant reduction in trade barriers (outcome) and a subsequent increase in trade (impact). This has been quite an achievement for the WTO even if the WTO has been less successful in liberalizing trade beyond goods.

This chapter has also identified a need to address economic disparities between richer and poorer countries. As a result of trade liberalization, inequalities can increase, which poses a development dilemma. While there are many international organizations dealing with development, this chapter has focused on the World Bank Group. It has not only highlighted the different policy programmes available but also stressed how the World Bank Group has (slowly) addressed its objectives over time as a result of negative feedback from previous outcomes. For instance, the World Bank Group now pays central attention to human development, including eradicating poverty, rather than the macro-level development of countries. Furthermore, the World Bank Group now prioritizes sustainable development, which does not come at the expense of the environment, rather than economic development per se.

The political system perspective of this book is also helpful in understanding how policy is made in the area of finance and monetary affairs. Once it appears that a country can no longer pay its bills, it can request support from the IMF (input). Further input comes from borrowing countries and the IMF staff, which assesses the situation and makes recommendations. The next step is political decision-making by the IMF executive directors (conversion) resulting in programme and operational decisions concerning the loans supplied to the indebted country and the conditions attached (output). The outcome will be the loan given to the country, whereas the impact of such a loan may be that the economic situation in the country stabilizes and that the country can ultimately return to the capital markets on its own.

Discussion questions

1. What are the main obstacles for the further formulation and specification of trade policy programmes within the WTO?
2. To what extent have World Bank's objectives changed over time and why?
3. What are the advantages and disadvantages of IMF conditionality?

Further reading

Matsushita, Mitsuo, Thomas J. Schoenbaum, Petros C. Mavroidis and Michael Hahn (2015). *The World Trade Organization: Law, Practice, and Policy*, 3rd edn, Oxford: Oxford University Press.

Momani, Bessma and Mark Hibben, eds (2024). *Oxford Handbook of the International Monetary Fund*, Oxford: Oxford University Press.

Weaver, Catherine (2008). *Hypocrisy Trap. The World Bank and the Poverty of Reform*, Ithaca, NY: Cornell University Press.

10

Climate and the environment

When it comes to climate change and environmental protection, states face similar dilemmas to those in security and the economy. While states may protect the environment within their own territories, for instance, by designating national parks or fining polluters (Hardin 1968), they may be less concerned about environmental protection beyond their borders. The trouble is that many environmental problems have a cross-border or even global dimension. The effects of river pollution – whether in the Nile or the Rhine – will be felt downstream. Increased greenhouse gas emission in one state may result in further global warming. In an anarchical international system, this may lead to a situation where states have an incentive to free ride on the efforts of other states. After all, if other states already reduce greenhouse gases, why bother to join them? If, however, all follow this strategy of free riding, not a single state would benefit and the environmental situation would worsen for all. Thus, the environmental dilemma describes a social trap in which behaviour aimed at gains for individual states places both the community of states collectively and also each state individually in a worse situation than would have been the case with effective international cooperation.

As with security policy and economic relations, international organizations offer states the opportunity to mitigate this environmental dilemma and achieve international cooperation (Ostrom 1990; Dietz, Ostrom and Stern 2003). Through international organizations, states can make binding agreements. International organizations can furthermore help to specify and monitor those agreements as well as adjudicate in disputes. Also, given the (scientific) complexity of many environmental problems, such as climate change or the biodiversity crisis, international organizations can play a key role in providing states with reliable information based on expert assessment. Unsurprisingly, a whole range of international organizations and regimes have been established, particularly since the 1970s, to address problems in the area of environmental protection. In this chapter, we analyse in detail the protection of the stratospheric ozone layer and the approach to climate change as examples to evaluate the activities of the United Nations (UN) – including the UN Environment Programme (UNEP) and the World Meteorological Organization (WMO) – in the environmental field.

Protection of the ozone layer

In 1974 two American scientists, Mario Molina and Sherwood Rowland, first drew attention to the depletion of the stratospheric ozone layer as a potential consequence of the emission of chlorofluorocarbons (CFCs). A lively scientific discussion followed about the validity of this observation, which had a lasting influence on policy programmes for the protection of the stratospheric ozone layer (Chasek, Downie and Brown 2010: Chapter 4; Haas 1992b; Wettestad 2002: 155). These scientific findings provided input for the international community, and international organizations such as UNEP (founded in 1972), to address this problem. Once all the member states were convinced about the scientific evidence, and the United States insisted on cooperation, the international community adopted policy programmes and operational activities. The outcome of these policy programmes and operational activities was a phasing out of CFCs, which ultimately had a positive impact on the ozone layer. Even though the relevant Montreal Protocol (1987) was agreed decades ago, it is still a good example of how the political system of international organizations works in practice. Moreover, it shows how international organizations can be effective in addressing international environmental problems.

Policy programme of UNEP

Based on input from scientists, UNEP, with the support of environmental non-governmental organizations (NGOs), pushed for a programme for the protection of the ozone layer (Andersen and Sharma 2002; Breitmeier 1996: 108–24). It did this initially by convening and preparing international conferences, in which state representatives were for the first time able to discuss the risks of the then-only-assumed depletion of the ozone layer and consider possible action. The international conference in Washington, DC of 1977 issued the World Plan of Action for the Ozone Layer, requesting an international agreement for the protection of the stratospheric ozone layer (Wettestad 1999: 125–6). However, it was not until 1982 that concrete steps were taken, pushed globally by environmental groups. The UNEP Governing Council set up an ad hoc working party charged with drafting a framework convention for the protection of the ozone layer (Andersen and Sharma 2002; Parson 2003).

The working party, consisting of government experts from twenty-two countries, met seven times up to 1985 in order to work out a draft convention. In lengthy intergovernmental negotiations the United States,

Canada and the Scandinavian countries – the Toronto Group – demanded the rapid phasing out of the use of CFCs. The European Economic Community (EEC) (which preceded the European Union, EU), with 45 per cent of the global production capacity of CFCs (ahead of the United States with 30 per cent), together with Japan and the Soviet Union, however, had different preferences. They were only prepared to accept freezing of production on the basis of existing capacity. They argued that the link between the use of CFCs and the depletion of the ozone layer had not yet been definitely proven (Breitmeier 1996: 108–16). In other words, the inputs from the different (groups of) states conflicted significantly. It made agreement on specific measures for the reduction in CFC production and consumption impossible at the time. The Vienna Convention for the Protection of the Ozone Layer was signed by twenty-two states on 22 March 1985, but it amounted to little more than a general statement. Furthermore, these states agreed to cooperate more closely in research and to exchange information (Parson 2003).

On the basis of new scientific information, and in particular the discovery of the hole in the ozone layer above the Antarctic (further input), the UNEP secretariat and the Toronto Group insisted on continuing negotiations for the internationally coordinated phasing out of CFC use (Canan and Reichman 2002; Haas 1992b: 189–213). In the search for a compromise, a negotiating marathon followed. However, the convergence of positions was a very slow process. The United States, the leader of the Toronto Group, was under pressure from the American public. Its initial demand was for a reduction of CFC production by 95 per cent. The EEC, on the other hand, was only prepared to accept a reduction of 20 per cent. Eventually, in 1987, the main negotiating parties agreed on the Montreal Protocol on Substances that Deplete the Ozone Layer – a regulative programme which foresaw a step-by-step phasing out aimed at reducing the global consumption of CFCs by 1999 to 50 per cent of the 1986 level (Andersen and Sharma 2002; Parson 2003).

The change in Europe's position on the Montreal Protocol of 1987 came about partly due to pressure exerted by Germany on its European partners for more far-reaching concessions. The main driving force, however, was the United States which had threatened to impose an import ban on products containing or produced with the use of CFCs. This threat clearly shows the importance of a state's (market) power in intergovernmental negotiations. Equally typical for intergovernmental negotiations, whose success depends on the consent of all (or most) negotiating parties, was the agreement of weaker states to the regulative programme following concessions granted by richer and more powerful countries. Developing countries, whose part in the worldwide consumption of CFCs amounted to 14 per cent, gained the concession of increasing their annual consumption of CFCs, independently of their then situation, to 300g per capita. In addition, they were promised technical aid to give them access to environmentally friendly alternatives and technologies (Andersen and Sharma 2002).

Yet the Montreal Protocol was only a beginning. Shortly after the signing of the original Montreal Protocol, scientific research not only proved clearly and beyond doubt the existence of a connection between CFC emissions and depletion of the ozone layer but also laid bare the insufficiency of the agreed limits to production and consumption (Canan and Reichman 2002). Based on such scientific input, in 1989 stricter measures were negotiated in Helsinki, as demanded by environmental protection groups and the expert community of atmospheric scientists. The EU, previously a reluctant participant in the negotiations, now became a driving force for a more rapid phasing out of the production and consumption of CFCs. In a non-binding declaration with eighty-one other states, it affirmed its readiness to accept a total ban on the production and consumption of CFCs by the year 2000. Furthermore, the developing countries were promised financial assistance in implementing the decisions (Breitmeier 1996: 127–9; Parson 2003).

At another conference in London (1990), the non-binding decisions reached in Helsinki were formalized by strengthening the Montreal Protocol through an amendment. The time allowed for the phase out was reduced so that it was envisaged that production and consumption of CFCs would cease completely by the year 2000. It was also agreed to set up the Multilateral Fund for the Implementation of the Montreal Protocol, aimed at subsidizing developing countries for the additional costs they were going to incur by complying with the ozone regulations. The Fund has since been replenished every three years since 1991, providing assistance of more than USD$6.2 billion to developing countries. The latest replenishment included a record of USD$965 million for three years (2024–6).

Interestingly, the London negotiations in 1990 were based on changing positions by the member states. The United States, which had previously welcomed the phasing out of production and consumption of CFCs, was now trying to slow things down, whereas the EU had joined the group of states that were pushing for a total end to production and consumption (Breitmeier 1996: 129–38). Nevertheless, it was possible to reduce the time allowed for compliance through negotiations leading to Protocol amendments at several subsequent conferences (Parson 2003; Wettestad 1999: 138–40). As efforts to end the production and use of CFCs proved very successful, the parties to the Montreal Protocol have started negotiations at their annual conferences to expand the ozone treaty into the much more contested area of climate change. For instance, during the summit in Kigali, Rwanda, in 2016, parties to the Montreal Protocol also agreed on phasing down hydrofluorocarbons (HFCs), emissions which have a significant impact on global warming. This broadening of the Montreal Protocol with the Kigali Amendment underlined the Protocol's success and its position in the broader climate regime (see below).

In global efforts to stop the depletion of the ozone layer, UNEP has offered a forum for intergovernmental negotiations and pushed the negotiating process along through the organization of conferences and the preparation of draft programmes (Wettestad 1999: 140–1). Like the many environmental groups and the expert community of atmospheric scientists that focused on the ozone problem, it acted as a catalyst for programme generation by putting the states permanently under pressure to act until they finally not only agreed on basic norms and rules to protect the ozone layer but subsequently continued to strengthen them (Andersen and Sharma 2002; Parson 2003). By 2009, all UN member states and the EU had ratified the Montreal Protocol, committing themselves to phase out provisions not only for CFCs but also for other ozone-depleting substances.

Operations of UNEP

The implementation of the policy programmes concerned with environmental pollution is generally in the hands of the states themselves (Breitmeier 1997; Chasek, Downie and Brown 2010). The competencies of international organizations in the implementation of the Vienna Convention of 1985, the Montreal Protocol of 1987 and the various revisions of the Montreal Protocol are limited to administering financial support for environmental protection efforts by developing countries and granting them technical assistance. Crucial support comes from the World Bank, UNEP, the UN Development Programme (UNDP) and the UN Industrial Development Organization (UNIDO), which serve as implementing agencies for programmes financed by the Multilateral Fund for the Implementation of the Montreal Protocol. The Multilateral Fund is managed by an Executive Committee, which comprises seven members from developed countries and seven members from developing countries and meets twice a year. The Executive Committee's main tasks include specifying criteria for project eligibility and monitoring their implementation, allocating resources among the four implementing agencies and approving country programmes and projects. In the fulfilment of these tasks the Executive Committee is assisted by the Fund Secretariat.

Additional operational activities, such as supervising compliance and sanctioning states for non-compliance, are not well defined. The only commitment imposed on states by the Montreal Protocol is the submission to the secretariat of an annual report on the production and consumption of CFCs. The secretariat then examines whether states have fulfilled their obligations (Bauer 2009; Greene 1998: 92–5; Victor 1998). The relatively high level of transparency inherent in the production and consumption of CFCs makes supervision of compliance by an international organization appear less urgent, since it is difficult for states clandestinely to withdraw from their agreed commitments. This holds all the more because of the existence, in most industrialized states, of environmental NGOs and green parties which keep a watchful eye on the implementation of international environmental agreements and are prepared to make public any breach of norms and rules (Greene 1998: 109–10). Domestic protest against such breaches can be seen as the functional equivalent of sanctioning by an international organization (Gemmill and Bamidele-Izu 2002; Zangl 1999: 98–9, 248–50).

A substantial part of the operational activities of international environmental organizations concerns information, expertise and scientific research. When analysing the policy programme on the protection of the ozone layer, much of the input came from scientific experts (see above). This was not a one-time input. It took time before states, including the EU, recognized the adverse effect of CFCs on the environment. So, it was about the repeated input of experts. The ozone layer regime is, in this respect, not exceptional. In many environment areas, international organizations rely heavily on such outside expertise. Moreover, importantly, they actively stimulate the acquisition of new information on policy problems as part of their operational activities. Both UNEP and the WMO made an important contribution to generating information about the depletion of the ozone layer and were especially successful in coordinating and disseminating international ozone research (Andersen and Sharma 2002; Canan and Reichman 2002). In particular, UNEP was instrumental in the formation of a transnational epistemic community of atmospheric scientists and, consequently, a scientific consensus on the ozone problem (Haas 1992b). The starting point was the creation in 1977 of the Coordinating Committee on the Ozone Layer (CCOL) following a meeting of experts in Washington, DC. The UNEP Governing Council had set up CCOL to promote scientific understanding of the ozone problem and to collect and publish scientific findings. The Committee, essentially composed of experts from state and non-state organizations dealing with the problem of ozone depletion, met eight times between 1977 and 1986. Its results were regularly published by UNEP in the *Ozone Layer Bulletin*.

Coordination of international ozone research by UNEP considerably hastened the establishment of a scientific consensus about the causes and effects of depletion of the ozone layer (Haas 1992b). UNEP, in collaboration with the WMO and a series of national research institutes, was able, during the 1990s, to publish a large number of important studies of the effects of greenhouse gases on the ozone layer and the world climate. To sum up the knowledge and state of the art concerning the ozone layer in 1985, UNEP and the WMO, jointly with other national and international environmental organizations, presented a three-volume stocktaking report, *Atmospheric Ozone*. This was seen at the time as the best and most comprehensive treatise on the state of the ozone layer (Canan and Reichman 2002).

These international information activities made it increasingly difficult for CFC-producing and hitherto hesitant states to justify their wait-and-see attitude towards ozone depletion, since there was no longer any uncertainty about the causal nexus between CFC emissions and depletion of the ozone layer (Canan and Reichman 2002). A final and decisive impetus for an international regulatory intervention in economic activities damaging the ozone layer came from a conference of experts in Würzburg, convened by UNEP in 1987. By comparing the research results of different scientists the last scientific doubts about the urgency of worldwide abandonment of CFC production and consumption were removed. Comparison of the scientific assumptions and models showed that even a reduction of CFC emissions by 50 per cent would only slow down, but not halt, the damage to the ozone layer. Furthermore, the experts were able to reach a consensus as to which individual substances in particular threatened the ozone layer. As a result of this activity, with the help of UNEP and the WMO, a transnational epistemic community of scientific experts was formed. The consensual knowledge of the experts put pressure on the state representatives to meet a few months later in Montreal (Andersen and Sharma 2002). This epistemic community definitively undermined the foundations of the argument to reject CFC reduction on the grounds of scientific uncertainty (Canan and Reichman 2002; Haas 1992b: 211–12).

Thanks to the continuing information activities of UNEP and the WMO, which acted as generators, disseminators and coordinators of epistemic knowledge, it soon became clear that the framework agreement reached in Montreal was insufficient. A report by the Ozone Trends Panel, a multinational group of researchers set up in 1986 by UNEP, the WMO and the US National Aeronautics and Space Administration (NASA) to examine and evaluate the many years of ozone measurement data, confirmed the causal nexus between CFC emissions and the depletion of the ozone layer. This report also showed the existence of a global depletion of the ozone layer in addition to the hole over the Antarctic. These new findings gave UNEP the scientific basis and the effective support of public opinion to move the states to adopt more far-reaching measures, culminating in a strengthening of the Montreal Protocol with the amendments noted above.

Evaluation of the organizations' effectiveness

The global ozone regime supported by UNEP, the WMO, a transnational expert community of atmospheric scientists and environmental NGOs is widely considered a success story and one of the most effective international environmental regimes (Greene 1998; Haas 1992c; Victor 1998; Wettestad 2002). In the late 1980s and early 1990s, global consumption and production of CFCs stopped expanding and began to decrease substantially (see Figure 10.1). By the mid-1990s, almost all developed countries had, by and large, phased out production and consumption of CFCs. Assisted by resources from the Montreal Protocol's Multilateral Fund, most developing countries devised programmes to do the same. This global decrease in the production and consumption of CFCs has continued to a point where production has virtually ceased and consumption has become marginal. Meanwhile, controls have been extended to hydrochlorofluorocarbons (HCFCs) and have proved successful in this area as well. Negotiations about

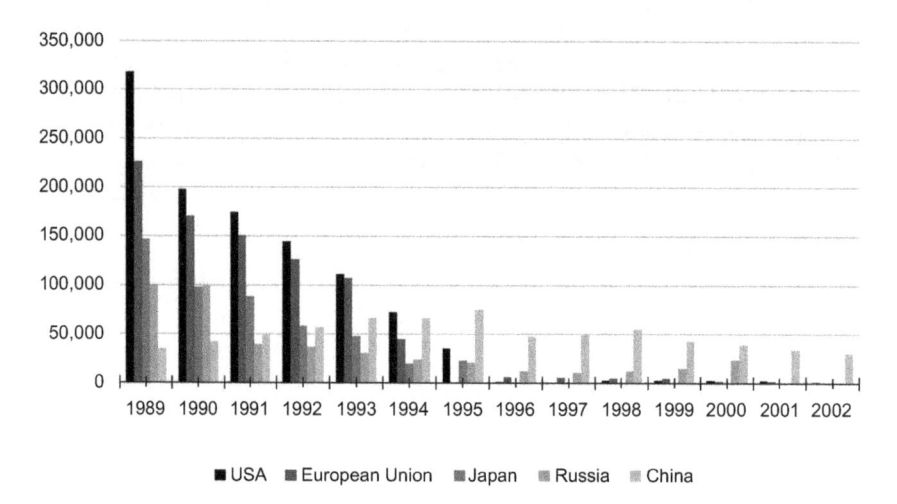

FIGURE 10.1 *Total chlorofluorocarbon (CFC) production major states, 1986–2003 (ODP tons). Note: ODP tons are metric tons of CFCs weighted by their Ozone Depletion Potential (ODP). Sources: Based on data from UNEP.*

the phasing out of hydrofluorocarbons (HFCs), which have even greater global warming potential than carbon dioxide, have also been successful, with the Rwanda summit in 2016 pointing to a further expansion of the ozone treaty into the issue area of climate change.

There is little doubt that the ozone regime as well as the collaboration of UNEP and the WMO with the transnational expert community have made these achievements possible (Greene 1998: 89–90). To be sure, the phasing out of the consumption of CFCs was relatively easy to achieve when compared to the reduction of greenhouse gas emissions (see below) because the gradual ban of CFCs 'only' affected particular, delimited industrial sectors, and alternative chemicals and technologies were available at a reasonable cost (Rittberger, Kruck and Romund 2010: 579). Nonetheless, it is fair to conclude that, without the presence of UNEP and the WMO and their cooperation with the transnational expert community:

> it is likely that there would have been less cooperation, that its form would have been less comprehensive (that is fewer pollutants covered and less sensitivity to related issues), that its enforcement would have been slower and less aggressive, and that the variation among national regulatory efforts would have been much broader. (Haas 1992c: 51)

Despite the success of UNEP and the WMO in establishing an international regime for the protection of the stratospheric ozone layer, this success story also points out that often (too) much time passes between the discovery of an environmental problem and the implementation of international measures to address it. In the ozone case, depletion of the ozone layer due to a delayed reaction to CFC emissions continued for decades; only recently this trend has reversed as the 'ozone hole' is becoming smaller (impact). In general, reaction time to environmental problems is too slow. This is at least in part related to prevalent intergovernmental decision-making procedures in programme generation and specification which slow down policy programme development and constrain the effectiveness of international environmental governance.

Climate change

For states, climate change poses a dilemma similar to the one encountered in combating ozone depletion. Although states share the ecological interest in reducing global greenhouse gas emissions in order to prevent or slow down climate change and particularly global warming, each state has an economic interest in not having to reduce household or industrial greenhouse gas emissions on its territory or at least to keep associated costs as low as possible. If all states therefore succumb to their short-term economic interest, they will forego their long-term ecological interest in slowing down or halting climate change, which has meanwhile progressed substantially (see Figure 10.2). Whereas the basic dilemmas are quite similar in both environmental issue areas, international organizations have not been nearly as successful in climate protection as they have been in dealing with the ozone problem. The scale of climate change is exponentially larger and

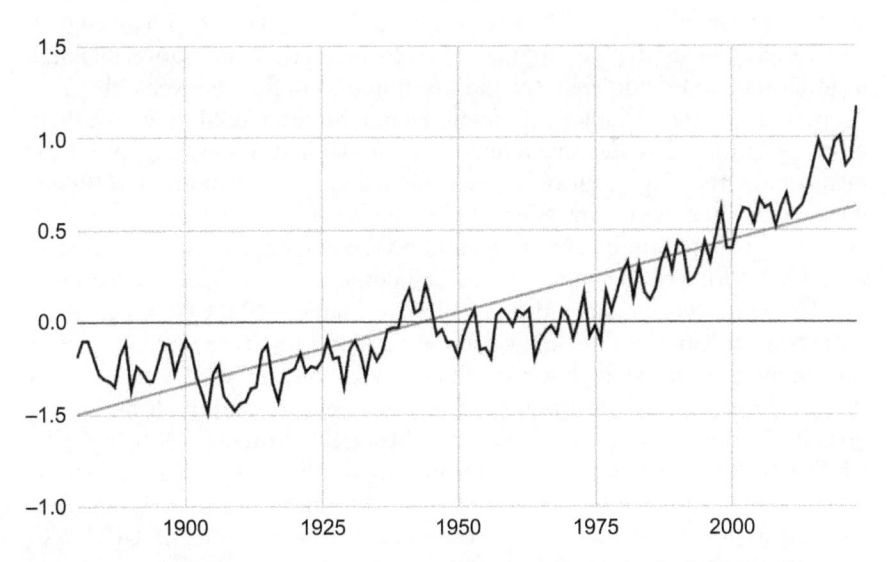

FIGURE 10.2 *Global rise of temperature, 1880–present (yearly deviation from the average temperature in the period 1951–80, °C)*. Source: Based on data from NASA's Goddard Institute for Space Studies (GISS).

the required energy transition cuts across all aspects of society. Addressing climate change requires clearly more than reducing specific emissions, such as CFCs, as in the case of the ozone layer.

Policy programme of the UN

The question of human-induced (anthropogenic) climate change was discussed by meteorologists as early as the 1960s and 1970s. At that time, the previously held belief that humankind could not endanger the global climate through environmental pollution, and in particular through carbon dioxide emissions, was challenged for the first time. Initially, both the scenario of the earth warming and that of its cooling seemed equally plausible. As the academic thesis of global warming through the greenhouse effect was gaining in strength, political efforts intensified to achieve a significant reduction in greenhouse gas emissions, particularly those of carbon dioxide. The intergovernmental negotiating process dealing with this issue was not only spurred by the advocacy activities of international NGOs, such as Greenpeace and the Worldwatch Institute, but was also influenced by international organizations, especially UNEP and the WMO (Chasek 2001: 124–33; Luterbacher and Sprinz 2001; Rowlands 1995: 65–98).

Impetus for international climate protection started to manifest itself in 1990 when the UN General Assembly set up an Intergovernmental Negotiating Committee (INC) which, supported by UNEP and the WMO, was given the task of presenting a plan for a framework convention on climate change in time for the 1992 Rio de Janeiro UN Conference on Environment and Development (the 'Earth Summit'). However, these intergovernmental negotiations were hindered by the continuing conflict between the EU, supported by the Alliance of Small Island States (AOSIS), which had more ambitious climate preferences, and the United States, supported by members of the Organization of Petroleum Exporting Countries (OPEC), which was more reluctant (Ott 1997: 205–8). Under the influence of a growing participation by environmental NGOs, a compromise was reached nevertheless for a framework convention in time for the 1992 Earth Summit. The UN Framework Convention on Climate Change (UNFCCC), signed by 150 states in Rio, does not oblige states explicitly to freeze or reduce their carbon dioxide emissions but commits them to 'the aim of returning . . . to their 1990 levels these anthropogenic emissions of carbon dioxide and other greenhouse gases not controlled by the Montreal Protocol' (Article 4 IIb, UNFCCC). In addition, the Convention provides for a regular reconvening of a Conference of the Parties (COP), with the aim of negotiating concrete agreements for the reduction of greenhouse gas emissions. The UNFCCC Climate Secretariat is tasked to support intergovernmental negotiations by organizing meetings and by analysing and reviewing climate change information and data reported by Parties (Wettestad 1999: 205–6).

During the COP in Kyoto (COP3) in 1997, the United States relaxed its resistance to EU demands for compulsory reductions in greenhouse gas emissions. In the Kyoto Protocol, the developed countries committed themselves to reductions in emissions of the six most important greenhouse gases by 2012 by an average of 5 per cent of their 1990 levels. The United States and the EU, as the two biggest polluters at that time, were supposed to reduce their emissions by 7 and 8 per cent, respectively (Aldy and Stavins 2007; Sprinz 1998; Wettestad 1999: 208–10). However, in order to enter into force, the Protocol needed to be ratified by developed nations accounting for at least 55 per cent of global greenhouse gas emissions. International climate policy was still a long way from a breakthrough, however, and subsequent negotiations were required before the Kyoto Protocol could come into effect. Importantly, the US Senate was unwilling to consent to the treaty after President Clinton had signed it. The Senate found it unacceptable that developing countries and emerging economies should initially be exempt from the obligation to reduce emissions. Thus, the Protocol came into force on 16 February 2005 without US participation (Aldy and Stavins 2007).

The Kyoto Protocol set targets for 2012, but since it took until 2005 to enter into force, the key question was not whether targets would be met but rather what successor agreement should be negotiated for after the commitment period. In other words, states were forced to start working on a successor agreement to the Kyoto Protocol. At the time of the Kyoto Protocol, the United States and the EU were by far the largest polluters. Therefore, they were the ones to make commitments in addressing climate change. Yet with the rise of China and the other emerging economies, it became quickly clear that those countries should be included in a successor agreement as well. For instance, as a result of economic growth, China overtook the EU in the early 2000s and the United States in the late 2000s in terms of its carbon dioxide emissions (Olivier, Janssens-Maenhout and Peters 2012: Figure 2.2). Making an agreement exclusively between the EU and the United States would therefore not make sense, because it would exclude the world's largest polluter.

Including China and the other emerging economies into a new agreement proved difficult. Even though China was now the largest polluter, its carbon footprint per capita was still much lower than those of the EU and the United States. It would therefore be difficult to insist that China and the other emerging countries would need to reduce their emissions at the same rate. The EU, which had been the self-declared leader of the climate change negotiations during the difficult time of President Bush's administration (2001–9), saw an opportunity to push for an ambitious legally binding new agreement at the Copenhagen summit (2009, COP15). The EU was, however, sidelined during the summit by the United States and China, which made a deal among themselves. It was now clear that the international community would not be able to produce a new agreement that would take effect after the expiration date of the Kyoto Protocol in 2012. It was indeed not until

2015, during the Paris summit (COP21), that states adopted the new Paris Agreement. The emphasis in this agreement is on Nationally Determined Contributions (NDCs) without an enforcement mechanism for states that fail to meet their targets. The Paris Agreement did give a significant boost to the Green Climate Fund (GCF), which helps developing countries in addressing climate change challenges.

The Paris Agreement itself is relatively concise with twenty-nine articles. While it is legally binding, it does not include many obligations for states. As it is not a treaty, it does not require ratification in the US Senate, which was a key lesson learned from the Kyoto Protocol. Yet this makes it also much easier for successive US presidents to withdraw from the agreement and to rejoin it again. In terms of its substance, the Paris Agreement notably states its objective of responding to climate change by '[h]olding the increase in the global average temperature to well below 2°C above pre-industrial levels and pursuing efforts to limit the temperature increase to 1.5°C above pre-industrial levels, recognizing that this would significantly reduce the risks and impacts of climate change' (Article 2(1)(a)). For this headline target superseding all the other ambitions of the Paris Agreement, it was agreed that '[e]ach Party shall prepare, communicate and maintain successive nationally determined contributions' (Article 4(2)). All these NDCs would be collected and monitored by the UNFCCC secretariat, and the COP meetings 'shall periodically take stock of the implementation of this Agreement' (Article 14).

Even though the Paris Agreement no longer solely includes commitments by Western states and Japan, as the Kyoto Protocol had done, the agreement continues to distinguish between the state parties. It notes that the agreement 'will be implemented to reflect equity and the principle of common but differentiated responsibilities and respective capabilities, in the light of different national circumstances' (Article 2(2)). In this respect, the Paris Agreement also stipulates that '[d]eveloped country Parties shall provide financial resources to assist developing country Parties with respect to both mitigation and adaptation' to climate change (Article 9). The Paris Agreement furthermore calls for technology transfer, capacity transfer and also highlights the Warsaw International Mechanism for Loss and Damage. The loss and damage mechanism refers to the principle that states adversely affected by climate change (e.g. small islands) should be compensated for costs incurred (e.g. moving parts of the population). The Paris Agreement entered into force on 4 November 2016.

In the years since the Paris Agreement, states have mostly worked on specifying the details and expanding the policy programme through the annual COP summits. A major returning point has been climate finance. Already before the Paris Agreement, states had agreed to an ambitious target of mobilizing US$100 billion a year by 2020, later extended to 2025, to address the needs of developing countries. According to the Organisation for Economic Co-operation and Development (OECD, n.d.), this target was reached in 2022 with US$50 billion coming from multilateral donors, US$41 billion via bilateral channels and another US$22 billion mobilized through the private sector. Another key issue was the adoption of a rulebook during COP24 in Katowice, Poland, on how countries can measure and report on their emissions. During COP26 in Glasgow, UK, states mentioned phasing out of coal power and subsidies for fossil fuels as relevant for the Paris Agreement. Furthermore, the COP27 in Sharm El Sheikh, Egypt, created a fund for loss and damage. While the subsequent COP meetings have therefore focused on developing the policy programme, they are also major climate events where tens of thousands of state delegates and non-state actors meet. Part of the purpose is thus also to sustain the climate action momentum, exchange information and strengthen the network and community of actors engaged in climate action.

Four days after the Paris Agreement entered into force in November 2016, Donald Trump was elected as US president which sent a shock through the climate community. Everyone expected President Trump to withdraw from the Paris Agreement, and he announced in June 2017 that he would do so. The Paris Agreement, however, stipulates that parties could only sent their notification of withdrawal three years after the agreement had entered into force (Article 28). The actual withdrawal would then still take one year. The United States could therefore only actually withdraw on 4 November 2020, which was the day after voters had elected Joe Biden as the next US president. President Biden then decided to rejoin the Paris Agreement on his first day in office in January 2021. Despite the legal details of the belated US withdrawal under Trump, this episode did set action against climate change seriously back. After all, it is the states themselves that need to deliver and the United States did little during the initial term of Trump. With President Trump announcing, on day one of his second term in January 2025, the US withdrawal from the Paris Agreement again, other states may also wonder whether they need to live up to their own commitments. This shows the cooperation dilemma involved in the area of environmental protection.

Operations of UNEP, the WMO and the Climate Secretariat

The UNFCCC, the Kyoto Protocol and the Paris Agreement assign a significant role to international organizations such as UNEP, the WMO or the UNFCCC Climate Secretariat for their implementation (Oberthür 2004; Yamin and Depledge 2004). As with the protection of the ozone layer, they are involved in the direct financing of environmental efforts by developing countries. Here, the Global Environmental Facility (GEF), established by the World Bank, UNEP and UNDP, enables developing countries to obtain financial assistance for the additional costs incurred in replacing old energy-sapping technologies that are harmful to the climate with modern energy-efficient ones. This is complemented by the GCF, which provides funding specifically for the area of climate change.

In the area of climate protection, international organizations also develop important operational activities. The UN Climate Secretariat, based in Bonn, for instance, maintains the registry for the NDCs established under the Paris Agreement. According to the Paris Agreement, countries make national commitments but should communicate these NDCs publicly to the secretariat. As such, it is possible to verify when countries are indeed living up to their own commitments. The secretariat also provides the technical expertise necessary to analyse and review all these NDCs. The secretariat does not have a monitoring, let alone a sanctioning, mechanism, but the public sharing of the NDCs provides some incentive for the different countries to comply.

Under the Enhanced Transparency Framework, operational since 2024, all state parties to the Paris Agreement need to submit every two years so-called transparency reports detailing their progress towards their NDCs. Technical experts then review all these submissions followed by an exchange between the state parties themselves. In addition, there is the Paris Agreement Implementation and Compliance Committee (PAICC) of twenty-four experts. The PAICC has a facilitatory role, for instance, if a state party does not submit its NDC or provides information on the progress made. The purpose is not sanctioning but rather helping state parties, even if the PAICC can report systemic issues to the COP. Still, monitoring of NDCs does happen under the Paris Agreement and information about countries' progress is clearly shared.

As with the ozone layer regime, the information activities of international organizations have had a lasting influence on protecting the world's climate. The intergovernmental negotiating processes which led to the UNFCCC and the Kyoto Protocol were shaped by the results of research into anthropogenic climate change supported by UNEP and the WMO (Rowlands 1995). Both organizations ensured that climate change was taken seriously as a global environmental problem and put on the political agenda in a timely fashion. The Intergovernmental Panel on Climate Change (IPCC), jointly established by UNEP and the WMO in 1988, proved especially important (Bolin 2007; Wettestad 1999: 221–4). Composed of researchers from the countries participating in the negotiations, the IPCC was tasked by UNEP and the WMO to conduct an audit of research into climate change and update it periodically. The IPCC's First Assessment Report in 1990 provided a detailed analysis of risks to the world's climate that resulted from growing greenhouse gas emissions. The report predicted that unchecked greenhouse gas emissions would lead to an increase in world temperatures of between 1.5 and 4.5°C on average by 2025. This assessment report was submitted to the second world climate conference (Geneva, 1990), which then asked the participating states to initiate negotiations immediately on an international framework convention on climate change (Breitmeier 1996: 164–6).

Even after the 1992 Rio Framework Convention was signed, the IPCC's contribution to the ensuing negotiations in the COPs remained decisive in helping to form a consensus, which was reinforced through its Second Assessment Report in 1995. An epistemic community of some 3,000 researchers assembled for this Report observed almost unanimously that climate change was due to accrued greenhouse gas emissions. They added that, if the existing emission trends were to continue, an average rise in temperature of about 2°C could be expected in the twenty-first century. The report also warned that sea levels would rise by about 50 cm (Rowlands 1995).

This second IPCC assessment report had its full impact on the first COP1 in 1995 in Berlin. Supporters of specific reduction commitments could point to the report in arguing for urgent action to counteract climate change, while opponents were finding it harder to dismiss the idea that greenhouse gas emissions are responsible for climate change. This helped to shift the balance of power between supporters and opponents, and it became possible to begin specific negotiations on a climate protocol to reduce emissions. The Third Assessment Report in 2001 confirmed that anthropogenic climate change would continue. It helped to underline yet again the vital need for global climate protection by curbing emissions. The Fourth Assessment Report of 2007 contained numerous, quite specific findings and prognoses on trends in global warming and on the ecological consequences of climate change, for example, for sea levels, vegetation zones and biodiversity. The 2007 IPCC report found unprecedented resonance not only among policymakers but also with the larger public. At the end of 2007, the IPCC (jointly with the former US vice president Al Gore) was even awarded the Nobel Peace Prize for its 'efforts to build up and disseminate greater knowledge about man-made climate change, and to lay the foundations for the measures that are needed to counteract such change' (Norwegian Nobel Committee 2007).

Thus the information activities of UNEP and the WMO helped considerably to reduce the uncertainties about the causal link between greenhouse gas emissions and climate change. They contributed to putting global climate change on the political agenda and pushed states to enter into negotiations leading to binding, though still modest, commitments to cutting their greenhouse gas emissions.

Evaluation of the organizations' effectiveness

UNEP and the WMO, in conjunction with environmental international NGOs, promoted a relatively early scientific recognition of the climate change problem and contributed to the rapid formation of a consensus among scholars and experts upon which international climate policy could be based. They have also furthered reaching an agreement on reducing greenhouse gas emissions in the Kyoto Protocol. The establishment of internationally binding emission reductions under the Kyoto Protocol was certainly no small achievement (see Aldy and Stavins 2007). The scale and the complexity of the problem – its truly global nature, the great incentives to free ride on the efforts of others and the need to regulate domestic level behaviour – have brought forth one of the most ambitious projects in the history of international law (Thompson 2010: 270).

Nonetheless, even taking into account the formidable challenge and exceptional difficulty of reducing global carbon dioxide emissions, the overall record of international organizations' effectiveness in addressing the global problem of climate change is sobering (Breitmeier 2009; Rittberger, Kruck and Romund2010: 594–5). Global greenhouse gas emissions have continued to increase and will likely only peak in 2025 (see Figure 10.3). Even if we can already see modest declines in the EU and the United States, global emissions need to be seriously reduced. Emerging economies, such as China and India were not bound to any reduction commitments under the Kyoto Protocol. The very basis of the Paris Agreement was furthermore the NDCs rather than international legally binding commitments. It is widely acknowledged among scientists (and many policymakers) that previous and current reduction commitments – under the Kyoto Protocol and the Paris Agreement – are insufficient to stop or significantly slow down global climate change (Aldy and Stavins 2007). Another big question is whether countries can achieve their NDCs in the longer term. On top of this, the announcement

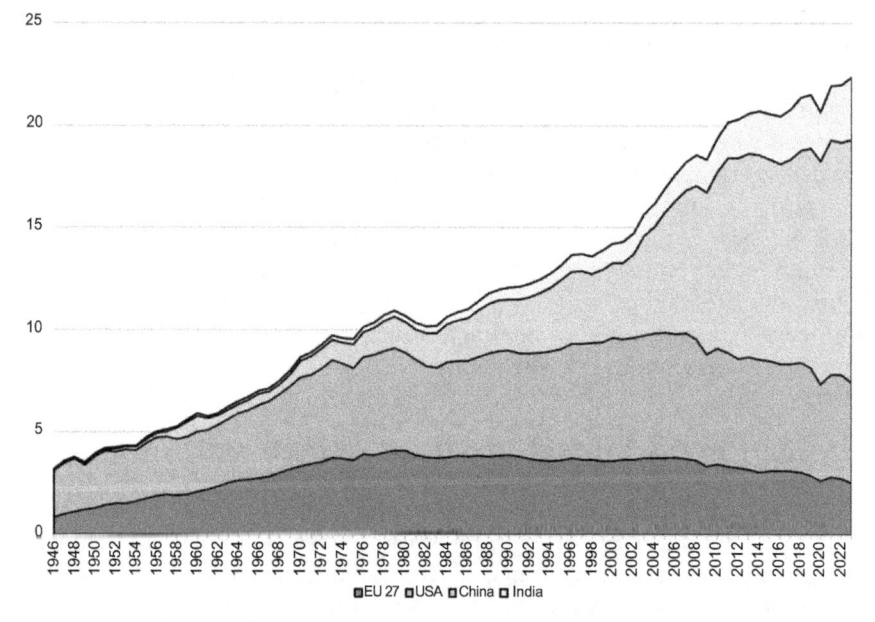

FIGURE 10.3 *Annual CO2 emissions (1946–date) of major economies (in billion tons). Source: Global Carbon Budget (2024) – with major processing by Our World in Data.*

of President Trump to again withdraw from the Paris Agreement hardly helps. Thus, not only on the impact level (mitigating climate change) but also on the outcome level (changing states' emission policies), international organizations are insufficiently effective.

Conclusion

In the area of environmental protection – both regarding the ozone layer and climate change – we can identify some clear dynamics by approaching international organizations as political systems. As a starting point, it is important to point out the input provided by scientists and the extensive lobbying of international NGOs and other transnational expert networks. It is also significant to pay attention to the input provided by states themselves. Here, we have identified changing constellations of states as well as changing preferences. While the EU was initially sceptical of international cooperation to address problems with the ozone layer, it has come out as one of the strongest supporters of global environmental cooperation, including in the area of climate change. The United States, at the same time, has also shifted its position. Particularly important these days is whether the US president is a Democrat or a Republican. Furthermore, China and the other emerging economies have become powerful actors in the field of environmental protection. Their input is also increasingly relevant.

The mode of decision-making is rather particular to the area of the environment. There is not a single, traditional, international organization where decisions are being made on a continuous basis. Rather, most of the decision-making takes place through COPs on an annual, or at least regular, basis. While intergovernmental bargaining between the states dominates, many of these COPs have also become major events (gatherings) where thousands of representatives from NGOs and the scientific community meet. Just organizing these events is already a major job for the relevant secretariats, such as the UNFCCC Climate Secretariat in Bonn. The fact that these conferences have become such big gatherings also puts tremendous pressure on states. Leaving the COPs without an agreement creates a significant disappointment in the broader public. In this sense, even though the prominent mode is intergovernmental negotiations, the process is rather institutionalized.

The output of international organizations in the area of environmental protection includes both policy programmes and operational activities. The policy programmes in both the area of the protection of the ozone layer and climate change provide ambitious targets and road maps on how to address environmental problems. The big question is implementation, which has been delegated to the member states themselves. While member states make clear commitments and communicate about them publicly, they ultimately remain responsible for achieving them. The monitoring and sanctioning mechanisms remain weak. This is one of the reasons why, particularly in the area of climate change, both the outcome (lower emissions) and impact (less global warming) are not fully achieved. With respect to the ozone layer, the international community has been more successful. It was, however, easier to phase out CFCs than greenhouse gases altogether. What the policy area of the environment also neatly shows is that the impacts of international organizations feed again into international organizations as input. If it becomes clear that the impact is insufficient, this creates feedback and returns to the agenda as a problem to be addressed.

Discussion questions

1. What explains the difference between international organizations' effectiveness in the issue areas of protection of the stratospheric ozone layer and containment of climate change?
2. What effects did the information activities of international organizations have in the field of environmental policymaking and why are they particularly relevant in this issue area?

Further reading

Allan, Jen Iris, Charles B. Roger, Thomas N. Hale, Steven Bernstein, Yves Tiberghien and Richard Balme (2023). 'Making the Paris Agreement: Historical Processes and the Drivers of Institutional Design', *Political Studies*, 71 (3): 914–34.

Bäckstrand, Karin, Jonathan W. Kuyper, Björn-Ola Linnér and Eva Lövbrand (2017). 'Non-state Actors in Global Climate Governance: From Copenhagen to Paris and Beyond', *Environmental Politics*, 26 (4): 561–79.

Falkner, Robert (2016). 'The Paris Agreement and the New Logic of International Climate Politics', *International Affairs*, 92 (5): 1107–25.

Keohane, Robert O. and David G. Victor (2011). 'The Regime Complex for Climate Change', *Perspectives on Politics*, 9 (1): 7–23.

11

Migration and human rights

The previous chapters have dealt with problems that states face when confronted with security dilemmas, mercantilism and the spillover effects of economic crises as well as global warming and environmental protection. The argument is that international organizations can help to address such problems, and the chapters have examined the policy programmes, operational activities and the effectiveness of the relevant international organizations. This chapter focuses on international cooperation with regard to individual human beings. We distinguish here between people who cross borders or are internally displaced (i.e. migrate) and the human rights of people in their own countries. While migration and human rights are as old as humans themselves, they have only relatively recently been perceived as an international 'problem' by states. As a result of major displacements during and after the First World War, states set up institutions in the context of the League of Nations to address this problem. Other forms of migration, such as workers moving from one country to another, were long considered domestic affairs of the destination states or at best were subject to policies of regional organizations (see Chapter 12). The immigration of people from around the world to the United States over the past two centuries, for instance, has largely been (and remains) an American rather than an international matter. Yet with the increasing human mobility as part of broader globalization during the post-Cold War era, migration is also increasingly considered an international problem in need for international organizations.

While migration also involves human rights questions, we are mostly concerned in this chapter about the human rights within states. The (lack of) protection of human rights within states does not directly involve a cross-border or international problem. Human rights violations in one country, after all, do not automatically affect the human rights situation in another country. The human rights dilemma derives 'only' from moral interdependencies across state borders: human rights violations in one state can give rise to moral outrage in other states resulting in an active international human rights policy (Risse and Sikkink 1999: 22–4). The existence of such international moral interdependencies crucially depends on the activities of transnational networks of human rights organizations, which construct local human rights violations as global problems requiring governance beyond the state. Even more than in other issue areas, global human rights problems are socially constructed rather than naturally given issues of international governance. Indeed, until rather recently, human rights were mostly considered domestic rather than international matters.

Despite increasingly strong global concern, individual states may still be reluctant to 'lecture' other states on human rights, let alone to unilaterally pursue sanctions in the case of human rights violations. For instance, Western states have been rather cautious to confront China over its human rights record, afraid that this may affect economic relations. Therefore, collective international cooperation, including through international organizations, is needed in order to bring about active human rights policies aimed at those states that violate such rights. Furthermore, delegating monitoring and compliance tasks to international organizations avoids individual states needing to point to each other. International organizations working jointly with civil society actors can contribute to achieving international cooperation in the issue area of human rights. Through generating reliable information about human rights violations and by mobilizing civil society, transnational networks of human rights organizations can exert pressure on governments to act against offending states (Finnemore and Sikkink 1998: 896–901; Risse and Sikkink 1999: 22–5). To understand the contributions of international organizations to international cooperation in the areas of migration and human rights, we concentrate on the activities of the United Nations (UN) system.

Migration and refugees

Migration covers everyone who crosses a border including workers, students, tourists, refugees and irregular migrants. In this section, we also include internally displaced people (IDP), who have been forced to flee their homes but have not crossed an international state border. Due to the different challenges related to the different forms of migration, states have established a variety of institutions and policies to deal with migration at both the domestic and international levels. The protection of refugees has long been subject to an international policy programme with the 1951 Refugee Convention at its core. Other forms of migration have been covered by different international institutions to the extent that they have been addressed at the international level. In 2018, however, under the UN framework, states adopted two parallel Global Compacts (for migration and on refugees) as stepping stones towards a more comprehensive policy programme. As international cooperation on refugees is more developed, this is discussed first in terms of the policy programme before analysing the policy programme on migration. Subsequently, the section examines the operational activities of the UN Refugee Agency (UNHCR) and International Organization for Migration (IOM) in in the area of refugees and migration.

Policy programme of the UN

During the First World War (1914–18), more than 10 million people are estimated to have been displaced. The large majority was displaced within the then-existing empires, but many also fled temporarily to neighbouring states. This immediately raised a whole range of questions from the definition and administration of refugees to lodging, subsistence and education, return but also health and security threats. With the Armenian genocide (1915–16), the collapse of the Ottoman Empire (1922) and the forced exchange of Greek and Turkish nationals as part of the Lausanne Treaty (1923), migration and refugees became an international problem for which the League of Nations set up a variety of institutions. Within this context, the 1933 Convention Relating to the International Status of Refugees was negotiated and ultimately ratified by nine European states. The problem of refugees became even larger during the Second World War (1939–45) with 40–60 million displaced people in Europe alone, for many of whom it was unclear which state they could be part of after 1945. In response, the UN Relief and Rehabilitation Agency (UNRRA, 1943–8) was set up and was succeeded by the International Refugee Organization (IRO, 1948–52), while the UN Relief and Works Agency for Palestinian Refugees (UNRWA) was set up in 1949. All of this formed the background to the UN refugee policy programme that was developed after the Second World War.

To understand the post-Second World War global refugee regime, it is first of all important to note that states did not envision a comprehensive, global and permanent policy programme. Indeed, the ambition was to 'wrap up' the problem of refugees and displacements in the years after the Second World War. The IRO, for instance, was set up purposefully as a temporary organization and when its mandate ran out, the responsibility for the remaining refugee camps was transferred to the European host countries. Likewise, the Office of the United Nations High Commissioner for Refugees, which was established in 1950, was not really a successor organization to the IRO. It was literally an office in Geneva, and it originally did not have an operational mandate like the IRO. Interestingly, the 1951 Refugee Convention only gave 'refugee' status to persons fleeing from prosecution as a result of 'events occurring before 1 January 1951' (Article 1(A)(2)) or to be even more precise 'events occurring *in Europe* before 1 January 1951' (Article 1(B)(1)(a), emphasis added). Despite the ambition to wind down the international refugee regime, it became quite quickly clear that the problems with refugees persisted beyond 1951 and were also global rather than exclusively European in nature. The small office of the UN

High Commissioner thus grew overtime into the large UNHCR (see further below), and the 1951 Convention became applicable worldwide through the 1967 Protocol.

While originally unintended, the 1951 Convention sets out a comprehensive and global policy programme on the status of refugees. It defines a refugee, apart from the mentioned restrictions above, as any person 'owing to well-founded fear of being persecuted for reasons of race, religion, nationality, membership of a particular social group or political opinion, is outside the country of his nationality and is unable or, owing to such fear, is unwilling to avail himself of the protection of that country' (Article 1(A)(2)). Excluded are those persons who 'committed a crime against peace, a war crime, or a crime against humanity' or 'ha[ve] been guilty of acts contrary to the purposes and principles of the UN' or have committed a serious non-political crime (Article 1(F)). Persons under protection or receiving assistance of UN organs or agencies (other than UNHCR), such as Palestinian refugees under UNRWA, or those who have settled in their destination countries also do not fall under the Convention (Article 1(D-E)). The definition of who constitutes a refugee is important, as it results in a range of rights for those recognized as refugees.

Perhaps most importantly, the 1951 Convention stipulates that states shall not expel or return refugees 'in any manner whatsoever to the frontiers of territories where [their] life or freedom would be threatened on account of [their] race, religion, nationality, membership of a particular social group or political opinion' (Article 33). They can also not punish refugees for 'illegal entry or presence' under the condition that 'they present themselves without delay to the authorities' (Article 31). States thus have to accept refugees and, with few exceptions, are not allowed to send them back. The Convention also grants refugees a range of rights in their host countries. These include non-discrimination and freedom of religion, the right to decent work, housing and property, the right to education and social protection, the access to justice and the right to be issued administrative documents. In other words, the 1951 Convention provided an extensive policy programme but was limited in time and geographical scope. Yet because 'new refugee situations' arose after 1951 – for instance, as a result of the Hungarian revolution and the wars in Algeria and Vietnam – no less than 146 states signed the 1967 Protocol, which lifted these restrictions and made the Convention essentially universally applicable. In addition, around half of the UN member states adopted two Conventions (1954, 1961) on stateless people to provide them with rights as well.

While the 1951 Convention remains the core legally binding policy programme on refugees, it also noted in the preamble that 'the grant of asylum may place *unduly heavy burdens on certain countries*, and that a satisfactory solution of a problem of which the United Nations has recognized the international scope and nature cannot therefore be achieved without international co-operation' (emphasis added). Refugees typically cross borders to safer countries in the region, which leads to pressure on these regional states. While burden-sharing challenges played a role throughout the Cold War and the post-Cold War period, with some relief through the operational activities of international organizations (see below), such challenges came high on the political agenda when the civil war in Syria (since 2011) displaced nearly 14 million people with around 1 million refugees coming to Western Europe. Even though half of them were displaced within Syria and another 5 million refugees hosted in Türkiye, Lebanon and Jordan, the EU member states pushed the UN to negotiate a Global Compact on Refugees in 2018 (alongside the Compact on Migration, below). The eventual document is not legally binding and burden sharing is based on voluntary contributions of states, but the Compact establishes institutional forums for states to discuss such issues and identifies a whole range of areas where states may be in need of support. The 2018 Compact, in this respect, specifies the policy programme defined by the 1951 Convention, but it also identifies burden sharing as a critical element in the global refugee regime.

For the broader policy area of migration, there is not such an identifiable policy programme at the global level, but there is rather a patchwork of agreements and institutions. The International Labour Organization (ILO), for instance, already in its 1919 Constitution recognizes the rights of migrant workers and has adopted the 1949 and 1975 Conventions outlining the rights of migrant workers with regard to non-discrimination in terms of employment conditions and taxes. In the UN human rights context, we find furthermore specific conventions such as the 1990 Convention on the Protection of the Rights of All Migrant Workers and Members of Their Families (see also below). And, importantly, several regional organizations, such as the EU or MERCOSUR, have their own policy programmes around freedom of movement and migration (see Chapter 12). It was, however, only from the early 2000s that the UN began actively talking about migration as an international issue and a phenomenon requiring international cooperation. It established a Global Migration Group (GMG) with the purpose of bringing relevant UN agencies together, which resulted in a variety of activities related to migration and human rights as well as migration and development. Migration within the UN context ultimately made it into the Sustainable Development Goals (SDGs) with the aim to 'facilitate orderly, safe, and responsible migration and mobility of people' (SDG 10.7). In 2018, the UN adopted the Global Compact for Migration following a contentious negotiations process.

The Global Compact for Migration includes twenty-three objectives to make migration 'safe, orderly and regular'. These are mostly practical measures to facilitate migration and make the lives of migrants easier, such as states providing accurate information about migration, ensure that migrants have the proper documentation, counter smuggling and trafficking of persons, manage borders better, facilitate remittances and establish mechanisms for social security. While states still have full sovereignty over which migrants can enter their countries, opponents of the Compact (such as the United States under the Trump administration) object to facilitating migration in the first place. On the other hand, by making migration more regular, the ambition of the Compact was also to counter 'irregular' migration by facilitating legal border crossings. For many countries around the globe – particularly in the Global South – it was also important that their nationals would be treated better when migrating to other countries. The Compact was endorsed by the UN General Assembly in December 2018, when 152 states voted in favour with 5 against (Czech Republic, Hungary, Israel, Poland and the United States) and 12 abstentions. While the Compact is not legally binding, it includes a range of operational activities for implementation, follow up and review.

Operations of the UNHCR and IOM

The UNHCR and IOM have become important operational organizations in the area of refugees and migration. The UNHCR provides international protection and humanitarian assistance to refugees, thereby implementing the 1951 Refugee Convention, whereas the IOM delivers migration services 'to ensure the orderly flow of migration movements throughout the world' (IOM Constitution 1951: preamble). Both organizations started in the early 1950s but have come a long way since. The UNHCR was, as mentioned above, initially only a (temporary) office to liaise with governments on refugee issues. Yet as refugee crises unfolded during the 1950s and subsequent decades, it soon developed operational activities. In 2003, its mandate became permanent 'until the refugee problem is solved' (UN General Assembly Resolution 58/153) and, as of 2024, UNHCR has a budget of US$10 billion and employs more than 20,000 staff members. The IOM was originally created under a different name and served mainly as a logistical agency to organize issues around the transport of migrants. It was actually not part of the UN until recently when in 2016 it formally became an affiliated organization. The IOM has a budget of US$3.5 billion and employs more than 22,000 staff members. As can be expected from a UN-affiliated organization, it has near-universal membership.

The UNHCR and the IOM have some policy roles to play. The UNHCR, for instance, is the guardian of the 1951 Refugee Convention and thus the main contact point for all refugee-related questions. Following the Global Compact for Refugees, it also organizes, for instance, the four-yearly Global Refugee Forum where states make pledges to ease the burden for host countries. The IOM has become the lead organization for the Global Compact on Migration, which includes engaging in the four-yearly International Migration Review Forum. But the majority of the operational activities of both organizations are about the implementation of the policy programmes on the ground in countries across the globe. The UNHCR works, for instance, in 136 countries, while the IOM is present in 172 countries with no less than 550 field offices.

The operational activities of UNHCR fall into three categories: responding to emergencies, providing protection to refugees and helping refugees build better futures. When we use the term of 'refugee', it is important to note that UNHCR now has a mandate to not only look after people with an official refugee status but also asylum seekers (who do not yet have a refugee status), stateless people and even IDPs. While IDPs fall outside the scope of the 1951 Refugee Convention, as they do not cross state borders, the UN General Assembly has long recognized the importance of UNHCR operational activities and asked UNHCR since the 1970s to also get involved in displacement crises within certain states. While for most of the post-Cold War period, there were between 35 and 45 million refugees around the globe (all combined), the number has increased threefold since 2011 from around 38 million to 120 million in 2024, of which around 32 million are UNHCR-mandated refugees, 68 million IDPs, 7 million asylum seekers, 6 million Palestinian refugees (under UNRWA) and 6 million other people in need of international protection, particularly from Venezuela. Around 69 per cent of refugees – excluding IDPs – live in neighbouring states.

The activities of UNHCR in terms of *responding to emergencies* are very visible. UNHCR defines an 'emergency' when there is a humanitarian crisis or disaster that threatens displacement and the rights of refugees, for which the local government and UNHRC offices are not equipped. UNHCR distinguishes between three levels of emergences. Level 1 emergencies involve the initial response and preparedness, while level 2 and 3 emergencies are more serious and are declared by the UNHCR High Commissioner. This is not subject to member states' negotiations, and the authority to declare emergencies thus falls under the operational autonomy of the agency. Because emergencies can happen at any time, UNHCR takes extensive preparatory measures so that it can provide up to 1 million refugees with immediate support on the ground – shelter, water and food, medical care and help to reunite families – within 72 hours after a declared emergency. UNHCR, in this respect, has stockpiles of relief items ready in warehouses around the world and preidentified staff members that can 'drop everything' they are normally working on in order to respond to an emergency. UNHCR also ensures that refugees can actually cross borders and reach safety. It also monitors through patrols whether governments and armed groups are blocking refugees to enter safe areas. UNHCR is the coordinating agency for the UN in this respect and also coordinates with local authorities and NGOs. Emergency response lasts maximum six months and can be prolonged by three months. In 2024, UNHCR managed forty-three active emergencies across twenty-five countries. It declared seven new level 3 emergencies including as a result of the escalating war in Sudan, the war in Lebanon and the hostilities in Syria. In its annual report, UNHCR also noted a record of nine emergencies in 2024 related to climate change and displacement (UNHCR 2025).

Providing protection to refugees is at the heart of the 1951 Convention and UNHCR's mandate. While the host countries that have signed the Convention bear a key responsibility in this regard, the operational activities of UNHCR provide support to these governments. UNHCR works with them on improving laws, policies and practices to ensure that the rights from the Convention (as well as the Convention on statelessness) are fully implemented. Yet state capacity around the world can be low and host countries are often not capable of providing sufficient assistance to refugees. Refugee camps can stay in place for years if not decades after the declared emergencies are over. The UNHCR Dadaab refugee 'complex' in Kenya, on the border with Somalia, was set up as a temporary shelter in 1991, but still more than 300,000 refugees lived there in 2023. In such camps, UNHCR may provide not only food and shelter but also services such as education and healthcare. The reality is, however, that the large majority of refugees (almost 80 per cent) do not live in camps but in cities. This is where the third operational activity of *building better futures* comes in as UNHCR seeks to help refugees rebuild their lives in the longer term. Education and access to schooling is, in this regard, critical as many UNHCR-registered refugees are under the age of eighteen. This requires for UNHCR to work with the host countries, which are responsible for providing education. The same goes for economic inclusion allowing refugees employment opportunities and starting businesses. The end game for the UNHCR is when refugees return to their home countries, when it is safe to do so, or when they are granted the nationality of their host countries. Under the 2018 Global Compact, UNHCR also has a resettlement scheme to alleviate the burden on several host countries. Nearly 100,000 refugees were resettled in 2023, mostly to the United States and Canada, though President Trump scrapped refugee resettlement in 2025.

The IOM has a partially overlapping operational mandate with the UNHCR (Bradley, Costello and Sherwood 2023; Pécoud 2018; Moretti 2021). While the UNHCR has traditionally focused on protection of refugees, the IOM has dealt with all sorts of logistical and administrative challenges surrounding migration more broadly. The IOM serves, in this respect, its member states rather than the individual migrant. The IOM has, however, also carved out a role for itself when it comes to crisis response and it mostly deals with refugees. Since the UNHCR was originally not established as an operational agency, because of US worries about Soviet influence over the UN system, the predecessors of the IOM were set up as a Western-dominated 'travel agency' to deal with the operational tasks of the closed IRO. This task of *migration management* remains a core activity today with a focus on orderly migration between countries. This includes supporting member states in immigration and border management, providing assistance to vulnerable migrants, providing assistance to facilitate the voluntary return of migrants as well as countering human trafficking. The IOM may help member states with setting up visa procedures or help them with the collection of migration data. The IOM has, in this respect, a fairly open-ended mandate and also assists migrants with social services such as access to healthcare (Bradley 2024). The second core task of the IOM concerns *crisis response*. For this task, the IOM may co-deploy alongside the UNHCR. The division of labour varies across crises and countries with the UNHCR focusing on protection and the IOM working on administration and also return. The IOM has played a particularly strong role in response to the refugee crisis in Venezuela where more than 6 million refugees have fled to neighbouring states since 2018.

Because the IOM developed originally outside the UN system and has been sponsored by the Western powers, it has been frequently criticized of doing the bidding of the United States and Europe with little regard to the rights of individual migrants. For instance, following the 2011 war in Libya, the IOM helped to repatriate 1.5 million foreign nationals, mostly from sub-Saharan countries, back to their home countries, thereby 'avoiding' that they would flee to European destinations (Brachet 2016). As such, it clearly contributed to restrictive European migration policies. Yet while much of the scholarship is highly critical of the IOM, Bradley, Costello and Sherwood (2023) also note that scholarship 'tends to be unclear about the standards to which IOM can and should be held to account' (p. 4). In many respects, the case of the IOM highlights a significant disconnect between a largely underdeveloped policy programme on migration and a very strong demand for operational activities in this area due to the increasing migration pressures around the world. This is, somewhat, atypical for international organizations, because oftentimes there are clearer policy programmes and weaker operational activities.

Evaluation of the organization's effectiveness

For more than a century, international organizations have been involved with migration and refugees. While various international institutions were originally set up to deal with what were seen as 'temporary' refugee problems, due to the two world wars, they ultimately became permanent organizations, even if this was only belatedly recognized with the UNHCR in 2003. Despite the cross-border nature of migration and refugees, it took a while to recognize these as international problems to be addressed by international organizations. Migration is still oftentimes considered as a state issue and responsibility to be dealt with exclusively at the level of states. Evaluating the UN policy programme and the operational activities of the UNHCR and the IOM is difficult. When considering the outputs and outcomes of both international organizations, many of the results are surely impressive. They are capable of rapid response, operate in difficult environments and provide services to many millions of refugees and other vulnerable migrants. There would be (more) human catastrophes around the globe if not for the work of both organizations and other humanitarian actors. Their contributions are also clearly recognized by states and other donors, which have supported both organizations for decades including as their mandates and operational activities have increased dramatically. That the initial restrictions of the UNHCR mandate (in Europe and before 1951) were lifted and that the organization can also address the question of IDPs shows that states have found the UNHCR a useful organization. The same can be said about the IOM, which is also seen as an effective tool by many member states.

Yet despite the clear demand for the services of UNHCR and IOM, it is also clear that both these international organizations are not fully achieving the goals for which they were originally set up. The number of refugees and particularly IDPs has significantly increased again in recent years as a result of the various conflicts around the world (see Figure 11.1). The UNHCR, in this respect, only offers limited solutions. Most refugees continue to stay refugees and do not return, naturalize in their host country or get resettled elsewhere in countries around the world. Some of the temporary camps under UNHCR protection exist for decades. The Global Compact has not resulted in a degree of burden sharing among host countries anywhere close to what is required. It is also clear that in Western states – the United States and Europe – there is a strong refugee fatigue and particularly European countries tend to struggle with administratively determining which asylum

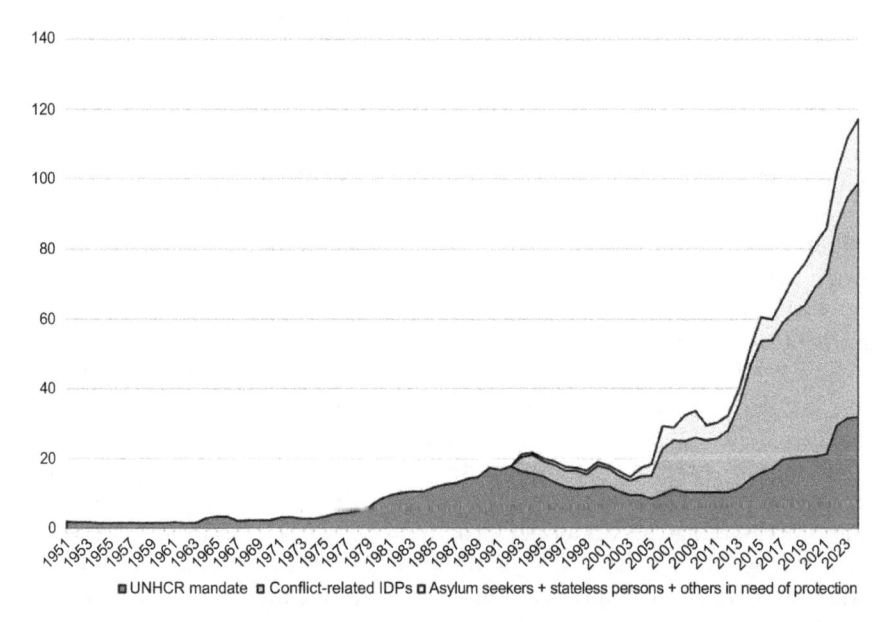

FIGURE 11.1 *Number of refugees and IDPs, 1951–2024. Source: Based on data from UNHCR.*

seekers qualify for refugee states. This is so despite the fact that the large majority of refugees are hosted in neighbouring countries outside of Europe and the United States. We have seen, in this respect, also a shift in terms of states relying more on the IOM (which serves states) than the UNHCR (which protects refugees). While the UNHCR and the IOM may therefore field impressive operations in terms of their output and outcomes, many states remain dissatisfied with their actual impact.

Global human rights protection

During the late nineteenth century and early twentieth century, the international community adopted a number of international humanitarian treaties touching upon human rights, including the Geneva Convention of 1864 and the Brussels Act against slavery of 1890. A major input for securing human rights internationally, however, was the reaction of states and civil society to the crimes against humanity committed by Nazi Germany during the Second World War (Krasner 1999: 106–10). This resulted in the adoption of the Universal Declaration of Human Rights by the UN General Assembly in 1948. During the past decades, the human rights violations by the politics of apartheid in South Africa, the massacre in Tiananmen Square in Beijing, violations against women in Iran, the Rwandan genocide and the atrocities committed in the wars in the Darfur region of Sudan, Ukraine and Gaza – to name but a few – have kept human rights issues on the international political agenda. At the same time, political and civil rights are increasingly contested and various human rights crises, such as China's repression of the Uyghurs, are barely discussed internationally.

Policy programme of the UN

The reactions of the international community to the atrocities committed by Nazi Germany during the Second World War provided significant input for the UN human rights regime developed after 1945. The Preamble to the UN Charter reaffirms 'faith in fundamental human rights, the dignity and worth of the human person, in the equal rights of men and women and of nations large and small'. However, the Charter does not mention the specific human rights which states have to guarantee beyond Article 55, which urges the promotion of 'universal respect for, and observance of, human rights and fundamental freedoms for all without distinction of race, sex, language, or religion'. Thus, initially, human rights protection by the UN remained limited.

The UN Economic and Social Council (ECOSOC) was charged with translating this general declaration into a human rights policy programme. To this end, as early as 1946, ECOSOC set up a Commission on Human Rights as a subsidiary body to develop programmes for international human rights protection. Until it was replaced by the UN Human Rights Council in 2006, the Commission on Human Rights – with the support of the Sub-Commission on the Promotion and Protection of Human Rights – represented the central forum for the intergovernmental negotiations in the UN on policy programmes for the protection of human rights. Initially, the decision-making process was dominated by the Western coalition of liberal democracies under the leadership of the United States. It was thus possible to reach an international consensus based on liberal ideas about what rights should henceforth be recognized and guaranteed as human rights. As a result, in 1948 the UN General Assembly adopted the Universal Declaration of Human Rights (GA Resolution 217A (III)). The General Assembly decision was taken by majority vote and the Declaration remained legally non-binding. The Declaration was significant nonetheless: it meant that human rights were now issues for the agenda of the principal organs of the UN. In other words, states' exercise of authority over their citizens was removed from their exclusive jurisdiction and the principle of non-interference in domestic affairs began to lose some of its validity insofar as human rights were concerned.

The Universal Declaration of Human Rights established a normative frame of reference. It was to be followed by the legally binding codification of human rights. Immediately after the adoption of the Declaration, the Commission on Human Rights proceeded with lengthy intergovernmental negotiations about the International Covenant on Civil and Political Rights and the International Covenant on Economic, Social and Cultural Rights. Both covenants had largely been negotiated by 1954, but it took the General Assembly until 1966 to formally adopt them and to recommend them to states for signature. Another ten years passed before a sufficient number of states had ratified them. They came into force in 1976. The number of parties to the covenants grew steadily throughout the 2000s and by 2024 stood at 173 (Civil Pact) and 171 (Social Pact), respectively.

The Universal Declaration of Human Rights and the two Covenants form the core of the UN's policy programme on human rights. They contain a large number of human rights norms. Each individual norm has a prescriptive status and together the human rights standards form an international normative structure (Donnelly 2006: 15; Ramcharan 2007; Risse and Ropp 1999; Tomuschat 2008: Chapter 3). The UN programme on human rights, starting with the dignity and equality of all people (Articles 1 and 2, Universal Declaration of Human Rights), formulates a canon of liberal rights for the protection of individuals against a state's arbitrary and excessive exercise of power (Articles 3 to 21, Universal Declaration of Human Rights; Articles 6 to 27, International Covenant on Civil and Political Rights). They include the right to life, liberty and personal security; protection against discrimination; prohibition of torture and slavery or servitude; protection of the private sphere; the right to freedom of thought, conscience and religion; the right to freedom of expression, assembly, association and movement; protection of the family; the right to marry; the right to equal access to public service and the right to take part in the government of one's country; the right to participate in elections; entitlement to equality before the law and to a fair and public hearing in courts of law; the right to legal assistance and to be presumed innocent until proved guilty; and the right of being convicted only on the basis of laws in existence at the time the offence was committed.

In addition, the UN programme mentions basic economic, social and cultural rights (Articles 22–27, Universal Declaration of Human Rights; International Covenant on Economic, Social and Cultural Rights). These include, among others, the right to sufficient food and an adequate standard of living as well as the right to physical and mental health; the right to work and to just and favourable conditions of work; the right to strike; the right to leisure, holidays and social security; and the right to education and to participation in the cultural and scientific life of one's country.

To these rights, others have been added in a series of conventions for the protection of human rights. The most important ones include the 1948 Convention on the Prevention and Punishment of the Crime of Genocide, the 1965 Convention on the Elimination of all Forms of Racial Discrimination, the 1979 Convention on the Elimination of all Forms of Discrimination against Women, the 1984 Convention against Torture and other Forms of Cruel, Inhuman and Degrading Treatment or Punishment, the 1989 Convention on the Rights of the Child, the 2006 Convention on the Rights of Persons with Disabilities and the 2006 Convention for the Protection of All Persons from Enforced Disappearance (see Table 11.1).

While the international community has thus developed an elaborate policy programme on human rights, and the number of ratifications for many of the conventions has increased over the past decades, the UN policy programme is also increasingly contested. For instance, an established principle of the UN policy programme is that all human rights are 'indivisible' and 'interdependent'. In this view, there is not such a thing as a less important right. Accordingly, the UN has long recognized that economic-social rights cannot go without civil and political rights (and the UN would not have been able to have the Civil Pact without the Social Pact). China and various other countries, however, have become much more vocal and obstructive, in recent years, by questioning the UN practice that all rights are equal. Instead, China actively champions a hierarchy of human rights prioritizing economic and social development of states over civil and political rights. It also underlines sovereignty with the implication that human rights should result from diplomatic consensus ('universal acceptance') rather than being a reflection of common humanity (Inboden 2021; Chen and Hsu 2021; Dukalskis 2023). Such contestation does not just affect UN operations, for instance, when voting in the Human Rights Council, but erodes the UN policy programme as such. China has been promoting its own model through rhetorical campaigns; additionally, it has been creating its own human rights

TABLE 11.1 *The main global Human Rights Conventions*

Convention	Treaty Body	Year Opened for Signature	Year Entered into Force	Number of Ratifications (2024)
Convention on the Prevention and Punishment of the Crime of Genocide	None	1948	1951	153
Convention on the Elimination of all Forms of Racial Discrimination	Committee on the Elimination of Racial Discrimination	1965	1969	182
International Covenant on Civil and Political Rights	Human Rights Committee	1966	1976	173
International Covenant on Economic, Social and Cultural Rights	Committee on Economic, Social and Cultural Rights	1966	1976	171
Convention on the Elimination of all Forms of Discrimination against Women	Committee on the Elimination of Discrimination against Women	1979	1981	189
Convention against Torture and other Forms of Cruel, Inhuman and Degrading Treatment or Punishment	Committee against Torture	1984	1987	173
Convention on the Rights of the Child	Committee on the Rights of the Child	1989	1990	196
Convention on the Protection of the Rights of All Migrant Workers and Members of Their Families	Committee on Migrant Workers	1990	2003	58
Convention on the Rights of Persons with Disabilities	Committee on the Rights of Persons with Disabilities	2006	2008	186
Convention for the Protection of All Persons from Enforced Disappearance	Committee on Enforced Disappearances	2006	2010	75

Source: Based on data from OHCHR.

forums and finding an increasing number of supportive states along the way. In this regard, the UN human rights policies are under considerable pressure.

Operations of the UN

The Commission on Human Rights was the main human rights-monitoring body of the UN until 2006 when it was replaced by the Human Rights Council through General Assembly Resolution 60/251. The Commission on Human Rights had increasingly suffered from a stand-off between Western states and a group of frequently criticized states trying to prevent country resolutions and the appointment of special rapporteurs (Mertus 2009; Ramcharan 2011). The Human Rights Council, which is a standing body, consists of forty-seven member states elected by the General Assembly. The membership rights of states with gross and systematic human rights violations can be suspended by a two-thirds majority vote of the General Assembly. Nonetheless, notorious human rights violators with a bad record are still frequently represented in the Human Rights Council. In 2024, for instance, members of the Human Rights Council included Algeria, Burundi, Cameroon, China, Cuba, Eritrea, Kazakhstan, Kyrgyzstan, Somalia, Sudan and Vietnam, all of which are classified as 'not free' by the human rights NGO Freedom House.

The supervisory procedures of the Human Rights Council resemble those at the disposal of the Commission on Human Rights (see Table 11.2). In the Universal Periodic Review (UPR) the compliance of all UN member states with their human rights obligations is assessed once every four and a half years (Etone, Nazir and Storey 2024). For that purpose, a working group, consisting of the members of the Council, is set up. It takes into account reports and comments from the state under review, the Office of the UN High Commissioner for Human Rights (OHCHR) and other UN and treaty organs, as well as civil society organizations. However, it mainly asks states to declare what actions they have taken to improve the human rights situations in their countries. Its main output is a final report ('outcome report') which documents the questions, comments and recommendations directed at the country under review, as well as the responses by the reviewed state. In the review that follows, the state must provide information on how it implemented the recommendations from the preceding review.

Special Procedures are mechanisms established by the Human Rights Council to address country-specific situations or global thematic issues. As of October 2024, there are forty-six thematic and fourteen country mandates. The mandate holders ('special rapporteurs' or 'independent experts') ask for information from governments on their human rights policies, carry out country visits and prepare reports as well as draft resolutions and provide technical assistance and capacity-building measures. The Special Procedures do not provide for hard sanctions in the case of states' non-compliance with

TABLE 11.2 *Monitoring procedures of the Human Rights Council*

Procedure	Object of Investigation	Providers of Relevant Information	Investigating Actors
Universal periodic review	Compliance with human rights obligations of all states	States under review, OHCHR, human rights treaty organs, NGOs	Working group of the Human Rights Council
Special procedures	Situation in specific countries; global thematic issues of human rights protection	Special rapporteurs, working groups of the Human Rights Council, states, NGOs	Special rapporteur, independent experts or working group of the Human Rights Council
Investigations	Alleged human rights violations in specific countries	Local government officials, civil society representatives, UN officials and national diplomats	Normally two to three senior members from different countries supported by the experts from the Office of the UN High Commissioner
Designated experts	Situation in specific countries	Local government officials, civil society representatives, UN officials and national diplomats	Independent expert appointed by the UN High Commissioner for Human Rights
Complaints procedure	Massive and systematic human rights violations by one state	Individuals, (state and non-state) organizations	Working Group on Communications, Working Group on Situations

Source: Website of the UN Human Rights Council.

their human rights obligations. The Human Rights Council – as well as the Security Council, General Assembly and secretary general – can also launch investigations, fact-finding missions and inquiry commissions, which normally consist of several high-level experts who will visit countries and report back over several years. More recently, it has mandated the UN High Commissioner to appoint also individual experts for mostly short-term country visits. Finally, the Human Rights Council uses complaints procedures which are open to individuals as well as organizations and generally correspond to the 1503 procedure of the Commission on Human Rights. Incoming complaints ('communications') are first examined by a Working

Group on Communications, which consists of five independent experts and assesses the admissibility of a communication. If the communication is admissible, it is transferred to the Working Group on Situations, which finally presents the Council with a report on proven human rights violations and policy recommendations for the respective country. Again, apart from suspension of membership in the Council, there are no sanctions beyond 'naming and shaming' available to the Human Rights Council.

Far-reaching collective sanctions against a state are only possible in cases where the UN Security Council declares the human rights violations of that state to be endangering international peace and security. This allows the Security Council to take all the measures listed in Chapter VII of the Charter (see Chapter 8). With the end of the Cold War, the Security Council redefined its role in implementing the human rights codified in the framework of the UN. Whereas before 1990 the Security Council did not take collective enforcement measures against perpetrators of human rights violations – with the exception of economic sanctions against the former Rhodesia and the arms embargo against South Africa (see Chapter 3) – the behaviour of the Security Council has changed somewhat (Forsythe 2006: 59–61). Since the early 1990s, the Security Council has agreed to enforcement measures in a substantial number of humanitarian crises such as those in Bosnia, Kosovo, Haiti, Somalia, East Timor, the Democratic Republic of Congo and Libya. At the same time, the Security Council has done little to counter human rights violations in Darfur during the 2000s or in Syria during the 2010s.

At least in part driven by motives to avoid costly military sanctions (Forsythe 2006: 98, 103; Rudolph 2001), the Security Council has revitalized another instrument of adjudication and sanctioning, namely that of international courts for the legal pursuit of individuals – rather than states – who are accused of being responsible for gross infringement of international humanitarian law. Acting under Article 29 of the UN Charter, the Security Council set up two international (ad hoc) tribunals for the former Yugoslavia and for Rwanda. With its Resolution 827 (1993), the Security Council, starting from the procedures adopted by the Allied Powers after the Second World War in Nuremberg and Tokyo, created the International Criminal Tribunal for the Former Yugoslavia (ICTY) in The Hague for the prosecution of persons accused of being responsible for serious violations of international humanitarian law. Later Security Council Resolutions 955 (1994) and 977 (1995) established the International Criminal Tribunal for Rwanda (ICTR). The offences prosecuted were genocide, crimes against humanity and war crimes. Both tribunals led to the arrest, handover and sentencing of a number of prominent war criminals. The ICTY indicted 161 high-profile persons and sentenced 90 persons for war crimes. This included, among others, Bosnian Serb leader Radovan Karadžić and General Ratko Mladic, both convicted of genocide. The ICTR had a lower exposure but sentenced the former prime minister of Rwanda, Jean Kambanda, to life imprisonment for genocide in 2000 (Gareis and Varwick 2005: 230).

Whereas the ICTY and the ICTR were clearly subsidiary organs of the UN, there have also been so-called hybrid tribunals with a mixed composition of national and international personnel. These hybrid tribunals, such as the Special Court for Sierra Leone (SCSL, 2002) or the Extraordinary Chambers in the Courts of Cambodia ('Khmer Rouge Tribunal', 2004), rested on a contractual agreement between the UN and the national government to address past international crimes in post-conflict societies (Goldstone 2007; Hoffmann-Van de Poll 2011).

The symbolic significance of these tribunals and their precursor role in relation to the Statute for an International Criminal Court, signed in Rome in 1998 by representatives of 120 states, is widely recognized (Boekle 1998: 14–16; Schabas 2011: 11–15). In contrast to the ICTY and the ICTR, the authority of the International Criminal Court (ICC) is not limited to prosecuting and sentencing gross violations of international humanitarian law on specific territories. It can sentence crimes against humanity, war crimes, crimes of aggression and genocide either committed on the territory of a country that has ratified its statute or committed by a citizen of such a country (Rudolph 2001). While the ICC is an independent international organization located in The Hague and is not part of the UN system, it maintains in general cooperative relations with the UN, in particular with the Security Council. The ICC prosecutor can initiate investigations on the basis of a referral from any state party or from the Security Council but also by his or her own initiative on the basis of information received from individuals or (civil society) organizations. State parties must cooperate with the Court, which also includes surrendering suspects upon request of the Court. As of 2024, 124 states have ratified the Rome Statute, with powerful states such as China, India, Russia and the United States still not being party to the ICC. The ICC has begun its work in 2002, conducting investigations, issuing arrest orders and hearing cases concerning situations in the Democratic Republic of Congo, Palestine, Uganda, Ukraine, the Central African Republic and Sudan.

Evaluation of the organization's effectiveness

The effectiveness of the UN's response to human rights violations must be assessed against the background of particularly challenging conditions for international cooperation in this field. International human rights protection affects the core of states' domestic sovereignty since it proscribes particular practices of rule within states. Authoritarian states, in particular, tend to reject their domestic practices of rule being subject to international scrutiny. Moreover, it is still debated in how far human rights constitute truly universal or culturally specific (above all Western liberal) values, which further complicates consensus on international human rights norms and their implementation (Jetschke 2006; Renteln 1990).

A first indication that UN activities in the human rights field can nonetheless have a positive impact on the human rights situation within member states might be that the global human rights situation has overall improved since the 1980s. This finding is underlined by a comparison of country ratings by the American NGO Freedom House. Freedom House rates all countries in the world based on criteria of political participatory rights and civil liberties. Figure 11.2 shows that between 1972 and 2024 the share of 'free' countries has increased whereas the proportion of 'not free' countries has become smaller, even though there has been a stagnation – and even backlash – since 2000. This improvement in the global human rights situation correlates with UN human rights activities being no longer limited to policy programme activities but increasingly including operational activities as well. However, this improvement of the global human rights situation (particularly in the field of political rights and civil liberties) might have many reasons, some of which are unrelated to the UN human rights regime. A closer look at the effectiveness of specific UN activities is warranted.

Some, mainly qualitative, studies suggest that international human rights norms had a positive impact on states' human rights policies during the Cold War and the early 1990s. Keck and Sikkink (1998) show that, especially in Latin America, transnational networks of human rights NGOs relied on international organizations' programme and operational activities in bringing about significant change in the human rights policies of particular states. In a similar vein, Risse, Ropp and Sikkink (1999) find evidence that cooperative efforts by transnationally operating networks

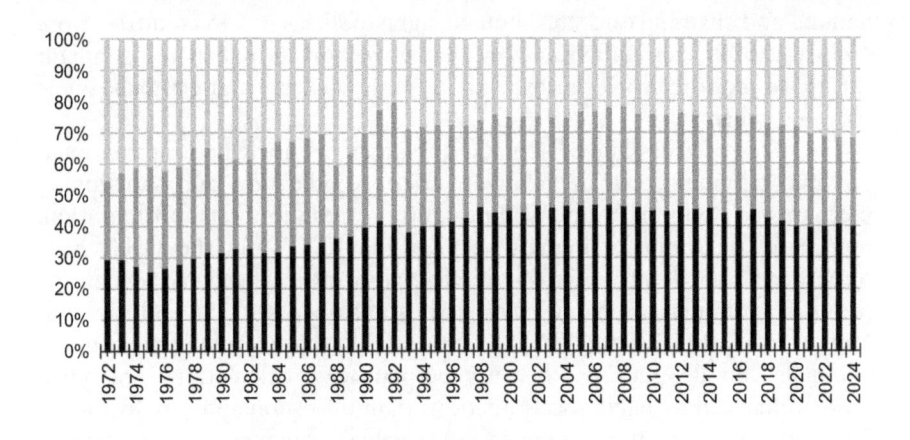

FIGURE 11.2 *Proportion of 'free', 'partly free' and 'not free' countries, 1972–2024* (in % of overall number of states, based on Freedom House Country Ratings). *Source: Based on data from Freedom House.*

of human rights NGOs, international organizations, Western states and domestic opposition groups have indeed brought about improvements in domestic human rights practices in eleven countries representing five different world regions – Northern Africa, sub-Saharan Africa, Southeast Asia, Latin America and Eastern Europe. Furthermore, UN human rights norms offer transnational human rights networks important arguments with which to convince democratic states to engage in more active human rights policies which then lead to improved human rights policies in, or even a democratic transition of, non-democratic countries (Klotz 1995; Risse, Ropp and Sikkink 1999). In a large-scale, statistical study, Simmons (2009) finds that, at state level, international human rights law has made a positive contribution to the respect for human rights, in particular in the fields of civil rights, equality for women, prevention of torture and the rights of the child. States' ratifications of treaties do lead over time to improved human rights practices by influencing legislative agendas, altering intrastate political coalitions and defining the terms of acceptable state action.

Naming and shaming of human rights violations is still the most common instrument of (promoting) international and transnational human rights enforcement. Thus, it is encouraging that states' practices of naming and shaming in UN organs are indeed based less on partisan ties among political allies and power politics and more on countries' actual human rights records and treaty commitments. This holds especially for the time after the end of the Cold War (Lebovic and Voeten 2006). However, naming and shaming by no means guarantees sustained norm compliance in political practice; its impact on the actual day-to-day human rights situation within countries is often limited. Hafner-Burton (2008) quantitatively analyses the effect of naming and shaming on states' human rights policies in 145 countries from 1975 to 2000. Her statistics show that governments put in the spotlight for abuses continue or even exacerbate some violations afterwards, while reducing others.

For cases of gross and systematic human rights atrocities, international criminal tribunals provide relatively hard adjudication and sanctioning mechanisms (Sikkink and Walling 2007). Despite their proliferation, international criminal tribunals such as the ICTY and the ICTR have often been regarded as relatively ineffective or at least inconsistent in the promotion of international justice (Barria and Roper 2005: 349; Hoffmann-Van de Poll 2011). Ku and Nzelibe (2006) doubt that international criminal tribunals can deter crimes because perpetrators' calculations are much more influenced by harsh local sanctions than uncertain and usually lighter international ones. Thus, pessimists are largely unconvinced of international criminal tribunals' transformative potential (Simmons and Danner 2010: 225–6; see Bloxham 2006; Goldsmith 2003). All-too bleak assessments of international criminal tribunals do not seem justified, though. It can be shown that international criminal tribunals had important influences on domestic values and cultural orientations towards violence (Kiss 2000; see also Sikkink and Walling 2007). Moreover, while there were certainly deficits in the reliability with which perpetrators of gross human rights violations were actually brought before the tribunals, sweeping claims that international criminal tribunals were unable to deter any atrocities are questionable on both methodological and empirical grounds (Akhavan 2001; Gilligan 2006; Scheffer 2002).

At any rate, these ad hoc international criminal tribunals were important precursors for the establishment of the ICC, which enjoys considerably broader authority. In an early study of the ICC's effects on member states' human rights policies in violent conflict, Simmons and Danner (2010) came to the conclusion that ratification of the Rome Statute is associated with tentative steps towards violence reduction and peace, at least in some countries, and that the ICC is potentially helpful as a mechanism for governments to credibly commit to reducing violence and get on the road to peaceful negotiations (Simmons and Danner 2010). At the same time, the ICC has been criticized particularly by African Union member states as only addressing human rights violations in Africa or more generally the Global South. This resulted in Burundi (2017) and Philippines (2019) leaving the ICC and South Africa threatening to do so. At the same time, the ICC has had its work cut out for it. In 2024, it was working on cases against sixty-five defendants, and the ICC prosecutors have not shied away from going after sitting heads of state and government including Omar al-Bashir from Sudan, Vladimir Putin from Russia and Benjamin Netanyahu from Israel. Indeed, the ICC has considerable investigative powers even if many defendants remain at large.

Conclusion

International organizations are playing a critical role in the area of migration and human rights. While migration and human rights were long considered sovereign and domestic issues, since the First World War, refugee protection is seen as an international problem. Whereas human rights violations are internationally discussed and addressed since the Second World War, issues around regular migration have only reached the international agenda in the past two decades. The legacy with refugees from both world wars has led to a clear policy programme in the legally binding 1951 Refugee Convention, while human rights have been developed in the 1948 Universal Declaration and the subsequent legally binding conventions and treaties. The policy programmes on migration are more fragmented, even if the 2018 Compact provides some guidance. In terms of operational activities, it is clear that refugees are most clearly protected through the activities of the UNHCR. While domestic publics, predominantly in the Western countries, may have little sympathy for regimes that violate human rights, UN operational activities in terms of the Human Rights Council have been more disappointing. It is clear that few countries are willing to take on China or other authoritarian regimes over their human rights records. Particularly in the past few years, international human rights norms and their compliance seem to be eroding. In the field of migration, the operational activities by the IOM remain almost entirely at the request of states. In this field, operational activities are least developed. Indeed, more ambitious policy programmes and operational activities for migration are to be found in regional organizations (see Chapter 12).

Much of the input for international organizations in the area of refugees, migration and human rights comes from outside developments. If a refugee crisis erupts, this is almost immediately brought to the attention of the UNHCR via the media and other channels (input). The UNHCR has offices around the world and can declare an emergency (conversion) which leads to deployments within seventy-two hours (output). Through the UPR, Special Procedures and the Complaints Procedure, instances of human rights violations are brought to the attention of the Human Rights Council by states, NGOs or even individuals (input). Through an investigation, the Human Rights Council subsequently converts this input into output, including the suspension of the offender from the Human Rights Council or 'naming and shaming'. Whether a solution is found in case of a refugee crisis, for instance, through the return, naturalization or resettlement of refugees, or whether human rights violations stop because of the pressures resulting from the UN proceedings (impact) is another question. At any rate, migration, refugees and human rights are clear examples of issue areas where the political system of international organizations works.

Discussion questions

1. To what extent are migration and human rights international or national problems?
2. Why do the policy programmes for refugees and migrants differ?
3. To what extent do international governmental organizations and (local as well as transnational) NGOs depend on one another's activities in bringing about improvements of states' human rights policies?

Further reading

Betts, Alexander (2009). *Protection by Persuasion: International Cooperation in the Refugee Regime*, Ithaca NY: Cornell University Press.

Orchard, Phil (2014). *A Right to Flee: Refugees, States, and the Construction of International Cooperation*, Cambridge: Cambridge University Press.

Simmons, Beth (2009). *Mobilizing for Human Rights. International Law in Domestic Politics*, Cambridge: Cambridge University Press, Chapters 2 and 5–8.

12

Regional cooperation

International organizations can be distinguished between those that deal with a specific task and those that have a much wider policy scope (see Chapter 1; also Hooghe, Lenz and Marks 2019). Task-specific international organizations seek to address a particular international problem and typically include all states affected by that problem: the membership of the organization follows the problem. In the last few of chapters, we have discussed many of such international organizations. From the World Trade Organization (WTO), providing a policy programme where its member states are not allowed to discriminate against each other, to the North Atlantic Treaty Organization (NATO), where allies commit to mutual defence in case of an armed attack, and the United Nations Framework Convention on Climate Change (UNFCCC), where the member states adopted the Paris Agreement and submitted the Nationally Determined Contributions (NDCs) for climate action, there are plenty of examples where international organizations have a relatively narrow scope and seek to address a particular international problem such as economic mercantilism, external security threats and climate change.

Such task-specific organizations contrast with general purpose organizations, which present a second and different type of international organizations. The cooperation logic here differs. Rather than focusing on a specific international problem, a like-minded group of states gets together first and they then decide to tackle a whole range of cross-border problems. Hooghe, Lenz and Marks (2019) argue that such international organizations are community-driven as the member states feel part of a certain community. Within such a community, member states may be more enthusiastic to cooperate and less reluctant to share sovereignty because they identify more strongly with the other member states. To better understand such general purpose organizations, we focus in this chapter on four regional international organizations: the European Union (EU), African Union (AU), Association of Southeast Asian Nations (ASEAN) and the Southern Common Market (MERCOSUR). General purpose organizations do not have to be regional. For example, the Commonwealth of Nations, consisting of former territories of the British Empire, the International Organization of La Francophonie (OIF), representing countries where the French language is used, and the Organisation of Islamic Cooperation (OIC) are also general purpose organizations, yet they span multiple regions. Nevertheless, regional organizations have become important forms of cooperation in international relations precisely because neighbouring states often encounter a range of cross-border problems and feel a joint responsibility to address them.

This book has a strong comparative focus by conceptualizing international organizations as political systems and comparing the input, conversion and output of different organizations across a range of policy areas and issues. There is also the temptation to compare regional organizations, and scholars have indeed developed an elaborate research agenda on comparative regionalism (e.g. Haas 1966; Acharya and Johnston 2007; Börzel and Risse 2016; Panke, Stapel and Starkmann 2020). One of the pitfalls here is to compare all regional organizations around the world to the EU, which is by far the most extensive regional organization when it comes to depth and breadth of integration and the sharing of sovereignty. Another pitfall is to expect that all other regional organizations will eventually follow the 'example' of the EU. While regional cooperation in Europe has, no doubt, been inspiring to some in the rest of the world, scholars of regional cooperation are sceptical that European ideas diffuse unidirectionally around the globe. They furthermore caution against regional comparisons that neglect the specificities of particular regional organizations, while encouraging us to appreciate the trajectory of individual regional organizations (e.g. De Lombaerde et al. 2010; Acharya 2012; Börzel and Risse 2016; Lenz 2021). There are more than seventy regional organizations around the world (Panke, Stapel and Starkmann 2020). This chapter discusses the EU, AU, ASEAN and MERCOSUR, which play important functions in their respective regions.

European Union

The EU has become one of the most important international organizations and the principal forum for cooperation for European countries. It is the international organization with the largest policy scope and highest degree of delegation (Hooghe, Lenz and Marks 2019: Figures 5.2 and 3.6). Even if policies such as defence, taxation, health, education and social policy formally remain state 'competences', the current twenty-seven member states also collaborate on and coordinate such 'core state powers' in the context of the EU (Genschel and Jachtenfuchs 2014). European laws harmonize, for example, value-added tax (VAT) throughout the Union and the member states collectively bought Covid-19 vaccines, thereby giving the EU a role in, respectively, taxation and health. What is more, the EU is not just a regional organization in which European member states work together. The

EU has also become an actor in its own right in international relations and represents its member states in a variety of other international institutions. For instance, both the EU and its member states are members of the Food and Agriculture Organization (FAO) and the WTO. Moreover, the presidents of the European Council and Commission participate in the Groups of 7 and 20 (G7/G20) on behalf of the membership. As such, some scholars consider the EU as an entity of its own kind (sui generis): more than an international organization but less than a state (Wallace 1982). Former Commission president Jacques Delors once dubbed it an 'unidentified political object'.

The current-day EU is normally traced to the Schuman Declaration (1950), in which the French foreign minister proposed a European Coal and Steel Community (ECSC) between six European countries (Segers and Van Hecke 2023). These countries then established the European Economic Community (EEC) through the Treaty of Rome (1957), which included an elaborate policy programme to establish a customs union and a common market through the gradual reduction of tariffs. The EEC developed during the Cold War expanding its scope to include a common agricultural policy as well as foreign policy consultations. It also welcomed new member states such as Denmark, Ireland and the UK (1973) and Greece, Spain and Portugal (1980s). With the Treaty of Maastricht (1992), the EEC was turned into a Union with a larger policy scope. The member states agreed, for instance, to adopt the Euro as a single currency. During the 1990s and 2000s, the EU further expanded its membership taking in no less than twelve Central and Eastern European states (2004 and 2007). The EU revised its treaties further in Amsterdam (1999), Nice (2001) and Lisbon (2007) to fine-tune its constitutional and institutional structure and to engage in more policy programmes and operational activities. Following Russia's war in Ukraine (2022), the EU agreed to open and speed up accession negotiations with Ukraine and various other Eastern European and Western Balkan countries. The membership of the EU will thus likely continue to evolve in the coming years and decade.

The Treaty on European Union (TEU) and the Treaty on the Functioning of the European Union (TFEU) form the constitutional basis of the EU (Hix and Høyland 2022). The former sets out the main objectives, values and principles of cooperation. It also defines the institutional structure of the EU. The latter, which is much longer, details the policy programmes of the EU. While both treaties are fundamental, the EU has also adopted more than 100,000 pages of secondary laws which make up the EU's *acquis communautaire*. Some of the policy programme and the operational activities are discussed below, but it is first important to describe its institutional structure (Hobson et al. 2021). The EU formally has seven institutions (see Box 12.1). The heads of state and government meet in the European Council and their ministers in ten different configurations of the Council. The European Parliament is the parliamentary assembly and includes 700+ directly elected politicians. The Commission serves as the secretariat and bureaucracy of the EU. It formulates policies and even has the exclusive right of initiative, and it implements various policy programmes through its operational activities. Quite often though, the member states themselves are in charge of implementation. The Council and the European Parliament act as 'co-legislators'. They are in charge of decision-making and in most policy areas, they both need to agree to the proposals of the Commission. The Council takes decisions mostly by qualified majority voting (requiring 55 per cent of member states representing 65 per cent of the EU population to be in favour), though in some areas unanimity remains the rule (such as foreign policy, taxation, citizenship and membership). The European Parliament decides also by majority.

Apart from these three core institutions, the EU has a powerful Court of Justice which can issue legally binding verdicts in case of disputes. The independent European Central Bank sets, among others, the interest rate for the Eurozone area, and the Court of Auditors audits the EU's finances to improve transparency and accountability. These seven institutions are, however, only the institutional tip of the iceberg. Within the Council, for instance, the member states have set up around 150 preparatory bodies where national diplomats meet on a daily basis. For this purpose, all member states have established permanent representations to the EU. These function as embassies and help member states to look after their interests in Brussels. These permanent representations each employ typically 100–200 diplomats, which are drawn from all national ministries. These include agricultural attachés, economic counsellors and even military advisers. The EU furthermore has eight 'bodies' including the European External Action Service (EEAS) for all foreign policy issues, the Committee of Regions, bringing regional politicians together, and the European Investment Bank, which provides loans to projects. In addition, there are about three dozen technical agencies dealing with food safety, police cooperation, border control or the approval of medicine. These agencies often report to the European Commission.

BOX 12.1 EU INSTITUTIONAL STRUCTURE

The EU has seven institutions according to the Treaty:

- European Parliament
- European Council
- Council (ten different configurations and 150 working groups)
- European Commission
- Court of Justice
- European Central Bank
- Court of Auditors

In addition, the EU has eight relevant bodies such as:

- European External Action Service
- Committee of the Regions
- European Investment Bank

The EU has also more than thirty agencies which engage in operational activities such as:

- European Aviation Safety Agency
- European Centre for Disease Prevention and Control
- European Chemicals Agency
- European Defence Agency
- European Food Safety Agency
- European Medicines Agency
- European Union Intellectual Property Office
- European Union Agency for Railways
- European Border and Coast Guard Agency (FRONTEX)

The policy programmes of the EU are extensive (Wallace et al. 2020). In fact, the TEU notes the ambition of 'creating an ever closer union among the peoples of Europe'. In many ways, the EU is historically a political project aimed to reconcile France and Germany after the Second World War and heal divisions across the European continent through successive enlargement rounds. It is nevertheless fair to say that the customs union and common market are central to the EU's policy programme as it has developed since the Treaty of Rome. The common market, the TFEU points out, 'shall comprise an area without internal frontiers in which the free movement of goods, persons, services and capital' (Article 26; the EU tends to refer to its

TABLE 12.1 *Different forms of economic cooperation*

Free trade area	No tariff or quotas on goods
Customs union	Free trade area plus a common external tariff
Common market	Free trade area plus free movement of people, services and capital
Economic union	Common market plus harmonization of economic policies

Source: Based on Balassa (1961: 2) and Nye (1968). An ideal common market often has a common external tariff (and is thus also a customs union) but this is not always the case.

common market as an internal or single market). This means that companies should be able to move their goods freely across the member states and offer their services elsewhere in the EU. Citizens should furthermore be able to travel, work, study, retire or start a company in a different member state. Citizens and companies should also be able to move capital across borders without restrictions. Importantly, this common market programme comes with a customs union (see Table 12.1). This implies that the member states trade with the rest of the world through a single EU foreign trade policy. The member states therefore use the same tariffs on products coming into the EU and apply the same customs standards. Once products have entered the EU, there are no further checks in line with the principle of the common market. The customs union also implies that the EU member states negotiate, as a single trading bloc, trade agreements with other countries.

Many of the other policies of the EU follow from the common market and the customs union, even if they were by no means automatically agreed by the member states. Indeed, the step towards economic (and monetary) union required decades of negotiations. Nevertheless, by having similar product standards, harmonized consumer protection, safety concerns for public health as well as environmental policies, the EU protects cross-border transactions and avoids a 'race to the bottom' or a situation where member states may invoke, for instance, public health concerns to ban products from other countries. In the famous *Cassis de Dijon* judgement of 1979, for instance, the European Court of Justice stated that products which are lawfully marketed in one member state cannot be prohibited in another member state. This implies an obligation of mutual recognition.

To ensure a 'level playing field' and to 'harmonize' the common market, EU member states also adopted laws on VAT and social policy including compulsory holidays and maternity leave. The EU further established strict competition and state aid rules to avoid unfair competition between companies. It also established the Schengen zone to allow citizens to travel between member states without passport checks. The adoption of the Euro as a single currency makes payments in the common market a lot easier.

In addition to many of these regulatory and monetary policies, the EU also established redistributive policies with a view to further strengthen the Union. Examples are the common agricultural and fisheries policies as well as the cohesion funds aimed to support poorer regions in Europe. The EU now spends a large part of its budget on research and innovation and has established the NextGenerationEU programme to help member states recover from Covid-19. While some view all these policy programmes as almost automatically resulting from the common market, this is not necessarily the case. Indeed, in other regional organizations we see common markets without similar regulatory and redistributive policy programmes.

Since the policy programmes of the EU are so extensive, it is difficult to summarize all the various operational activities here. As noted, a lot of effort has gone into specifying and implementing the common market programme. In 1985, for instance, the European Commission published a famous plan to 'complete' the common market, which involved removing all sorts of trade barriers that still existed among the member states. The 100,000 pages of *acquis* have furthermore been mentioned, which includes a variety of EU laws, including legally binding regulations (e.g. to prohibit mobile phone roaming charges) and directives which provide member states with targets that they need to achieve through domestic legislation (e.g. common rules for the generation, distribution and supply of electricity). When countries want to join the EU, they have to go through a year-long 'screening process' to assess the extent to which their legislation aligns with that of the EU. Specification has therefore been an important operational activity that has kept the EU busy over the decades.

The EU institutions, notably the European Commission, and the various EU bodies and agencies also play a key role in implementation. This includes the implementation of both the regulatory and distributive policy programmes. Under the competition policy programme, for instance, the European Commission decides whether large companies can acquire or merge with other companies. During the Covid-19 pandemic, to give another example, the European Medicines Agency had to assess the effectiveness and safety of vaccines. The European Commission also checks national plans for the NextGenerationEU fund and disburses research and innovation funds directly to research institutions across Europe. In many other cases, the member states themselves are in charge of implementation. Following the Russian invasion of Ukraine, the EU member states agreed to repeated rounds of sanctions against Russia including travel bans and freezing the assets of Russian nationals. It was up to the individual member states, however, to track such assets, via their banks and property registries, and subsequently freeze them. Similarly, as part of the Schengen zone, the EU has developed clear rules that border guards need to follow, but it is ultimately the national border guards in the member states that implement such rules when checking who can enter the Schengen zone from abroad.

While the EU is an example of a centralized international organization, where many decisions are formulated and agreed in Brussels, Luxembourg and Strasbourg, much of the actual implementation remains in the hands of the member states themselves.

Because implementation is key to its success, the EU has developed a large range of operational activities with respect to monitoring, adjudication and sanctioning non-compliant member states (Tallberg 2000, 2002b). The European Commission is considered, in this respect, the 'guardian of the treaties' and can start infringement procedures against member states that fail to implement EU law. This starts with a formal letter of notification, to which the member state can reply, followed by a reasoned opinion which is a formal request to comply with EU law. In case member states do not take the necessary measures, the Commission may decide to bring the matter in front of the European Court of Justice. The Court's ruling is binding, and the Commission may ask the Court to impose penalties (sanctions) on the member state. While the European Commission opens up to 1,000 infringement procedures each year, less than 5 per cent of those cases end up before the Court. The large majority of cases is closed after the initial letter of notification and the response by the member state. Interestingly, the compliance of member states with EU law varies significantly. Scholars suggest a number of reasons. Some have to do with domestic politics in member states, while others are about the administrative capacity that member states have available to implement complex EU laws on time (e.g. Mastenbroek 2005; Börzel 2022).

It is difficult to assess the effectiveness of regional organizations, such as the EU, precisely because their policy programmes are so broad. Individual policy programmes often have specific goals and their achievement can be measured, but the EU deals with so many different policies. When it concerns purely trade in goods, it is interesting to note that both trade within the common market (intra-EU) and trade with other regions of the world (extra-EU) have gone up considerable since the early 1990s, even if intra-EU trade is in volume almost twice as large than extra-EU trade. The EU, in this sense, has clearly created wealth for its member states and citizens. The EU has also created opportunities for citizens in terms of free movement and equal treatment that are difficult to measure in economic numbers. When thinking more broadly about the contemporary EU, it is also clear that this regional organization has 'muddled through' various crises, including the Eurozone crisis, migration and asylum crisis, Brexit and rule of law crises (Zeitlin, Laffan and Nicoli 2019). While the EU and its member states have stepped up a number of times, for instance, in handling the Eurozone crisis with bailouts and establishing new Eurozone institutions, the divergence in member states positions and the growth in Euroscepticism in domestic politics have become a constraining factor for European cooperation (Hooghe and Marks 2009). The politicization of the

EU is, however, also an indicator that the EU is having a clear impact in terms of regional cooperation. It is precisely because the EU matters to their lives that people care.

African Union

The AU is the largest regional organization in Africa with fifty-five member states thereby covering the entire continent. It also has a considerable policy scope dealing with all sorts of policies from peace and security to sustainable development, democratization and human rights. While its first objective is to 'achieve greater unity and solidarity between the African countries and the peoples of Africa' (AU Constitutive Act 2000: Article 3(a)), which resonates with the EU's 'ever closer union', there are also very obvious differences with the EU discussed above. First, the historical experience differed with decolonization and pan-Africanism playing a central role in the origins of the AU. Second, while the EU was developed around its common market, the AU in fact does not have a single common market. Rather, it relies on eight Regional Economic Communities (RECs), such as the East African Community and the Southern African Development Community which are regional organizations in their own right, to provide partially overlapping free trade areas, custom unions and common markets, even if the AU's objective remains to establish a continent-wide African Economic Community. Third, the AU has a lower degree of delegation than the EU, and the AU institutions struggle in terms of their authority and resources. As such, it is important to discuss the AU as a regional organization on its own terms.

Following decolonialization after the Second World War, thirty-one newly independent African states established the Organization of African Unity (OAU) in 1963 (Makinda, Okumu and Mickler 2016). They were inspired by pan-African ideas of the need for self-reliance in the face of colonialism and racism, the common history and bonds between African people as well as the unity of the continent. This was an important driver, as the African continent had previously been (artificially) split by colonial powers, hence the idea of a united Africa was not an automaticity. Against this background, the OAU Charter also states the 'sovereign equality' of all the member states (Article III). The newly independent African states were not going to dominate each other, as the colonial powers had done. The Charter also noted strict non-interference in each other's internal affairs and respect for each other's sovereignty and inalienable right to independent existence. This is therefore very different from the EU, which from the beginning has been based on the notion of shared sovereignty and authority over vital resources such as coal and steel to avoid interstate conflict. The OAU members would also support the decolonization and 'total emancipation' of the African territories which are still dependent (e.g. Angola and Mozambique or South Africa under apartheid), and importantly, they would not choose sides in the Cold War between the United States and Soviet Union but rather remain non-aligned.

The policy programme of the original OAU can therefore be seen as a pan-African attempt to stick together and stand strong against outside interference and major powers that might have been tempted to divide and rule the newly independent African states once more. The policy programme was thus restricted, and operational activities remained limited. Economic and development issues were left to other international organizations, such as the United Nations (UN). Trade was organized in the regional African organizations. The OAU remained weak and toothless as it failed to respond to most conflicts within African countries. The OAU developed nonetheless. In 1981, it adopted an African Charter on Human and Peoples' Rights and ten years later, in 1991, it adopted the Treaty Establishing the African Economic Community as an integral part of the OAU. The next step was the creation of the AU (2002), which formally replaced the OAU as the main regional organization in Africa (Pecker and Rukare 2002). The AU, which will be discussed in the remainder of this section, is much more progressive in its aims than the OAU reflecting also the post-Cold War era. The AU Constitutive Act (2000), for instance, promotes democratic principles, human rights and health (Article 3), issues that contrast with the non-interference principles of the OAU. The AU can also suspend member states (Article 30), which it has recently done after various military coups in, for instance, Mali and Sudan. The Constitutive Act includes proactive policy programmes on peace and security and economic development as well. Furthermore, rather than staying non-aligned and outside global politics, the AU wants 'the continent to play its rightful role in the global economy and in international negotiations' (Article 3(i)).

The Constitutive Act provides the constitutional structure of the AU along with another seventy-plus treaties, constitutions, conventions, charters, agreements and protocols adopted under the framework of the OAU and AU. The 1991 Treaty Establishing the African Economic Community is, in this regard, an important example and also paved the way to the establishment of the AU. In terms of the institutional structure, the AU Constitutive Act lists no less than nine organs. These include the Assembly consisting of the heads of state and government, the Executive Council of national ministers and the Permanent Representative Committee of the ambassadors accredited to the AU headquarters in Addis Ababa, Ethiopia. The Assembly and the Executive Council take decisions by consensus, or failing which, by a two-thirds majority. The Pan-African Parliament brings together 265 representatives of African legislatures. It has several roles, such as to examine and discuss the work of the AU, even if it does not have formal decision power. The Commission, consisting of a chairperson, a deputy chairperson and eight commissioners, serves as the secretariat of the organization. While the Constitutive Act foresees a Court of Justice as an organ, it was never established. Instead, it was 'merged' with the already existing African Court on Human and Peoples' Rights into the African Court of Justice and Human Rights. The AU financial institutions are another organ but consist of three still-to-be-established institutions, namely the African Central Bank, the African Monetary Fund and the African Investment Bank. In addition to these nine organs, the AU established a Peace and Security Council (PSC) as an additional organ through a protocol in 2002. It consists of fifteen members elected by the Executive Council.

BOX 12.2 AU INSTITUTIONAL STRUCTURE

The AU has ten organs according to the Treaty and PSC protocol:

- Assembly of the Union
- Executive Council
- Pan-African Parliament
- Court of Justice (never established)
- Commission
- Peace and Security Committee
- Permanent Representatives Committee
- Specialized Technical Committees
- Economic, Social and Cultural Council
- Financial Institutions

The organ of Financial Institutions of the AU consists of three institutions:

- African Central Bank (planned)
- The African Monetary Fund (planned)
- African Investment Bank (planned)

The AU has also a variety of linked agencies and bodies including:

- Africa Centre for Disease Control and Prevention
- African Court on Justice and Human Rights
- African Energy Commission
- African Space Agency

In terms of its policy programme, as noted above, the AU has a rather broad scope and a much more extensive programme (Article 3 of the Constitutive Act) than its preceding OAU. At the same time, the AU builds on policy programmes of a range of other (regional) institutions and initiatives with only partially overlapping memberships. For instance, while the AU has long had a human rights programme, only thirty-four member states have ratified the protocol establishing the African Court on Human and Peoples' Rights. It therefore makes sense to discuss here the peace and security policy programme, the African Economic Community policy programme and the Agenda 2063 policy programme. In terms of peace and security, the Constitutive Act notes the respect of borders, the peaceful resolution of conflicts, non-interference, peaceful coexistence and the prohibition of the use of force as core principles (Article 4). Yet it also includes 'the right of the Union to intervene in a Member State pursuant to a decision of the Assembly in respect of grave circumstances, namely: war crimes, genocide and crimes against humanity' and 'the right of Member States to request intervention from the Union in order to restore peace and security' (Article 4(h)(j)). In other words, the AU as a regional organization has a security mandate to intervene (militarily) in its member states under certain conditions. In a way, this resembles the UN policy programme on peace and security (see Chapter 8) and just as the UN has developed operational activities on this basis, so has the AU (see below).

The mentioned African Economic Community, established by Treaty in 1991, provides for the economic policy programme of the AU. This policy programme set out a gradual agenda of six stages to ultimately achieve an African economic and monetary union by 2028. The logic was that the AU would build on the eight RECs, thereby gradually achieving African economic integration. First, all African countries would need to become part of one such regional bloc and each of these blocs would establish a free trade area and customs union by 2021. The next steps would be then a continent-wide free trade area and customs union. While progress in the eight RECs has been uneven, the AU agreed to the African Continental Free Trade Area (AfCFTA) in 2018 which so far forty-four member states have ratified. The AfCFTA provides a gradual path to eliminate tariffs and foster cooperation on non-tariffs issues such as intellectual property. In a sense, it also resembles the WTO policy programme with a most favoured nation treatment and dispute settlement procedures including an appellate body. These attempts at creating economic integration by the AU have been subsumed under the broader 2063 Agenda of the AU. Celebrating fifty years since the OAU, the AU put forward an ambitious policy programme in 2013 for the next fifty years under the label 'Agenda 2063: the Africa we want'. This is a policy programme for the decades with African aspirations in terms of inclusive growth and sustainable development, an integrated continent with peace and security as well as good governance, rule of law, human rights and justice, a strong cultural identity, people-driven and Africa being an influential global player and partner. These seven aspirations of Agenda 2063 are spread over the five decades and include various goals and flagship projects, not unlike the worldwide UN Sustainable Development Goals (SDGs).

In terms of operational activities, it is important to point at the implementation of the AU peace and security policy programme. Through the 2002 PSC Protocol, the AU launched several operational activities and established relevant institutions under what is called the African Peace and Security Architecture. This includes, among others, early warning, peacebuilding capacities, humanitarian action, a panel of the wise and the establishment of the African Standby Force (Vines 2013; Williams 2014; Darkwa 2017). In collaboration with the RECs, the AU has authorized more than twenty peace support operations across the continent and has been involved in the implementation of several large ones including the AU Mission in Somalia (AMISOM, 2007–22) and AU Transition Mission in Somalia (ATMIS, since 2022) with no less than 22,000 troops (Williams 2018) or the joint AU-UN mission in Darfur (UNAMID, 2008–21) with 21,600 troops. The AU was particularly active with peace operations in the 2000s and 2010s. However, because of the increasing gridlock at the UN and the downsizing of UN peacekeeping (see Chapter 8), part of the burden of peacekeeping in Africa now seems to shift back to the AU with a variety of new military missions launched in 2022. The UN has, in this respect, also agreed in 2023 to fund the majority of the budget of AU missions.

When it comes to other operational activities, the AU has been less active. It has helped to specify the policy programme including the operationalization of the 2063 Agenda. The AU does not engage in clear monitoring or adjudication activities. While the Court of Justice was foreseen in the Constitutive Act, it was never established as such. The African Court on Justice and Human Rights, which developed from the African Court on Human and Peoples' Rights, has a very broad jurisdiction including the interpretation and application of the Constitutive Act (Article 28(a) of 2008 Protocol). Yet the 'African Court', as it is generally referred to, largely remains focused on human rights (it even still carries the old name on its website) rather than adjudicating about AU issues more generally. The AfCFTA does include a separate dispute settlement mechanism and an appellate body to adjudicate over trade matters, but so far disputes have been dealt within the RECs bodies or the WTO. The AU and its RECs can uniquely suspend membership and sanction member states, for instance, for non-democratic coups, which is a practice that has been used repeatedly including in the 2020s. Such measures are thus taken to safeguard the democratic nature of the membership; by contrast, in the EU, for instance, sanctions can be imposed for non-compliance with legislation (while the EU has largely failed to effectively address the democratic backsliding of some of its member states).

Regional cooperation in Africa does not lack ambitions. From policy programmes to bring peace and security in the AU to economic integration resulting in an economic and monetary union and the aspirations of the

2063 Agenda, the member states have repeatedly set the bar high for themselves. When speaking of effectiveness, as per the definitions of Chapter 7, most of such goals have not been achieved. Effectiveness is thus low by the traditional definition of goal achievement. At the same time, African regional cooperation has come a long way from the initial aims of the OAU established more than sixty years ago when decolonization was still ongoing. African states have set up elaborate sets of overlapping institutions, developed considerable peace and security policies and operations, used regional institutions as building blocks for the purpose of economic integration and set out strong pan-Africanism aspiration in the 2063 Agenda. Even if some of these aspirations remain 'moonshots', in the words of the AU, it is striking that for all its diversity, the African continent through the AU is pursuing common goals. This does, of course, not distract from the fact that many conflicts take place in Africa, that 60 per cent of the global poor live in sub-Saharan Africa and that the continent and the AU remain heavily dependent on external financial support. The challenges for the AU therefore remain immense.

Association of Southeast Asian Nations

Asia is the largest continent and unlike the AU in Africa, it does not have a continent-wide regional organization. In this chapter, we focus on ASEAN as an example of regional cooperation (Beeson 2009). ASEAN with its ten member states is a relevant organization, but it does not include major Asian powers such as China, India, Japan and Russia as members. Indeed, the rationale of ASEAN was and is for smaller states to bond together under Indonesian leadership to balance against the major Asian powers. ASEAN has, however, facilitated more extended forms of regional cooperation including 'ASEAN Plus Three' cooperation (including China, Japan and South Korea), the East Asia Summit (including Australia, New Zealand, Russia and the United States) and the ASEAN Regional Forum (including Bangladesh, India, Pakistan and the EU). Through these different institutional frameworks, concentric circles around ASEAN proper, ASEAN member states have thus not only been able to establish an institutionalized dialogue with major Asian powers but have also brought in relevant non-Asian powers. While ASEAN, like other regional organizations, currently has a wide scope, it originally focused more on security than on trade. As exporting countries, ASEAN member states were mostly interested in global trade (extra-ASEAN) rather than trading with each other (intra-ASEAN). Over time, however, ASEAN has become the most comprehensive regional organization in Asia in terms of its scope (Panke, Stapel and Starkmann 2020: 95–6).

When five states signed the ASEAN Declaration in Bangkok in 1967, bipolarity and the Cold War were very much on their mind. With the war in neighbouring Vietnam (1955–75) intensifying, Indonesia, Malaysia, Thailand, the Philippines and Singapore were worried to be caught up in the geopolitics of China, the Soviet Union and the United States as well as conflicts between each other including between Indonesia and Malaysia. The short Declaration though was also short on security. Economic growth and welfare instead were seen as means to regional security. Nevertheless, the fallout of the communist victory in Vietnam led to the first ASEAN summit and the adoption of the 1976 Treaty of Amity and Cooperation, while the subsequent Vietnamese invasion of Cambodia occupied ASEAN for much the remainder of the Cold War. This process was driven by what is known as the 'ASEAN way' with policies of non-intervention and the peaceful settlements of conflicts through extensive consultation and consensus building (Acharya 1997). After the end of the Cold War, ASEAN developed its policy programme by agreeing to the ASEAN Free Trade Area (AFTA), expanded its membership to ten states and set up the ASEAN Regional Forum in 1994. ASEAN's focus shifted to increasing economic growth with the 1997 Asian financial crisis providing further impetus. Eventually the member states adopted the 2007 ASEAN Charter, which would serve as a constitutional framework and thus codify, to a significant extent, the processes and practices of the organization (Leviter 2010).

Despite the 'ASEAN way' of informality and informal consultation as a means of cooperation, ASEAN has been legalized and institutionalized in the recent decades. It possesses an extensive constitutional and institutional structure. The 2007 Charter clearly makes up the constitutional structure of ASEAN along with a number of separate agreements and treaties such as the 1976 Treaty of Amity and Cooperation and the 1992 AFTA on the Common Effective Preferential Tariff (CEPT) (Woon 2015). There are currently more than eighty of such legal instruments (as of 2024). In addition, there are partially overlapping yet separate constitutional structures for ASEAN Plus Three, the East Asian Summit and the ASEAN Regional Forum. In terms of the institutional structure, ASEAN has a Summit, a Coordination Council, three Community Councils dealing with political-security, economic and socio-cultural affairs, Sectoral Ministerial Bodies and a Committee of Permanent Representatives. All of these take decisions on the basis of consultation and consensus. ASEAN furthermore has a secretary general and a Secretariat since 1976 as well as National Secretariats which serve as contact points in the member states. There is a Human Rights Body and an ASEAN Foundation to support community and identity building. Annex 1 and 2 of the ASEAN Charter include a very long list of all sorts of ministerial bodies as well as entities associated with ASEAN including business and civil society organizations. ASEAN Plus Three, the East Asian Summit and the ASEAN Regional Forum have their own structures such as preparatory units, but they are administered through the ASEAN Secretariat. With such an elaborate institutional structure, it is difficult to claim that ASEAN remains 'informal' compared to other organizations, yet clearly the emphasis is on permanent consultation among the member states rather than the delegation of powers to the ASEAN Secretariat.

> ### BOX 12.3 ASEAN INSTITUTIONAL STRUCTURE
>
> The ASEAN Charter lists nine organs:
>
> - Summit
> - Coordinating Council
> - Community Councils (Political-Security, Economic, Socio-Cultural Councils)
> - Sectoral Ministerial Bodies
> - Secretary general and Secretariat
> - Committee of Permanent Representatives
> - National Secretariats
> - Human Rights Body
> - ASEAN Foundation
>
> Annex I of the ASEAN Charter lists all the ministerial bodies and other institutions linked to the three communities. Annex II lists a whole range of entities associate to ASEAN. Some of these entities include:
>
> - Inter-Parliamentary Assembly
> - ASEAN Automotive Federation
> - ASEAN Insurance Council
> - ASEAN Chess Confederation
> - ASEAN Fisheries Federation

The policy programme of ASEAN consists of its political-security, economic and socio-cultural cooperation. In terms of political and security cooperation, it follows a number of core principles such as respect for the independence and territorial integrity of the member states and non-interference in internal affairs (Charter, Article 2), which were previously mentioned in the Treaty of Amity and Cooperation. It importantly also includes the principle of a shared commitment and collective responsibility in enhancing regional peace, security and prosperity, thus giving ASEAN a regional role beyond its membership. The centrality and proactiveness of ASEAN is mentioned here as well. The policy programme includes the objective to create a single market and production base and to alleviate poverty. There is a specific emphasis on human development and promoting the ASEAN identity

(Charter, Article 1). In addition to the policy programme listed in the Charter, it is worth mentioning the agreements under AFTA relating to trade in goods (1992), services (1995), investment (1998), movement of persons (2012), complemented by the ASEAN Vision 2020 (adopted in 1997) aimed at making ASEAN a highly competitive economic region. Internal trade is, however, less important as previously mentioned than trade with the rest of the world. Therefore, ASEAN member states have tried to collectively phase out their external tariffs. These external tariffs are, however, set and administered by the member states as ASEAN – unlike, say, the EU – is not a customs union. To promote external trade, ASEAN has also negotiated free trade agreements with relevant countries such as Australia, China, India, Japan and New Zealand. In 2022, after a decade of negotiations, the Regional Comprehensive Economic Partnership (RCEP) entered into force. It is a free trade agreement that covers all ASEAN members and the five mentioned states.

To develop the AFTA policy programme, ASEAN has developed a considerable number of operational activities particularly with regard to the specification of policies. Precisely because the member states are in charge of their own external tariffs, ASEAN, through consultation, has adopted all sorts of tariffs reduction schedules. The same goes for investment and the movement of people. It has also specified details for the mutual recognition of services, from engineering services to dental practitioners. The implementation of AFTA and the ASEAN Economic Community has, however, been made more difficult due to the large differences in the member states' economies. Singapore, for instance, is much more open and richer than some of the newer ASEAN members such as Cambodia and Laos. The phasing out of tariffs does not automatically mean more trade as non-tariff barriers (e.g. product requirements or languages on labelling) also prevent cross-border trade. While the ASEAN Secretariat monitors the AFTA, it does not have enforcement powers. AFTA does include a dispute settlement mechanism but it is not actively used. When ASEAN member states have a trade dispute, they prefer to use the WTO dispute settlement mechanism. The ASEAN Secretariat provides some economic operational activities, including offering macroeconomic monitoring, giving expert advice and gathering statistics.

Similar things can also be said about the other policy areas where operational activities tend to be limited as well. Most of the implementation of the ASEAN policy programme is done by the member states themselves, including through their intergovernmental consultative bodies. In the area of the political security community, there has been a stronger emphasis on activities in the realm of non-traditional security threats such as human smuggling, illicit drugs, border management and counterterrorism. The ASEAN Secretariat remains modest in size with only a few hundred officials and runs few operational activities itself. It is in this respect also interesting that ASEAN has National Secretariats alongside the centralized secretariat in Indonesia. While the Treaty of Amity and Cooperation already included a dispute settlement mechanism for conflict resolution among the member states, ASEAN countries have also been keen to develop informal mechanisms including a diplomacy of accommodation, consultation and consensus, networking, agreeing to disagree or third-party mediation (Caballero-Anthony 1998). In other words, in practice, the 'ASEAN way' is not necessarily about the formal institutional structure, which is solidly in place, but rather about how member states develop operational activities and about their approach towards these institutions. There is a clear policy programme but the implementation and follow up is mostly decentralized through the member states or organized through member state consultations.

The effectiveness of ASEAN is a matter of debate among scholars who disagree on whether ASEAN as a regional organization has contributed to the security and prosperity of its member states (Jones and Smith 2007; Ravenhill 2009; Stubbs 2019). For instance, some argue that the absence and mitigation of conflict within ASEAN over the decades is not a surprise given the decline of interstate conflict around the world at this time. In this view, the absence and mitigation of conflict within ASEAN cannot be credited to ASEAN as a regional organization. A similar argument can be made about globalization and free trade which has gone up significantly in the post-Cold War period. At the same time, it is clear that ASEAN has made progress in achieving its stated goals of the peaceful coexistence of its member states and increasing economic integration between the member states. A complex question is that it is not always clear what 'ASEAN' exactly is. The Treaty of Amity and Cooperation now includes more than fifty states including from Europe and the Americas. AFTA has been expanded with the conclusion of RCEP and includes ASEAN plus five other key states. A big debate about the effectiveness of ASEAN concerns the future. With geopolitical competition heating up (also) in Asia, ASEAN member states are immediately affected by the conflict in the South China Sea for instance. Such geopolitical tensions put in question ASEAN's model of cooperative security based on consultations and outreach to other relevant Asian powers and global actors through the various platforms (Beeson 2022). While such geopolitical pressures might stimulate further integration, just as when ASEAN was created in 1967, it is unclear whether the current organizational set-up is fit for that purpose.

MERCOSUR: Southern Common Market

Various regional organizations provide cooperation in the Americas. There is a long tradition of pan-Americanism going back to the nineteenth century and the Monroe Doctrine of keeping the European colonial powers – and later Soviet influence – out of the Western Hemisphere. The Organization of American States (OAS), founded in 1948, and including most North, Central and South American states, is the regional embodiment of this. At the same time, the independent Latin American states have long worried about excessive US influence and have therefore tried to stick together. There is also a case for sub-regional cooperation. The community of Caribbean states, which joined forces in the regional organization CARICOM (1973-date), clearly faces different types of challenges than the United States, Mexico and Canada (USMCA Agreement, formerly North American Free Trade Agreement (NAFTA) since 1994) or the four states of the Andean Community (Bolivia, Colombia, Ecuador and Peru since 1969). We could have introduced any of these regional organizations here, which all have constitutional and institutional structures as well as policies and operational activities. Our focus is however on the Southern Common Market (MERCOSUR) between Argentina, Bolivia, Brazil, Paraguay and Uruguay. With five states, MERCOSUR does not have the largest membership. Founded only in 1991, it is also not the oldest. Yet it is one of the largest trading blocks around the world along with ASEAN/AFTA/RCEP, EU, USMCA and the AU/AfCFTA. It also has a customs union with a common external tariff. This makes MERCOSUR a significant regional organization to study. MERCOSUR, compared to the other three regional organizations in this chapter, however, has a more limited scope.

MERCOSUR was established by Argentina, Brazil, Paraguay and Uruguay through the Treaty of Asunción of 1991 (Gardini 2010). There had been previous attempts at regional cooperation in Latin America, but the parallel democratization of Argentina (1983) and Brazil (1985), and both states opening up to the world, provided the momentum for the bilateral Foz do Iguaçu Declaration (1985) and Buenos Aires Act (1990), which aimed for a customs union between both countries. This was part of a broader attempt at reconciliation between the countries, which included further agreements such as nuclear non-proliferation. Paraguay and Uruguay joined the negotiations leading to the Treaty of Asunción which had the ambition to establish a common market by the end of 1994 while establishing a common external tariff of up to 35 per cent on imports. MERCOSUR was in this respect not just about trade between the member states but also protecting domestic industries in Argentina and Brazil from global competition (Council on Foreign Relations 2023). MERCOSUR survived the economic crises in Latin America during the 1990s and through fairly lengthy accession processes, Venezuela (2012) and Bolivia (2024) eventually joined the organization as new members. Venezuela, though, was suspended as a member in 2016 under the 1998 Ushuaia Protocol on Democratic Commitment, which notes that the full application of democratic institutions is an essential condition for the development of the integration process within MERCOSUR. Most other South American states, such as Chile and Peru, have become associate members of MERCOSUR. They receive tariff reductions but are not part of the common market and the institutional organs of the organization.

The 1991 Treaty of Asunción along with the 1994 Protocol of Ouro Preto, which formally set up the customs union, and the 1998 Ushuaia Protocol on Democratic Commitment thus make up the constitutional structure of MERCOSUR. Under the 1991 Treaty, MERCOSUR has two institutions: the Council, which consists of ministers, and the Common Market Group as the executive body. Under the 1994 Protocol, four organs were added including a Trade Commission, Joint Parliamentary Commission, Economic-Social Consultative Forum and an administrative secretariat. All the decisions are taken by consensus, which makes sense given the small number of member states and the prominence of Argentina and Brazil. The 1991 Protocol of Brasilia and the subsequent 2002 Protocol of Olivos set up a dispute settlement mechanism with the possibility of establishing an ad hoc arbitration court and a permanent review tribunal. In 2005, the Constitutive Protocol of the MERCOSUR Parliament was adopted and, over time, MERCOSUR added additional bodies thereby gradually expanding its policy scope.

BOX 12.4 MERCOSUR INSTITUTIONAL STRUCTURE

The 1991 Treaty of Asunción lists two organs:

- Council
- Common Market Group

The 1994 Protocol of Ouro Preto adds four organs:

- Trade Commission (MTC)
- Joint Parliamentary Commission (JPC)
- Economic-Social Consultative Forum (ESCF)
- Administrative Secretariat (MAS)

Additional organs and bodies include:

- Ad hoc arbitration court and permanent review tribunal
- MERCOSUR Parliament
- Social Institute
- Creation of the Institute of Public Policies on Human Rights

The policy programme of MERCOSUR centres on its common market and customs union. The 1991 Treaty, in this regard, briefly notes the ambition to achieve 'the free movement of goods, services and factors of production between countries' by means of eliminating tariffs among the member states as well as 'the establishment of a common external tariff and the adoption of a common trade policy' when dealing with the rest of the world (Article 1). In addition, the member states committed to coordinating their economic and sectoral policies and harmonizing their legislation to strengthen regional integration, hinting in the direction of economic union (see Table 12.1). The Treaty also included as Annex I its trade liberalization programme, which provided a schedule to eliminate tariffs within three and a half years until the end of 1994 and included a range of transition rules for the different member states.

While MERCOSUR set out an ambitious common market and customs union programme as part of its 1991 Treaty, it was also largely an incomplete contract. The phasing out of internal tariffs on goods between the member states was clear, but much of the rest of the policy programme needed specification. The first challenge has, in this respect, been non-tariff barriers among the member states. As tariffs came down, non-tariff barriers such as quotas and product licenses went up. Technical and regulatory measures applying to certain goods are another persistent non-tariff barrier. It has similarly been difficult for MERCOSUR to establish a common external tariff, as there remain many exceptions with the member states setting their own rates, even if tariffs have generally come down. MERCOSUR has further specified its treaty programme with regard to the freedom of movement of persons. Not only is MERCOSUR now mentioned on the cover of passports, nationals of the member states and associated states only need a national identity card (not a passport) to travel within the MERCOSUR area. MERCOSUR citizens also have the right to take residence and work in the other member states. Beyond the common market, MERCOSUR has also adopted a variety of protocols dealing with economic and social harmonization with regard to civil and criminal procedure, transportation, education, labour law and the environment. MERCOSUR has also set up a fund for structural convergence of the member states, largely paid for by Brazil, which includes mainly infrastructure projects. All such specifications have been the result of member states' negotiations in the relevant organs of the institutional structure and are implemented by the member states themselves.

The effectiveness of MERCOSUR is mixed at best. The initial policy programme of the early 1990s brought a very significant reduction, almost abolishment, of tariffs, which in turn resulted in a very strong increase in trade between the member states. Furthermore, MERCOSUR has managed to expand its scope beyond merely trade in goods and has also made steps towards a common market with the freedom of movement of persons as well as the harmonization of several economic policies. At the same time, intra-MERCOSUR trade also remained a fraction of the total trade of MERCOSUR member states. While import plus export within MERCOSUR was about US$100 billion in 2023, total trade with the rest of the world was US$685 billion. This is a very different ratio from, for instance, the EU where intra-EU trade exceeds extra-EU trade. Part of the problem is that the member states have not been able to do away with non-tariff barriers among them and that there remain too many exceptions to the common external tariff. In this sense, MERCOSUR is not a fully fledged free trade area, let alone a common market.

Conclusion

This chapter has studied regional cooperation in Europe, Africa, Asia and South America through the regional organizations of the EU, AU, ASEAN and MERCOSUR. The logic behind such regional cooperation is that a group of like-minded countries together try to address a set of cross-border cooperation problems. While the scope of the EU, AU and ASEAN are indeed broad, and there is clearly evidence of community and identity building in these organizations, MERCOSUR remains centred around trade even if it has also introduced citizenship policies. Each of these organizations has developed over time a clear constitutional structure and an elaborate set of institutions, yet there are also notable differences. The EU, in particular, has centralized policymaking and relies heavily on the monitoring as well as the enforcement powers of its institutions. Its common market is sacrosanct, and harmonization and mutual recognition have been the magic words to further integration over time. The AU, in contract, relies more heavily on its RECs for economic cooperation and is still building its free trade area. ASEAN has found its own 'ASEAN way' to regional integration relying primarily on consultation and consensus among its member states instead of legalized procedures. It is also a central actor in a range of cooperation formats and dialogues that bring in other states. MERCOSUR has been less open to external members and has adopted a common market and customs union, whose purpose was a common external tariff. At the same time, it has clearly not gone as far as the EU in developing all sorts of policy programmes in support of this common market. It also does not have comparable dispute settlement and compliance mechanisms.

The origins and history of each of these different regional organizations are also relevant. While the EU and MERCOSUR developed economic policy programmes around previous rival member states, the AU and ASEAN were much more informed by decolonialization and staying out of geopolitics via non-alignment during the Cold War. Non-interference in internal affairs and the peaceful resolution of disputes are therefore key principles in both the AU and ASEAN. If member states of these two regional organizations do not stick together, outsiders may take advantage. What is striking is that each of these regional organizations has been heavily influenced by the wave of globalization and democratization of the post-Cold War era. The EU prospered enormously, while the AU adopted a more progressive Constitutive Act. Both the ASEAN/AFTA and MERCOSUR economic policies were directly linked to the opportunities of the end of bipolarity. The EU, ASEAN and AU also developed an external role as regional players in this period by engaging in conflict management and cooperative security including beyond the borders of their member states. The fact that geopolitics is intensifying again may imply that the future is less bright for these organizations.

What this chapter has also made clear is that the EU truly stands out as a regional organization in terms of its constitutional and institutional structure as well as its policy programmes and operational activities. It therefore does not necessarily make a lot of sense to compare the other regional organizations (and their trajectories) to the EU. Indeed, of the four regional organizations studied in this chapter, the EU is the only one where member states trade more with each other (intra-EU) than with the rest of the world (extra-EU). For ASEAN members, the initial ambition was not necessarily intra-ASEAN trade as the export markets were elsewhere. The same goes for AU and MERCOSUR member states. But the analysis of the AU, ASEAN and MERCOSUR also tells us something about the EU. The story of the EU is often presented as one of 'spillover' where a free trade area almost automatically led to a customs union, competition policy, an economic and monetary union and the harmonization of laws (from product standards to the number of holidays) (e.g. Haas 1968; Jones, Kelemen and Meunier 2016). Comparative regionalism shows that this is not the case. There are various forms of regional cooperation (see Table 12.1). The overlapping free trade areas in Africa and Asia, where countries can still set and administer external tariffs, are an antidote to harmonization and centralization. European regional integration therefore really is different.

Discussion questions

1. What are the core differences between regional organizations and the task-specific international organizations discussed in the previous chapters?
2. Does it make sense to compare regional organizations? What are the potential downsides of such a comparison?
3. To what extent is regional cooperation a solution to the increasing gridlock in international organizations with a universal membership? Discuss by providing examples.

Further reading

Acharya, Amitav (1997). 'Ideas, Identity, and Institution-building: From the "ASEAN Way" to the "Asia-Pacific Way"?', *The Pacific Review*, 10 (3): 319–46.

Börzel, Tanja A. and Thomas Risse, eds (2016). *The Oxford Handbook of Comparative Regionalism*, Oxford: Oxford University Press.

Hix, Simon and Bjørn Høyland (2022). *The Political System of the European Union*, 4th edn, London: Bloomsbury Publishing.

Williams, Paul D. (2018). *Fighting for Peace in Somalia: A History and Analysis of the African Union Mission (AMISOM), 2007–2017*, Oxford: Oxford University Press.

PART IV

Conclusion

13

The future of international organizations

In this book, we have shown that international organizations through their policy programmes and operational activities contribute to addressing international problems. We have argued that the creation and implementation of international norms and rules depends on the existence and internal workings of international organizations. By considering international organizations as political systems, we can identify how they convert inputs into outputs and thus respond to developments in the international environment. This approach is important, because it allows us to analyse how exactly different international organizations convert similar inputs into different outputs. While our evaluations of the effectiveness of international organizations have also shown that they are no panacea, international organizations are nonetheless key actors in global governance and the broader international environment.

Many of the international organizations we know have been created in the post-war and post-Cold War period. Even if they were inspired by older institutions, the United Nations (UN) system, most regional organizations and most international organizations dealing with security, trade, the environment, migration and human rights developed against the background of Cold War bipolarity and American hegemony since 1989. While many of these international organizations remain central to international relations, there is also wide consensus among scholars and other observers that world politics is changing and that such changing world politics, in turn, challenges many established international organizations. From the Trump administration's 'America First' to the assertiveness of China under president Xi and the effects of the Russian war against Ukraine, international organizations seem to be at the receiving end of international politics. This raises the question whether the current set of international organizations is still fit for purpose. To assess whether the future of international organizations is bright or bleak, we consider four key contemporary challenges to international organizations in this concluding chapter:

- The legitimacy of international organizations and contestation
- Gridlock within international organizations and new cooperation challenges
- Emerging powers and power shifts in international organizations
- The geopoliticization of international organizations

These challenges put considerable pressures on many international organizations, yet while some may cause a systemic crisis *of* international organizations, others may 'only' cause problems *within* international organizations. Indeed, throughout this concluding chapter we reflect on whether these challenges spell trouble for individual organizations or more broadly for international organizations as vehicles for cooperation (cf. Eilstrup-Sangiovanni and Hofmann 2020). Importantly, these four challenges frequently overlap. For instance, great power rivalry between China and the United States may result in contestation, gridlock, geopoliticization and efforts to negotiate power shifts in international organizations. Nonetheless, these are also different types of challenges, distinguished in the academic literature, and we therefore present them one by one. In the conclusion of the chapter, we consider what this 'crisis' of international organizations means for their future as part of international relations.

Legitimacy and contestation

One of the most prominent research agendas on international organizations in recent years has been the study of their legitimacy and contestation. Legitimacy is defined as the recognition of not only member states but also other relevant societal audiences that international organizations have the 'right to rule' in a particular policy area (e.g. Binder and Heupel 2015; Tallberg and Zürn 2019). Questions of legitimacy became particularly prominent after the 'Battle of Seattle' (1999) when no less than 40,000 protestors demonstrated against a Ministerial Conference of the World Trade Organization (WTO), as they objected to economic globalization in the WTO policy programme. Legitimacy questions are raised, however, about many international organizations. For instance, to what extent has the International Monetary Fund (IMF) the legitimacy to impose harsh conditionality on states and to what extent has the UN the right to freeze the bank account of suspected terrorists? Also, their democratic deficit has been cited as an issue that impairs the legitimacy of international organizations and thus contributes to their contestation. Various scholars have therefore studied the legitimacy crises of international organizations

(Tallberg and Zürn 2019; Deitelhoff and Zimmermann 2020). Such crises are significant, as contrary to states, international organizations typically cannot rely on material resources of power (e.g. coercion and the use of force) to compensate for a lack of legitimacy (Reus-Smit 2007). When the stakeholders perceive that international organizations no longer have the 'right to rule', international organizations may lose support and go on a pathway towards decline or fall into desuetude.

When considering the legitimacy of different political systems, researchers often distinguish between 'input', 'throughput' and 'output' legitimacy (Easton 1965; Scharpf 2009; Schmidt 2013). Input legitimacy is about whether relevant actors – states and non-state actors including citizens – perceive that they have adequate representation in international organizations and that their inputs and demands are sufficiently considered. Throughput legitimacy is about actors perceiving that policy programmes and operational activities are properly formulated and implemented by international organizations (within the 'black box') with a sufficient amount of transparency, openness, inclusiveness and accountability. Output legitimacy then refers to whether actors consider that the outputs of international organizations have the right impact for them. It is possible for different actors to value different types of legitimacy differently. Some states care deeply for input legitimacy and symbolic representation in international organizations. They want a seat at the table and be heard; for them, it is about sovereign equality and respect. Other states care largely about output legitimacy: as long as international organizations continue to provide them with cooperation gains, they are less interested in providing input. Some states, like the United States, have put lots of focus on throughput and the quality of policymaking within international organizations (Grigorescu 2007).

A prominent argument on the legitimacy of international organizations is made by Zürn (2018) and his co-authors. He argues that international organizations have gained a lot more authority over time and now 'rule' over a great many policy areas. They are no longer just concerned with technical international cooperation but have also become 'intrusive' in the domestic affairs of their member states (Börzel and Zürn 2021). The increase in their authority has thus made the democracy deficit of international organizations more and more pressing (Zürn 2018; Louis and Maertens 2021; Kreuder-Sonnen and Rittberger 2023). This, in turn, triggers the politicization of international organizations in domestic politics. To put it differently, the output of international organizations potentially favours certain groups over others, which creates a domestic political conflict in many of the member states. Politicians now increasingly have to 'look over their shoulders' when they try to address problems through international organizations. Domestic politics has therefore become a constraining factor for international organizations (Hooghe and Marks 2009). In addition to politicization, international organizations may also be increasingly contested by a variety of state and non-state actors and may see their legitimacy decline as a result of it. While many scholars support this 'endogenous' argument, in which the empowerment of international organizations over time leads to contestation, we should also consider the political games played at the member states level. (Populist) parties, for instance, cleverly use and blame international organizations in domestic debates to gain more votes in elections (Hooghe and Marks 2009; De Vries, Hobolt and Walter 2021). By portraying international organizations as part of unaccountable global and liberal elites, who promote their private interests at the cost of 'normal people', they have brought politics to international organizations.

The exact drivers for politicization and contestation remain subject of debate, but empirical research has indeed highlighted a gap in the extent to which elites and normal citizens have 'confidence' in international organizations. Dellmuth et al. (2022) have compared the legitimacy beliefs of elites (political party, bureaucratic, media, civil society, research and business elites) and normal citizens in Brazil, Germany, the Philippines, Russia and the United States, asking elites and normal citizens exactly the same questions about six well-known international organizations: the International Criminal Court (ICC), IMF, UN, World Bank, World Health Organization (WHO) and WTO. They find that, except for the Philippines, elites in all countries have more confidence in each of the international organizations than normal citizens (Dellmuth et al. 2022: Figures 5.1 and 5.4). Confidence of elites and citizens in international organizations most closely relates to the confidence that they have in (national) government institutions, but confidence also varies across the countries and international organizations. While the more technical WHO typically ranks the highest in terms of confidence (the survey was conducted before the Covid-19 pandemic), civil society elites tend to be most sceptical about international economic organizations such as the World Bank, IMF and WTO (Dellmuth et al. 2022: Figure 5.8). Civil society elites, in general, have less confidence in international organizations than bureaucratic elites (Dellmuth et al. 2022: Figure 5.7).

The elite–citizens gap is thus real when it comes to the legitimacy of international organizations. This is a challenge because elites provide much of the input of international organizations and citizens having to cope with the output. At the same time, scholars have also questioned whether we can really speak of a global legitimacy 'crisis' of international organizations. Kentikelenis and Voeten (2021) have, for instance, analysed speeches that national politicians gave at the UN between 1970 and 2018. They looked for evidence of politicians voicing demands, such as a call for serious reform, or even threatening to exit the existing global order, and they found that such demands are surprisingly at an all-time low. While during the 1970s there were strong calls for a New International Economic Order (NIEO) by recently decolonized states, such voices now seem muted. Similarly, Sommerer et al. (2022a) show that while various international organizations have faced considerable legitimacy challenges since the mid-1990s, such 'crises' are institution-specific (Sommerer et al. 2022a: Figure 3.9). In other words, there is no such thing as a single worldwide legitimacy crisis. Moreover, they find that various international organizations have used legitimacy crises to reform and actually increase their power. Recent scholarship has also studied the responses of international organizations themselves and has shown that international organizations engage in self-legitimation practices and proactively adapt or resist contestation (Schmidtke and Lenz 2024; Dijkstra et al. 2025). Many international organizations have also set up press and public relations departments in an effort to better get their message across to stakeholders and improve their legitimacy (e.g. Ecker-Ehrhardt 2018).

The British withdrawal from the EU (Brexit) has inspired much of the academic scholarship on the politicization and contestation of international organizations. The EU is clearly an example of an international organization with high authority. Its output has also been politicized and contested in domestic debates, including in the UK. And the UK did withdraw after then prime minister David Cameron accepted a membership referendum following pressures by the populist UK Independence Party. Brexit is, however, only one example. It is not possible, more generally for all international organizations, to draw a direct line from the authority of international organizations to domestic contestation to state withdrawal. Indeed, academic research shows that states withdraw from international organizations mostly for geopolitical reasons, such as a divergence in the preferences of member states, and not for domestic political reasons (Von Borzyskowski and Vabulas 2019). There is also no clear link between the authority of international organizations and the extent to which states criticize and withdraw from international organizations (Dijkstra and Ghassim 2024). States' strategies vary significantly even when they are dissatisfied with an international organization (Daßler, Heinkelmann-Wild and Kruck 2024). While the legitimacy of international organizations is a clear concern, it is therefore seen as a challenge *within* individual international organizations rather than a systemic challenge *of* international organizations.

Gridlock and new cooperation challenges

Gridlock is a second challenge for international organizations and global governance. Hale, Held and Young (2013) ask themselves, for instance, why 'efforts to address the most pressing issues of our time seem to have stalled?' (p. 2). In part they are concerned about the ability of international organizations to continue to function amid a divergence in the support and demands of a variety of actors. For instance, gridlock in the UN Security Council over issues such as the wars in Ukraine (2022) and Gaza (2023) prevents it from productively addressing threats to international peace and security. Yet they also identify a 'governance gap' between the need to address new cooperation challenges – such as migration, climate change and digitalization – and the ability of international organizations to keep up.

Hale, Held and Young (2013: Table 1.1) clarify four 'pathways' or causes of gridlock. First, they note the growing multipolarity in the international system, which results in increased transaction costs of cooperation, legitimacy dilemmas and a divergence of interest (see further below under emerging powers). Second, they point at institutional inertias in international organizations, which exhibit not only a high degree of path dependency but also the persistence of specific cognitive beliefs. Third, they note that cooperation problems have become harder as the scope of (new) cooperation challenges is wider and as they penetrate more deeply into societies. Finally, they point at fragmentation in global governance which also brings transaction costs and excessive flexibility. Hale, Held and Young (2013) thus relate the problem of gridlock not just to power-based explanations but also to the structure of international problems and the institutional landscape. Indeed, they argue that gridlock is largely self-reinforcing as international cooperation in the post-war era has deepened the interdependence of states. Once such interdependencies are coupled with the rise of nationalist parties in domestic politics, it becomes exceedingly difficult to move 'through' or 'beyond' gridlock. On the basis of detailed case studies across different policy areas, Hale and Held (2017, 2018) find seven mechanisms out of gridlock – such as domestic mobilization, leadership, technical processes and more autonomous international organizations – but their ultimate conclusion is bleak: international cooperation has become difficult.

A persistent answer to gridlock in the traditional (post-war) international organizations seems to be to organize governance functions through other types of international institutions. The ambition of the Groups of 7 and 20 (G7/G20), for instance, has long been to give some political direction and coordinate the various gridlocked international organizations. The idea here is that the individual international organizations may have difficulty in overcoming divisions among their member states and can therefore benefit from top-level political coordination by the leaders of some of the world's largest economies. The G7 and G20 are part of a much larger set of informal international institutions which do not necessarily have a treaty or a standing secretariat but still seek to tackle international and cross-border problems. The number of informal intergovernmental organizations, a specific subset of informal international institutions, has grown spectacularly since the end of the Cold War from around 40 to 140 in 2015 (Vabulas and Snidal 2021). At the same time, transnational public-private governance initiatives – international institutions that also include private actors – have increased from 74 to 559 in 2014 (Westerwinter, Abott and Bierste 2021).

In other words, we seem to witness an evolution in the institutional formats of cooperation. Verdicts on apparent shifts away from gridlocked international organizations differ. Roger (2020) traces the preference of policymakers for such 'weakly-legalized organizations' back to the 1970s and argues that informal institutions have allowed states to address more complex international problems with more flexibility. Reshaping the legal structure of the global system, however, has also resulted in a decline in the quality of the policy response to international problems. Roger (2020), in this respect, explicitly sees informal solutions as substituting for the policies of formal international organizations. Not all scholars, however, agree. Slaughter (2005), for instance, has argued that global governance is not just a set of international institutions, let alone a world government, but rather a network in which government officials, such as 'police investigators, financial regulators, even judges and legislators', continuously and closely work together to address international problems. From this perspective, new cooperation challenges cannot be solved by directives from the UN in New York but require a proverbial village. Along these lines, she notes that even though the Paris Agreement on Climate Change is non-binding and '[b]y the standards of a traditional treaty . . . falls woefully short', this is precisely its strength as 'tackling a problem as complex and fast-moving as climate change would be impossible with permanent, binding commitments' (Slaughter 2015). She continues that '[t]he Paris agreement is . . . not law. It is a bold move toward public problem solving on a global scale. And it is the only approach that could work' (ibid.).

While informal international institutions can be shortcuts, which can be established without great expense (Abbott and Faude 2021), they rarely offer the same type of governance functions as formal international organizations. The scale of international organizations (such as the UN, EU or WTO) is very different from many of the informal institutions. What is more, many international institutions are oftentimes positioned within or around formal international organizations (Westerwinter, Abbott and Biersteker 2021). Smaller groups of states may, for instance, meet informally to iron out their differences before they participate in the broader international organizations. Such informal 'minilateralism' makes sense when political divergences exist or problems are complex. Or national leaders may meet at the margins of a high-level meeting of an international organization to also tackle other business in informal institutional institutions. In other words, these informal institutions do not always stand on themselves.

Scholars have also introduced the concept of orchestration to make sense of the relationship between formal international organizations and other international institutions as well as non-state and private actors (e.g. Abbott and Snidal 2010; Abbott et al. 2015). They argue that the performance of international organizations should not just be assessed on the basis of policy programmes and operational activities that international organizations carry out themselves. Instead, we should also consider the policies and activities that international organizations 'orchestrate' by, for instance, 'reaching out to private actors and [other] institutions, collaborating with them, and supporting and shaping their activities' (Abbott and Snidal 2010: abstract). In various chapters in this book, for instance, we have seen how international organizations engage with like-minded actors and their communities not only in the areas of climate and the environment but also in the field of peace and security and human rights. Orchestration is a form of indirect governance where international organizations and their secretariats can play a central hub function. Indirect governance is also a way to address policy problems if direct governance is gridlocked. In conclusion, it therefore appears that while gridlock across international organizations can drive the creation of alternative forms of cooperation – thereby creating a crisis *of* international organizations – oftentimes international organizations remain at the heart of the regimes underlying these new forms of cooperation.

Emerging powers and power shifts

One of the most significant challenges to international organizations concerns global power shifts with the emerging powers demanding a stronger position across the various international institutions. While many international organizations were set up and dominated by Western states in the post-war and post-Cold War eras, the 'rise of the rest' has raised questions about the balance of power within established international organizations in terms of input and representation and the need for institutional reform. The original challenge of the emerging powers was targeted at international economic organizations, because it was their rapid economic growth that made them more important actors in international relations. For instance, O'Neill (2001), who coined the term 'BRICs', argued that Brazil, Russia, India and China with their large market economies should become part of an expanded G7. Brazil and India then targeted the WTO during the Doha Development Round (mid-2000s), while China argued that IMF quotas and votes should reflect its increased weight in the world economy in the wake of the economic and financial crisis (2007–8) (Zangl et al. 2016). The demands for the reform of international institutions have since spread to other policy areas as well. Emerging powers now also openly contest established institutions, block proceedings and have established parallel institutions. Overall, this constitutes a considerable challenge to international organizations.

Scholars have already wondered for some time what 'space' there is for 'would-be great powers' in a liberal global order (Hurrell 2006) and how to negotiate such change in a 'resilient status quo' (Kahler 2013) as there is a long-term understanding that hegemonic transition requires institutional adjustment (Gilpin 1981, see also Paul 2016; Kruck and Zangl 2020). Although Ikenberry (2008: 24) has argued that the liberal international order – including the various international organizations – is 'easy to join' and 'hard to overturn', emerging powers not only wanted to join this order but also claim their rightful place. The emerging powers, in this regard, do not just demand that their increasing economic weight is reflected in the number of votes and seats at the table in international organizations, but that they are also properly represented on the basis of their (large) populations. China and India want a 'democratization' of international organizations by which they mean that they as states should get more representation because they represent a larger number of citizens. This also includes the recognition of a multipolar world and the sovereignty of states. The extent to which the emerging powers are successful in pursuing institutional reform in international organizations, scholars show, is dependent on their ability to issue credible threats, develop outside options such as alternative institutions and build coalitions (e.g. Zangl et al. 2016; Lipscy 2017; Schirm 2010). We have witnessed more representation – particularly for China – across international organizations since the early 2010s. In the WTO, emerging powers clearly have a stronger position now than in the 1990s or 2000s. In the IMF and the World Bank, they have received more quotas. Nationals from the emerging powers now also lead more international organizations, including in the UN system, and the staff in international secretariats has also become gradually more representative of the world's population (Parízek and Stephen 2021).

The 'battle' over institutional adjustment in international organizations is often portrayed as a zero-sum game, in which the West needs to give up historical privileges to the emerging powers (and countries in the Global South). Yet scholars also note that the process matters through which the adjustment of international organizations takes place (Kruck and Zangl 2020). There are a variety of strategies at play that affect how precisely adjustments take place. A prominent one is strategic co-optation (Kruck and Zangl 2019) by which Western states might try to divide and rule emerging powers and offer some of them a better deal within international organizations. For Western states, it is typically more appealing to engage with Brazil, India and South Africa than with China and Russia (see also below). The Brazilian national Roberto Azevêdo was therefore, for instance, appointed as WTO Director-General; he was then succeeded by the Nigerian national Ngozi Okonjo-Iweala. India was furthermore co-opted into the nuclear non-proliferation regime after being treated as a nuclear pariah for decades (Frankenbach, Kruck and Zangl 2021). The creation of the G20, which includes a whole range of emerging powers, can also be seen as putting a strategic layer over the G7. Instead of expanding the G7 in response to demands for representation, the G20 is an additional forum where China and Russia are 'boxed in' through the presence of a range of other Western allies such as Australia, Saudi Arabia, South Korea and Türkiye (Fioretos 2020).

Much of the academic literature is therefore about making space for the emerging powers and adjusting the existing international organizations. Yet in recent years, it has also become clearer that countries such as China do not just want to have more power in the existing order but have also started to challenge the liberal international order including its international organizations (Lake, Martin and Risse 2021; Weiss and Wallace 2021). As Weiss and Wallace (2021: abstract) note, 'Chinese Communist Party rule chafe against many of the fundamental principles of the [liberal international order], but could coexist with a return to Westphalian principles and markets that are embedded in domestic systems of control.' In other words, China has started to pursue, at least with regard to some international organizations, a revisionist policy that takes aim at the authority and (liberal) intrusiveness of international organizations and other institutions. While China is happy with the UN Security Council which represents the type of Westphalian forum where great powers have veto power, it likes the UN Human Rights Council a lot less. Such diverging views on global order by China, and also other emerging powers, have the potential to create a crisis *of* international organizations rather than a crisis *within* international organizations. First, it is revisionist in terms of which cooperation problems should be addressed at the international level. Second, it also challenges the core functions of international organizations in terms of monitoring state compliance and adjudicating in case of state conflicts. As we have discussed earlier in this book, international organizations are often a solution to defection and freerider problems (e.g. Keohane 1984; Abbott and Snidal 1998). They go beyond Westphalian principles of state sovereignty.

China and other rising powers often hold an alternative vision of global order and increasingly pursue it through the BRICS (even if China does not fully dominate this institution). While originally an acronym used by the Goldman Sachs investment bank to lump together several emerging economies (O'Neill 2001), it has grown into a venerable international institution with annual summits by the leaders of the participating states. It can be best understood as an alternative to the Western G7 and is increasingly presented as a counter-hegemonic institution. While the BRICS are a diverse group of countries, and subject to regular divide-and-rule tactics by the West, scholars do point at some convergence in the positions of the BRICS (Papa, Zhen and O'Donnell 2023). This has become particularly prominent since the Russian war against Ukraine (2022). China and Russia adopted a 'no limits' all-encompassing partnership, and China has provided Russia with political backing since the start of the war. The BRICS furthermore welcomed five new members (Egypt, Ethiopia, Indonesia, Saudi Arabia and the United Arab Emirates) in 2024–5 and accepted another dozen as partner states. During the 2024 Summit, Russia claimed that the expanded BRICS now represented the 'global majority' (thereby hijacking a concept that is sometimes used instead of the Global South) with the clear implication that the West is now the 'global minority'.

Part of China's and the BRICS approach to international organizations has also been the creation of alternative and parallel institutions in what has been conceptualized as competitive or 'contested' multilateralism (Morse and Keohane 2014). In the Durban Declaration of 2013, the BRICS countries not only provided a long list of demands for the reform of existing international institutions but also initiated the process of creating the New Development Bank ('BRICS bank') as a potential competitor to the World Bank. Even more importantly, China started to establish its own international organizations. While it had already been part of the regional Shanghai Cooperation Organisation (SCO) with Russia since 2001, it created the Asian Infrastructure Investment Bank (AIIB) along with its Belt and Road Initiative (BRI) in 2013. These hardly stand on themselves. Stephen (2021) identifies, for instance, more than twenty international institutions that China has helped to initiate between 1990 and 2017. There is an academic debate on the extent to which these China-led international institutions are part of the existing global order or are part of China's emerging regional hegemony. The AIIB, for instance, has been co-developed by the World Bank and includes many of the features of other regional development banks. It is nevertheless clear that global power shifts are not confined to an institutional adjustment of existing international organizations but has wider implications.

Geopoliticization of international organizations

A final challenge concerns the geopoliticization of international organizations. While we have already discussed politicization and contestation above as well as gridlock resulting from geopolitics and the emerging powers demanding global governance reform, geopoliticization is different. It is about (ab)using international organizations and other institutions to score points against geopolitical rivals. Geopolitization starts from the understanding that geopolitics is no longer just about territory and the battlefield, but that great power rivalry (for instance, between China and the United States) also plays out at other sites, such as international institutions (Agnew 2022; Heimann et al. 2024). Indeed, issues that were previously not considered geopolitical (e.g. intellectual property rights) can be framed by rivals in geopolitical terms. In the wake of the Russian war in Ukraine, almost all matters in the relationship between Russia and the West are now seen through a geopolitical zero-sum lens. If Russia then 'wins' something, such as a leadership position in the secretariat of an international organization, the West 'loses'. In other words, international organizations have also become vehicles for geopolitics. Geopolitics is thus entering the political system of international organization through the inputs of great powers. This may, in turn, undermine their productive functions.

There are many recent examples of the geopoliticization of international organizations. When, for instance, the Covid-19 pandemic broke out, President Trump blamed China for 'the virus'. He also stopped funding the World Health Organization (WHO) in 2020 and set in motion the process of US withdrawal from the WHO. Trump argued that the WHO was too lenient on China and that China had failed to report the outbreak to the WHO. The United States had similar fights with China at the WTO and the Universal Postal Union (UPU), and it worked hard to prevent the appointment of a Chinese national as Director-General of the World Intellectual Property Organization (WIPO). The Russian war in Ukraine has also resulted in geopolitical fights at various international organizations. In the Council of Europe, states immediately voted to expel Russia as a member in 2022, while Western states in the Organization for Security and Cooperation in Europe (OSCE) noted that there can no longer be 'business as usual' with Russia, that is, continuing to work together in the OSCE as if there was no war ongoing. This in turn paralysed the organization. Poland, for instance, refused the Russian delegation visas to the OSCE Ministerial Council in Lodz in 2022. Russia subsequently blocked the appointment of all leadership positions in 2024. The OSCE has not had an agreed budget anymore since 2022 and is on the pathway to decline (e.g. Schuette and Dijkstra 2023).

While some of these are simply petty fights between rivals, what makes the geopoliticization of international organizations important is that there is something at stake. As this book has shown, international organizations have become authoritative actors in international relations with policy programmes setting norms and rules as well as operational activities to implement them. If one can control (or capture) international organizations (e.g. Urpelainen and Van de Graaf 2015), one can subsequently direct their authority in a way that tilts the balance of power at the expense of rivals. Farrell and Newman (2019) provide a key example when the United States geopoliticized ('weaponized' in their words) the Society for Worldwide Interbank Financial Telecommunication (SWIFT). SWIFT is a non-state organization located in Belgium in charge of linking nearly all financial institutions around the world. It is therefore the key operator that can provide secure international payments. Through extraterritorial US sanctions, backed up by EU sanctions, SWIFT disconnected all Iranian banks from its systems in 2012, thereby massively complicating international payments to Iran. The purpose was to weaken Iran's economy. SWIFT was also used for sanctions against Russia in 2022. While SWIFT is not an international organization, it is a useful example to understand how geopoliticization can work and how the authority of international organizations can be instrumentalized for geopolitical objectives. The argument of Farrell and Newman (2019) indeed is that states can use their interdependencies for geopolitical purposes.

Such geopoliticization is problematic for international organizations as it affects their productive functions. The UN Security Council is, of course, the place to discuss geopolitics, but if the work of the Security Council gets entirely geopoliticized due to heightened great power rivalries, this also clearly has consequences for the rest of what the UN does, including the eleven ongoing peacekeeping operations and the more than 60,000 blue helmets. The same goes for other international organizations. When China and the United States fought over geopolitics at the WHO during the

Covid-19 pandemic in 2020, WHO staff had greater difficulty to actually address the pandemic. Particularly when the United States stopped paying contributions and put in motion the process to leave the organization, WHO leadership had to dedicate valuable time to political crisis management and fund raising. The trouble with geopoliticization is also that states will then pursue alternative routes outside international organizations. The SWIFT sanctions on Russia have had only a limited effect as Russia continued to find ways to trade with other states. In fact, the BRICS have the ambition to set up their own systems and to 'de-dollarize' the world economy, for instance, by trading directly in their own currencies.

Even though geopolitics clearly affects international organizations, results in gridlocks and demands for institutional adjustment, it is also clear that there are barriers to the geopoliticization and institutional capture of international organizations. As we noted previously in this book, international organizations are precisely created for situations in which the preferences of member states are neither mutually exclusive nor harmoniously in agreement. In other words, it is part of the job of international organizations to absorb the different inputs of the member states and to convert them into common policies and activities. Collective security organizations, such as the UN, would have no purpose if all the member states always acted peacefully. It is precisely because states do not always act in line with the principles of the UN Charter that the UN has a set of institutions at its disposal to reduce and mitigate the conflicting interests of its member states. From this perspective, geopolitics may create a crisis *within* certain international organizations but does not lead us to question international organizations as cooperation platforms as such.

Conclusion

The challenges of legitimacy crises, gridlock, power shifts and geopoliticization put international organizations under pressure. It is clear that various international organizations find it increasingly difficult to carry out their mandates to the fullest. Faced with disagreeing member states and their conflicting demands, international organizations may not be able to adopt the necessary decisions. They may also struggle when they are not given the necessary resources, such as budget and staff, to implement ambitious policy programmes and operational activities. At the same time, many of the mentioned challenges play out *within* or around the political system of international organizations. They do not necessarily challenge international organizations or global order in general (Eilstrup-Sangiovanni and Hofmann 2020). Nonetheless, these challenges do raise questions about the future of international organizations in terms of their position in international relations.

When considering the current challenges to international organizations, it is worth remembering that historically international organizations have proven resilient. International organizations have previously survived wars between their member states, major economic crises, changing international problems, power transitions and domestic challenges. The paradox is that international organizations are created to address international problems, so demand for international organizations is ironically high when international relations are restless. Scholars show, in this respect, that while international organizations are occasionally dissolved, the major international organizations tend to survive longer (Debre and Dijkstra 2021a; Dijkstra and Debre 2022; Eilstrup-Sangiovanni 2021; Gray 2018). Indeed, major international organizations perform core governance functions, can be difficult to replace and tend to have considerable buy-in from member states and supporting stakeholders. The League of Nations is an example of an international organization that was eventually dissolved, but this remains an exception rather than a rule. Indeed, even the mandate, institutions, buildings, personnel and 'soul' of the League lived on in the UN which was established after the Second World War (Wessel 2011; Dijkstra, Debre and Heinkelmann-Wild 2024). The bottom line is that many international organizations are quite robust and can handle a challenge or two.

International organizations have thus been set up to absorb the different inputs from a variety of actors, but they are also important actors in their own right when they get challenged. The central actors within international organizations – such as the international secretariats – can be surprisingly proactive in responding and ensuring the survival of their organizations (Dijkstra et al. 2025). The World Bank has been proactive in helping to develop the China-initiated AIIB promoting its own international standards along the way. The Secretariat of the UN Framework Convention on Climate Change (UNFCCC) has cultivated and orchestrated a large supportive network of substate and non-state actors in support of its mission to address global warming. Even if the International Criminal Court (ICC) has been accused in the past of a 'bias' due to which it only investigates African nationals, in recent years it has issued arrest warrants for Russian president Vladimir Putin and Israeli prime minister Benjamin Netanyahu. Across the board, international organizations have become much more active in terms of public diplomacy in order to better communicate their purpose and activities and get their narratives across. In other words, international organizations are also responsive actors that can cope with and counter many of the challenges discussed in this chapter.

With all the contestation of international organizations, it is sometimes also easy to forget that the world needs to be governed. There are simply too many international problems that demand the involvement of international organizations. While states and other actors can contest their representation within the institutional structure of international organizations or object to specifics of policy programmes and operational activities, ultimately the underlying rationale for international organizations rarely disappears (Klabbers 2022: 197). We should, in this respect, also try to avoid to focus entirely on those instances where international organizations find it exceedingly difficult to act and ignore the fact that there are 350 international organizations around the globe. The web of international organizations and other international institutions is thick. Diplomats and officials in international organizations around the world work day in day out on addressing all sorts of international problems. Only by paying close attention to their work, indeed by going into the black box which is the political system of international organizations, we can truly understand world affairs.

Discussion questions

1. What is the difference between a crisis of international organizations and a crisis within international organizations? Please provide examples.
2. To what extent does domestic politics facilitate or constrain cooperation within international organizations?
3. Why is China contesting international organizations even though it has benefited economically from its membership in organizations such as the WTO?

Further reading

Dellmuth, Lisa, Jan Aart Scholte, Jonas Tallberg and Soetkin Verhaegen (2022). 'The Elite–citizen Gap in International Organization Legitimacy', *American Political Science Review*, 116 (1): 283–300.

Dijkstra, Hylke, Laura von Allwörden, Leonard Schütte and Giuseppe Zaccaria (2025). *The Survival of International Organizations: Institutional Responses to Existential Challenges*, Oxford: Oxford University Press.

Lake, David A., Lisa L. Martin and Thomas Risse (2021). 'Challenges to the Liberal Order: Reflections on International Organization', *International Organization*, 75 (2): 225–57.

Weiss, Jessica Chen, and Jeremy L. Wallace (2021). 'Domestic Politics, China's Rise, and the Future of the Liberal International Order', *International Organization*, 75 (2): 635–64.

REFERENCES

Abbott, Kenneth W. and Benjamin Faude (2021). 'Choosing Low-cost Institutions in Global Governance', *International Theory*, 13 (3): 397–426.

Abbott, Kenneth W., Philipp Genschel, Duncan Snidal and Bernhard Zangl, eds (2020). *The Governor's Dilemma: Indirect Governance Beyond Principals and Agents*, Oxford: Oxford University Press.

Abbott, Kenneth W., Philipp Genschel, Duncan Snidal, and Bernhard Zangl, eds (2015). *International Organizations as Orchestrators*, Oxford: Oxford University Press.

Abbott, Kenneth W., Robert O. Keohane, Andrew Moravcsik, Anne-Marie Slaughter and Duncan Snidal (2000). 'The Concept of Legalization', *International Organization*, 54 (3): 401–20.

Abbott, Kenneth W. and Duncan Snidal (1998). 'Why States Act through Formal International Organizations', *Journal of Conflict Resolution*, 42 (1): 3–32.

Abbott, Kenneth W. and Duncan Snidal (2000). 'Hard and Soft Law in International Governance', *International Organization*, 54 (3): 421–56.

Abbott, Kenneth W. and Duncan Snidal (2010). 'International Regulation without International Government: Improving IO Performance through Orchestration', *The Review of International Organizations*, 5 (3): 315–44.

Abbott, Kenneth W. and Duncan J. Snidal, eds (2021). *The Spectrum of International Institutions: An Interdisciplinary Collaboration on Global Governance*, London: Routledge.

Abiew, Francis Kofi (1999). *The Evolution of the Doctrine and Practice of Humanitarian Intervention*, The Hague: Kluwer Law International.

Abouharb, M. Rodwan and David L. Cingranelli (2009). 'IMF Programs and Human Rights, 1981–2003', *The Review of International Organizations*, 4 (1): 47–72.

Acharya, Amitav (1997). 'Ideas, Identity, and Institution-building: From the "ASEAN Way" to the "Asia-Pacific Way"?', *The Pacific Review*, 10 (3): 319–46.

Acharya, Amitav (2012). 'Comparative Regionalism: A Field Whose Time Has Come?', *The International Spectator*, 47 (1): 3–15.

Acharya, Amitav (2022). 'Race and Racism in the Founding of the Modern World Order', *International Affairs*, 98 (1): 23–43.

Acharya, Amitav and Alastair Iain Johnston, eds (2007). *Crafting Cooperation: Regional International Institutions in Comparative Perspective*, Cambridge: Cambridge University Press.

Adebajo, Adekeye (2023). 'Post-colonial Global Governance', in Thomas G. Weiss and Rorden Wilkinson (eds), *International Organization and Global Governance*, 216–29, London: Routledge.

Adler, Emanuel and Michael Barnett (1998). 'A Framework for the Study of Security Communities', in Emanuel Adler and Michael Barnett (eds), *Security Communities*, 29–65, Cambridge: Cambridge University Press.

Adler, Emanuel and Peter M. Haas (1992). 'Conclusion: Epistemic Communities, World Order, and the Creation of a Reflective Research Program', *International Organization*, 46:(1): 367–90.

Adler, Emanuel and Vincent Pouliot (2011). 'International practices', *International Theory*, 3 (1): 1–36.

Adler-Nissen, Rebecca and Pouliot Vincent Pouliot (2014). 'Power in Practice: Negotiating the International Intervention in Libya', *European Journal of International Relations*, 20 (4): 889–911.

Agnew, John (2022). *Hidden Geopolitics: Governance in a Globalized World*, Lanham, MD: Rowman & Littlefield.

Akhavan, Payam (2001). 'Beyond Impunity: Can International Criminal Justice Prevent Future Atrocities?', *American Journal of International Law*, 95 (1): 7–31.

Aldy, Joseph E. and Stavins Robert N. Stavins (2007). 'Introduction: International Policy Architecture for Global Climate Change', in Joseph E. Aldy and Robert N. Stavins (eds), *Architectures for Agreement. Addressing Global Climate Change in the Post-Kyoto World*, 1–30, Cambridge: Cambridge University Press.

Alger, Chadwick (2002). 'The Emerging Role of NGOs in the UN System. From Article 71 to a People's Millennium Assembly', *Global Governance*, 8 (1): 93–117.

Alter, Karen J. (2001). *Establishing the Supremacy of European Law: The Making of an International Rule of Law in Europe*, Oxford: Oxford University Press.

Alter, Karen J. (2008). 'Agents or Trustees? International Courts in Their Political Context', *European Journal of International Relations*, 14 (1): 33–63.

Amerasinghe, Chittharanjan F. (2005). *Principles of the Institutional Law of International Organizations*, 2nd edn, Cambridge: Cambridge University Press.

Andersen, Stephen O. and Madhava K. Sharma (2002). *Protecting the Ozone Layer. The United Nations History*, London: Earthscan.

Archibugi, Daniele, David Held and Martin Köhler, eds (1998). *Re-imagining Political Community. Studies in Cosmopolitan Democracy*, Cambridge: Polity Press.

Armstrong, David, Lorna Lloyd and John Redmond (1996). *From Versailles to Maastricht. International Organisation in the Twentieth Century*, London: Macmillan.

Auerswald, David P. and Stephen M. Saideman (2014). *NATO in Afghanistan: Fighting Together, Fighting Alone*, Princeton, NJ: Princeton University Press.

Balassa, Bela (1961). *The Theory of Economic Integration*, London: George Allen & Unwin.

Barnett, Michael N. and Martha Finnemore (2004). *Rules for the World. International Organizations in Global Politics*, Ithaca, NY: Cornell University Press.

Barria, Lilian A. and Steven D. Roper (2005). 'How Effective are International Criminal Tribunals? An Analysis of the ICTY and the ICTR', *The International Journal of Human Rights*, 9 (3): 349–68.

Bauer, Steffen (2009). 'The Ozone Secretariat: The Good Shepherd of Ozone Politics', in Frank Biermann and Bernd Siebenhüner (eds), *Managers of Global Change. The Influence of International Environmental Bureaucracies*, 225–44, Cambridge, MA: The MIT Press.

Bayerlein, Louisa, Christoph Knill and Yves Steinebach (2020). *A Matter of Style: Organizational Agency in Global Public Policy*, Cambridge: Cambridge University Press.

Beach, Derek (2004). 'The Unseen Hand in Treaty Reform Negotiations: The Role and Influence of the Council Secretariat', *Journal of European Public Policy*, 11 (3): 408–39.

Beck, Peter J. (1981). 'The Winter War in the International Context: Britain and the League of Nations' Role in the Russo-Finnish Dispute, 1939–1940', *Journal of Baltic Studies*, 12 (1): 58–73.

Becker, Jordan (2024). 'Pledge and Forget? Testing the Effects of NATO's Wales Pledge on Defense Investment', *International Studies Perspectives*, 25 (4): 490–517.

Becker, Jordan, Sarah E. Kreps, Paul Poast and Rochelle Terman (2024). 'Transatlantic Shakedown: Presidential Shaming and NATO Burden Sharing', *Journal of Conflict Resolution*, 68 (2–3): 195–229.

Beeson, Mark (2009). *Institutions of the Asia-Pacific: ASEAN, APEC and Beyond*, London: Routledge.

Beeson, Mark (2022). 'Decentered? ASEAN's Struggle to Accommodate Great Power Competition', *Global Studies Quarterly*, 2 (1): ksab044.

Benner, Thorsten, Stephan Mergenthaler and Philipp Rotmann (2011). *The New World of UN Peace Operations: Learning to Build Peace?* Oxford: Oxford University Press.

Bercovitch, Jacob (2007). 'Mediation in International Conflicts', in Ira W. Zartman (ed.), *Peacemaking in International Conflict. Methods and Techniques*, 163–94, Washington, DC: United States Institute of Peace Press.

Bickerton, Christopher J., Dermot Hodson and Uwe Puetter (2015). 'The New Intergovernmentalism: European Integration in the Post-Maastricht Era', *Journal of Common Market Studies*, 53 (4): 703–22.

Biermann, Frank and Bernd Siebenhüner, eds (2009). *Managers of Global Change. The Influence of International Environmental Bureaucracies*, Cambridge, MA: The MIT Press.

Biermann, Frank, Bernd Siebenhüner and Anna Schreyögg (2009). *International Organizations in Global Environmental Governance*, London: Routledge.

Biermann, Frank, Kenneth Abbott, Steinar Andresen, Karin Bäckstrand, Steven Bernstein, Michele M. Betsill et al. (2012). 'Navigating the Anthropocene: Improving Earth System Governance', *Science*, 335 (6074): 1306–07.

Binder, Martin and Monika Heupel (2015). 'The Legitimacy of the UN Security Council: Evidence from Recent General Assembly Debates', *International Studies Quarterly*, 59 (2): 238–50.

Blackwill, Robert D. (2016). *War by Other Means: Geoeconomics and Statecraft*, Cambridge, MA: Harvard University Press.

Bloxham, Donald (2006). 'Beyond 'Realism' and Legalism: A Historical Perspective on the Limits of International Humanitarian Law', *European Review*, 14 (4): 457–70.

Boekle, Henning (1998). 'Die Vereinten Nationen und der internationale Schutz der Menschenrechte: Eine Bestandsaufnahme', *Aus Politik und Zeitgeschichte*, 46–47: 3–17.

Bolin, Bert (2007). *A History of the Science and Politics of Climate Change. The Role of the Intergovernmental Panel on Climate Change*, Cambridge: Cambridge University Press.

Bosco, David (2014). *Rough Justice: The International Criminal Court's Battle to Fix the World, One Prosecution at a Time*, Oxford: Oxford University Press.

Bown, Chad P. and Joost Pauwelyn, eds (2010). *The Law, Economics and Politics of Retaliation in WTO Dispute Settlement*, Cambridge: Cambridge University Press.

Börzel, Tanja A. (2022). *Why Noncompliance: The Politics of Law in the European Union*, Ithaca NY: Cornell University Press.

Börzel, Tanja A. and Thomas Risse, eds (2016). *The Oxford Handbook of Comparative Regionalism*, Oxford: Oxford University Press.

Börzel, Tanja A. and Michael Zürn (2021). 'Contestations of the Liberal International Order: From Liberal Multilateralism to Postnational Liberalism', *International Organization*, 75 (2): 282–305.

Brachet, Julien (2016). 'Policing the Desert: The IOM in Libya Beyond War and Peace', *Antipode*, 48 (2): 272–92.

Bradley, Megan (2024). "'We're an Organization that Does Stuff': The International Organization for Migration, Logistics and Expert Authority in Migration Governance', *Geopolitics*, advance online publication.

Bradley, Megan, Cathryn Costello and Angela Sherwood, eds (2023). *IOM Unbound?: Obligations and Accountability of the International Organization for Migration in an Era of Expansion*, Cambridge: Cambridge University Press.

Braithwaite, John and Peter Drahos (2000). *Global Business Regulation*, Cambridge: Cambridge University Press.

Brandsma, Gijs Jan and Jens Blom-Hansen (2017). *Controlling the EU Executive?: The Politics of Delegation in the European Union*, Oxford: Oxford University Press.

Breitmeier, Helmut (1996). *Wie entstehen globale Umweltregime? Der Konfliktaustrag zum Schutz der Ozonschicht und des globalen Klimas*, Opladen: Leske & Budrich.

Breitmeier, Helmut (1997). 'International Organizations and the Creation of Environmental Regimes', in Oran R. Young (ed.), *Global Governance. Drawing Insights from the Environmental Experience*, 87–114, Cambridge, MA: The MIT Press.

Breitmeier, Helmut (2009). 'Regieren in der globalen Umweltpolitik. Eine gemischte Bilanz zwischen Erfolgs- und Problemfällen', in Helmut Breitmeier, Michèle Roth and Dieter Senghaas (eds), *Sektorale Weltordnungspolitik. Effektiv, gerecht und demokratisch?* 150–70, Baden-Baden: Nomos.

Brühl, Tanja (2003). *Nichtregierungsorganisationen als Akteure internationaler Umweltverhandlungen. Ein Erklärungsmodell auf der Basis der situationsspezifischen Ressourcennachfrage*, Frankfurt/M.: Campus.

Buzan, Barry, Ole Waever and Jaap de Wilde (1998). *Security. A New Framework for Analysis*, Boulder, CO: Lynne Rienner.

Caballero-Anthony, Mely (1998). 'Mechanisms of Dispute Settlement: The ASEAN Experience', *Contemporary Southeast Asia*, 20 (1): 38–66.

Canan, Penelope and Nancy Reichman (2002). *Ozone Connection. Expert Networks in Global Environmental Governance*, Sheffield: Greenleaf Publishing.

Carr, Edward H. (1939). *The Twenty Years' Crisis, 1919–1939. An Introduction to the Study of International Relations*, New York: St Martin's Press.

Chadwick, C. F. (2014). *Pioneer in the Study of the Political Process and on NGO Participation in the United Nations*, Heidelberg: Springer.

Chasek, Pamela S. (2001). *Earth Negotiations. Analyzing Thirty Years of Environmental Diplomacy*, Tokyo: United Nations University Press.

Chasek, Pamela S., David L. Downie and Janet Welsh Brown (2010). *Global Environmental Politics*, 5th edn, Boulder, CO: Westview.

Chatfield, Charles (1997). 'Intergovernmental and Nongovernmental Associations to 1945', in Jackie G. Smith, Charles Chatfield and Ron Pagnucco (eds), *Transnational Social Movements and Global Politics. Solidarity Beyond the State*, Syracuse, 19–41, New York: Syracuse University Press.

Chayes, Abram and Antonia Chayes (1995). *The New Sovereignty. Compliance with International Regulatory Agreements*, Cambridge, MA: Harvard University Press.

Checkel, Jeffrey T. (2005). 'International Institutions and Socialization in Europe: Introduction and Framework', *International Organization*, 59 (4): 801–26.

Chen, Titus C. and Chiahao Hsu (2021). 'China's Human Rights Foreign Policy in the Xi Jinping Era: Normative Revisionism Shrouded in Discursive Moderation', *The British Journal of Politics and International Relations*, 23 (2): 228–47.

Chesterman, Simon (2003). *Just War or Just Peace? Humanitarian Intervention and International Law*, Oxford: Oxford University Press.

Chesterman, Simon, ed. (2007). *The UN Secretary-General in World Politics*, Cambridge: Cambridge University Press.

Chimni, B. S. (2006). 'The World Trade Organization, Democracy and Development: A View From the South', *Journal of World Trade*, 40 (1): 5–36.

Chorev, Nitsan (2012). *The World Health Organization Between North and South*, Ithaca, NY: Cornell University Press.

Christiansen, Thomas and Christine Reh (2009). *Constitutionalizing the European Union*, Basingstoke: Palgrave Macmillan.

Clavin, Patricia (2013). *Securing the World Economy: The Reinvention of the League of Nations, 1920–1946*, Oxford: Oxford University Press.

Claude, Inis L. (1996). 'Peace and Security: Prospective Roles for the Two United Nations', *Global Governance*, 2 (3): 289–98.

Coase, Ronald (1960). 'The Problem of Social Cost', *Journal of Law and Economics*, 3: 1–44.

Cohn, Theodore H. (2002). *Governing Global Trade. International Institutions in Conflict and Convergence*, Burlington, VT: Ashgate.

Coleman, James S. (1990). *Foundations of Social Theory*, Cambridge, MA: Belknap Press of Harvard University Press.

Copelovitch, Mark (2010). *The International Monetary Fund in the Global Economy: Banks, Bonds, and Bailouts*, Cambridge: Cambridge University Press.

Corbett, Richard (2002). *The European Parliament's Role in Closer EU Integration*, Basingstoke: Palgrave Macmillan.

Cortell, Andrew P. and Susan Peterson (2006). 'Dutiful Agents, Rogue Actors, or Both? Staffing, Voting Rules, and Slack in the WHO and WTO', in Darren

G. Hawkins, David A. Lake, Daniel L. Nielson and Michael J. Tierney (eds), *Delegation and Agency in International Organizations*, 255–80, Cambridge: Cambridge University Press.

Cortright, David and George A. Lopez, eds (2002). *Smart Sanctions. Targeting Economic Statecraft*, Lanham, MD: Rowman & Littlefield.

Council on Foreign Relations (2023). 'Mercosur: South America's Fractious Trade Bloc', *CFR*. https://www.cfr.org/backgrounder/mercosur-south-americas-fractious-trade-bloc

Cox, Robert W. (1969). 'The Executive Head: An Essay on Leadership in International Organization', *International Organization*, 23 (2): 205–30.

Cox, Robert W. (1981). 'Social Forces, States and World Orders: Beyond International Relations Theory', *Millennium*, 10 (2): 126–55.

Cox, Robert W. (1983). 'Gramsci, Hegemony and International Relations: An Essay in Method', *Millennium*, 12 (2): 162–75.

Cox, Robert W. (2023). 'Critical Theory', in Thomas G. Weiss and Rorden Wilkinson (eds), *International Organization and Global Governance*, 168–80, London: Routledge.

Cronin, Bruce (2008). 'International Consensus and the Changing Legal Authority of the UN Security Council', in Bruce Cronin and Ian Hurd (eds), *The UN Security Council and the Politics of International Authority*, 57–79, London: Routledge.

Cueto, Marcos, Theodore M. Brown, and Elizabeth Fee (2019). *The World Health Organization: A History*, Cambridge: Cambridge University Press.

Darkwa, Linda (2017). 'The African Standby Force: The African Union's Tool for the Maintenance of Peace and Security', *Contemporary Security Policy*, 38 (3): 471–82.

Daßler, Benjamin, Tim Heinkelmann-Wild and Andreas Kruck (2024). 'How Negative Institutional Power Moderates Contestation: Explaining Dissatisfied Powers' Strategies towards International Institutions', *The Review of International Organizations*, advance online publication.

Davey, William (2014). 'WTO and Rules-based Dispute Settlement: Historical Evolution, Operational Success, and Future Challenges', *Journal of International Economic Law*, 17 (3): 679–700.

Davis, Christina L. and Krzysztof J. Pelc (2017). 'Cooperation in Hard Times: Self-Restraint of Trade Protection', *Journal of Conflict Resolution*, 61 (2): 398–429.

De Lombaerde, Philippe, Fredrik Söderbaum, Luk Van Langenhove and Francis Baert (2010). 'The Problem of Comparison in Comparative Regionalism', *Review of International Studies*, 36 (3): 731–53.

De Vries, Catherine E., Sara B. Hobolt and Stefanie Walter (2021). 'Politicizing International Cooperation: The Mass Public, Political Entrepreneurs, and Political Opportunity Structures', *International Organization*, 75 (2): 306–32.

Debre, Maria Josepha and Hylke Dijkstra (2021a). 'Institutional Design for a Post-liberal Order: Why Some International Organizations Live Longer Than Others', *European Journal of International Relations*, 27 (1): 311–39.

Debre, Maria Josepha and Hylke Dijkstra (2021b). 'COVID-19 and Policy Responses by International Organizations: Crisis of Liberal International Order or Window of Opportunity?', *Global Policy*, 12 (4): 443–54.

De Wilde, Jaap (2008). 'Environmental Security Deconstructed', in Hans Günter Brauch et al. (eds), *Globalisation and Environmental Challenges*, 595–602, Mosbach: AFES-Press.

Di Salvatore, Jessica, Magnus Lundgren, Kseniya Oksamytna and Hannah M. Smidt (2022). 'Introducing the Peacekeeping Mandates (PEMA) Dataset', *Journal of Conflict Resolution*, 66 (4–5): 924–51.

Di Salvatore, Jessica and Andrea Ruggeri (2017). 'The Effectiveness of Peace Keeping Operations', *Oxford Research Encyclopedias, Politics*. https://oxfordre.com/politics/display/10.1093/acrefore/9780190228637.001.0001/acrefore-9780190228637-e-586

Deitelhoff, Nicole (2009). 'The Discursive Process of Legalization: Charting Islands of Persuasion in the ICC Case', *International Organization*, 63 (1): 33–66.

Deitelhoff, Nicole and Lisbeth Zimmermann (2020). 'Things We Lost in the Fire: How Different Types of Contestation Affect the Robustness of International Norms', *International Studies Review*, 22 (1): 51–76.

Dellmuth, Lisa, Jan Aart Scholte, Jonas Tallberg and Soetkin Verhaegen (2022). *Citizens, Elites, and the Legitimacy of Global Governance*, Oxford: Oxford University Press.

Denizer, Cevdet, Daniel Kaufmann and Aart Kraay (2013). 'Good Countries or Good Projects? Macro and Micro Correlates of World Bank Project Performance', *Journal of Development Economics*, 105: 288–302.

Deutsch, Karl W. et al. (1957). *Political Community and the North Atlantic Area. International Organization in the Light of Historical Experience*, Princeton, NJ: Princeton University Press.

Dietz, Thomas, Elinor Ostrom and Paul C. Stern (2003). 'The Struggle to Govern the Commons', *Science*, 302 (5652): 1907–12.

Dijkstra, Hylke (2015a). 'Shadow Bureaucracies and the Unilateral Control of International Secretariats: Insights from UN Peacekeeping', *The Review of International Organizations*, 10 (1): 23–41.

Dijkstra, Hylke (2015b). 'Functionalism, Multiple Principals and the Reform of the NATO Secretariat after the Cold War', *Cooperation and Conflict*, 50 (1): 128–45.

Dijkstra, Hylke (2016). *International Organizations and Military Affairs*, London: Routledge.

Dijkstra, Hylke (2017). 'Collusion in International Organizations: How States Benefit from the Authority of Secretariats', *Global Governance*, 23 (4): 601–18.

Dijkstra, Hylke and Maria J. Debre (2022). 'The Death of Major International Organizations: When Institutional Stickiness is Not Enough', *Global Studies Quarterly*, 2 (4): ksac048.

Dijkstra, Hylke, Maria J. Debre and Tim Heinkelmann-Wild (2024). 'Governance Abhors a Vacuum: The Afterlives of Major International Organisations', *The British Journal of Politics and International Relations*, 26 (3): 759–78.

Dijkstra, Hylke and Farsan Ghassim (2024). 'Are Authoritative International Organizations Challenged More? A Recurrent Event Analysis of Member State Criticisms and Withdrawals', *The Review of International Organizations*, advance online publication.

Dijkstra, Hylke, Laura von Allwörden, Leonard Schütte and Giuseppe Zaccaria (2025). *The Survival of International Organizations: Institutional Responses to Existential Challenges*, Oxford: Oxford University Press.

Donnelly, Jack (2006). *International Human Rights*, 3rd edn, Boulder, CO: Westview.

Doyle, Michael W. (1986). 'Liberalism and World Politics', *American Political Science Review*, 80 (4): 1151–69.

Doyle, Michael W. and Nicholas Sambanis (2000). 'International Peacebuilding: A Theoretical and Quantitative Analysis', *American Political Science Review*, 94 (4): 779–802.

Dreher, Axel, Valentin Lang and Bernhard Reinsberg (2024). 'Aid Effectiveness and Donor Motives', *World Development*, 176: 106501.

Dreher, Axel, Jan-Egbert Sturm and James Raymond Vreeland (2009a). 'Global Horse Trading: IMF Loans for Votes in the United Nations Security Council', *European Economic Review*, 53 (7): 742–57.

Dreher, Axel, Jan-Egbert Sturm and James Raymond Vreeland (2009b). 'Development Aid and International Politics: Does Membership on the UN Security Council Influence World Bank Decisions?', *Journal of Development Economics*, 88 (1): 1–18.

Drezner, Daniel W. (2007). *All Politics is Global: Explaining International Regulatory Regimes*, Princeton, NJ: Princeton University Press.

Drezner, Daniel W. (2011). 'Sanctions Sometimes Smart: Targeted Sanctions in Theory and Practice', *International Studies Review*, 13 (1): 96–108.

Driscoll, David D. (1998). *Was ist der Internationale Währungsfonds?* Washington, DC: Internationaler Währungsfonds, Abteilung Öffentlichkeitsarbeit.

Dryzek, John S. (2016). 'Institutions for the Anthropocene: Governance in a Changing Earth System', *British Journal of Political Science*, 46 (4): 937–56.

Dukalskis, Alexander (2023). 'A Fox in the Henhouse: China, Normative Change, and the UN Human Rights Council', *Journal of Human Rights*, 22 (3): 334–50.

Dunleavy, Patrick (1985). 'Bureaucrats, Budgets and the Growth of the State: Reconstructing an Instrumental Model', *British Journal of Political Science*, 15 (3): 299–328.

Easton, David (1965). *A Framework for Political Analysis*, Englewood Cliffs, NJ: Prentice Hall.

Ecker-Ehrhardt, Matthias (2018). 'Self-legitimation in the Face of Politicization: Why International Organizations Centralized Public Communication', *The Review of International Organizations*, 13 (4): 519–46.

Eckersley, Robyn (2010). 'Green Theory', in Tim Dunne, Milja Kurki and Steve Smith (eds), *International Relations Theories. Discipline and Diversity*, 2nd edn, 257–77, Oxford: Oxford University Press.

Eckhard, Steffen and Jörn Ege (2016). 'International Bureaucracies and Their Influence on Policy-making: A Review of Empirical Evidence', *Journal of European Public Policy*, 23 (7): 960–78.

Eichengreen, Barry (1996). *Globalizing Capital. A History of the International Monetary System*, Princeton, NJ: Princeton University Press.

Eilstrup-Sangiovanni, Mette (2021). 'What Kills International Organisations? When and Why International Organisations Terminate', *European Journal of International Relations*, 27 (1): 281–310.

Eilstrup-Sangiovanni, Mette and Stephanie C. Hofmann (2020). 'Of the Contemporary Global Order, Crisis, and Change', *Journal of European Public Policy*, 27 (7): 1077–89.

Einhorn, Jessica P. (2001). 'The World Bank's Mission Creep', *Foreign Affairs*, 80 (5): 22–35.

Ege, Jörn (2020). 'What International Bureaucrats (really) Want: Administrative Preferences in International Organization Research', *Global Governance: A Review of Multilateralism and International Organizations*, 26 (4): 577–600.

Ege, Jörn, Michael W. Bauer, Nora Wagner and Eva Thomann (2023). 'Under What Conditions Does Bureaucracy Matter in the Making of Global Public Policies?', *Governance*, 36 (4): 1313–33.

Elgström, Ole and Christer Jönsson (2000). 'Negotiation in the European Union: Bargaining or Problem-Solving?', *Journal of European Public Policy*, 7 (5): 684–704.

Elsig, Manfred and Mark A. Pollack (2014). 'Agents, Trustees, and International Courts: The Politics of Judicial Appointment at the World Trade Organization', *European Journal of International Relations*, 20 (2): 391–415.

Escobar, Arturo (1995). *Encountering Development: The Making and Unmaking of the Third World*, Princeton, NJ: Princeton University Press.

Etone, Damian, Amna Nazir and Alice Storey, eds (2024). *Human Rights and the UN Universal Periodic Review Mechanism: A Research Companion*, London: Routledge.

Falkner, Robert (2012). 'Global Environmentalism and the Greening of International Society', *International Affairs*, 88 (3): 503–22.

Farrell, Henry, and Abraham L. Newman (2019). 'Weaponized Interdependence: How Global Economic Networks Shape State Coercion', *International Security*, 44 (1): 42–79.

Finnemore, Martha (1993). 'International Organizations as Teachers of Norms: The United Nations Educational, Scientific, and Cultural Organization and Science Policy', *International Organization*, 47 (4): 565–98.

Finnemore, Martha and Kathryn Sikkink (1998). 'International Norm Dynamics and Political Change', *International Organization*, 52 (4): 887–917.

Fioretos, Orfeo (2011). 'Historical Institutionalism in International Relations', *International Organization*, 65 (2): 367–99.

Fioretos, Orfeo (2020). 'Rhetorical Appeals and Strategic Cooptation in the Rise and Fall of the New International Economic Order', *Global Policy*, 11 (S3): 73–82.

Forsythe, David (2006). *Human Rights in International Relations*, 2nd edn, Cambridge: Cambridge University Press.

Fortna, Virginia Page (2004a). 'Does Peacekeeping Keep Peace? International Intervention and the Duration of Peace after Civil War', *International Studies Quarterly*, 48 (2): 269–92.

Fortna, Virginia Page (2004b). 'Interstate Peacekeeping: Causal Mechanisms and Empirical Effects', *World Politics*, 56 (4): 481–519.

Fortna, Virginia Page (2008). *Does Peacekeeping Work? Shaping Belligerents' Choices after Civil War*, Princeton, NJ: Princeton University Press.

Fortna, Virginia Page and Lisa Morjé Howard (2008). 'Pitfalls and Prospects in the Peacekeeping Literature', *Annual Review of Political Science*, 11: 283–301.

Forster, Timon, Alexander E. Kentikelenis, Bernhard Reinsberg, Thomas H. Stubbs and Lawrence P. King (2019). 'How Structural Adjustment Programs Affect Inequality: A Disaggregated Analysis of IMF Conditionality, 1980–2014', *Social Science Research*, 80: 83–113.

Forster, Timon, Alexander E. Kentikelenis, Thomas H. Stubbs and Lawrence P. King (2020). 'Globalization and Health Equity: The Impact of Structural Adjustment Programs on Developing Countries', *Social Science & Medicine*, 267: 112496.

Frankenbach, Patrick, Andreas Kruck and Bernhard Zangl (2021). 'India's Recognition as a Nuclear Power: A Case of Strategic Cooptation', *Contemporary Security Policy*, 42 (4): 530–53.
Friedrich, Carl J. (1968). *Trends of Federalism in Theory and Practice*, New York: Praeger.
Galtung, Johan (1969). 'Violence, Peace, and Peace Research', *Journal of Peace Research*, 6 (3): 167–91.
Gareis, Sven Bernhard and Johannes Varwick (2005). *The United Nations. An Introduction*, Basingstoke: Palgrave Macmillan.
Geck, Angela (2024). *The Power to Persuade: Strategic Arguing at the World Trade Organization*, Toronto: University of Toronto Press.
Gemmill, Barbara and Abimbola Bamidele-Izu (2002). 'The Role of NGOs and Civil Society in Global Environmental Governance', in Daniel C. Esty and Maria H. Ivanova (eds), *Global Environmental Governance. Options & Opportunities*, 1–24, New Haven, CT: Yale School of Forestry and Environmental Studies.
Genschel, Philipp and Markus Jachtenfuchs, eds (2014). *Beyond the Regulatory Polity?: The European Integration of Core State Powers*, Oxford: Oxford University Press.
Gardini, Gianluca (2010). *The Origins of Mercosur: Democracy and Regionalization in South America*, London: Palgrave Macmillan.
Gilbert, Christopher L. and David Vines (2000). 'The World Bank: An Overview of Some Major Issues', in Christopher L. Gilbert and David Vines (eds), *The World Bank. Structure and Policies*, 10–38, Cambridge: Cambridge University Press.
Gill, George (1996). *The League of Nations. From 1929 to 1946*, Garden City Park, NY: Avery.
Gilligan, Michael J. (2006). 'Is Enforcement Necessary for Effectiveness? A Model of the International Criminal Regime', *International Organization*, 60 (4): 935–67.
Gilpin, Robert (1981). *War and Change in World Politics*, Cambridge: Cambridge University Press.
Gilpin, Robert (1987). *The Political Economy of International Relations*, Princeton, NJ: Princeton University Press.
Gilpin, Robert (2000). *The Challenge of Global Capitalism. The World Economy in the 21st Century*, Princeton, NJ: Princeton University Press.
Girod, Desha M. and Jennifer L. Tobin (2016). 'Take the Money and Run: The Determinants of Compliance with Aid Agreements', *International Organization*, 70(1): 209–39.
Goldsmith, Jack L. (2003). 'The Self-defeating International Criminal Court', *Chicago Law Review*, 70 (1): 89–104.
Goldstein, Judith and Robert O. Keohane (1993). 'Ideas and Foreign Policy: An Analytical Framework', in Judith Goldstein and Robert O. Keohane (eds), *Ideas and Foreign Policy. Beliefs, Institutions, and Political Change*, 3–30, Ithaca, NY: Cornell University Press.
Goldstein, Judith L., Douglas Rivers and Michael Tomz (2007). 'Institutions in International Relations: Understanding the Effects of the GATT and the WTO on World Trade', *International Organization*, 61 (1): 37–67.
Goldstone, Richard (2007). 'International Criminal Courts and Ad-hoc Tribunals', in Thomas G. Weiss and Sam Daws (eds), *The Oxford Handbook on the United Nations*, 463–78, Oxford: Oxford University Press.

Goodrich, Leland M. (1947). 'From League of Nations to United Nations', *International Organization*, 1 (1): 3–21.

Grabenwarter, Christoph (2005). *Europäische Menschenrechtskonvention*, 2nd edn, Munich: Beck.

Graham, Erin R. (2023). *Transforming International Institutions: How Money Quietly Sidelined Multilateralism at the United Nations*, Oxford: Oxford University Press.

Gray, Julia (2018). 'Life, Death, or Zombie? The Vitality of International Organizations', *International Studies Quarterly*, 62, (1): 1–13.

Gray, Julia (2024). 'The Life Cycle of International Cooperation: Introduction to the Special Issue', *The Review of International Organizations*, 19 (4): 641–64.

Green, Duncan & Griffith, Matthew (2002). 'Globalization and Its Discontents', *International Affairs*, 78 (1): 49–68.

Greene, Owen (1998). 'The System of Implementation Review in the Ozone Regime', in David G. Victor, Kal Raustiala and Eugene B. Skolnikoff (eds), *The Implementation and Effectiveness of International Environmental Commitments. Theory and Practice*, 89–136, Cambridge, MA: MIT Press.

Grieco, Joseph M. (1988). 'Anarchy and the Limits of Cooperation: A Realist Critique of the Newest Liberal Institutionalism', *International Organization*, 42 (3): 485–507.

Grigorescu, Alexandru (2007). 'Transparency of Intergovernmental Organizations: The Roles of Member States, International Bureaucracies and Nongovernmental Organizations', *International Studies Quarterly*, 51 (3): 625–48.

Grigorescu, Alexandru (2015). *Democratic Intergovernmental Organizations?* Cambridge: Cambridge University Press.

Gruber, Lloyd (2000). *Ruling The World: Power Politics and The Rise of Supranational Institutions*, Princeton, NJ: Princeton University Press.

Gutner, Tamar and Alexander Thompson (2010). 'The Politics of IO Performance: A Framework', *The Review of International Organizations*, 5 (3): 227–48.

Guzman, Andrew T. (2008). *How International Law Works*, Oxford: Oxford University Press.

Haas, Ernst B. (1964). *Beyond the Nation State. Functionalism and International Organization*, Stanford, CA: Stanford University Press.

Haas, Ernst B. (1967). 'The Uniting of Europe and the Uniting of Latin America', *Journal of Common Market Studires*, 5: 315.

Haas, Ernst B. (1968). *The Uniting of Europe. Political, Social, and Economic Forces 1950–1957*, Stanford, CA: Stanford University Press.

Haas, Peter M. (1989). 'Do Regimes Matter? Epistemic Communities and Mediterranean Pollution Control', *International Organization*, 43 (3): 377–403.

Haas, Peter M. (1990). *Saving the Mediterranean. The Politics of International Environmental Cooperation*, New York: Columbia University Press.

Haas, Peter M. (1992a). 'Introduction: Epistemic Communities and International Policy Coordination', *International Organization*, 46 (1): 1–35.

Haas, Peter M. (1992b). 'Banning Chlorofluorocarbons: Epistemic Community Efforts to Protect Stratospheric Ozone', *International Organization*, 46 (1): 187–224.

Haas, Peter M. (1992c). 'Obtaining Environmental Protection through Epistemic Communities', in Ian H. Rowlands and Malory Greene (eds), *Global*

Environmental Change and International Relations, 38–59, Basingstoke: Palgrave Macmillan. .

Hafner-Burton, Emilie M. (2008). 'Sticks and Stones: Naming and Shaming the Human Rights Enforcement Problem', *International Organization*, 62 (3): 689–716.

Häge, Frank M. (2013). 'Coalition Building and Consensus in the Council of the European Union', *British Journal of Political Science*, 43 (3): 481–504.

Hale, Thomas and David Held (2017). *Beyond Gridlock*, Hoboken, NJ: John Wiley & Sons.

Hale, Thomas and David Held (2018). 'Breaking the Cycle of Gridlock', *Global Policy*, 9 (1): 129–37.

Hale, Thomas, David Held and Kevin Young (2013). *Gridlock: Why Global Cooperation is Failing When We Need It Most*, London: Polity Press.

Hardin, Garrett (1968). 'The Tragedy of the Commons', *Science,* 162 (3859): 1243–48.

Harbom, Lotta and Peter Wallensteen (2010). 'Armed Conflicts, 1946–2009', *Journal of Peace Research*, 47 (4): 501–09.

Hasenclever, Andreas (2001). *Die Macht der Moral in der internationalen Politik. Militärische Interventionen westlicher Staaten in Somalia, Ruanda und Bosnien-Herzegowina,* Frankfurt/M.: Campus.

Hasenclever, Andreas, Peter Mayer and Volker Rittberger (1997). *Theories of International Regimes*, Cambridge: Cambridge University Press.

Haug, Sebastian, Rosemary Foot and Max-Otto Baumann (2024). 'Power Shifts in International Organisations: China at the United Nations', *Global Policy*, 15: 5–17.

Hauser, Heinz and Kai-Uwe Schanz (1995). *Das neue GATT. Die Welthandelsordnung nach Abschluss der Uruguay-Runde,* 2nd edn, Munich: Oldenbourg.

Hawkins, Darren G., David A. Lake, Daniel L. Nielson and Michael J. Tierney (2006). 'Delegation Under Anarchy: States, International Organizations, and Principal-agent Theory', in Darren G. Hawkins, David A. Lake, Daniel L. Nielson and Michael J. Tierney (eds), *Delegation and Agency in International Organizations*, 3–38, Cambridge: Cambridge University Press. .

Heimann, Gadi, Andreasl Kruck, Deganit Paikowsky and Bernhard Zangl (2025). 'Cooptation in Great Power Rivalries: A Conceptual Framework', *Contemporary Security Policy*, advance online publication, 46 (1): 8–36.

Heinzel, Mirko (2022). 'International Bureaucrats and Organizational Performance. Country-specific Knowledge and Sectoral Knowledge in World Bank Projects', *International Studies Quarterly*, 66 (2): sqac013.

Heinzel, Mirko, Ben Cormier and Bernhard Reinsberg (2023). 'Earmarked Funding and the Control–performance Trade-off in International Development Organizations', *International Organization*, 77 (2): 475–495.

Helleiner, Eric (1994). *States and the Reemergence of Global Finance. From Bretton Woods to the 1990s,* Ithaca, NY: Cornell University Press.

Helm, Carsten and Detlef Sprinz (2000). 'Measuring the Effectiveness of International Environmental Regimes',*Journal of Conflict Resolution*, 44 (5): 630–52.

Hernández, Gleider (2014). *The International Court of Justice and The Judicial Function*, Oxford: Oxford University Press.

Herranz-Surrallés, Anna, Chad Damro and Sandra Eckert (2024). 'The Geoeconomic Turn of the Single European Market? Conceptual Challenges and Empirical Trends', *Journal of Common Market Studies*, 62 (4): 919–37.

Herz, John H. (1950). 'Idealist Internationalism and the Security Dilemma', *World Politics*, 2 (2): 157–80.

Higgott, Richard (2001). 'Economic Globalization and Global Governance: Towards a Post-Washington Consensus?', in Volker Rittberger (ed.), *Global Governance and the United Nations System*, 127–57, Tokyo: United Nations University Press.

Hinsley, Francis Harry (1963). *Power and the Pursuit of Peace: Theory and Practice in the History of Relations between States*, Cambridge: Cambridge University Press.

Hix, Simon and Bjørn Høyland (2022). *The Political System of the European Union*, 4th edn, London: Bloomsbury.

Hix, Simon, Abdul Noury and Gerard Roland (2006). 'Dimensions of Politics in the European Parliament', *American Journal of Political Science*, 50 (2): 494–520.

Hodson, Dermot, Uwe Puetter, Sabine Saurugger and John Peterson (2021). *The Institutions of the European Union*, Oxford: Oxford University Press.

Hoekman, Bernard M. and Petros C. Mavroidis (2016). *World Trade Organization (WTO): Law, Economics, and Politics*, London: Routledge.

Hoffmann-Van de Poll, Frederike (2011). *A Quest for Accountability. The Effects of International Criminal Tribunals and Courts on Impunity*, Berlin: Berliner Wissenschaftsverlag.

Honig, Dan (2019). 'When Reporting Undermines Performance: The Costs of Politically Constrained Organizational Autonomy in Foreign Aid Implementation', *International Organization*, 73 (1): 171–201.

Hooghe, Liesbet, Tobias Lenz and Gary Marks (2019). *A Theory of International Organization*, Oxford: Oxford University Press.

Hooghe, Liesbet and Gary Marks (2009). 'A Postfunctionalist Theory of European Integration: From Permissive Consensus to Constraining Dissensus', *British Journal of Political Science*, 39 (1): 1–23.

Hooghe, Liesbet and Gary Marks (2015). 'Delegation and Pooling in International Organizations', *The Review of International Organizations*, 10 (3): 305–28.

Hooghe, Liesbet, Gary Marks, Tobias Lenz, Jeanine Bezuijen, Besir Ceka and Svet Derderyan (2017). *Measuring International Authority: A Postfunctionalist Theory of Governance, Volume III*, Oxford: Oxford University Press.

Hopewell, Kristen (2015). 'Different Paths to Power: The Rise of Brazil, India and China at the World Trade Organization', *Review of International Political Economy*, 22 (2): 311–38.

Hopewell, Kristen (2022). 'How China Lost its Wolf Pack: The Fracturing of the Emerging-power Alliance at the WTO', *International Affairs*, 98 (6): 1915–35.

Hopmann, P. Terrence (1995). 'Two Paradigms of Negotiation: Bargaining and Problem Solving', *The Annals of the American Academy of Political and Social Science*, 542 (1): 24–47.

Hughes, Steve and Nigel Haworth (2010). *The International Labour Organisation*, London: Routledge.

Hüller, Thorsten and Mathias Leonard Maier (2006). 'Fixing the Codex? Global Food-safety Governance', in Christian Joerges and Ernst-Ulrich Petersmann (eds), *Constitutionalism, Multilevel Trade Governance and Social Regulation*, 267–300, Oxford: Oxford University Press.

Hultman, Lisa, Jacob Kathman and Megan Shannon (2014). 'Beyond Keeping Peace: United Nations Effectiveness in the Midst of Fighting', *American Political Science Review*, 108 (4): 737–53.

Human Security Report Project (2010). *Human Security Report 2009/2010. The Causes of Peace and the Shrinking Costs of War*, Vancouver: Human Security Report Project.

Hurd, Ian (2007). *After Anarchy. Legitimacy and Power in the UN Security Council*, Princeton, NJ: Princeton University Press.

Hurrell, Andrew (2006). 'Hegemony, Liberalism and Global Order: What Space for Would-be Great Powers?', *International Affairs*, 82 (1): 1–19.

Huysmans, Jef (2000). 'The European Union and the Securitization of Migration', *Journal of Common Market Studies*, 38 (5): 751–77.

IAEA (n.d.). *Mission Statement*. https://www.iaea.org/about/mission (accessed 28 July 2018).

Iida, Keisuke (2004). 'Is WTO Dispute Settlement Effective?', *Global Governance*, 10 (2): 207–25.

Ikenberry, G. John (2008). 'The Rise of China and the Future of the West – Can the Liberal System Survive', *Foreign Affairs*, 87: 23–37.

Ikenberry, G. John (2011). *Liberal Leviathan: The Origins, Crisis, and Transformation of the American World Order*, Princeton, NJ: Princeton University Press.

Ikenberry, G. John (2020). *A World Safe for Democracy: Liberal Internationalism and the Crises of Global Order*, New Haven CT: Yale University Press.

Inboden, Rana Siu (2021). *China and the International Human Rights Regime*, Cambridge: Cambridge University Press.

Independent Evaluation Office of the IMF (IEO) (2011). *IMF Performance in the Run-Up to the Financial and Economic Crisis. IMF Surveillance in 2004–07*, Washington, DC: Evaluation Report.

Ingram, Paul, Jeffrey Robinson and Marc L. Busch (2005). 'The Intergovernmental Network of World Trade: IGO Connectedness, Governance and Embeddedness', *American Journal of Sociology*, 111 (3): 824–58.

International Commission on Intervention and State Sovereignty (ICISS) (2001). *Responsibility to Protect. Report of the International Commission on Intervention and State Sovereignty*, Ottawa, ON: International Development Research Center.

International Monetary Fund (IMF) (n.d.). *IMF Lending*. https://www.imf.org/en/About/Factsheets/IMF-Lending (accessed: 26 November 2024).

Jackson, John H. (1999). *The World Trading System. Law and Policy of International Economic Relations*, 2nd edn, Cambridge: Cambridge University Press.

Jackson, John H. (2004). 'Effektivität und Wirksamkeit des Streitbeilegungsverfahrens der WTO', in Bernhard Zangl and Michael Zürn (eds), *Verrechtlichung – Baustein für Global Governance?* 99–118, Bonn: Dietz.

Jacobson, Harold K. (1984). *Networks of Interdependence. International Organizations and the Global Political System*, 2nd edn, New York: Knopf.

Jentleson, Bruce W. and Rebecca L. Britton (1998). 'Still Pretty Prudent: Post-Cold War American Public Opinion on the Use of Military Force', *Journal of Conflict Resolution*, 42 (4): 395–417.

Jervis, Robert (1976). *Perception and Misperception in International Politics: New edition*, Princeton NJ: Princeton University Press.

Jervis, Robert (1983). 'Security Regimes', in Stephen D. Krasner (ed.), *International Regimes*, 357–78, Ithaca, NY: Cornell University Press.

Jetschke, Anja (2006). 'Weltkultur vs. Partikularismus: Die Universalität der Menschenrechte im Lichte der Ratifikation von Menschenrechtsverträgen', *Die Friedens-Warte*, 81 (1): 25–49.

Johnson, Tana (2014). *Organizational Progeny: Why Governments are Losing Control over the Proliferating Structures of Global Governance*, Oxford: Oxford University Press.

Johnston, Alastair Iain (2007). *Social States: China in International Institutions, 1980–2000*, Princeton, NJ: Princeton University Press.

Johnstone, Ian (2008). 'The Security Council as Legislature', in Bruce Cronin and Ian Hurd (eds), *The UN Security Council and the Politics of International Authority*, 80–104, London: Routledge.

Jones, David Martin and Michael L. R. Smith (2007). 'Making Process, Not Progress: ASEAN and the Evolving East Asian Regional Order', *International Security*, 32 (1): 148–84.

Jones, Erik, Daniel R. Kelemen and Sophie Meunier (2016). 'Failing Forward? The Euro Crisis and the Incomplete Nature of European Integration', *Comparative Political Studies*, 49 (7) 1010–34.

Jones, Kent (2009). *The Doha Blues. Institutional Crisis and Reform in the WTO*, Oxford: Oxford University Press.

Jönsson, Christer and Jonas Tallberg (1998). 'Compliance and Post-agreement Bargaining', *European Journal of International Relations*, 4 (4): 371–408.

Jørgensen, Knud Erik, ed. (2009). *The European Union and International Organizations*, London: Routledge.

Jupille, Joseph, Walter Mattli and Duncan Snidal (2013). *Institutional Choice and Global Commerce*, Cambridge: Cambridge University Press.

Kahler, Miles (1995). *International Institutions and the Political Economy of Integration*, Washington, DC: Brookings Institution.

Kahler, Miles (2013). 'Rising Powers and Global Governance: Negotiating Change in a Resilient Status Quo', *International Affairs*, 89 (3): 711–29.

Kaldor, Mary (1999). *New and Old Wars: Organised Violence in a Global Era*, Hoboken, NJ: John Wiley & Sons.

Kanbur, Ravi and David Vines (2000). 'The World Bank and Poverty Reduction: Past, Present and Future', in Christopher L. Gilbert and David Vines (eds), *The World Bank. Structure and Policies*, 87–107, Cambridge: Cambridge University Press.

Kant, Immanuel (1991 [1795]). 'Perpetual Peace: A Philosophical Sketch', in Hans Reiss (ed.), *Kant. Political Writings*, 2nd edn, 93–130, Cambridge: Cambridge University Press.

Karlsrud, John (2015). 'The UN at War: Examining the Consequences of Peace-enforcement Mandates for the UN Peacekeeping Operations in the CAR, the DRC and Mali', *Third World Quarterly*, 36 (1): 40–54.

Katzenstein, Peter J. (1996). 'Introduction: Alternative Perspectives on National Security', in Peter J. Katzenstein (ed.), *The Culture of National Security. Norms and Identity in World Politics*, 1–32, New York: Columbia University Press.
Keck, Margaret E. and Kathryn Sikkink (1998). *Activists Beyond Borders. Advocacy Networks in International Politics*, Ithaca, NY: Cornell University Press.
Keleman, Daniel R. (2002). 'The Politics of "Eurocratic" Structure and the New European Agencies', *West European Politics*, 25 (4) 93–118.
Keller, Helen and Alec Stone Sweet, eds (2008). *A Europe of Rights. The Impact of the ECHR on National Legal Systems*, Oxford: Oxford University Press.
Kentikelenis, Alexander E., Thomas H. Stubbs and Lawrence P. King (2016). 'IMF Conditionality and Development Policy Space, 1985–2014', *Review of International Political Economy*, 23 (4): 543–82.
Kentikelenis, Alexander and Erik Voeten (2021). 'Legitimacy Challenges to the Liberal World Order: Evidence from United Nations Speeches, 1970–2018', *The Review of International Organizations*, 16 (4): 721–54.
Keohane, Robert O. (1984). *After Hegemony. Cooperation and Discord in the World Political Economy*, Princeton, NJ: Princeton University Press.
Keohane, Robert O. (1989). 'Neoliberal Institutionalism: A Perspective on World Politics', in Robert O. Keohane (ed.), *International Institutions and State Power. Essays in International Relations Theory*, 1–20, Boulder, CO: Westview.
Keohane, Robert O., Andrew Moravcsik and Anne-Marie Slaughter (2000). 'Legalized Dispute Resolution: Interstate and Transnational', *International Organization*, 54 (3): 457–88.
Keohane, Robert O. and Joseph S. Nye Jr. (1977). *Power and Interdependence*, New York: Longman.
Keohane, Robert O. and David G. Victor (2011). 'The Regime Complex for Climate Change', *Perspectives on Politics*, 9 (1): 7–23.
Kiewiet, D. Roderick and Mathew D. McCubbins (1991). *The Logic of Delegation. Congressional Parties and the Appropriations Process*, Chicago, IL: University of Chicago Press.
Kilby, Christopher (2000). 'Supervision and Performance: The Case of World Bank Projects', *Journal of Development Economics*, 62 (1): 233–59.
Kindleberger, Charles (1974). *The World in Depression, 1929–1939*, Berkeley, CA: University of California Press.
Kiss, Elizabeth (2000). 'Moral Ambition Within and Beyond Political Constraints', in Robert I. Rotberg and Dennis Thompson (eds), *In Truth v. Justice: The Morality of Truth Commissions*, 68–98, Princeton, NJ: Princeton University Press.
Klabbers, Jan (2022). *An Introduction to International Organizations Law*, Cambridge: Cambridge University Press,.
Kleine, Mareike (2013). 'Trading Control: National Fiefdoms in International Organizations', *International Theory*, 5 (3): 321–46.
Klotz, Audie (1995). *Norms in International Relations. The Struggle against Apartheid*, Ithaca, NY: Cornell University Press.
Kolb, Robert (2013). *The International Court of Justice*, Oxford: Hart Publishing.
Kortendiek, Nele (2024). *Global Governance on the Ground: Organizing International Migration and Asylum at the Border*, Oxford: Oxford University Press.

Koops, Joachim, Norrie MacQueen, Thierry Tardy and Paul D. Williams, eds (2015). *The Oxford Handbook of United Nations Peacekeeping Operations*, Oxford: Oxford University Press.

Koremenos, Barbara, Charles Lipson and Duncan Snidal (2001). 'The Rational Design of International Institutions', *International Organization*, 55 (4): 761–800.

Krasner, Stephen D. (1983). 'Structural Causes and Regime Consequences: Regimes as Intervening Variables', in Stephen D. Krasner (ed.), *International Regimes*, 1–21, Ithaca, NY: Cornell University Press.

Krasner, Stephen D. (1985). *Structural Conflict. The Third World against Global Liberalism*, Berkeley, CA: University of California Press.

Krasner, Stephen D. (1991). 'Global Communications and National Power. Life on the Pareto Frontier', *World Politics*, 43 (3): 336–66.

Krasner, Stephen D. (1999). *Sovereignty. Organized Hypocrisy*, Princeton, NJ: Princeton University Press.

Kreuder-Sonnen, Christian (2019). *Emergency Powers of International Organizations: Between Normalization and Containment*, Oxford: Oxford University Press.

Kreuder-Sonnen, Christian and Berthold Rittberger (2023). 'The LIO's Growing Democracy Gap: An Endogenous Source of Polity Contestation', *Journal of International Relations and Development*, 26 (1): 61–85.

Kreuder-Sonnen, Christian and Bernhard Zangl (2025). 'The Politics of IO Authority Transfers: Explaining Informal Internationalisation and Unilateral Renationalization', *Journal of European Public Policy*, 32 (4): 954–79.

Kruck, Andreas (2011). *Private Ratings, Public Regulations. Credit Rating Agencies and Global Financial Governance*, Basingstoke: Palgrave Macmillan.

Kruck, Andreas and Bernhard Zangl (2019). 'Trading Privileges for Support: the Strategic Co-optation of Emerging Powers into International Institutions', *International Theory*, 11 (3): 318–43.

Kruck, Andreas and Bernhard Zangl (2020). 'The Adjustment of International Institutions to Global Power Shifts: A Framework for Analysis', *Global Policy*, 11 (S3) 5–16.

Ku, Julian and Jide Nzelibe (2006). Do International Criminal Tribunals Deter or Exacerbate Humanitarian Atrocities? *Washington University Law Quarterly*, 84 (4): 777–833.

Kucik, Jeffrey and Eric Reinhardt (2008). 'Does Flexibility Promote Cooperation? An Application to the Global Trade Regime', *International Organization*, 62(3): 477–505.

Kuziemko, Ilyana and Eric Werker (2006). 'How Much is a Seat on the Security Council Worth? Foreign Aid and Bribery at the United Nations', *Journal of Political Economy*, 114 (5): 905–30.

Kwa, Aileen (2003). *Power Politics in the WTO*, Bangkok: Focus on the Global South.

Lake, David A., Lisa L. Martin and Thomas Risse (2021). 'Challenges to the Liberal Order: Reflections on International Organization', *International Organization*, 75 (2): 225–57.

Lall, Ranjit (2017). 'Beyond Institutional Design: Explaining the Performance of International Organizations', *International Organization*, 71 (2): 245–80.

Lebovic, James H. and Erik Voeten (2006). 'The Politics of Shame: The Condemnation of Country Human Rights Practices in the UNHCR', *International Studies Quarterly*, 50 (4): 861–88.
Lee, Kelley (2009). *The World Health Organization (WHO)*, London: Routledge.
Leitner, Kara and Simon Lester (2005). 'WTO Dispute Settlement 1995–2004: A Statistical Analysis', *Journal of International Economic Law*, 8 (1): 231–44.
Lenshow, Andrea (2010). 'Environmental Policy: Contending Dynamics of Policy Change', in Helen Wallace, Mark A. Pollack and Alasdair Young (eds), *Policy-Making in the European Union*, 6th edn, 307–29, Oxford: Oxford University Press.
Lenz, Tobias (2021). *Interorganizational Diffusion in International Relations: Regional Institutions and the Role of the European Union*, Oxford: Oxford University Press.
Leviter, Lee (2010). 'The ASEAN Charter: ASEAN Failure or Member Failure', *New York University Journal of International Law and Politics*, 43 (1): 159–210.
Levy, Marc A. (1993). 'European Acid Rain: The Power of Tote-board Diplomacy', in Peter M. Haas, Robert O. Keohane and Marc A. Levy (eds), *Institutions for the Earth. Sources of Effective International Environmental Protection*, 75–132, Cambridge, MA: MIT Press.
Lewis, Jeffrey (1998). 'Is the "Hard Bargaining" Image of the Council Misleading? The Committee of Permanent Representatives and the Local Elections Directive', *Journal of Common Market Studies*, 36 (4): 479–504.
Lewis, Jeffrey (2005). The Janus Face of Brussels: Socialization and Everyday Decision Making in the European Union, *International Organization*, 59 (4): 937–71.
Lin, Justin and Ha-Joon Chang (2009). 'Should Industrial Policy in Developing Countries Conform to Comparative Advantage or Defy It? A Debate between Justin Lin and Ha-Joon Chang', *Development Policy Review*, 27 (5): 483–502.
Linklater, Andrew (1990). 'The Problem of Community in International Relations', *Alternatives*, 15 (2): 135–53.
Linklater, Andrew (1998). *The Transformation of Political Community. Ethical Foundations of the Post-Westphalian Era*, Cambridge: Polity Press.
Lipscy, Phillip Y. (2017). *Renegotiating the World Order: Institutional Change in International Relations*, Cambridge: Cambridge University Press.
Lipson, Charles (1984). 'International Cooperation in Economic and Security Affairs', *World Politics*, 37 (1): 1–23.
Littoz-Monnet, Annabelle (2017). 'Expert Knowledge as a Strategic Resource: International Bureaucrats and the Shaping of Bioethical Standards', *International Studies Quarterly*, 61 (3): 584–95.
Littoz-Monnet, Annabelle and Juanita Uribe (2023). 'Methods Regimes in Global Governance: The Politics of Evidence-making in Global Health', *International Political Sociology*, 17 (2): olad005.
Lombardi, Domenico and Ngaire Woods (2008). 'The Politics of Influence: An Analysis of IMF Surveillance', *Review of International Political Economy*, 15 (5): 711–39.
Louis, Marieke and Lucile Maertens (2021). *Why International Organizations Hate Politics: Depoliticizing the World*, London: Routledge.
Lowi, Theodore J. (1964). 'American Business, Public Policy, Case Studies, and Political Theory', *World Politics*, 16 (4): 677–715.

Luard, Evan (1977). *International Agencies. The Emerging Framework of Interdependence*, London: Macmillan.
Luard, Evan (1982). *A History of the United Nations. The Years of Western Domination 1945–1955*, New York: St Martin's Press.
Lundgren, Magnus, Theresa Squatrito, Thomas Sommerer and Jonas Tallberg (2024). 'Introducing the Intergovernmental Policy Output Dataset (IPOD)', *The Review of International Organizations*, 19 (1): 117–46.
Luterbacher, Urs and Detlef Sprinz, eds (2001). *International Relations and Global Climate Change*, Cambridge, MA: MIT Press.
Lyall, Francis (2011). *International Communications: The International Telecommunication Union and the Universal Postal Union*, London: Routledge.
Madsen, Jakob B. (2001). 'Trade Barriers and the Collapse of World Trade during the Great Depression', *Southern Economic Journal*, 67 (4): 848–68.
Majone, Giandomenico (1994). 'The Rise of the Regulatory State in Europe', *West European Politics*, 17 (3): 77–101.
Majone, Giandomenico (1997). 'The New European Agencies: Regulation by Information', *Journal of European Public Policy*, 4 (2): 262–75.
Makinda, Samuel M., F. Wafula Okumu and David Mickler (2016). *The African Union: Addressing the Challenges of Peace, Security, and Governance*, London: Routledge.
Malone, David M. (2007). 'The Security Council', in Thomas G. Weiss and Sam Daws (eds), *The Oxford Handbook on the United Nations*, 117–35, Oxford: Oxford University Press.
Mansfield, Edward D. and Eric Reinhardt (2008). 'International Institutions and the Volatility of International Trade', *International Organization*, 62 (4): 621–52.
Manulak, Michael W. (2017). 'Leading by Design: Informal Influence and International Secretariats', *The Review of International Organizations*, 12 (4): 497–522.
March, James G. and Johan P. Olsen (1989). *Rediscovering Institutions. The Organizational Basis of Politics*, New York: Free Press.
Marchisio, Sergio and Antonietta Di Blase (1991). *The Food and Agriculture Organization (FAO)*, Dordrecht: Martinus Nijhoff.
Marshall, Katherine (2008). *The World Bank. From Reconstruction to Development to Equity*, London: Routledge.
Martin, Lisa L. (2006). 'Distribution, Information, and Delegation to International Organizations: The Case of IMF Conditionality', in Darren Greg, David A. Lake, Daniel L. Nielson and Michael J. Tierney (eds), *Delegation and Agency in International Organizations*, 140–64, Cambridge: Cambridge University Press.
Mastenbroek, Ellen (2005). 'EU Compliance: Still a "Black Hole"?', *Journal of European Public Policy*, 12 (6): 1103–20.
Matsushita, Mitsou, Thomas J. Schoenbaum and Petros C. Mavroidis (2004). *The World Trade Organization. Law, Practice and Policy*, Oxford: Oxford University Press.
McCubbins, Mathew D., Roger G. Noll & Barry R. Weingast (1987). 'Administrative Procedures as Instruments of Political Control', *Journal of Law, Economics, & Organization*, 3 (2): 243–77.

McCubbins, Mathew D. and Thomas Schwartz (1984). 'Congressional Oversight Overlooked: Police Patrols Versus Fire Alarms', *American Journal of Political Science*, 28 (1): 165–79.

McKeown, Ryder (2009). 'Norm Regress: US Revisionism and the Slow Death of the Norture Norm', *International Relations*, 23 (1): 5–25.

Mead, Walter Russell (2002). *Special Providence: American Foreign Policy and How it Changed the World*, London: Routledge.

Mearsheimer, John J. (1995). 'The False Promise of International Institutions', *International Security*, 19 (3): 5–49.

Mearsheimer, John J. (2001). *The Tragedy of Great Power Politics*, New York: Norton.

Mearsheimer, John J. (2014). 'Why the Ukraine Crisis is the West's Fault: The Liberal Delusions that Provoked Putin'. *Foreign Affairs*, 93 (5): 1–12.

Mearsheimer, John J. (2019). 'Bound to Fail: The Rise and Fall of the Liberal International Order'. *International Security*, 43 (4): 7–50.

Merrills, John Graham (2017). *International Dispute Settlement*, 6th edn, Cambridge: Cambridge University Press.

Mertus, Julie A. (2009). *The United Nations and Human Rights: A Guide for a New Era*, London: Routledge.

Meunier, Sophie and Kalypso Nicolaidis (2019). 'The Geopoliticization of European Trade and Investment Policy', *Journal of Common Market Studies*, 57 (S1): 103–13.

Mitchell, Ronald (1994). 'Regime Design Matters: Intentional Oil Pollution and Treaty Compliance', *International Organization*, 48 (3): 425–58.

Mitrany, David (1933). *The Progress of International Government*, New Haven, CT: Yale University Press.

Mitrany, David (1966). *A Working Peace System*, Chicago, IL: Quadrangle.

Momani, Bessma (2004). 'American Politicization of the International Monetary Fund', *Review of International Political Economy*, 11 (5): 880–904.

Mondré, Aletta (2009). 'Judizialisierungsprozesse im Sicherheitsbereich: Friedensbedrohungen vor dem UN-Sicherheitsrat', in Bernhard Zangl (ed.), *Auf dem Weg zu internationaler Rechtsherrschaft? Streitbeilegung zwischen Politik und Recht*, 119–59, Frankfurt/M.: Campus.

Moravcsik, Andrew (1995). 'Explaining International Human Rights Regimes: Liberal Theory and Western Europe', *European Journal of International Relations*, 1 (2): 157–89.

Moravcsik, Andrew (1998). *The Choice for Europe. Social Purpose and State Power from Messina to Maastricht*, Ithaca, NY: Cornell University Press.

Moretti, Sebastien (2021). 'Between Refugee Protection and Migration Management: The Quest for Coordination between UNHCR and IOM in the Asia-Pacific Region', *Third World Quarterly*, 42 (1): 34–51.

Morgenthau, Hans (1948). *Politics Among Nations. The Struggle for Power and Peace*, New York: Alfred A. Knopf.

Morris, Justin (2013). 'Libya and Syria: R2P and the Spectre of the Swinging Pendulum', *International Affairs*, 89 (5): 1265–83.

Morse, Julia C. and Robert O. Keohane (2014). 'Contested Multilateralism', *The Review of International Organizations*, 9: 385–412.

Moschella, Manuela (2010). *Governing Risk. The IMF and Global Financial Crises*, Basingstoke: Palgrave Macmillan.

Murphy, Craig N. (1994). *International Organization and Industrial Change: Global Governance since 1850*, Cambridge: Polity Press.
Murphy, Craig N. (2006). *The United Nations Development Programme: A Better Way?* Cambridge: Cambridge University Press.
Mumby, Jane (2023). *Dismantling the League of Nations: The Quiet Death of an International Organization, 1945–8*, London: Bloomsbury Publishing.
Narlikar, Amrita (2004). *International Trade and Developing Countries. Bargaining Coalitions in the GATT & WTO*, London: Routledge.
Narlikar, Amrita and Diana Tussie (2003). 'The G20 at the Cancun Ministerial: Developing Countries and Their Evolving Coalitions in the WTO', *World Economy*, 27 (7): 947–66.
Neumann, Iver B. (1996). 'Self and Other in International Relations', *European Journal of International Relations*, 2 (2): 139–74.
Newell, Peter and Harriet Bulkeley (2010). *Governing Climate Change*, London: Routledge.
Nielson, Daniel L., Michael J. Tierney and Catherine Weaver (2006). 'Bridging the Rationalist-constructivist Divide: Re-engineering the Culture of the World Bank', *Journal of International Relations and Development*, 9 (1): 107–39.
North, Douglass C. (1990). *Institutions, Institutional Change and Economic Performance*, Cambridge: Cambridge University Press.
Norwegian Nobel Committee (2007). *The Nobel Peace Prize 2007*. https://www.nobelprize.org/prizes/peace/2007/summary/ (accessed: 8 June 2025).
Nye, Joseph S. (1968). 'Comparative Regional Integration: Concept and Measurement', *International Organization*, 22 (4): 855–80.
Oberthür, Sebastian (2004). 'Verrechtlichung in der internationalen Umweltpolitik: Tendenzen, Gründe, Wirkungen', in Michael Zürn and Bernhard Zangl (eds), *Verrechtlichung – Baustein für Global Governance?* 119–39, Bonn: Dietz.
Odell, John S., ed. (2006). *Negotiating Trade. Developing Countries in the WTO and NAFTA*, Cambridge: Cambridge University Press.
Odell, John S. (2010). 'Three Islands of Knowledge about Negotiation in International Organizations', *Journal of European Public Policy*, 17 (5): 619–32.
O'Neill, Jim (2001). *Building Better Global Economic BRICs*, vol. 66, New York: Goldman Sachs.
Oksamytna, Kseniya (2023). *Advocacy and Change in International Organizations: Communication, Protection, and Reconstruction in UN Peacekeeping*, Oxford: Oxford University Press.
Oksamytna, Kseniya and Magnus Lundgren (2021). 'Decorating the "Christmas Tree": The UN Security Council and the Secretariat's Recommendations on Peacekeeping Mandates', *Global Governance: A Review of Multilateralism and International Organizations*, 27 (2): 226–50.
Olivier, Jos G. J., Greet Janssens-Maenhout and Jeroen A. H. W. Peters (2012). *Trends in Global CO2 Emissions*, The Hague: Netherlands Environmental Assessment Agency & EU Joint Research Centre. http://edgar.jrc.ec.europa.eu/CO2REPORT2012.pdf (accessed: 27 July 2018).
Organisation for Economic Co-operation and Development (OECD, n.d.). 'Climate Finance and the USD 100 billion Goal', *OECD*. https://www.oecd.org/en/topics/sub-issues/climate-finance-and-the-usd-100-billion-goal.html (accessed: 8 June 2025).

Osiander, Andreas (1994). *The States System of Europe 1640–1990. Peacemaking and the Conditions of International Stability*, Oxford: Clarendon Press.

Ostermann, Falk and Wolfgang Wagner (2023). 'Introducing the International Treaty Ratification Votes Database', *Foreign Policy Analysis*, 19 (4): orad023.

Ostrom, Elinor (1990). *Governing the Commons: The Evolution of Institutions for Collective Action*, Cambridge: Cambridge University Press.

Ott, Hermann E. (1997). 'Das internationale Regime zum Schutz des Klimas', in Thomas Gehring and Sebastian Oberthür (eds), *Internationale Umweltregime. Umweltschutz durch Verhandlungen und Verträge*, 201–18, Opladen: Leske & Budrich.

Packer, Corinne A. A. and Donald Rukare (2002). 'The New African Union and Its Constitutive Act', *American Journal of International Law*, 96 (2): 365–79.

Panel on United Nations Peace Operations (2000). Report of the Panel on United Nations Peace Operations (The Brahimi Report).

Panke, Diana (2012). 'Lobbying Institutional Key Players: How States Seek to Influence the European Commission, the Council Presidency and the European Parliament', *Journal of Common Market Studies*, 50 (1): 129–50.

Panke, Diana and Ulrich Petersohn (2016). 'Norm Challenges and Norm Death: The Inexplicable?', *Cooperation and Conflict*, 51 (1): 3–19.

Panke, Diana, Sören Stapel and Anna Starkmann (2020). *Comparing ‚Regional Organizations: Global Dynamics and Regional Particularities*, Bristol: Bristol University Press.

Papa, Mihaela, Zhen Han and Frank O'Donnell (2023). 'The Dynamics of Informal Institutions and Counter-hegemony: Introducing a BRICS Convergence Index', *European Journal of International Relations*, 29 (4): 960–89.

Pape, Matthias (1997). *Humanitäre Intervention. Zur Bedeutung der Menschenrechte in den Vereinten Nationen*, Baden-Baden: Nomos.

Parízek, Michal (2017). 'Control, Soft Information, and the Politics of International Organizations Staffing', *The Review of International Organizations*, 12 (4): 559–83.

Parízek, Michal and Matthew D. Stephen (2021). 'The Increasing Representativeness of International Organizations' Secretariats: Evidence from the United Nations System, 1997–2015', *International Studies Quarterly*, 65 (1): 197–209.

Parson, Edward A. (2003). *Protecting the Ozone Layer. Science, Strategy, and Negotiation in the Shaping of a Global Environmental Regime*, Oxford: Oxford University Press.

Parson, Edward E. (1993). 'Protecting the Ozone Layer', in Peter M. Haas, Robert O. Keohane and Marc A. Levy (eds), *Institutions for the Earth. Sources of Effective International Environmental Protection*, 27–74, Cambridge, MA: MIT Press.

Parsons, Craig (2003). *A Certain Idea of Europe*, Ithaca, NY: Cornell University Press.

Paterson, Matthew (2013). 'Green Theory', in Burchill, Scott et al. (eds), *Theories of International Relations*, 5th edn, 266–90, Basingstoke: Palgrave Macmillan.

Patz, Ronny and Klaus H. Goetz (2019). *Managing Money and Discord in the UN: Budgeting and Bureaucracy*, Oxford: Oxford University Press.

Paul, Thazha V., ed. (2016). *Accommodating ‚Rising Powers: Past, Present, and Future*, Cambridge: Cambridge University Press.

Pauly, Louis W. (1997). *Who Elected the Bankers? Surveillance and Control in the World Economy*, Ithaca, NY: Cornell University Press.

Pedersen, Susan (2007). 'Back to the League of Nations', *The American Historical Review*, 112 (4): 1091–17.

Pelc, Krzysztof J. (2009). 'Seeking Escape: The Use of Escape Clauses in International Trade Agreements', *International Studies Quarterly*, 53 (2): 349–68.

Pevehouse, Jon, Timothy Nordstrom, Roseanne McManus and Anne Spencer Jamison (2020). 'Tracking Organizations in the World: The Correlates of War IGO Version 3.0 datasets', *Journal of Peace Research*, 57 (3): 492–503.

Pécoud, Antoine (2018). 'What Do We Know About the International Organization for Migration?', *Journal of Ethnic and Migration Studies*, 44 (10): 1621–38.

Pillinger, Mara, Ian Hurd and Michael N. Barnett (2016). 'How to Get Away with Cholera: The UN, Haiti, and International Law', *Perspectives on Politics*, 14 (1): 70–86.

Pollack, Mark A. (2003). *The Engines of European Integration. Delegation, Agency, and Agenda Setting in the European Union*, Oxford: Oxford University Press.

Pouliot, Vincent (2016). *International Pecking Orders: The Politics and Practice of Multilateral Diplomacy*, Cambridge: Cambridge University Press.

Puetter, Uwe (2014). *The European Council and the Council: New Intergovernmentalism and Institutional Change*, Oxford: Oxford University Press.

Ramcharan, Bertrand (2007). 'Norms and Machinery', in Thomas G. Weiss and Sam Daws (eds), *The Oxford Handbook on the United Nations*, 439–62, Oxford: Oxford University Press.

Ramcharan, Bertrand (2011). *The UN Human Rghts Council*, London: Routledge.

Ravenhill, John (2009). 'East Asian Regionalism: Much Ado About Nothing?', *Review of International Studies*, 35 (S1): 215–35.

Reinalda, Bob (2009). *Routledge History of International Organizations: From 1815 to the Present Day*, London: Routledge.

Reinsberg, Bernhard, Alexander Kentikelenis, Thomas Stubbs and Lawrence King (2019). 'The World System and the Hollowing Out of State Capacity: How Structural Adjustment Programs Affect Bureaucratic Quality in Developing Countries', *American Journal of Sociology*, 124 (4): 1222–57.

Reinsberg, Bernhard, Mirko Heinzel and Christian Siauwijaya (2024). 'Earmarked Funding to International Organizations: Introducing the Earmarked Funding Dataset', *The Review of International Organizations*. https://doi.org/10.1007/s11558-024-09548-1

Renteln, Alison D. (1990). *International Human Rights. Universalism vs. Relativism*, London: Sage.

Reykers, Yf, John Karlsrud, Malte Brosig, Stephanie C. Hofmann, Cristiana Maglia and Pernille Rieker (2023). 'Ad hoc Coalitions in Global Governance: Short-notice, Task-and Time-specific Cooperation', *International Affairs*, 99 (2): 727–45.

Reus-Smit, Christian (2007). 'International Crises of Legitimacy', *International Politics*, 44: 157–74.

Risse, Thomas (2000). '"Let's argue!": Communicative Action in World Politics', *International Organization*, 54 (1): 1–41.

Risse, Thomas and Stephen C. Ropp (1999). 'International Human Rights Norms and Domestic Change: Conclusions', in Thomas Risse, Stephen C. Ropp and Kathryn Sikkink (eds), *The Power of Human Rights. International Norms and Domestic Change*, 234–78, Cambridge: Cambridge University Press.

Risse, Thomas, Stephen C. Ropp and Kathryn Sikkink, eds (1999). *The Power of Human Rights. International Norms and Domestic Change*, Cambridge: Cambridge University Press.

Risse, Thomas and Kathryn Sikkink (1999). 'The Socialization of International Human Rights Norms into Domestic Practices', in Thomas Risse, Stephen C. Ropp and Kathryn Sikkink (eds), *The Power of Human Rights. International Norms and Domestic Change*, 1–38, Cambridge: Cambridge University Press.

Risse-Kappen, Thomas (1995). 'Bringing Transnational Relations Back In Introduction', in Thomas Risse-Kappen (ed.), *Bringing Transnational Relations Back In. Non-State Actors, Domestic Structures and International Institutions*, 3–33, Cambridge: Cambridge University Press.

Ritchie, Nick (2019). 'A Hegemonic Nuclear Order: Understanding the Ban Treaty and the Power Politics of Nuclear Weapons', *Contemporary Security Policy*, 40: 409–34.

Rittberger, Berthold (2005). *Building Europe's Parliament. Democratic Representation Beyond the Nation State*, Oxford: Oxford University Press.

Rittberger, Volker, Andreas Kruck and Anne Romund (2010). *Grundzüge der Weltpolitik. Theorie und Empirie des Weltregierens*, Wiesbaden: VS Verlag für Sozialwissenschaften.

Rixen, Thomas, Lora Anne Viola and Michael Zürn, eds (2016). *Historical Institutionalism and International Relations: Explaining Institutional Development in World Politics*, Oxford: Oxford University Press.

Roberts, Adam (1996). 'The United Nations: Variants of Collective Security', in Ngaire Woods (ed.), *Explaining International Relations Since 1945*, 309–36, Oxford: Oxford University Press.

Roberts, Anthea, Henrique Choer Moraes and Victor Ferguson (2019). 'Toward a Geoeconomic order in International Trade and Investment', *Journal of International Economic Law*, 22 (4): 655–76.

Roger, Charles B. (2020). *The Origins of Informality: Why the Legal Foundations of Global Governance are Shifting, and Why It Matters*, Oxford: Oxford University Press.

Rosendorf, Peter R. and Helen V. Milner (2001). 'The Optimal Design of International Trade Institutions: Uncertainty and Escape', *International Organization*, 55 (4): 829–57.

Rowlands, Ian H. (1995). *The Politics of Global Atmospheric Change*, Manchester: Manchester University Press.

Rudolph, Christopher (2001). 'Constructing an Atrocities Regime: The Politics of War Crimes Tribunals', *International Organization*, 55 (3): 655–91.

Ruggeri, Andrea, Han Dorussen and Theodora-Ismene Gizelis (2018). 'On the Frontline Every Day? Subnational Deployment of United Nations Peacekeepers', *British Journal of Political Science*, 48 (8): 1005–25.

Ruggie, John Gerard (1982). 'International Regimes, Transactions, and Change: Embedded Liberalism in the Postwar Economic Order', *International Organization*, 36 (2): 379–415.

Ruggie, John Gerard (1992). 'Multilateralism: The Anatomy of an Institution', *International Organization*, 46 (3): 561–98.

Ruggie, John Gerard (1994). 'Trade, Protectionism and the Future of Welfare Capitalism', *Journal of International Affairs*, 48 (1): 1–11.

Rynning, Sten (2012). *NATO in Afghanistan: The Liberal Disconnect*, Stanford CA: Stanford University Press.

Rynning, Sten (2024). *NATO: From Cold War to Ukraine, a History of the World's Most Powerful Alliance*, New Haven, CT: Yale University Press.

Sandholtz, Wayne and John Zysman (1989). '1992 – Recasting the European Bargain', *World Politics*, 42 (1): 95–128.

Schabas, William (2011). *An Introduction to the International Criminal Court*, 4th edn, Cambridge: Cambridge University Press.

Scharpf, Fritz W. (2009). 'Legitimacy in the Multilevel European Polity', *European Political Science Review*, 1 (2): 173–204.

Scheffer, David J. (2002). 'Staying the Course with the International Criminal Court', *Cornell International Law Journal*, 35: 47–100.

Schimmelfennig, Frank, Thomas Winzen, Tobias Lenz, Jofre Rocabert, Loriana Crasnic, Cristina Gherasimov, Jana Lipps and Densua Mumford (2020). *The Rise of International Parliaments: Strategic Legitimation in International Organizations*, Oxford: Oxford University Press,.

Schirm, Stefan A. (2007). *Internationale Politische Ökonomie. Eine Einführung*, 2nd edn, Baden-Baden: Nomos.

Schirm, Stefan A. (2010). 'Leaders in Need of Followers: Emerging Powers in Global Governance', *European Journal of International Relations*, 16 (2): 197–221.

Schmidt, Vivien A. (2013). 'Democracy and Legitimacy in the European Union Revisited: Input, Output and "Throughput"', *Political Studies*, 61 (1): 2–22.

Schmidtke, Henning and Tobias Lenz (2024). 'Expanding or Defending Legitimacy? Why International Organizations Intensify Self-legitimation', *The Review of International Organizations*, 19 (4): 753–84.

Schmitt, Daniella (2009). *Do Transitional Administrations Fail? A Comparative Study of the Kosovo and East Timor Experiences*, Saarbrücken: Südwestdeutscher Verlag für Hochschulschriften.

Schöfer, Till and Clara Weinhardt (2022). 'Developing-country Status at the WTO: The Divergent Strategies of Brazil, India and China', *International Affairs*, 98 (6): 1937–57.

Schroeder, Michael Bluman (2014). 'Executive Leadership in the Study of International Organization: A Framework for Analysis', *International Studies Review*, 16 (3): 339–61.

Schuette, Leonard and Hylke Dijkstra (2023). 'When an International Organization Fails to Legitimate: The Decline of the OSCE', *Global Studies Quarterly*, 3 (4): ksad057.

Schulze, Peter M. (2002). 'NGOs', in Helmut Volger (ed.), *A Concise Encyclopedia of the United Nations*, 378–87, The Hague: Kluwer Law International.

Scott, George (1973). *The Rise and Fall of the League of Nations*, Southampton: Hutchinson.

Segers, Mathieu and Steven Van Hecke, eds (2023). *The Cambridge History of the European Union: Volume 2, European Integration Inside-Out*, Cambridge: Cambridge University Press.

Senti, Richard (2000). *WTO – System und Funktionsweise der Welthandelsordnung*, Zurich: Schultheiss.
Shepherd, Laura (2008). *Gender, Violence and Security: Discourse as Practice*, London: Zed Books.
Shepsle, Kenneth A. (1997). *Analyzing Politics. Rationality, Behaviour and Institutions*, New York: Norton.
Sikkink, Kathryn and Carrie Booth Walling (2007). 'The Impact of Human Rights Trials in Latin America', *Journal of Peace Research*, 44 (4): 427–45.
Simmons, Beth (2009). *Mobilizing for Human Rights. International Law in Domestic Politics*, Cambridge: Cambridge University Press.
Simmons, Beth and Allison Danner (2010). 'Credible Commitments and the International Criminal Court', *International Organization*, 64 (2): 225–56.
Slaughter, Anne-Marie (2005). *A New World Order*, Princeton, NJ: Princeton University Press.
Slaughter, Anne-Marie (2015). 'The Paris Approach to Global Governance', *Project Syndicate*, 28 December. https://www.project-syndicate.org/commentary/paris-agreement-model-for-global-governance-by-anne-marie-slaughter-2015-12
Smith, Jackie, Charles Chatfield and Ron Pagnucco, eds (1997). *Transnational Social Movements and Global Politics. Solidarity Beyond the State*, Syracuse, NY: Syracuse University Press.
Sommerer, Thomas, Hans Agné, Fariborz Zelli and Bart Bes (2022a). *Global Legitimacy Crises: Decline and Revival in Multilateral Governance*, Oxford: Oxford University Press.
Sommerer, Thomas, Theresa Squatrito, Jonas Tallberg and Magnus Lundgren (2022b). 'Decision-making in International Organizations: Institutional Design and Performance', *The Review of International Organizations*, 17 (4): 815–45.
Sommerer, Thomas and Jonas Tallberg (2019). 'Diffusion Across International Organizations: Connectivity and Convergence', *International Organization*, 73 (2): 399–433.
Sperling, James and Mark Webber (eds) (2025). *The Oxford Handbook of NATO*, Oxford: Oxford University Press.
Spero, Joan Edelman and Jeffrey A. Hart (2003). *The Politics of International Economic Relations*, 6th edn, London: Routledge.
Sprinz, Detlef F. (1998). 'Internationale Klimapolitik', *Die Friedens-Warte*, 73 (1): 25–44.
Sprinz, Detlef F. and Carsten Helm (1999). 'The Effect of Global Environmental Regimes: A Measurement Concept', *International Political Science Review*, 20 (4): 359–69.
Steffek, Jens, Claudia Kissling and Patrizia Nanz, eds (2008). *Civil Society Participation in European and Global Governance. A Cure for the Democratic Deficit?* Basingstoke: Palgrave Macmillan.
Steinberg, Richard (2002). 'In the Shadow of Law or Power? Consensus-based Bargaining and Outcomes in the GATT/WTO', *International Organization*, 56 (2): 339–74.
Steinwand, Martin C. and Randall W. Stone (2008). 'The International Monetary Fund: A Review of the Recent Evidence', *Review of International Organizations*, 3: 123–49.
Stephen, Matthew D. (2021). 'China's New Multilateral Institutions: A Framework and Research Agenda', *International Studies Review*, 23 (3): 807–34.

Stiglitz, Joseph (2002). *Globalization and Its Discontents*, New York: Norton.
Stone, Randall W. (2011). *Controlling Institutions: International Organizations and the Global Economy*, Cambridge: Cambridge University Press.
Strange, Susan (1996). *The Retreat of the State: The Diffusion of Power in the World Economy*, Cambridge: Cambridge University Press.
Stubbs, Richard (2019). 'ASEAN Sceptics versus ASEAN Proponents: Evaluating Regional Institutions', *The Pacific Review*, 32 (6): 923–50.
Stubbs, Thomas, Bernhard Reinsberg, Alexander Kentikelenis and Lawrence King (2020). 'How to Evaluate the Effects of IMF Conditionality: An Extension of Quantitative Approaches and an Empirical Application to Public Education Spending', *The Review of International Organizations*, 15: 29–73.
Sweeney, Gareth and Yuri Saito (2009). 'An NGO Assessment of the New Mechanisms of the UN Human Rights Council', *Human Rights Law Review*, 9 (2): 203–23.
Tallberg, Jonas (2000). 'The Anatomy of Autonomy: An Institutional Account of Variation in Supranational Influence', *Journal of Common Market Studies*, 38 (5): 843–64.
Tallberg, Jonas (2002a). 'Delegation to Supranational Institutions: Why, How, and with What Consequences?', *West European Politics*, 25 (1): 23–46.
Tallberg, Jonas (2002b). 'Paths to Compliance: Enforcement, Management, and the European Union', *International Organization*, 56 (3): 609–43.
Tallberg, Jonas (2006). *Leadership and Negotiation in the European Union*, Cambridge: Cambridge University Press.
Tallberg, Jonas (2010). 'The Power of the Chair: Formal Leadership in International Cooperation', *International Studies Quarterly*, 54 (1): 241–65.
Tallberg, Jonas, Thomas Sommerer, Theresa Squatrito and Christer Jönsson (2013). *The Opening Up of International Organizations: Transnational Access in Global Governance*, Cambridge: Cambridge University Press.
Tallberg, Jonas, Thomas Sommerer, Theresa Squatrito and Magnus Lundgren (2016). 'The Performance of International Organizations: A Policy Output Approach', *Journal of European Public Policy*, 23 (7): 1077–96.
Tallberg, Jonas and Michael Zürn (2019). 'The Legitimacy and Legitimation of International Organizations: Introduction and Framework', *The Review of International Organizations*, 14: 581–606.
Talmon, Stefan (2000). 'Law of the Sea', in Helmut Volger (ed.), *A Concise Encyclopedia of the United Nations*, 356–66, The Hague: Kluwer Law International.
Tanaka, Yoshifumi (2018). *The Peaceful Settlement of International Disputes*, Cambridge: Cambridge University Press.
Tannenwald, Nina (1999). 'The Nuclear Taboo: The United States and the Normative Basis of Nuclear Non-use', *International Organization*, 53 (3): 433–68.
Tetzlaff, Rainer (1996). *Weltbank und Währungsfonds – Gestalter der Bretton-Woods-Ära. Kooperations- und Integrationsregime in einer sich dynamisch entwickelnden Weltgesellschaft*, Opladen: Leske & Budrich.
Thakur, Ramesh, Andrew F. Cooper and John English, eds (2005). *International Commissions and the Power of Ideas*, Tokyo: United Nations University Press.

Thompson, Alexander (2006). 'Coercion through IOs: The Security Council and the Logic of Information Transmission', *International Organization*, 60 (1): 1–34.

Thompson, Alexander (2010). 'Rational Design in Motion: Uncertainty and Flexibility in the Global Climate Regime', *European Journal of International Relations*, 16 (2): 269–96.

Tickner, J. Ann and Laura Sjoberg (2010). 'Feminism', in Tim Dunne, Milja Kurki and Steve Smith (eds), *International Relations Theories. Discipline and Diversity*, 2nd edn, 195–212, Oxford: Oxford University Press.

Tomuschat, Christian (2008). *Human Rights. Between Idealism and Realism*, 2nd edn, Oxford: Oxford University Press.

Trondal, Jarle, Martin Marcussen, Torbjörn Larsson and Frode Veggeland (2010). *Unpacking International Organisations: The Dynamics of Compound Bureaucracies*, Oxford: Oxford University Press.

True, Jacqui (2013). 'Feminism', in Scott Burchill et al. (eds), *Theories of International Relations*, 5th edn, 241–65, Basingstoke: Palgrave Macmillan.

Tsebelis, George (2002). *Veto Players. How Political Institutions Work*, Princeton, NJ: Princeton University Press.

Underdal, Arild (1992). 'The Concept of Regime "Effectiveness"', *Cooperation and Conflict*, 27 (3): 227–40.

Underdal, Arild (1998). 'Explaining Compliance and Defection: Three Models', *European Journal of International Relations*, 4 (1): 5–30.

Underdal, Arild (2002). 'One Question, Two Answers', in Edward L. Miles, Arild Underdal, Steinar Andresen, Jorgen Wettestad, Jon Birger Skaerseth and Elaine M.Carlin (eds), *Environmental Regime Effectiveness. Confronting Theory with Evidence*, 3–45, Cambridge, MA: MIT Press.

Underdal, Arild (2004). 'Methodological Challenges in the Study of Regime Consequences', in Arild Underdal and Oran R. Young (eds), *Regime Consequences. Methodological Challenges and Research Strategies*, 27–48, Dordrecht: Kluwer Law International.

Underhill, Geoffrey, Jasper Blom and Daniel Mügge (2010). 'Introduction: The Challenges and Prospects of Global Financial Integration', in Geoffrey Underhill, Jasper Blom and Daniel Mügge (eds), *Global Financial Integration Thirty Years On. From Reform to Crisis*, 1–21, Cambridge: Cambridge University Press.

UNHCR (2025). *2024 Impact Report: Response to New Emergencies and Protracted Crises*, Geneva: UNHCR.

Union of International Associations (n.d.). *The Yearbook of International Organizations*. https://uia.org/yearbook/ (accessed: 18 November 2024).

United Nations (2004). *The Blue Helmets. A Review of United Nations Peacekeeping*, New York: United Nations Department of Public Information.

United Nations (n.d.). *Chapter VII Resolutions and Resolutions by Year (1995–2022)*. https://main.un.org/securitycouncil/sites/default/files/chapter_vii_resolutions.pdf (accessed: 27 November 2024).

United Nations General Assembly (2003). *Implementing Actions Proposed by the United Nations High Commissioner for Refugees to Strengthen the Capacity of His Office to Carry Out Its Mandate* (resolution 58/153), 22 December.

United Nations General Assembly (2005). *World Summit Outcome Document*, A/RES/60/1-. http://www.un.org/en/development/desa/population/migration/generalassembly/docs/globalcompact/A_RES_60_1.pdf (accessed: 28 July 2018).

Urpelainen, Johannes (2012). 'Unilateral Influence on International Bureaucrats: An International Delegation Problem', *Journal of Conflict Resolution*, 56 (4): 704–35.

Urpelainen, Johannes and Thijs Van de Graaf (2015). 'Your Place or Mine? Institutional Capture and the Creation of Overlapping International Institutions', *British Journal of Political Science*, 45 (4): 799–827.

Urquhart, Brian (1995). 'The United Nations in the Middle East: A 50-year Retrospective', *Middle East Journal*, 49 (4): 573–81.

Vabulas, Felicity and Duncan Snidal (2013). 'Organization without Delegation: Informal Intergovernmental Organizations (IIGOs) and the Spectrum of Iintergovernmental Arrangements', *The Review of International Organizations*, 8 (2): 193–220.

Vabulas, Felicity and Duncan Snidal (2021). 'Cooperation under Autonomy: Building and Analyzing the Informal Intergovernmental Organizations 2.0 dataset', *Journal of Peace Research*, 58 (4): 859–69.

Van den Bossche, Peter and Werner Zdouc (2021). *The Law and Policy of the World Trade Organization: Text, Cases, and Materials*, 5th edn, Cambridge: Cambridge University Press.

Van der Pijl, Kees (1998). *Transnational Classes and International Relations*, London: Routledge.

Van Rythoven, Eric (2020). 'The Securitization Dilemma', *Journal of Global Security Studies*, 5 (3): 478–93.

Vaubel, Roland (1996). 'Bureaucracy at the IMF and the World Bank: A Comparison of the Evidence', *World Economy*, 19 (2): 195–210.

Vaubel, Roland, Axel Dreher and Uğurlu Soylu (2007). 'Staff Growth in International Organizations: A Principal-agent Problem? An Empirical Analysis', *Public Choice*, 133 (3–4): 275–95.

Victor, David (1998). 'The Operation and Effectiveness of the Montreal Protocol's Non-compliance Procedure', in David G. Victor, Kal Raustiala and Eugene B. Skolnikoff (eds), *The Implementation and Effectiveness of International Environmental Commitments. Theory and Practice*, 137–76, Cambridge, MA: MIT Press.

Vines, Alex (2013). 'A Decade of African Peace and Security Architecture', *International Affairs*, 89 (1): 89–109.

Viola, Lora Anne (2020). *The Closure of the International System: How Institutions Create Political Equalities and Hierarchies*, Cambridge: Cambridge University Press.

Voeten, Erik (2000). 'Clashes in the Assembly', *International Organization*, 54 (2): 185–215.

Voeten, Erik (2005). 'The Political Origins of the UN Security Council's Ability to Legitimize the Use of Force', *International Organization*, 59 (3): 527–57.

Volgy, Thomas J., Elisabeth Fausett, Keith A. Grant and Stuart Rodgers (2008). 'Identifying Formal Intergovernmental Organizations', *Journal of Peace Research*, 45 (6): 837–50.

Von Allwörden, Laura (2025). 'When Contestation Legitimizes: The Norm of Climate Change Action and the US Contesting the Paris Agreement', *International Relations*, 39 (1): 52–75.

Von Borzyskowski, Inken and Felicity Vabulas (2019). 'Hello, Goodbye: When Do States Withdraw from International Organizations?', *The Review of International Organizations*, 14: 335–66.

Vreeland, James Raymond (2007). *The International Monetary Fund. Politics of Conditional Lending*, London: Routledge.

Wallace, Helen (2010). 'An Institutional Anatomy and Five Policy Modes', in Helen Wallace, Mark A. Pollack and Alasdair A. Young (eds), *Policy- Making in the European Union*, 6th edn, 69–104, Oxford: Oxford University Press.

Wallace, Helen, Pollack, Mark A., Roederer-Rynning, Christilla, and Young, Alasdair R. (Eds) (2020). *Policy-Making in the European Union*, 8th edition. Oxford: Oxford University Press.

Wallace, William (1982). 'Europe as a Confederation: The Community and the Nation-State', *Journal of Common Market Studies*, 21 (1): 57–68.

Wallander, Celeste A. (2000). 'Institutional Assets and Adaptability: NATO after the Cold War', *International Organization*, 54 (4): 705–35.

Wallander, Celeste A. and Robert O. Keohane (1999). 'Risk, Threat, and Security Institutions', in Helga Haftendorn, Robert O. Keohane and Celeste A. Wallander (eds), *Imperfect Unions. Security Institutions over Space and Time*, 21–47, Oxford: Oxford University Press.

Wallensteen, Peter and Patrik Johansson (2016). 'The UN Security Council: Decisions and Actions', in Sebastian von Einsiedel, David M. Malone and Bruno Stagno Ugarte (eds), *The UN Security Council in the 21st Century*, 27–54, Boulder, CO: Lynne Rienner.

Wallensteen, Peter and Isak Svensson (2014). 'Talking Peace: International Mediation in Armed Conflicts', *Journal of Peace Research*, 51 (2): 315–27.

Walter, Barbara F., Lise Morje Howard and V. Page Fortna (2021). 'The Extraordinary Relationship between Peacekeeping and Peace', *British Journal of Political Science*, 51 (4): 1705–22.

Walters, Francis Paul (1952). *A History of the League of Nations*, Oxford: Oxford University Press.

Waltz, Kenneth N. (1959). *Man, the State, and War: A Theoretical Analysis*, New York: Columbia University Press.

Waltz, Kenneth N. (1979). *Theory of International Politics*, New York: McGraw-Hill.

Waltz, Kenneth N. (1986). 'Reflections on Theory of International Politics: A Response to My Critics', in Robert O. Keohane (ed.), *Neorealism and Its Critics*, 322–46, New York: Columbia University Press.

Waltz, Kenneth N. (1990). 'Neorealist Thought and Neorealist Theory', *Journal of International Affairs*, 44, (1): 21–38.

Waters, Sarah (2004). 'Mobilising against Globalisation: Attac and the French Intellectual', *West European Politics*, 27 (5): 854–74.

Weaver, Catherine (2008). *Hypocrisy Trap. The World Bank and the Poverty of Reform*, Ithaca, NY: Cornell University Press.

Weinlich, Silke (2014). *The UN Secretariat's Influence on the Evolution of Peacekeeping*, London: Palgrave Macmillan.

Weiss, Jessica Chen and Jeremy L. Wallace (2021). 'Domestic Politics, China's Rise, and the Future of the Liberal International Order', *International Organization*, 75 (2): 635–64.

Weiss, Thomas G., Tatiana Carayannis and Richard Jolly (2009). 'The 'Third' United Nations', *Global Governance*, 15 (1): 123–42.

Weiss, Thomas G., David P. Forsythe, Roger A. Coate and Kelly-Kate Pease (2007). *The United Nations and Changing World Politics*, 5th edn, Boulder, CO: Westview Press.

Wendt, Alexander (1992). 'Anarchy Is What States Make of It', *International Organization*, 46 (2): 391–425.

Wendt, Alexander (1999). *Social Theory of International Politics*, Cambridge: Cambridge University Press.

Wertheim, Stephen (2020). *Tomorrow, the World: The Birth of U.S. Global Supremacy*, Cambridge MA: Harvard University Press.

Wessel, Ramses A. (2011). 'Dissolution and Succession: The Transmigration of the Soul of International Organizations', in Jan Klabbers and Åsa Wallendahl (eds), *Research Handbook on the Law of International Organizations*, Cheltenham: Edward Elgar Publishing.

Westerwinter, Oliver, Kenneth W. Abbott and Thomas Biersteker (2021). 'Informal Governance in World Politics', *The Review of International Organizations*, 16: 1–27.

Wettestad, Jorgen (1999). *Designing Effective Environmental Regimes. The Key Conditions*, Cheltenham: Edward Elgar.

Wettestad, Jorgen (2002). 'The Vienna Convention and Montreal Protocol on Ozone-Layer Depletion', in Edward L. Miles, Arild Underdal, Steinar Andresen, Jorgen Wettestad, Jon Birger Skjaerseth and Elaine M. Carlin (eds), *Environmental Regime Effectiveness. Confronting Theory with Evidence*, 149–69, Cambridge, MA: MIT Press.

Whitfield, Teresa (2007). 'Good Offices and "Groups of Friends"', in Simon Chesterman (ed.), *Secretary or General? The UN Secretary-General in World Politics*, 86–101, Cambridge: Cambridge University Press.

Wiener, Antje (2014). *A Theory of Contestation*, London: Springer.

Wiener, Antje (2018). *Contestation and Constitution of Norms in Global International Relations*, Cambridge: Cambridge University Press.

Wilkinson, Rorden (2000). *Multilateralism and the World Trade Organisation. The Architecture and Extension of International Trade Regulation*, London: Routledge.

Williams, Paul D. (2014). 'Reflections on the Evolving African Peace and Security Architecture', *African Security*, 7 (3): 147–62.

Williams, Paul D. (2018). *Fighting for Peace in Somalia: A History and Analysis of the African Union Mission (AMISOM), 2007–2017*, Oxford: Oxford University Press.

Williamson, John (1990). 'What Washington Means by Policy Reform', in John Williamson (ed.), *Latin American Adjustment. How Much Has Happened?* 5–38, Washington, DC: Institute for International Economics.

Wilson, Woodrow (1917/18). *President Wilson's Great Speeches and Other History Making Documents*, Chicago, IL: Stanton & Van Vliet.

Wolf, Klaus Dieter (1981). *Die dritte Seerechtskonferenz der Vereinten Nationen. Beiträge zur Reform der internationalen Ordnung und Entwicklungstendenzen im Nord-Süd-Verhältnis*, Baden-Baden: Nomos.

Wonka, Arndt and Berthold Rittberger (2010). 'Credibility, Complexity and Uncertainty: Explaining the Institutional Independence of 29 EU Agencies', *West European Politics*, 33 (4): 730–52.

Woods, Ngaire (2000). 'The Challenges of Multilateralism and Governance', in Christopher L. Gilbert and David Vines (eds), *The World Bank. Structure and Policies*, 132–56, Cambridge: Cambridge University Press.

Woon, Walter (2015). *The ASEAN Charter: A Commentary*, Singapore: National University of Singapore Press.

World Bank (n.d.). *The World Bank Data: Trade (% of GDP)*. https://data.worldbank.org/indicator/NE.TRD.GNFS.ZS (accessed: 27 July 2018).

World Bank Group (2014). *A Stronger, Connected, Solutions World Bank Group*, Washington, DC: The World Bank Group.

World Bank Group (2024). *IBRD Callable Capital*, Washington, DC: World Bank. https://documents1.worldbank.org/curated/en/099041224122018248/pdf/BOSIB1f97f66160061aff5128284597b03e.pdf

Yamin, Farhana and Joanna Depledge (2004). *The International Climate Change Regime. A Guide to Rules, Institutions and Procedures*, Cambridge: Cambridge University Press.

Young, Oran R. (1979). *Compliance and Public Authority. A Theory with International Applications*, Baltimore, MD: Johns Hopkins University Press.

Young, Oran R., eds (1999). *The Effectiveness of International Environmental Regimes: Causal Connections and Behavioral Mechanisms*, Cambridge, MA: The MIT Press.

Young, Oran R. (2001). 'Inferences and Indices: Evaluating the Effectiveness of International Environmental Regimes', *Global Environmental Politics*, 1 (1): 99–121.

Young, Oran R (2017). *Governing Complex Systems: Social Capital for the Anthropocene*, Cambridge, MA: The MIT Press.

Zangl, Bernhard (1999). *Interessen auf zwei Ebenen. Internationale Regime in der Agrarhandels-, Währungs- und Walfangpolitik*, Baden-Baden: Nomos.

Zangl, Bernhard (2008). 'Judicialization Matters! A Comparison of Dispute Settlement under GATT and the WTO', *International Studies Quarterly*, 52 (4): 825–54.

Zangl, Bernhard, Frederick Heußner, Andreas Kruck and Xenia Lanzendörfer (2016). 'Imperfect Adaptation: How the WTO and the IMF Adjust to Shifting Power Distributions among Their Members', *The Review of International Organizations*, 11 (2): 171–96.

Zeitlin, Jonathan, Francesco Nicoli and Brigid Laffan (2019). 'Introduction: The European Union Beyond the Polycrisis? Integration and Politicization in an Age of Shifting Cleavages', *Journal of European Public Policy*, 26 (7): 963–76.

Zürn, Michael (2000). 'Democratic Governance Beyond the Nation-state: The EU and Other International Institutions', *European Journal for International Relations*, 6 (2): 183–222.

Zürn, Michael (2018). *A Theory of Global Governance: Authority, Legitimacy, and Contestation*, Oxford: Oxford University Press.

Zürn, Michael, Martin Binder and Matthias Ecker-Ehrhardt (2012). 'International Authority and Its Politicization', *International Theory*, 4 (1): 69–106.

INDEX

Adler-Nissen, Rebecca   27
African Continental Free Trade Area
   (AfCFTA)   247
African Economic Community   247
African Standby Force   247
African Union (AU)   1, 41, 67, 130,
   161, 243–8
al-Bashir, Omar   147, 233
Alliance of Small Island States
   (AOSIS)   204
Al-Qaida   75
Amazon   5
American NGO Freedom House   231
Amnesty International   5, 52, 80
Appellate Body   78, 119, 174,
   177
Arctic Council   5
armed conflicts   152
Armenian genocide   215
Asian financial crisis   50
Asian Infrastructure Investment Bank
   (AIIB)   105
Asia-Pacific Economic Cooperation
   (APEC)   7–8
Association of Southeast Asian Nations
   (ASEAN)   49, 67, 249–53
AU Constitutive Act   245
autonomous international
   organizations   24, 266
Azevêdo, Roberto   269

Basel Committee on Banking
   Supervision (BCBS)   127–8
Biden, Joe   207
bilateral disputes   49
bilateral free trade agreements   177
Board of Governors   73
Bradley, Megan   221

Brazil, Russia, India, China and South
   Africa (BRICS)   1, 88, 105,
   268, 270, 273
Bretton Woods Agreement   49, 103,
   104, 187
British Empire   237
Brussels Act against slavery   222
Buenos Aires Act   254
bureaucratic cultures   27
Burundi   119, 233
Bush, J.   84

Cameron, David   265
causal beliefs   26
centralization   21
centralized international
   organizations   21
Chimni, B. S.   178
chlorofluorocarbons (CFCs)   123,
   196
Churchill, Winston   104, 107
Citigroup   5
civil society actors   214
climate and environment
   greenhouse gas emission   195
   organizations' effectiveness   201–3
   UNEP
      operations of   199–201
      organizations'
         effectiveness   209–11
      policy programme of   196–201
   WMO and Climate
      Secretariat   207–9
Codex Alimentarius Commission
   (CAC)   45, 126
cognitive condition   60
cognitive support   59
Cold War   42

Commission on Human Rights 51, 224
Committee of Permanent Representatives (COREPER) 76
communication 44–5
Comprehensive Development Framework (CDF) 183
Concert of Europe 37
Conference of the Parties (COP) 98, 204
Congress of Vienna 36
Connally, John 50
constitutional structure 66
Constitutive Act 245, 246, 248
constructivism 29
constructivist theory 24–9
contemporary theories 32
Convention on the Protection of the Rights of All Migrant Workers and Members of Their Families 217
cooperative security 161–3
Coordinating Committee on the Ozone Layer (CCOL) 200
Copenhagen summit 205
COP in Kyoto (COP3) 205
Costello, Cathryn 221
Council for Trade in Goods 173
Council for Trade in Services 173
Council for Trade-Related Aspects of Intellectual Property Rights (TRIPS Council) 48
Council of Europe 78
Council of Ministers, the Committee of Permanent Representatives (COREPER) 106
courts of justice 77–8
Covid-19 pandemic 1
Crimean War (1853–6) 37
critical theories 29–31
cultural identity 247
customary international law 68

Danner, Allison 233
Davis, Christina L. 176
decision-making, in international organizations
conferences 103–6
courts 118–19
operational decisions 114
plenary organs and executive councils 106–14
programme decisions 102–3
secretariats and agencies 114–18
delegated decision-making
courts 118–19
secretariats and agencies 115–18
delegation 7, 8, 21–3, 244, 250
Delian League 153
de Saint-Pierre, Abbé 36
developmental disparities
development and trade 56
financing development 54–6
disparities, in development 178–9
Dispute Settlement Body (DSB) 174
Dispute Settlement Understanding (DSU) 173
Doha Round 170, 172, 176
domestic politics 16, 263
Doyle, Michael W. 151

Earth Summit 204
East-West relations 42
Economic and Financial Committee 76
Economic and Social Council (UN) (ECOSOC) 68, 74, 79–80
Economic Commission for Europe (ECE) 57
economic cooperation 241
Eisenhower, Dwight 40, 154
Enhanced Transparency Framework 208
environmental dilemma 195
epistemic communities 26
European Central Bank (ECB) 117
European Commission 77, 87, 242
European Convention on Human Rights (ECHR) 53, 131
European Council and Commission 238
European Court of Human Rights 53
European Court of Justice (ECJ) 118, 130, 241, 242
European Economic and Social Committee (EESC) 80, 96

European Economic Community
    (EEC)   103, 238
European External Action Service
    (EEAS)   87, 239
European Medicines Agency   242
European Movement   53
European Parliament   94, 95
European Semester   128
European Social Charter   53
European Union (EU)   1, 31, 237–43
Executive Board of the UN
    Development Programme
    (UNDP)   74
executive councils, international
    organizations of   74–6
Extended Credit Facility (ECF)   189
Extended Fund Facility (EFF)   189
External experts   99
extra-EU trade   175

Farrell, Henry   272
federalism   19
financial resources   89
First World War   37, 46, 215
Flexible Credit Line (FCL)   189
Food and Agriculture Organization
    (FAO)   45, 238
Foreign Affairs Council   73
Franco-German War   37
functionalism   19

Gaddafi regime   161, 164
Gates Foundation   89
gender-emancipatory discourses   31
General Agreement on Tariffs and
    Trade (GATT)   46, 123,
    186
General Assembly   72, 73, 140
General Council   48
General Motors   5
General Postal Union   44
Geneva Convention   37, 50
geopoliticization, of international
    organizations   271–3
Global Compact for Migration   217,
    222
global economic crises
    monetary relations   49–50
    trade relations   46–9

Global Environmental Facility
    (GEF)   207
Global Fund   89
Global North   33
Global Refugee Forum   218
Global South   33, 178, 218
Goldstein, Judith L.   176
Great Depression   46
Green Climate Fund (GCF)   206
greenhouse gas emissions   210
Greenpeace/Transparency
    International   5
green theory approaches   31
gross domestic product (GDP)   157,
    159, 175
Group of 20 (G20)   5
Group of 77 (G77)   73
Groups of 7 and 20 (G7/G20)   266
Gulf Organization for Industrial
    Consulting (GOIC)   6
Gulf War   141

Hafner-Burton, Emilie M.   232
Hague Congress   53
Hale, Thomas   265–6
Havana Charter   47
Heavily Indebted Poor Countries
    (HIPC) initiative   189
Held, David   265–6
Hooghe, Liesbet   236
Human Rights Council (HRC)   52,
    227, 228, 234
human rights violations   20, 213, 232
    protection of   51–2
    regional protection of   53
Human Rights Watch   52
hybrid tribunals   230
hydrochlorofluorocarbons
    (HCFCs)   201
hydrofluorocarbons (HFCs)   202

Independent Evaluation Group   185
Independent Evaluation Office
    (IEO)   191
indirect governance   267
informal consultations   111
institutional design   20
institutionalism   24, 29, 33
institutionalist theory   18–24, 35

institutional structure   66
intensive transgovernmentalism   107
Intergovernmental Negotiating Committee (INC)   204
Intergovernmental Panel on Climate Change (IPCC)   97, 208
internally displaced people (IDP)   214
International Atomic Energy Agency (IAEA)   4, 89, 128
International Bank for Reconstruction and Development (IBRD)   179
International Bureau for Weights and Measures in Paris   44
International Civil Aviation Organization (ICAO)   44
international commerce   45
  communication   44–5
  social regulation   45–6
  transport   42–4
International Court of Justice (ICJ)   130, 145
International Covenant on Civil and Political Rights   51
International Covenant on Economic, Social and Cultural Rights   51
International Criminal Court (ICC)   1, 75, 119, 130, 274
International Criminal Tribunal for the Former Yugoslavia (ICTY)   229
International Development Association (IDA)   54, 179
International Finance Corporation (IFC)   54, 179
international institutions
  definition   4
  neo-institutionalist theory   20
  social constructivism   25
  subcategory of   4
International Labour Organization (ILO)   1, 46, 74, 95, 217
International Maritime Organization (IMO)   44
International Monetary Fund (IMF)   8, 18, 31, 46, 71, 89, 103, 124, 168, 262
  operations of   188–91

  organization's effectiveness   191–2
  policy programme of   186–8
international non-governmental organization (NGO)   37
International Organization for Migration (IOM)   31, 215
International Organization of La Francophonie (OIF)   237
international organizations   2–4
  ad hoc international conferences   5
  centralized   3
  constitutional and institutional structures of   9
  constitutional structure of   66–9
  contemporary challenges   262
  decentralized   7
  decision-making (see decision-making, in international organizations)
  decisions and activities of   10–11
  democratization of   269
  emerging powers and power shifts   268–71
  environmental protection   195
  general purpose   6
  geopoliticization of   271–3
  Gridlock and new cooperation challenges   265–8
  history of
    developmental disparities   53–6
    environmental degradation   56–8
    global economic crises   46–50
    human rights violations   50–3
    international commerce   42–6
    war and power politics   36–42
  institutional structure of
    courts of justice   77–8
    executive councils   74–6
    non-governmental actors, representation of   79–80
    parliamentary assemblies   78–9
    permanent secretariats   76–7
    plenary organs   71–4
  international and cross-border problems   35
  legitimacy and contestation   262–5
  multilateral cooperation   9
  organization's effectiveness   150–3, 163–4

permanent secretariat and
    correspondence address 5
policy programmes 122–5
political system of 9, 84
programme 3, 7
task-specific 3, 6
types of 6, 7
universal membership 7
international regimes 4
International Security Assistance Force
    (ISAF) 160
International Telecommunication
    Union (ITU) 44
International Trade Organization
    (ITO) 46–7
International Union of Railways
    (UIC) 44
International Whaling Commission
    (IWC) 1, 20, 89, 129
intra-EU trade 175

Kant, Immanuel 36
Karadžić, Radovan 229
Kellogg–Briand Pact 38
Kennedy Round 172
Kigali Amendment 198
Korean War 147
Kosovo conflict 148
Ku, Julian 232
Kyoto Protocol 58, 98, 205, 206,
    208–10

League of Nations 37, 39, 85, 274
legitimacy 262–5
Lenz, Tobias 236
Lisbon Treaty 105
long-term international
    cooperation 17

market access 176
Marks, Gary 236
Marxist theorists 29
McNamara, Robert 182
Mediation Support Unit 144
MERCOSUR 169, 253–6
migration and human rights
    global human rights protection
        organization's
            effectiveness 230–3
    UN operations 227–30
    UN Policy programme 223–7
and refugees
    organization's
        effectiveness 221–3
    UNHCR and IOM
        operations 218–21
    UN Policy programme 215–18
migration management 220
military enforcement 141
Millennium Declaration 92
Millennium Development Goals
    (MDGs) 92
Mladic, Ratko 229
Monroe Doctrine 85
Montreal Protocol 83, 196–9, 201,
    204
Multilateral Fund 199
Multilateral Investment Guarantee
    Agency (MIGA) 179
Multi-Party Interim Appeal Arbitration
    Arrangement (MPIA) 175

Napoleonic Wars (1803–15) 36
Nationally Determined Contributions
    (NDCs) 91, 236
neocolonialism 179
neo-institutionalism 19
neo-realism 16
Netanyahu, Benjamin 52, 147, 274
New Development Bank (NDB) 88,
    105
New International Economic Order
    (NIEO) 30, 179, 263
Newman, Abraham L. 272
NextGenerationEU programme 241
Non-Aligned Movement (NAM) 30,
    87
non-governmental actors
    demands of 96
    policy deliberations 96
    policymaking processes 95
    representation of 79–80
non-governmental organizations
    (NGOs) 2, 28, 57, 83, 107,
    174
non-military enforcement 147
Non-Proliferation Treaty (NPT) 31,
    86

non-tariff barriers 48, 170, 256
normative idealism 25
North Atlantic Alliance 153
North Atlantic Council (NAC) 119, 156
North Atlantic Treaty Organization (NATO) 31, 40, 67, 78, 103, 139, 140, 153–5, 159, 162, 166, 236
  NATO Council 155
  NATO Defence Planning Process (NDPP) 158
  operations of 156–63
  policy programme of 154–6
Nuclear Non-Proliferation Treaty (NPT) 123
Nzelibe, Jide 232

Office of the UN High Commissioner for Human Rights (OHCHR) 227
operational activities
  adjudication 129–30
  implementation 126–8
  monitoring 128–9
  sanctions 130–2
  specification 126
operational decisions 101, 102
Organisation for Economic Co-operation and Development (OECD) 1, 183, 206
Organisation of Islamic Cooperation (OIC) 237
Organization for Security and Co-operation in Europe (OSCE) 78, 95, 272
Organization of African Unity (OAU) 244
Organization of American States (OAS) 253
Organization of Islamic Cooperation (OIC) 1, 87
Organization of the Petroleum Exporting Countries (OPEC) 1
organization's effectiveness 230–3
  evaluation of 150–3, 163–4
  International Monetary Fund (IMF) 191–2
  international organizations 150–3, 163–4
  ozone layer protection 201–3
  refugees 221–3
  World Bank 183–5
  World Trade Organization (WTO) 175–8
Ottoman Empire 215
ozone layer protection
  organizations' effectiveness 201–3
  UNEP
    operations of 199–201
    policy programme of 196–201
Ozone Trends Panel 201

Pan-African Parliament 245
Paris Agreement 9, 58, 69, 86, 206–8, 210
Paris summit 206
parliamentary assemblies 78–9
Peace and Security Council (PSC) 245
peace enforcement 145–8
peaceful settlement of disputes 143–5
peacekeeping 40, 148–50
Pelc, Krzysztof J. 176
permanent secretariats 76–7
PfP programme 161–2
plenary organs, international organizations of 71–4
policy effectiveness 132–3
policy programmes
  binding nature 124–5
  binding obligations 124–5
  objectives 123–4
political actors
  administrative staff 91–4
  communities of experts 97–8
  governments of member states 84–91
  interest groups 95–7
  parliamentarians 94–5
political human rights 28
political-security community 252
postcolonialists 29
Pouliot, Pouliot Vincent 27
Preamble of UN Charter 51
principal–agent relationship 22, 23
'Prisoner's Dilemma' 19–20, 167
programme decisions 119

protectionism   46
Protocol amendments   198
PSC Protocol (2002)   247
Putin, Vladimir   52, 147, 233

Rapid Credit Facility (RCF)   189
Rapid Financing Instrument
     (RFI)   189
realism   24, 26, 29, 33
realist theory   16–18
redistributive programmes   124
Refugee Convention   7, 68, 215, 219
Regional Comprehensive Economic
     Partnership (RCEP)   251
Regional Economic Communities
     (RECs)   244
regional organization
   African Union   243–8
   ASEAN   249–53
   European Union   237–43
   MERCOSUR   253–6
regulatory programmes   123
Resolute Support Mission   160
Resolution 3314 (XXIX)   141
responsibility to protect (R2P)   52, 142
Rhine Navigation Act   42
Rhine River Commission   6, 43, 59
right to rule   263
right to self-defence   141
Rio Framework Convention   209
Rivers, Douglas   176
Roger, Charles B.   266, 267
Roosevelt, Franklin D.   51, 104, 107
Russia   86
Rwandan genocide   222

Sambanis, Nicholas   151
Schuman Declaration   238
Second World War   2
security communities   25
Security Council   31, 39, 40, 42, 52, 87, 92, 112, 116, 140–4, 146–9
security dilemma   26
Shanghai Cooperation Organisation
     (SCO)   271
Sherwood, Angela   221
Simmons, Beth   233

Single European Act   68
Smithsonian Agreement   188
social constructivism   25, 27, 33
social groups   28
socialization   107
social regulation   45–6
social trap   195
Society for Worldwide Interbank
     Financial Telecommunication
     (SWIFT)   272
Southern Common Market
     (MERCOSUR)   74, 168
Special Drawing Rights (SDRs)   50, 73, 188
Special Procedures   52, 227, 234
Stalin, Joseph   86, 107
Stand-By Arrangements (SBA)   189
Standby Credit Facility (SCF)   189
Statute for an International Criminal
     Court   230
Stephen, Matthew D.   271
Strategic Concepts   155
Structural Adjustment Programmes
     (SAPs)   182
Sub-Commission on the Promotion
     and Protection of Human
     Rights   224
summit declaration   88
supranational agents   23
Supreme Headquarters Allied Powers
     Europe (SHAPE)   157
Sustainable Development Goals
     (SDGs)   127, 183, 217

tariff barriers   170
task-specific organizations   22
theories, of international organizations
   constructivist theory   24–9
   contemporary theories of   32
   critical theories   29–31
   institutionalist theory   18–24
   realist theory   16–18
Third Assessment Report   209
Thirty Years War (1618–48)   36
Tiananmen Square protests   87
Tokyo Round   172
Tomz, Michael   176
Toronto Group   197
trade policy   33, 49, 56, 103

INDEX

Trade Policy Committee 76
Trade Policy Review Body
    (TPRB) 173
Trade Policy Review Mechanism 48
transactionalism 25
Transatlantic Trade and Investment
    Partnership (TTIP) 177
transnational advocacy networks 96
transnational capitalist class
    (TCC) 178
transnational networks 26
transnational social movements 96
Trans-Pacific Partnership (TPP) 177
transport 42–4
Treaties of Maastricht 68
Treaties of Westphalia 8
Treaty of Amity and
    Cooperation 249–253
Treaty of Amsterdam 79
Treaty of Asunción 254
Treaty of Lisbon 79
Treaty of Maastricht 79, 238
Treaty of Mutual Cooperation and
    Security 153
Treaty of Nice 79
Treaty of Rome 238, 240
Treaty on European Union
    (TEU) 238
Treaty on the Functioning of the
    European Union (TFEU) 67,
    238
Treaty on the Non-Proliferation of
    Nuclear Weapons 4
Truman 47
Trump, Donald 84, 158, 164,
    177, 178, 207, 211, 261,
    271

UN Environment Programme
    (UNEP) 58
  operations of 199–201, 207–9
  organizations' effectiveness 201–3
  policy programme of 196–9
United Nations (UN) 1, 21, 31, 39,
    244, 261
  Office for the Coordination of
      Humanitarian Affairs
      (OCHA) 118

Office of the High Commissioner
    for Human Rights
    (OHCHR) 129
operations of 142–50
peacekeeping operations 150
policy programme of 140–2,
    204–7
UN Assistance Mission in Iraq
    (UNAMI) 144
UN Charter 69, 96, 104, 130,
    141
UN Charter and ECOSOC
    Resolutions 1296
    (XLIV) 79, 96
UN Conference on Trade
    and Development
    (UNCTAD) 56, 67
UN Development Programme
    (UNDP) 55, 118, 124, 127,
    199
UN Economic and Social Council
    (ECOSOC) 223
UN Entity for Gender Equality and
    the Empowerment of Women
    (UN WOMEN) 67
UN Framework Convention
    on Climate Change
    (UNFCCC) 58, 91, 133,
    204, 274
UN General Assembly 22, 114,
    141, 222
UN High Commissioner for Human
    Rights (OHCHR) 52
UN Human Rights
    Conventions 51
UN Human Rights Council 224
UN Industrial Development
    Organization (UNIDO) 56,
    124, 199
UN Iran–Iraq Military Observer
    Group (UNIIMOG) 149
United Nations Children's Fund
    (UNICEF) 127
United Nations Environment
    Programme (UNEP) 83
United Nations Framework
    Convention on Climate
    Change (UNFCCC) 236

INDEX

United Nations Industrial Development Organization (UNIDO) 67, 89
United Nations Monitoring, Verification and Inspection Commission (UNMOVIC) 117
United Nations Special Commission (UNSCOM) (1991–7) 117
UN Peacekeeping Force in Cyprus (UNFICYP) 149
UN Population Fund (UNFPA) 89
UN Refugee Agency (UNHCR) 7, 118, 127, 215
UN Relief and Rehabilitation Agency 215
UN Security Council 18, 24, 41, 52, 59, 75, 81, 86, 96, 106, 113, 115, 132, 160, 165, 270, 272
UN Special Commissions 117
UN Special Organs and Specialized Agencies 75
UN Sustainable Development Goals (SDGs) 247
United States 17–18, 37, 38, 73, 83, 85, 197–8, 249
Universal Declaration of Human Rights 51, 222, 224
Universal Periodic Review (UPR) 52, 227
Uruguay Round 48, 170, 172

value-added tax (VAT) 237
Vienna Convention for the Protection of Ozone Layer 58, 197, 199
Volgy, Thomas J. 5

Warsaw Pact 41

Warsaw Treaty Organization 40
Washington Consensus 182
Wilson, Woodrow 85
Wilsonianism 85
Wolfensohn, James D. 183
Working Group on Communications 228
World Bank 8, 33, 46, 56, 81, 89, 124, 127, 168, 274
  operations of 181–3
  organization's effectiveness 183–5
  policy programme of 179–81
World Bank's Executive Boards 18
World Conference on Human Rights in Vienna 52
World Food Programme (WFP) 124, 127
World Health Organization (WHO) 1, 45, 86, 92, 127, 271
World Meteorological Organization (WMO) 57, 97
World Plan of Action for the Ozone Layer 196
World Trade Charter 47
World Trade Organization (WTO) 3, 31, 46, 78, 87, 123, 168, 236
  operations of 171–5
  organization's effectiveness 175–8
  policy programme of 168–71
  WTO Appellate Body 119, 193

Xi, Jinping 261

Yalta conference 104
Young, Kevin 265–6

zone of possible agreement (ZOPA) 109
Zürn, Michael 263